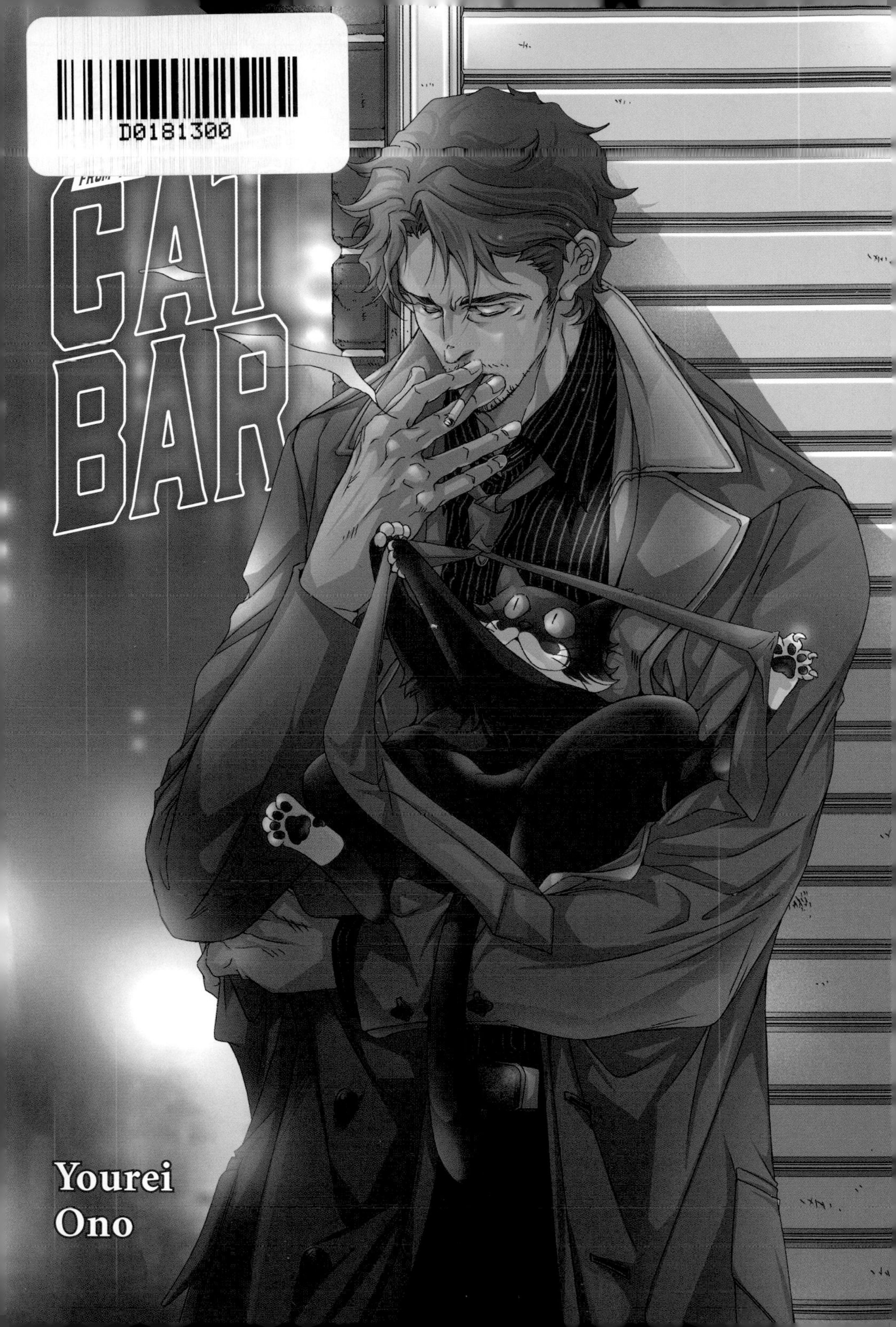
FROM
CAT
BAR
Yourei
Ono

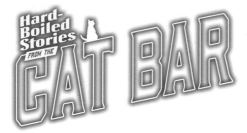

Hard-Boiled Stories from the CAT BAR

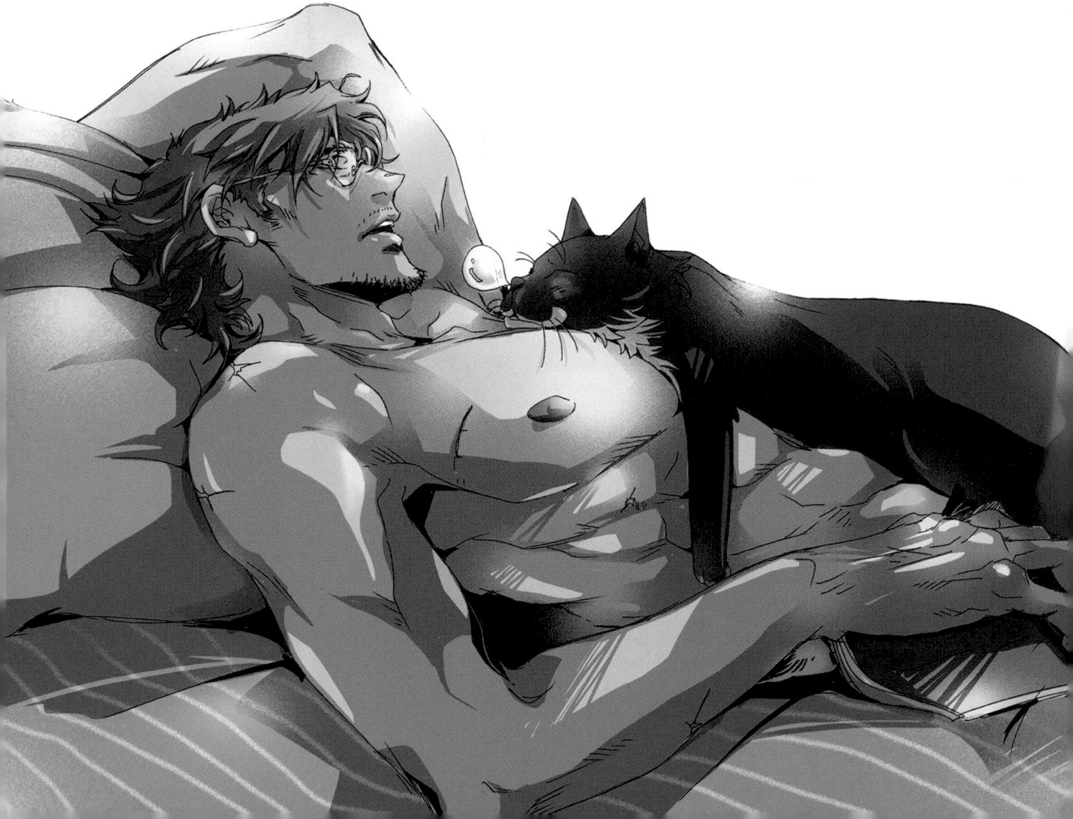

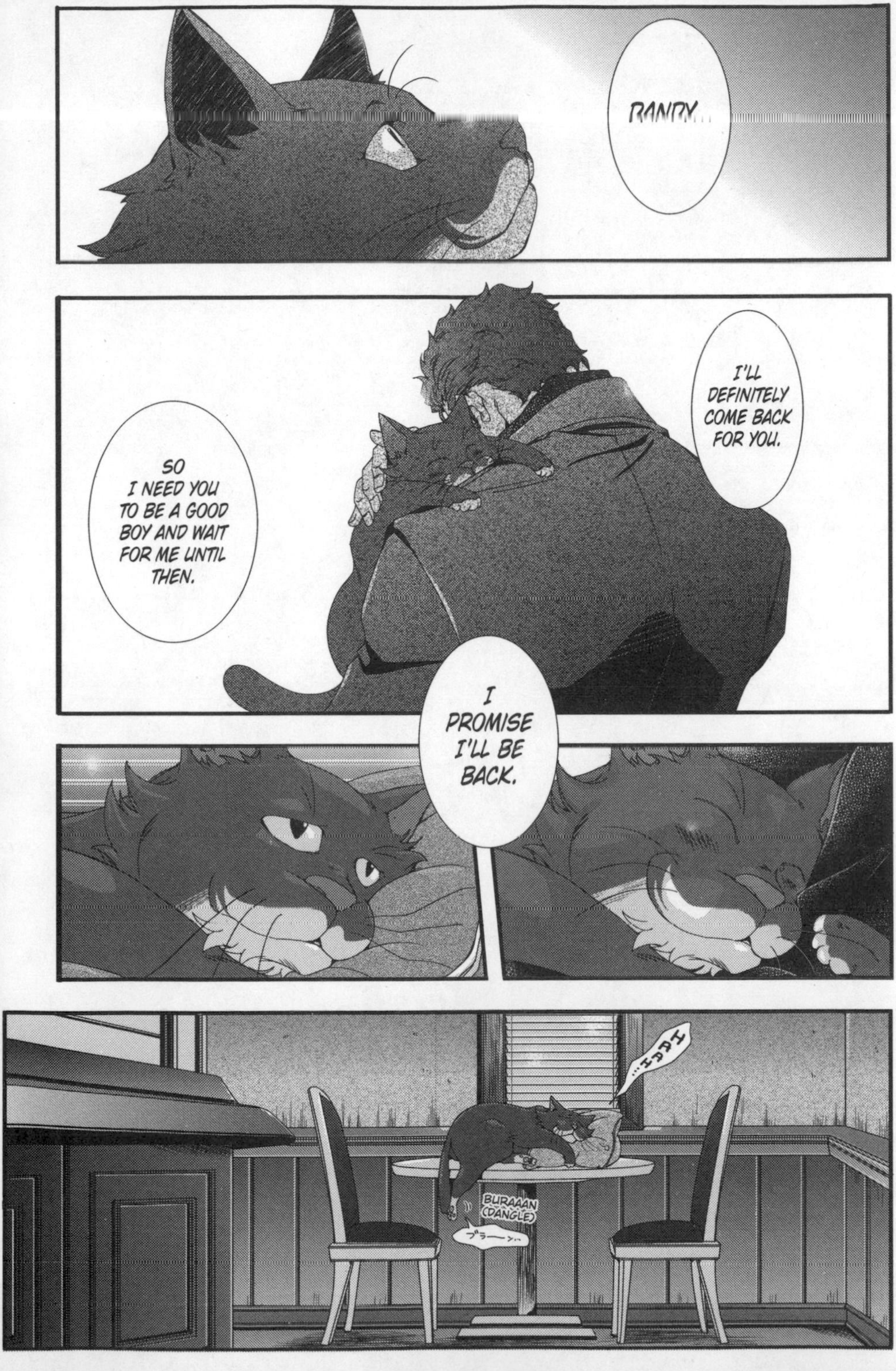
RANDY...
I'LL DEFINITELY COME BACK FOR YOU.
SO I NEED YOU TO BE A GOOD BOY AND WAIT FOR ME UNTIL THEN.
I PROMISE I'LL BE BACK.
BURAAAN (DANGLE)
ブラーン…

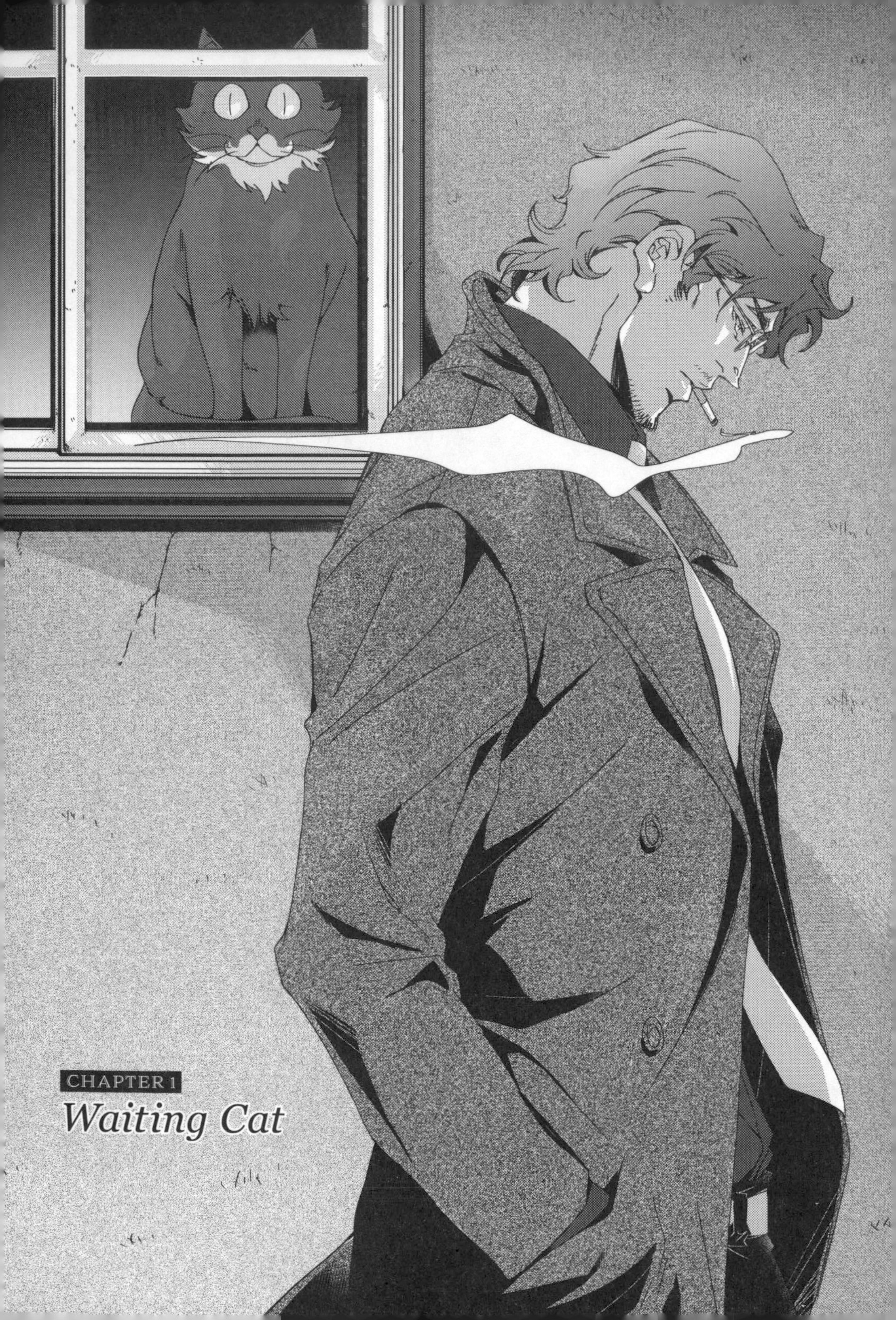

CHAPTER 1

Waiting Cat

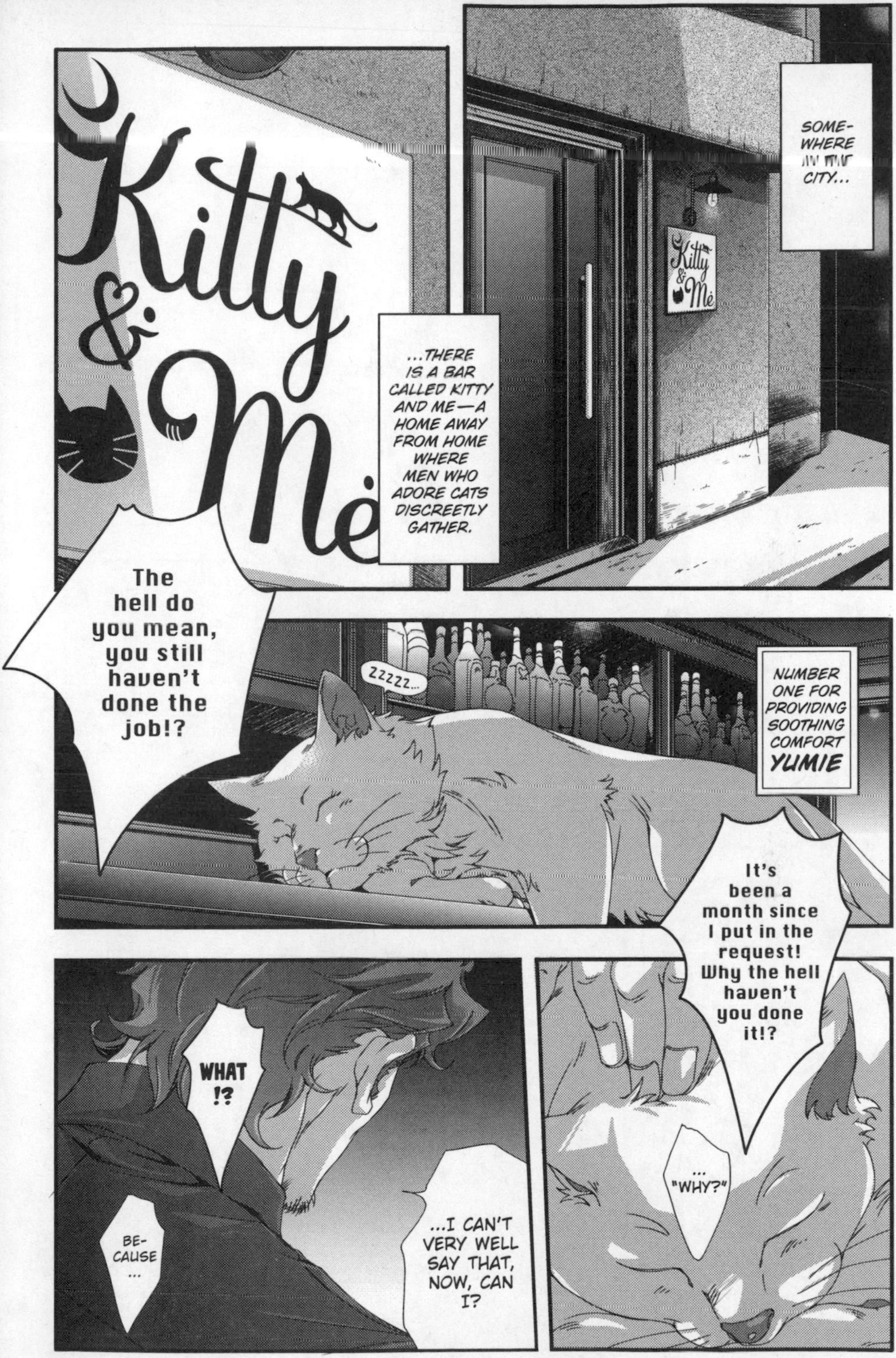

SOME-WHERE
CITY...
Kitty & Mė
...THERE IS A BAR CALLED KITTY AND ME—A HOME AWAY FROM HOME WHERE MEN WHO ADORE CATS DISCREETLY GATHER.
Kitty & Mė
The hell do you mean, you still haven't done the job!?
NUMBER ONE FOR PROVIDING SOOTHING COMFORT YUMIE
ZZZZZ...
It's been a month since I put in the request! Why the hell haven't you done it!?
... "WHY?"
WHAT!?
...I CAN'T VERY WELL SAY THAT, NOW, CAN I?
BE-CAUSE...

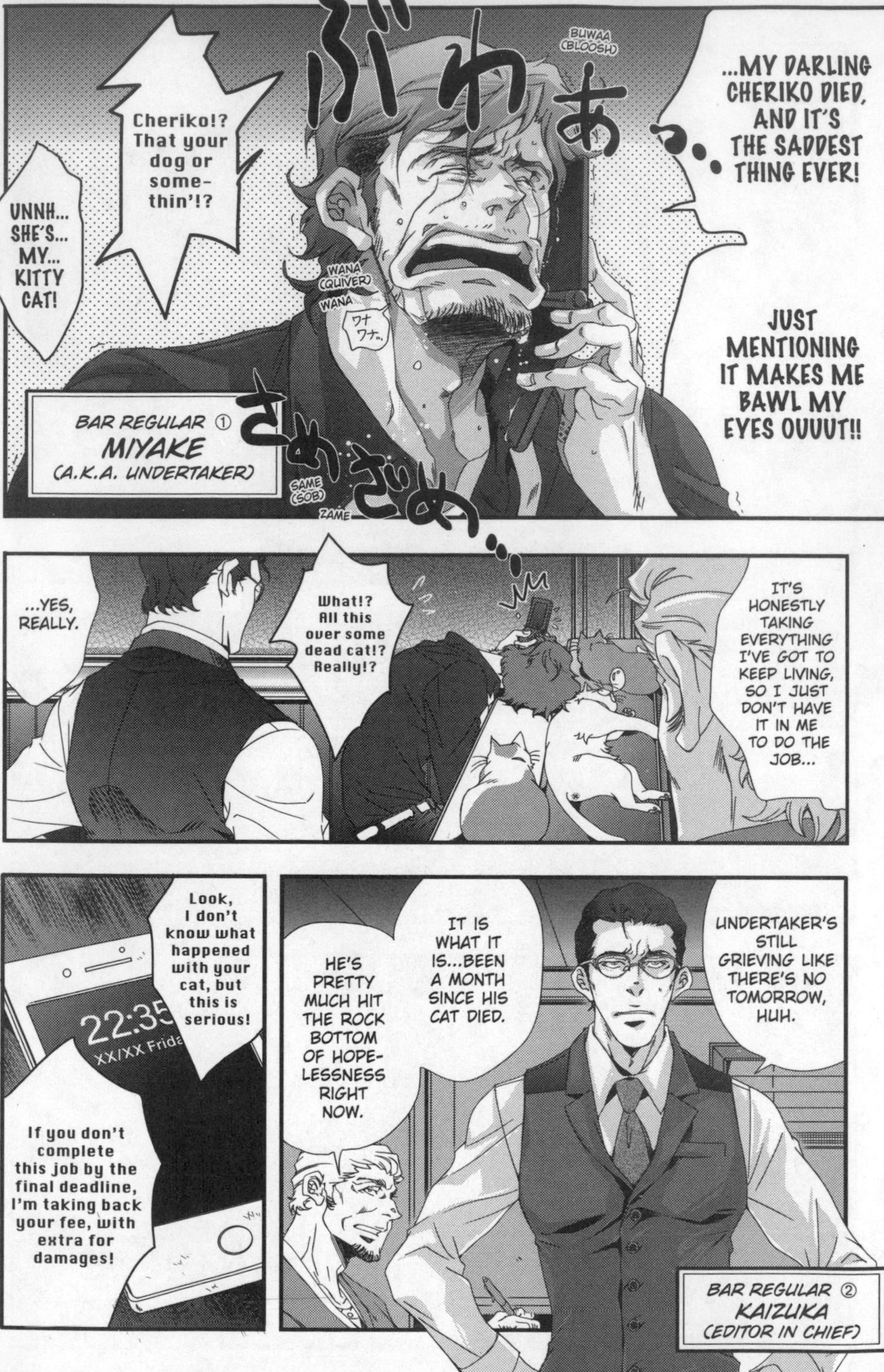

...MY DARLING CHERIKO DIED, AND IT'S THE SADDEST THING EVER!
ぶわぁっ
BUWAA (BLOOSH)
JUST MENTIONING IT MAKES ME BAWL MY EYES OUUUT!!
Cheriko!? That your dog or some-thin'!?
WANA (QUIVER) WANA
ワナワナ
UNNH... SHE'S... MY... KITTY CAT!
BAR REGULAR ① MIYAKE (A.K.A. UNDERTAKER)
さめざめ
SAME (SOB) ZAME
IT'S HONESTLY TAKING EVERYTHING I'VE GOT TO KEEP LIVING, SO I JUST DON'T HAVE IT IN ME TO DO THE JOB...
What!? All this over some dead cat!? Really!?
...YES, REALLY.
UNDERTAKER'S STILL GRIEVING LIKE THERE'S NO TOMORROW, HUH.
IT IS WHAT IT IS...BEEN A MONTH SINCE HIS CAT DIED.
HE'S PRETTY MUCH HIT THE ROCK BOTTOM OF HOPE-LESSNESS RIGHT NOW.
BAR REGULAR ② KAIZUKA (EDITOR IN CHIEF)
Look, I don't know what happened with your cat, but this is serious!
22:35
XX/XX Frida
If you don't complete this job by the final deadline, I'm taking back your fee, with extra for damages!

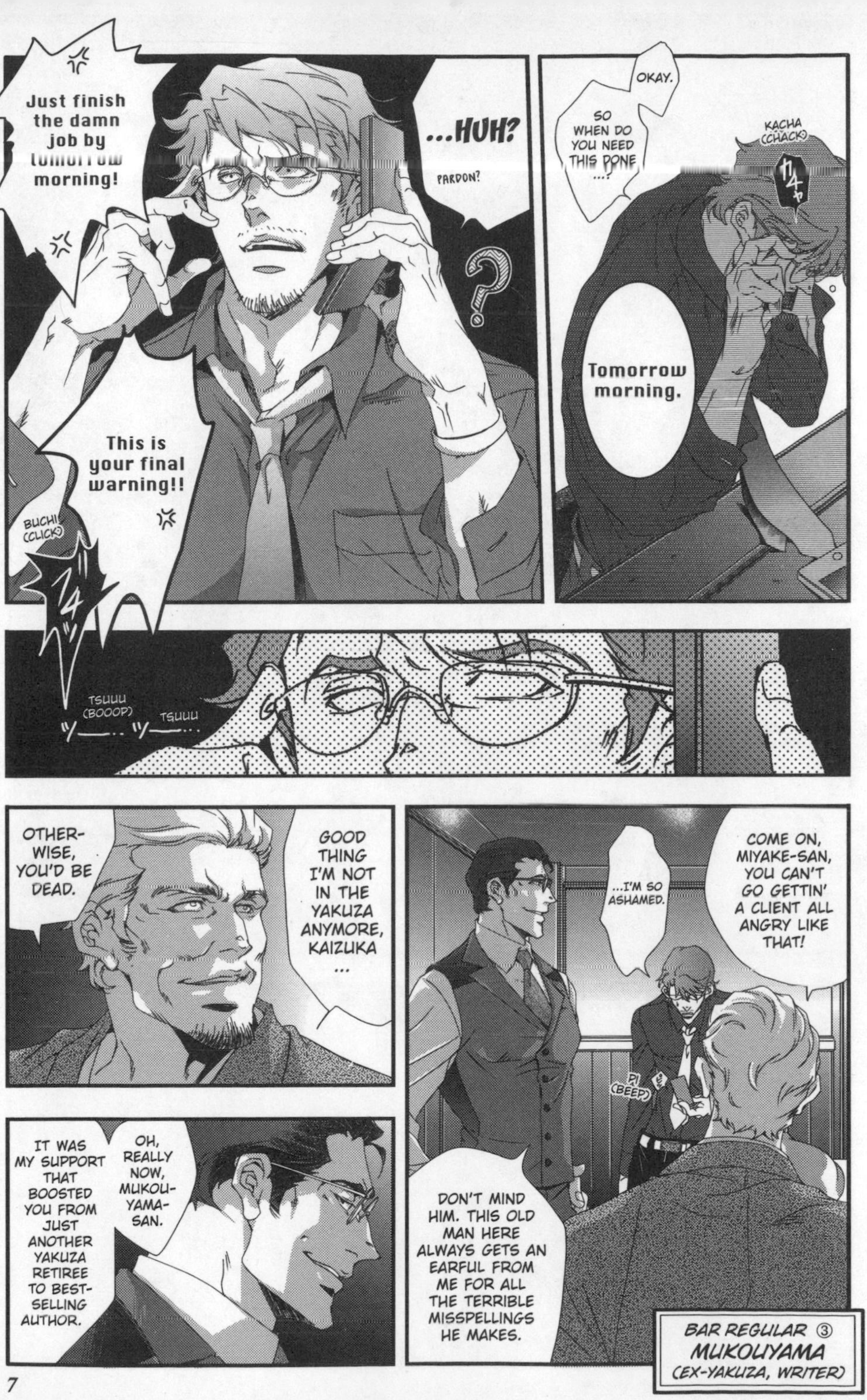
OKAY.
SO WHEN DO YOU NEED THIS DONE ...?
KACHA (CHACK)
Tomorrow morning.
Just finish the damn job by tomorrow morning!
...HUH?
PARDON?
This is your final warning!!
BUCHI (CLICK)
TSUUU (BOOOP) TSUUU
COME ON, MIYAKE-SAN, YOU CAN'T GO GETTIN' A CLIENT ALL ANGRY LIKE THAT!
...I'M SO ASHAMED.
PI (BEEP)
GOOD THING I'M NOT IN THE YAKUZA ANYMORE, KAIZUKA ...
OTHER-WISE, YOU'D BE DEAD.
DON'T MIND HIM. THIS OLD MAN HERE ALWAYS GETS AN EARFUL FROM ME FOR ALL THE TERRIBLE MISSPELLINGS HE MAKES.
BAR REGULAR ③ MUKOUYAMA (EX-YAKUZA, WRITER)
OH, REALLY NOW, MUKOU-YAMA-SAN.
IT WAS MY SUPPORT THAT BOOSTED YOU FROM JUST ANOTHER YAKUZA RETIREE TO BEST-SELLING AUTHOR.

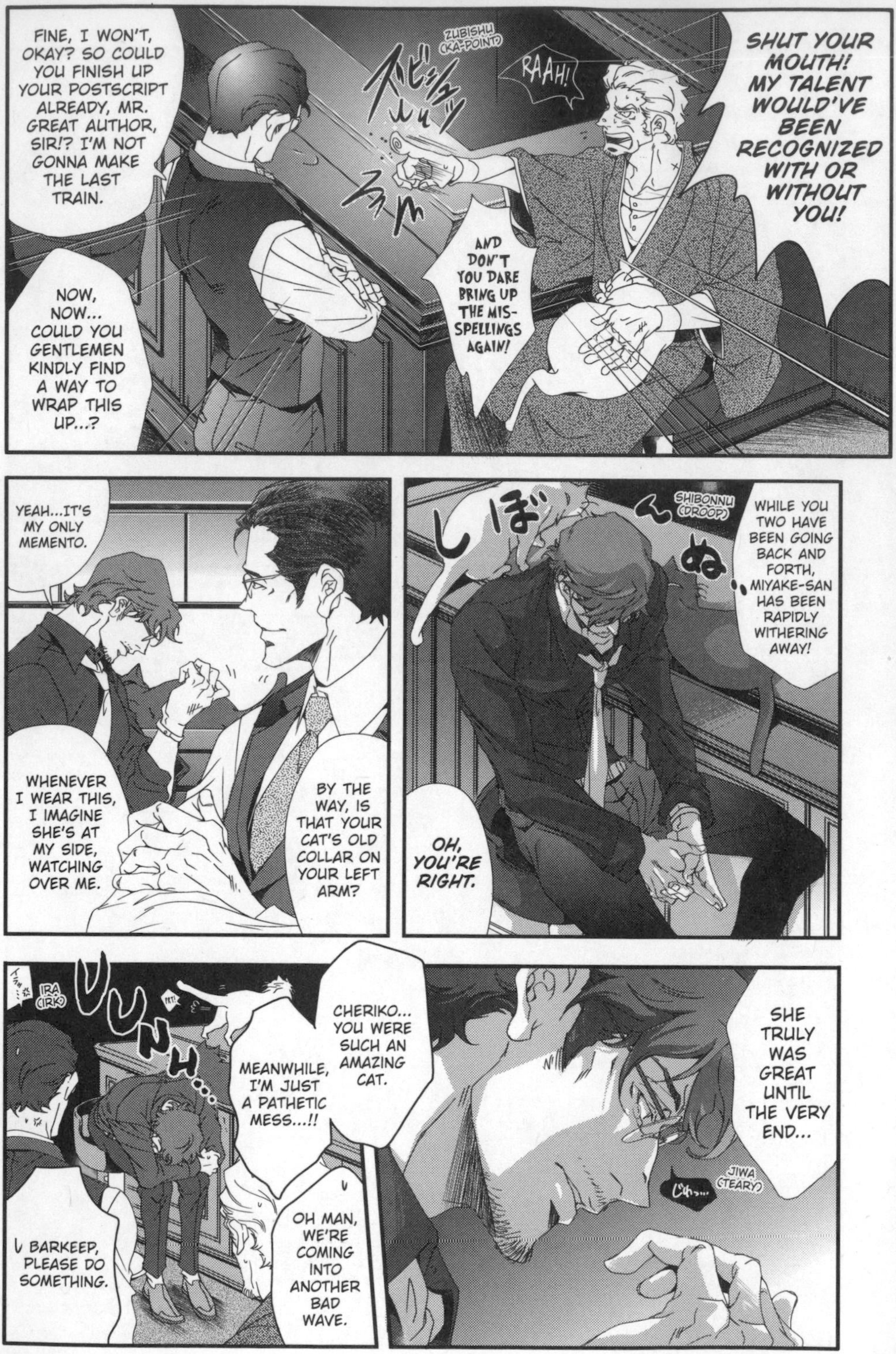
SHUT YOUR MOUTH! MY TALENT WOULD'VE BEEN RECOGNIZED WITH OR WITHOUT YOU!
RAAH!
ZUBISHU (KA-POINT)
AND DON'T YOU DARE BRING UP THE MIS-SPELLINGS AGAIN!
FINE, I WON'T, OKAY? SO COULD YOU FINISH UP YOUR POSTSCRIPT ALREADY, MR. GREAT AUTHOR, SIR!? I'M NOT GONNA MAKE THE LAST TRAIN.
NOW, NOW... COULD YOU GENTLEMEN KINDLY FIND A WAY TO WRAP THIS UP...?
SHIBONNU (DROOP)
WHILE YOU TWO HAVE BEEN GOING BACK AND FORTH, MIYAKE-SAN HAS BEEN RAPIDLY WITHERING AWAY!
OH, YOU'RE RIGHT.
BY THE WAY, IS THAT YOUR CAT'S OLD COLLAR ON YOUR LEFT ARM?
YEAH...IT'S MY ONLY MEMENTO.
WHENEVER I WEAR THIS, I IMAGINE SHE'S AT MY SIDE, WATCHING OVER ME.
SHE TRULY WAS GREAT UNTIL THE VERY END...
JIWA (TEARY)
CHERIKO... YOU WERE SUCH AN AMAZING CAT.
MEANWHILE, I'M JUST A PATHETIC MESS...!!
UUNH...
IRA (IRK)
OH MAN, WE'RE COMING INTO ANOTHER BAD WAVE.
BARKEEP, PLEASE DO SOMETHING.

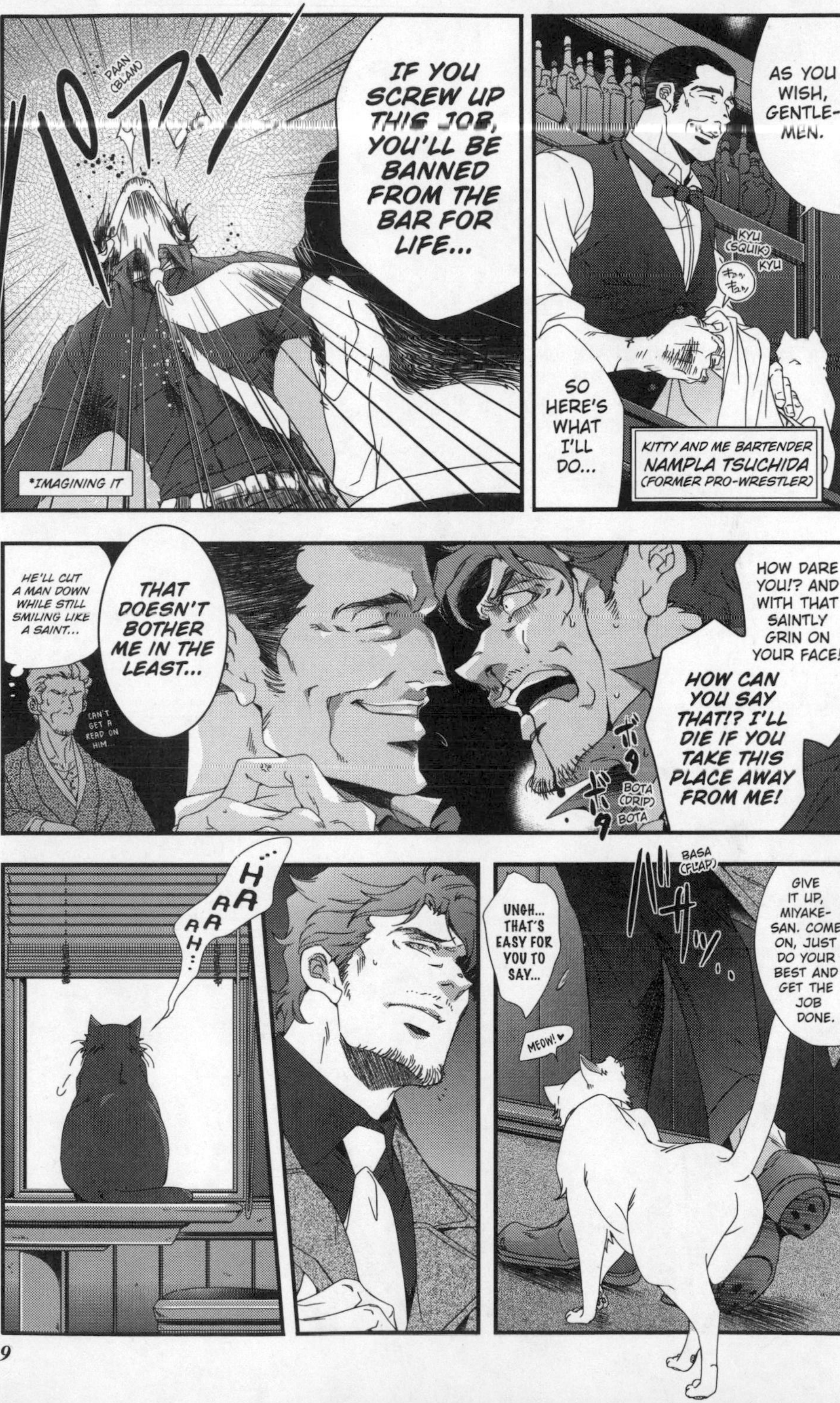
AS YOU WISH, GENTLEMEN.
KYU (SQUIK) KYU
SO HERE'S WHAT I'LL DO...
KITTY AND ME BARTENDER NAMPLA TSUCHIDA (FORMER PRO-WRESTLER)
IF YOU SCREW UP THIS JOB, YOU'LL BE BANNED FROM THE BAR FOR LIFE...
PAAN (BLAM)
*IMAGINING IT
HOW DARE YOU!? AND WITH THAT SAINTLY GRIN ON YOUR FACE!
HOW CAN YOU SAY THAT!? I'LL DIE IF YOU TAKE THIS PLACE AWAY FROM ME!
BOTA (DRIP) BOTA
THAT DOESN'T BOTHER ME IN THE LEAST...
HE'LL CUT A MAN DOWN WHILE STILL SMILING LIKE A SAINT...
CAN'T GET A READ ON HIM...
BASA (FLAP)
GIVE IT UP, MIYAKE-SAN. COME ON, JUST DO YOUR BEST AND GET THE JOB DONE.
UNGH... THAT'S EASY FOR YOU TO SAY...
MEOW! ♥
...HAAAH...

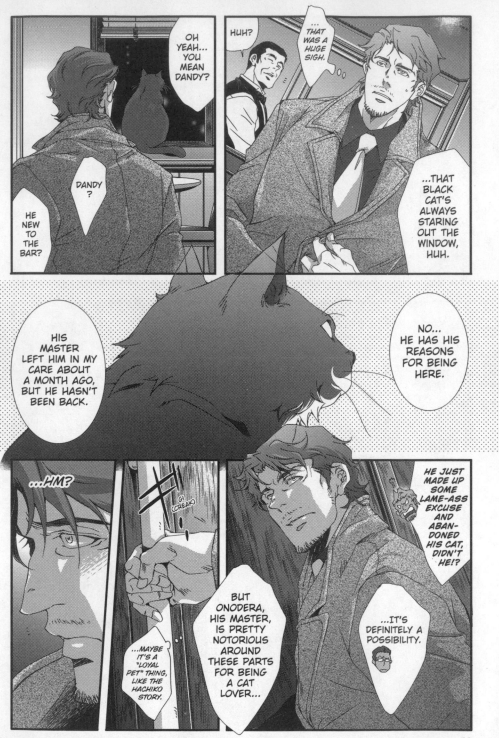

...THAT WAS A HUGE SIGH.
...THAT BLACK CAT'S ALWAYS STARING OUT THE WINDOW, HUH.
HUH?
OH YEAH... YOU MEAN DANDY?
DANDY?
HE NEW TO THE BAR?
NO... HE HAS HIS REASONS FOR BEING HERE.
HIS MASTER LEFT HIM IN MY CARE ABOUT A MONTH AGO, BUT HE HASN'T BEEN BACK.
HE JUST MADE UP SOME LAME-ASS EXCUSE AND ABANDONED HIS CAT, DIDN'T HE!?
...IT'S DEFINITELY A POSSIBILITY.
BUT ONODERA, HIS MASTER, IS PRETTY NOTORIOUS AROUND THESE PARTS FOR BEING A CAT LOVER...
...MAYBE IT'S A "LOYAL PET" THING, LIKE THE HACHIKO STORY.
GI (CREAK)
...HM?

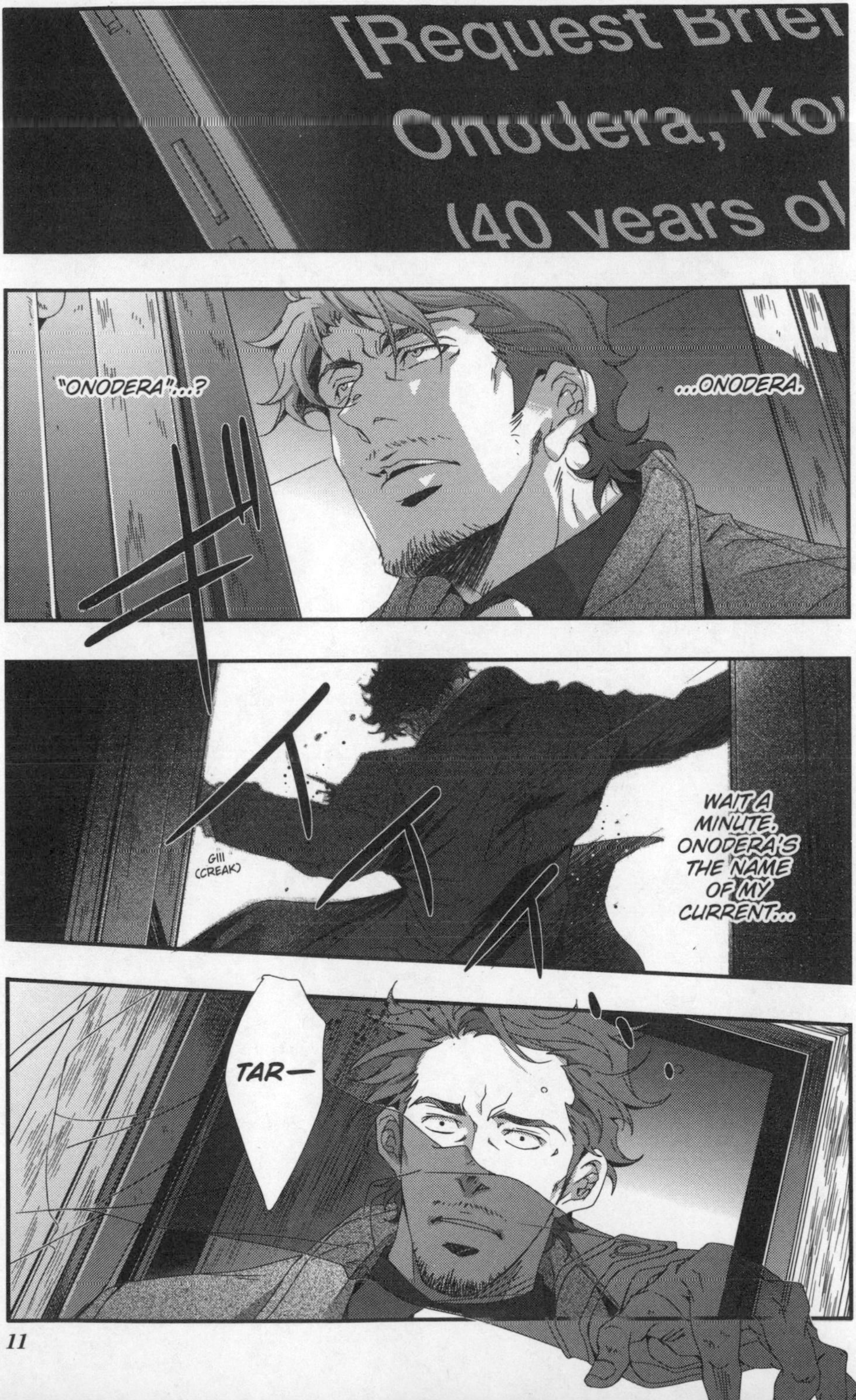
[Request Brie
Onodera, Ko
(40 years o
...ONODERA.
"ONODERA"...?
WAIT A MINUTE. ONODERA'S THE NAME OF MY CURRENT...
GIII (CREAK)
TAR—

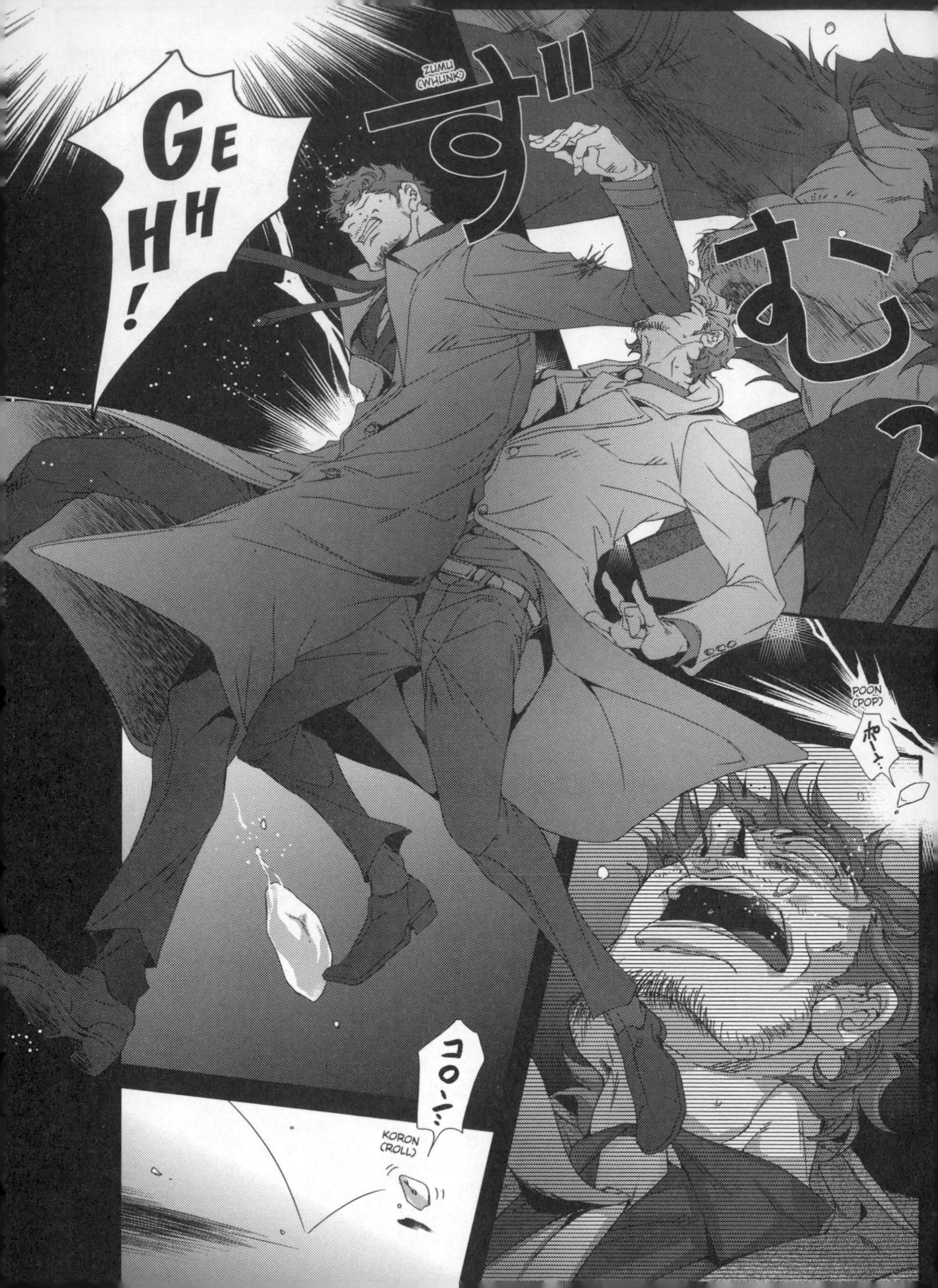
ずむっ
ZUMU (WHUNK)
GEHHH!
ポーン…
POON (POP)
コローン…
KORON (ROLL)

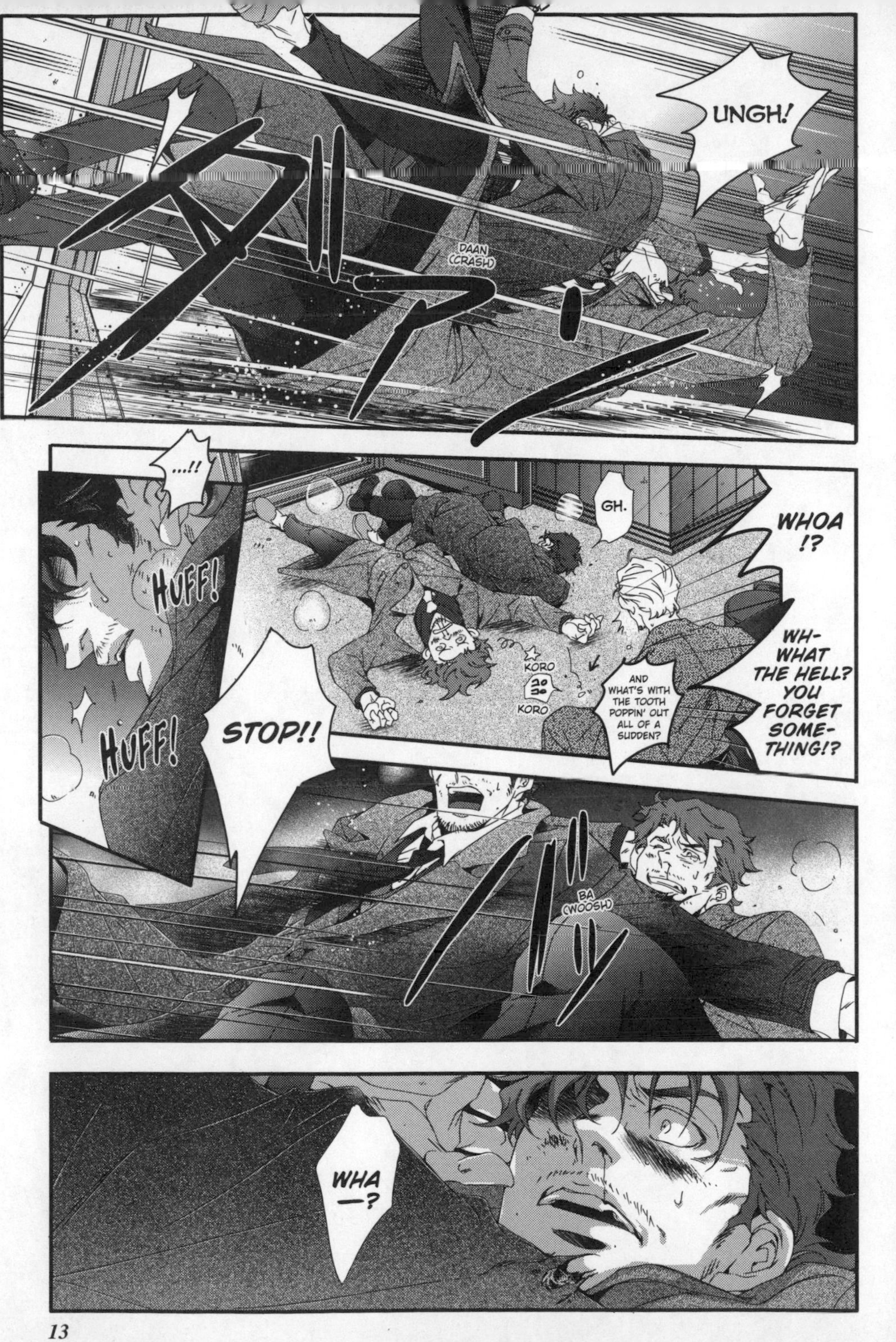
UNGH!
DAAN (CRASH)
WHOA !?
WH-WHAT THE HELL? YOU FORGET SOME-THING!?
GH.
AND WHAT'S WITH THE TOOTH POPPIN' OUT ALL OF A SUDDEN?
KORO KORO
BA (WOOSH)
...!!
HUFF!
HUFF!
STOP!!
WHA—?

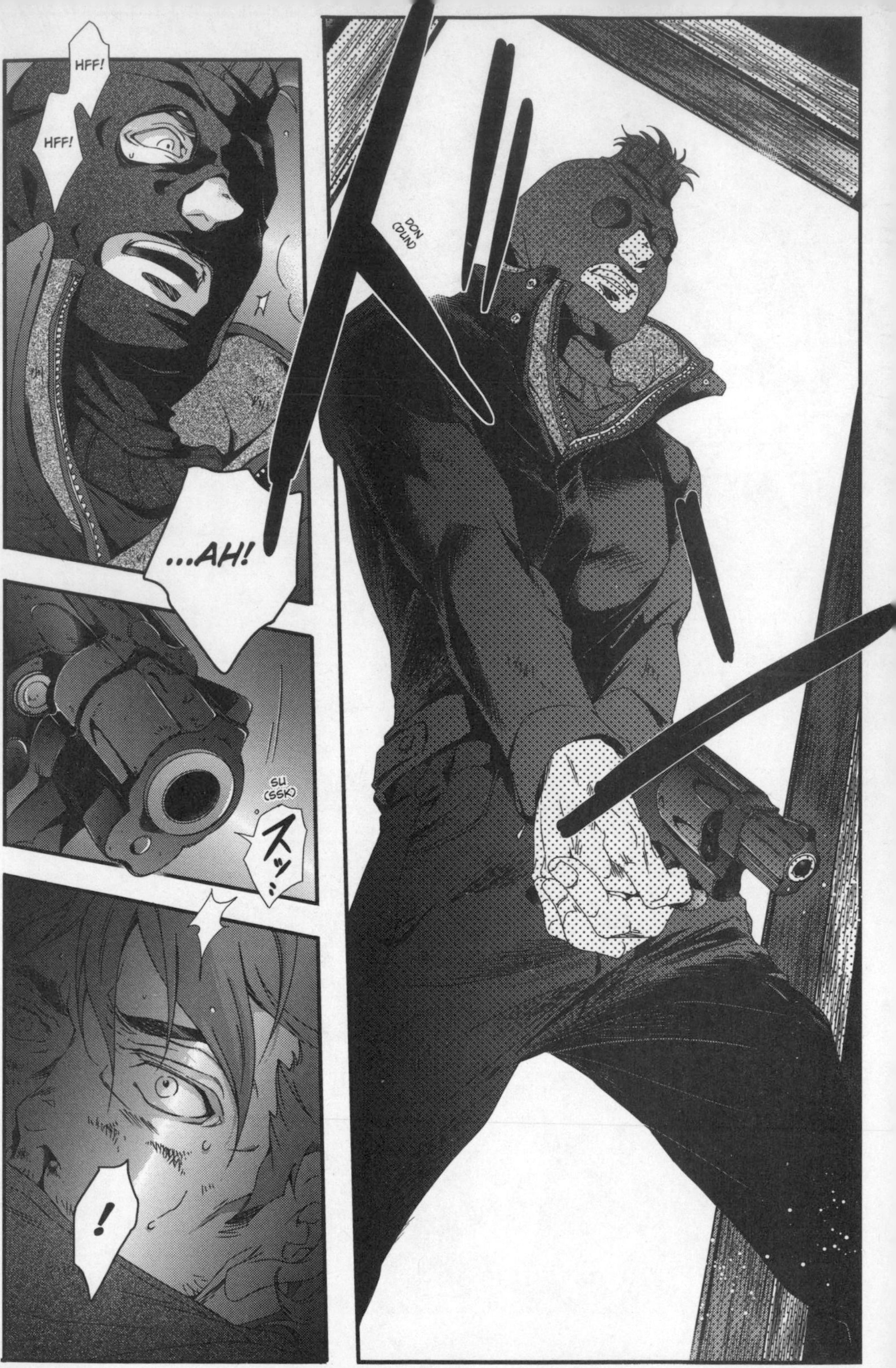
DON (DUN)
HFF!
HFF!
...AH!
SU (SSK)
スッ
!

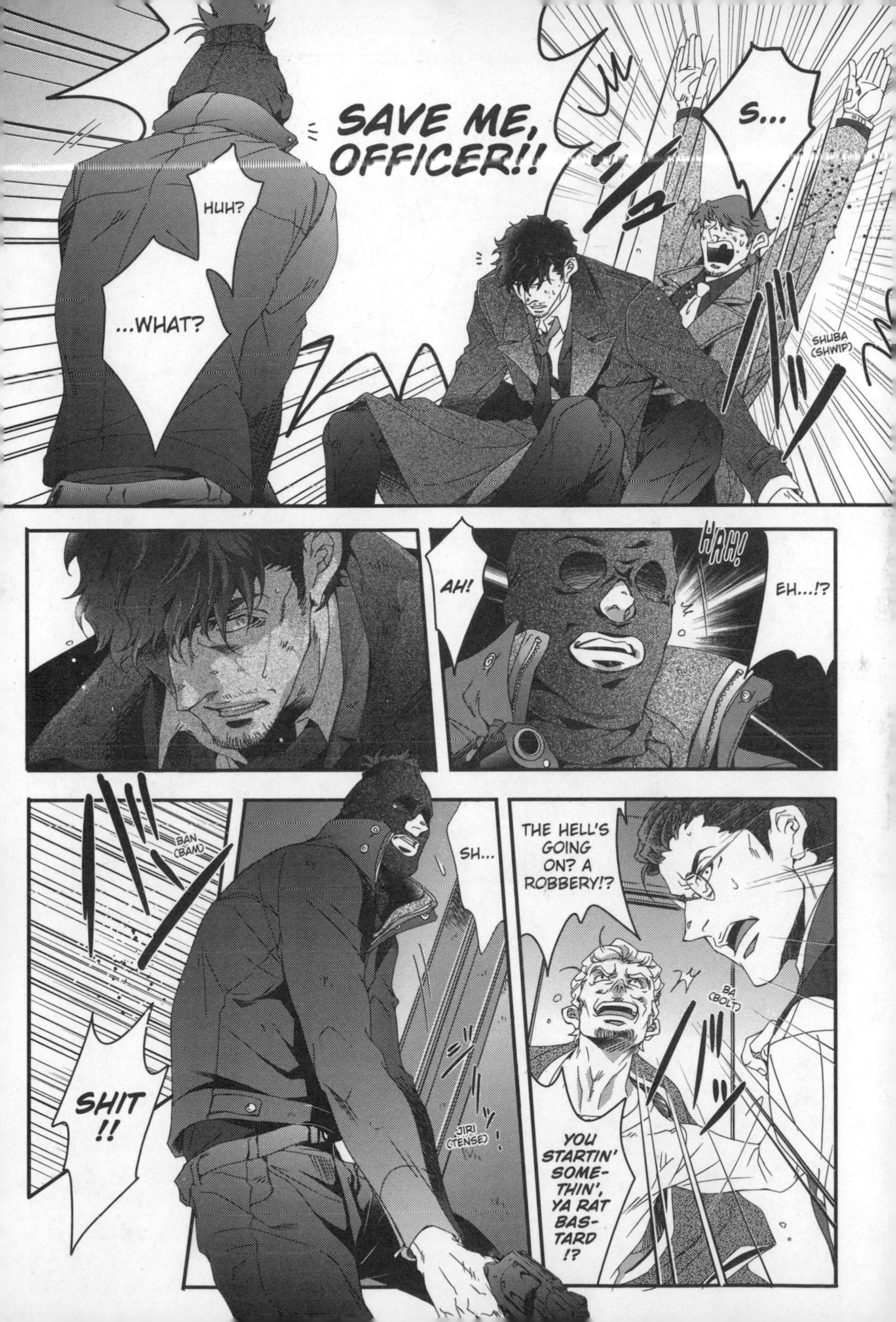
S...
SAVE ME, OFFICER!!
SHUBA (SHWIP)
HUH?
...WHAT?
HAH!
EH...!?
AH!
THE HELL'S GOING ON? A ROBBERY!?
BA (BOLT)
YOU STARTIN' SOME-THIN', YA RAT BAS-TARD !?
SH...
BAN (BAM)
SHIT !!
JIRI (TENSE)

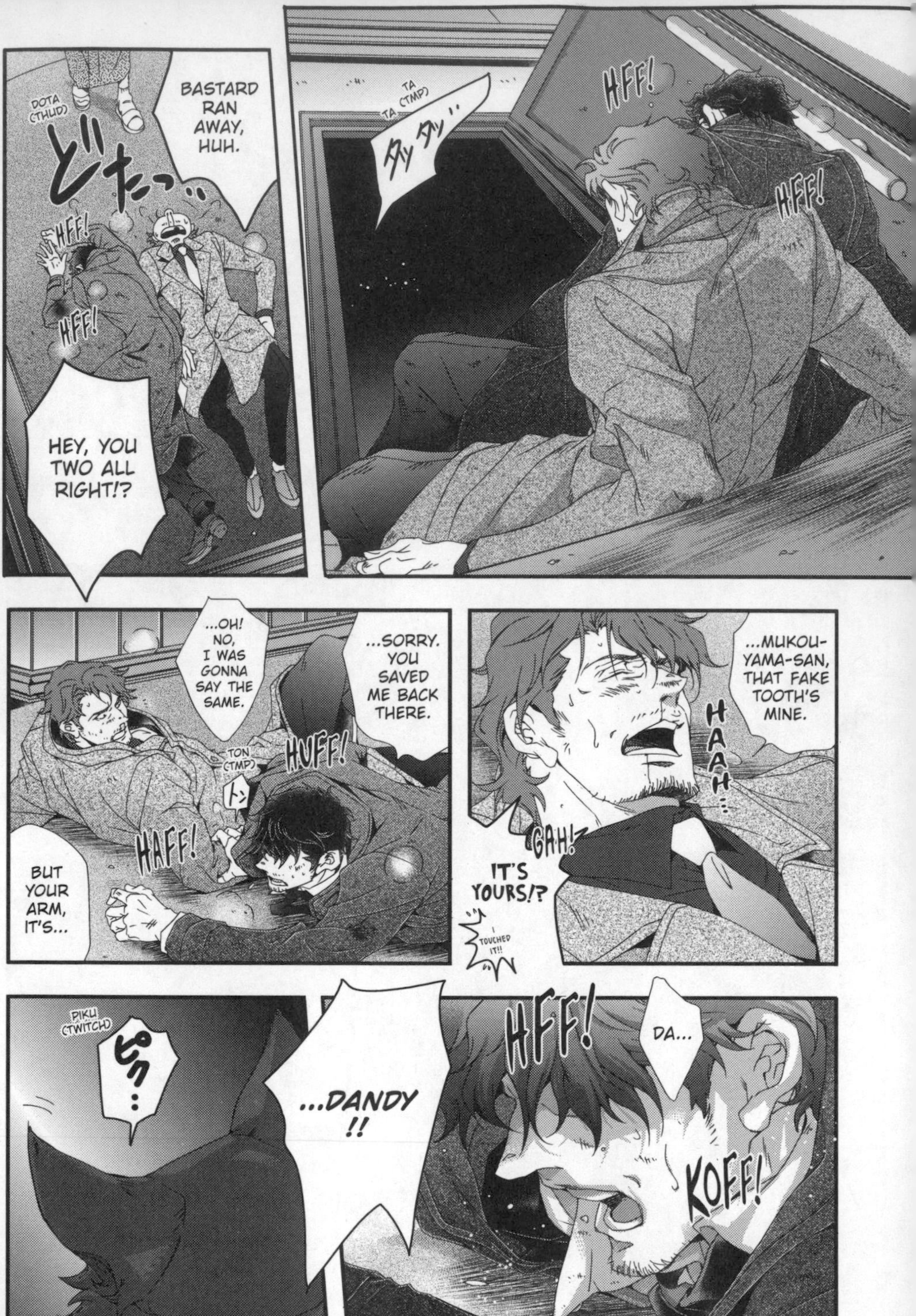
TA TA (TMP)
タッタッ
HFF!
HFF!
DOTA (THUD)
どたっ…
HFF!
HFF!
BASTARD RAN AWAY, HUH.
HEY, YOU TWO ALL RIGHT!?
...MUKOU-YAMA-SAN, THAT FAKE TOOTH'S MINE.
HAAAH...
GAH!
IT'S YOURS!?
I TOUCHED IT!!
...SORRY. YOU SAVED ME BACK THERE.
...OH! NO, I WAS GONNA SAY THE SAME.
TON (TMP)
トン
HUFF!
HAFF!
BUT YOUR ARM, IT'S...
DA...
HFF!
KOFF!
...DANDY!!
PIKU (TWITCH)
ピク…

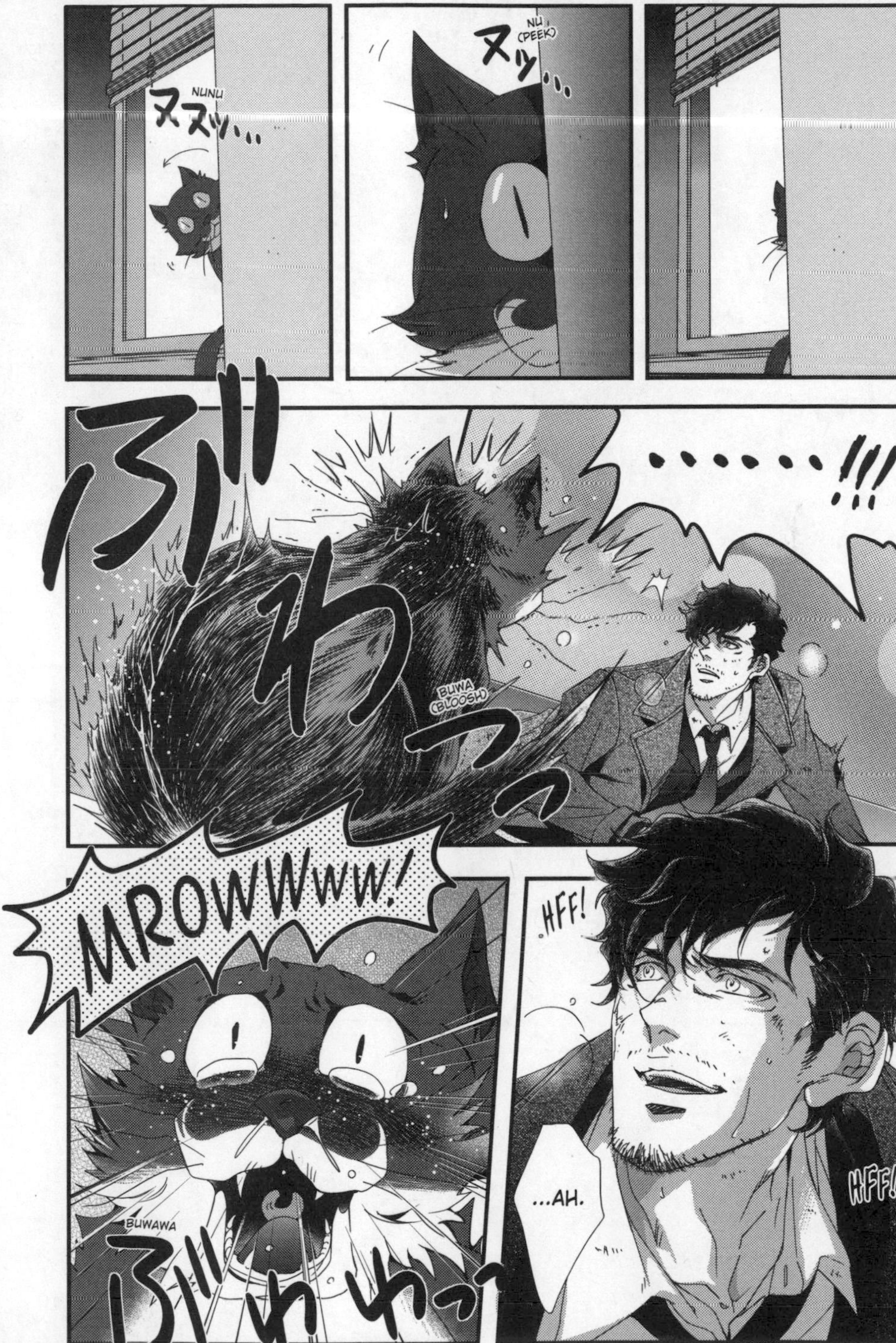
ヌッ..
NU (PEEK)
ヌヌッ...
NUNU
......!!!
ぶわっ
BUWA (BLOOSH)
HFF!
...AH.
HFF!
MROWWWW!
ぶわわっ
BUWAWA

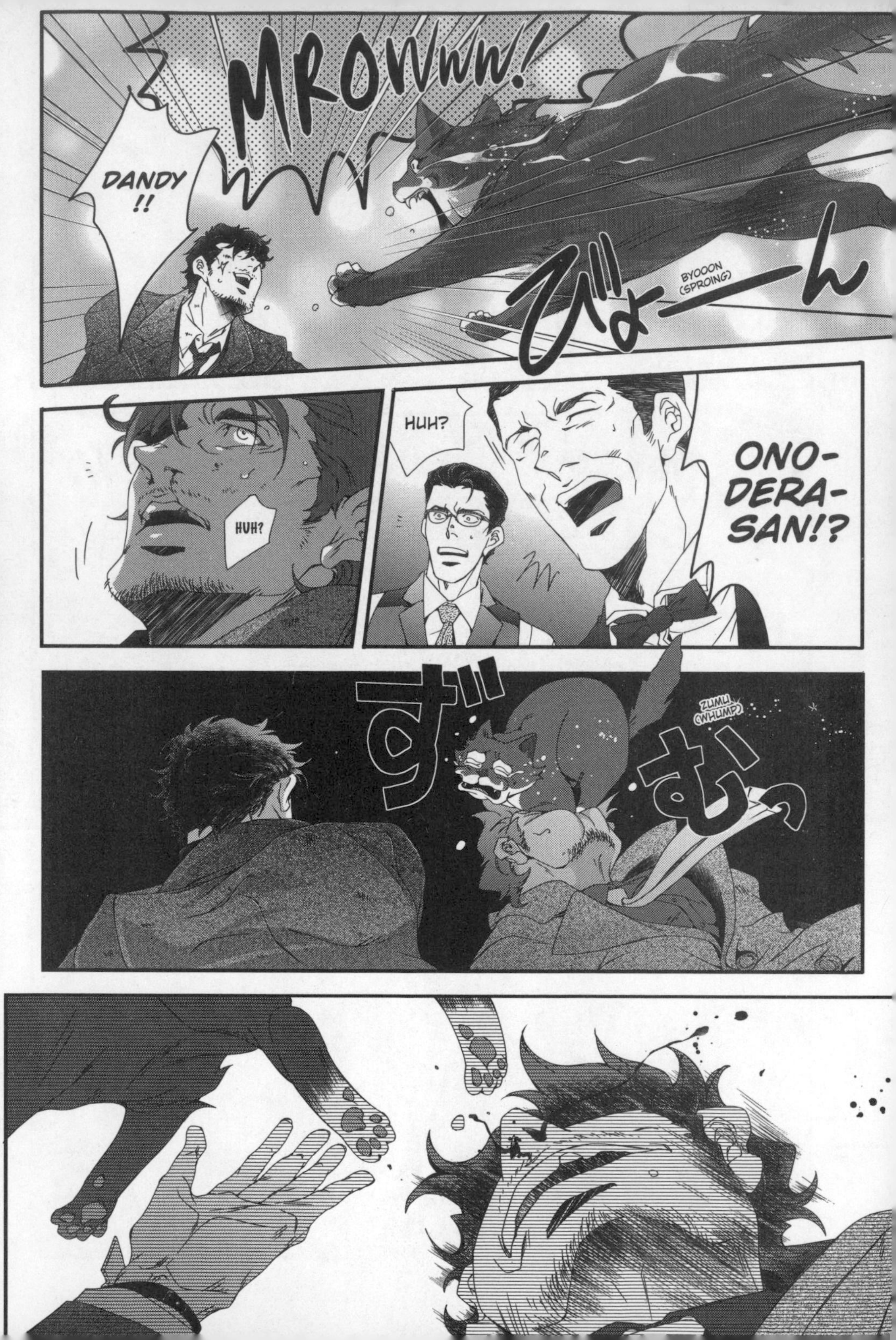
MROWWW!
DANDY !!
BYOOON (SPROING)
ONO-DERA-SAN!?
HUH?
HUH?
ZUMU (WHUMP)

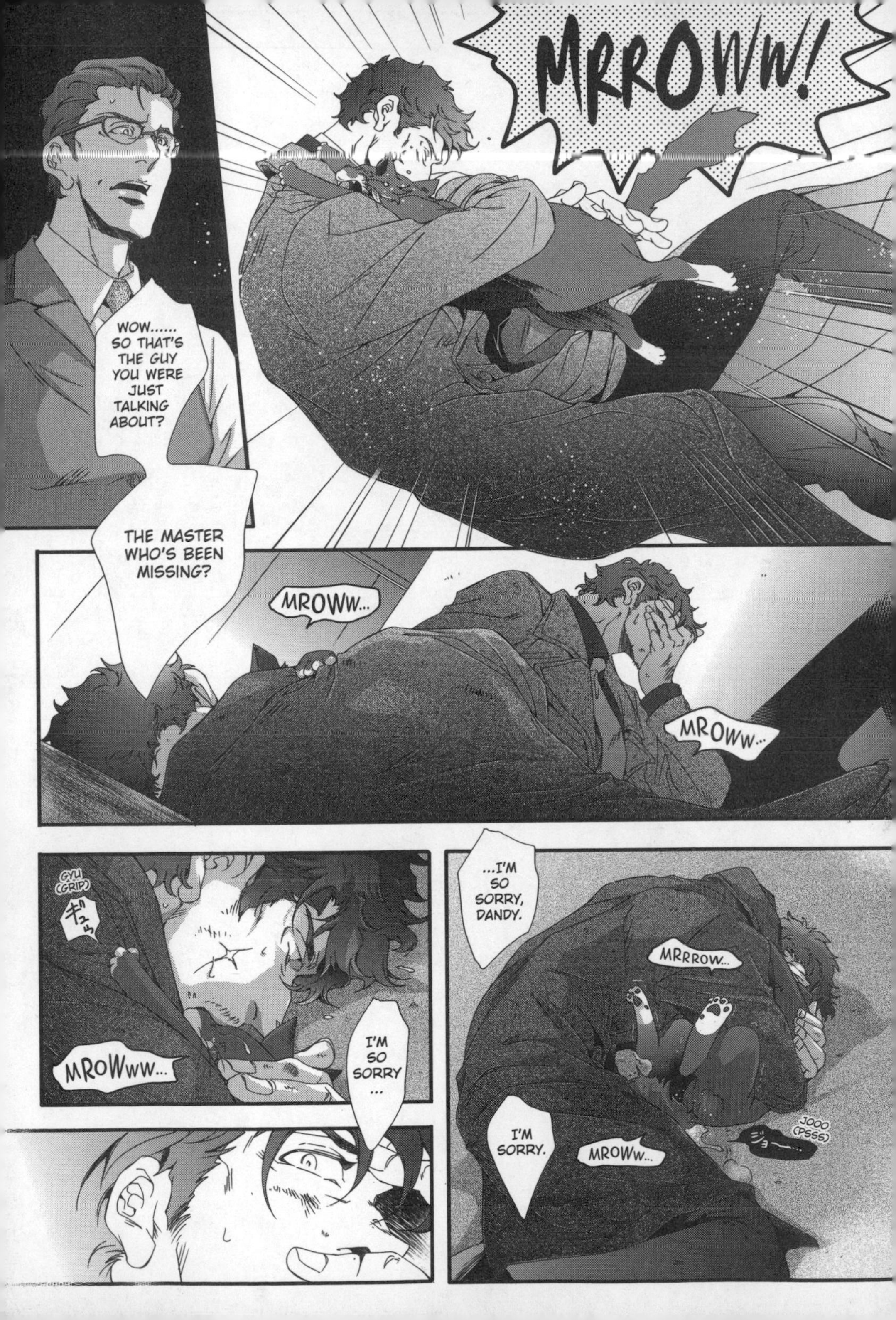
MRROWW!
WOW...... SO THAT'S THE GUY YOU WERE JUST TALKING ABOUT?
THE MASTER WHO'S BEEN MISSING?
MROWw...
MROWw...
...I'M SO SORRY, DANDY.
MRRROW...
JOOO (PSSS)
I'M SORRY.
MROWw...
GYU (GRIP)
ギュ
MROWww...
I'M SO SORRY ...

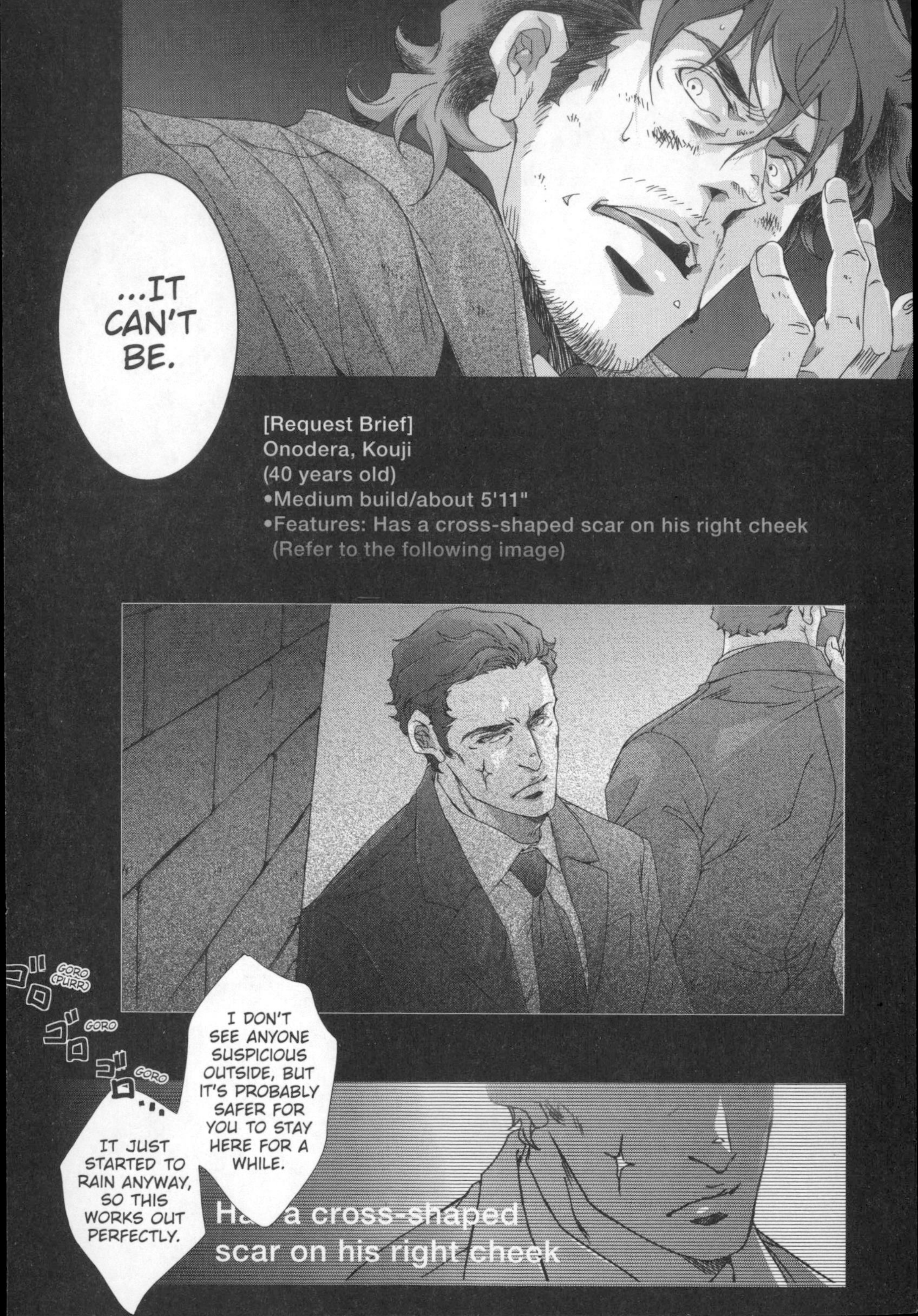
...IT CAN'T BE.
[Request Brief]
Onodera, Kouji
(40 years old)
•Medium build/about 5'11"
•Features: Has a cross-shaped scar on his right cheek
(Refer to the following image)
ゴロ GORO (PURR)
ゴロ GORO
ゴロ... GORO
I DON'T SEE ANYONE SUSPICIOUS OUTSIDE, BUT IT'S PROBABLY SAFER FOR YOU TO STAY HERE FOR A WHILE.
IT JUST STARTED TO RAIN ANYWAY, SO THIS WORKS OUT PERFECTLY.
Ha a cross-shaped scar on his right cheek

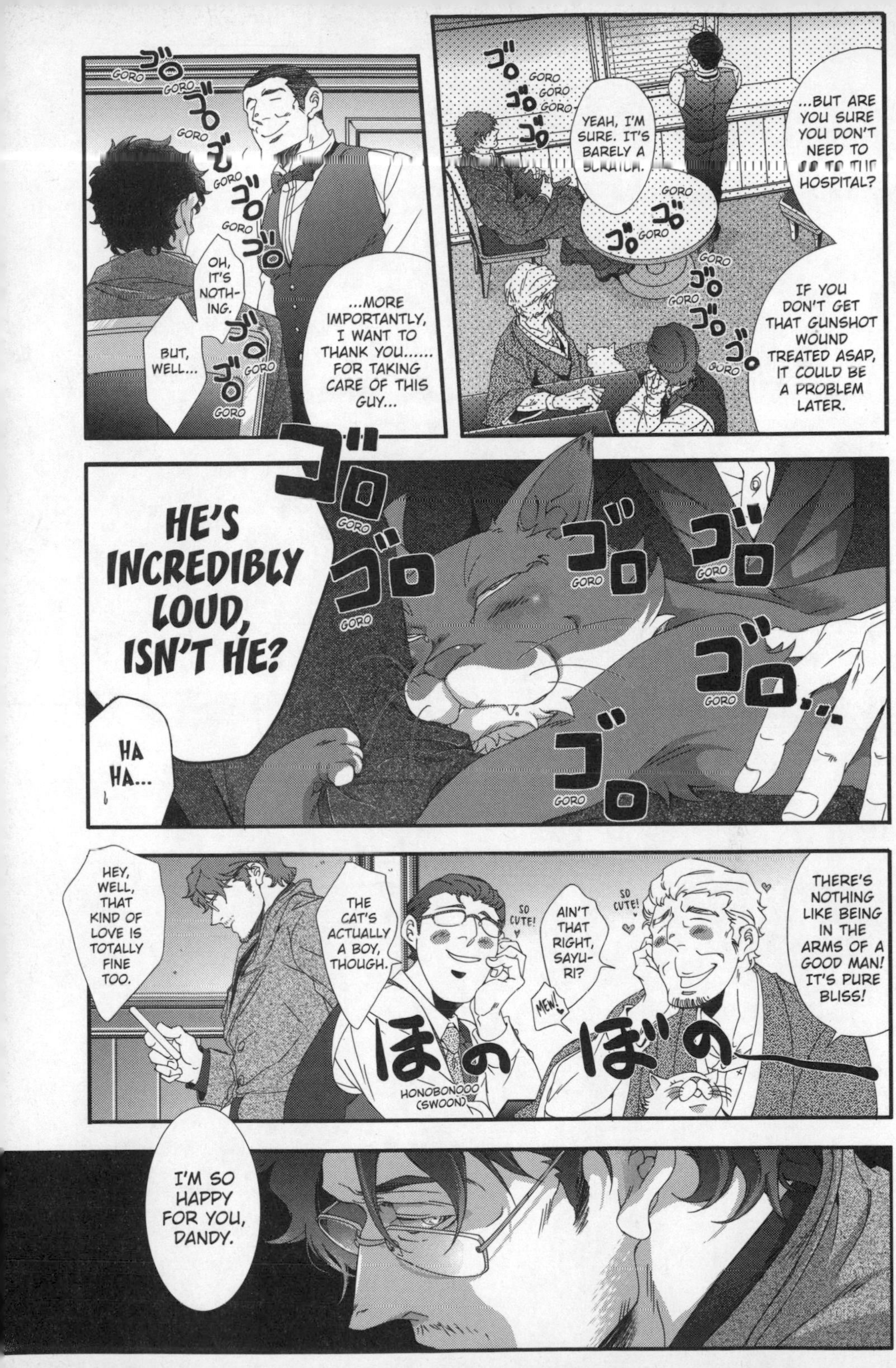
...BUT ARE YOU SURE YOU DON'T NEED TO GO TO THE HOSPITAL?
YEAH, I'M SURE. IT'S BARELY A SCRATCH.
ゴロ GORO ゴロ GORO ゴロ GORO
IF YOU DON'T GET THAT GUNSHOT WOUND TREATED ASAP, IT COULD BE A PROBLEM LATER.
ゴロ GORO ゴロ GORO ゴロ GORO
...MORE IMPORTANTLY, I WANT TO THANK YOU...... FOR TAKING CARE OF THIS GUY...
OH, IT'S NOTHING.
BUT, WELL...
ゴロ GORO ゴロ GORO ゴロ GORO
ゴロ GORO ゴロ GORO ゴロ GORO
ゴロ... GORO ゴロ GORO
HE'S INCREDIBLY LOUD, ISN'T HE?
HA HA...
THERE'S NOTHING LIKE BEING IN THE ARMS OF A GOOD MAN! IT'S PURE BLISS!
SO CUTE!
AIN'T THAT RIGHT, SAYURI?
MEW!
SO CUTE!
THE CAT'S ACTUALLY A BOY, THOUGH.
HEY, WELL, THAT KIND OF LOVE IS TOTALLY FINE TOO.
ほのぼの— HONOBONOOO (SWOON)
I'M SO HAPPY FOR YOU, DANDY.

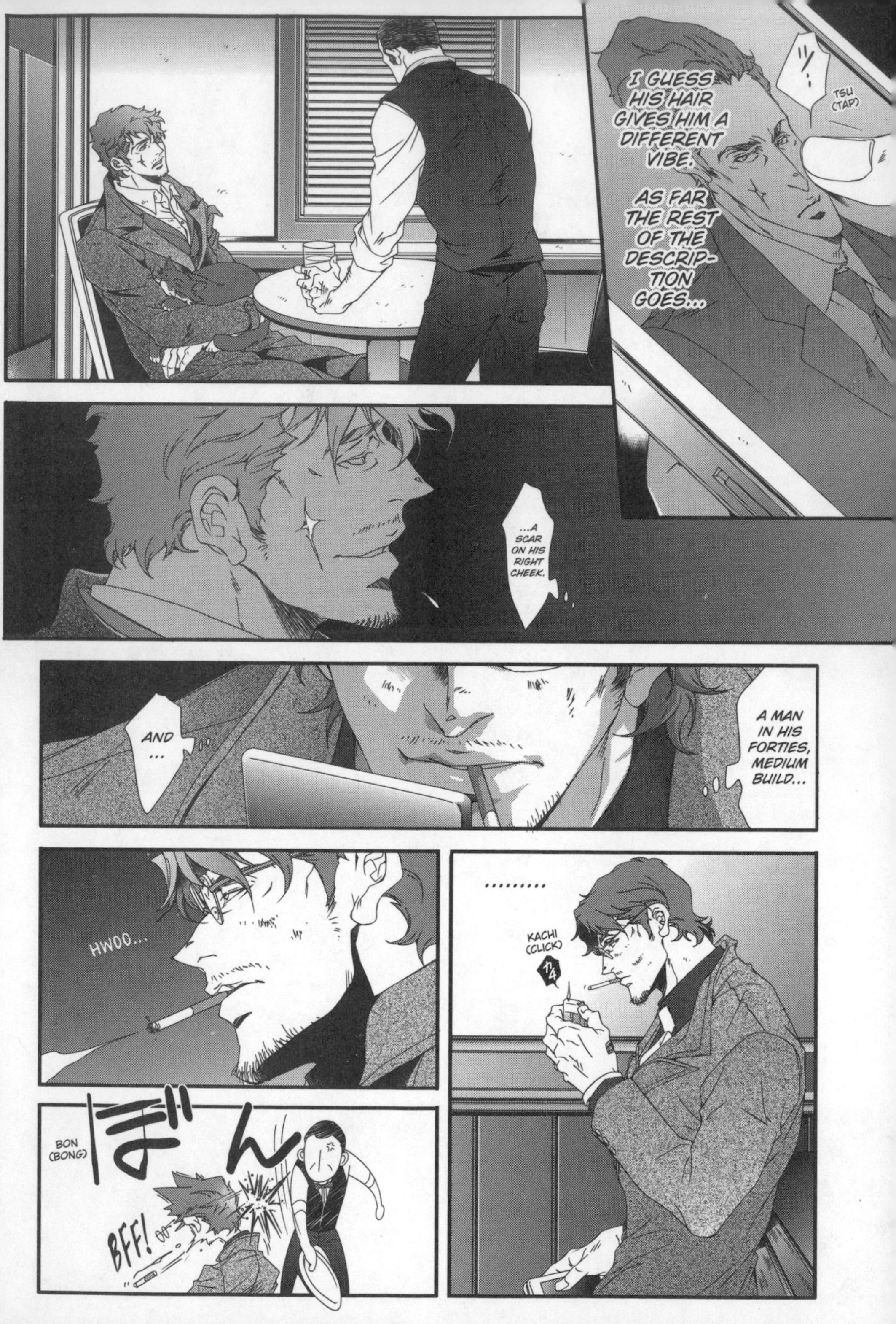
TSU (TAP)
I GUESS HIS HAIR GIVES HIM A DIFFERENT VIBE.
AS FAR THE REST OF THE DESCRIPTION GOES...
...A SCAR ON HIS RIGHT CHEEK.
A MAN IN HIS FORTIES, MEDIUM BUILD...
AND ...
....
KACHI (CLICK)
カチ
HWOO...
BON (BONG)
ぼん
BFF!

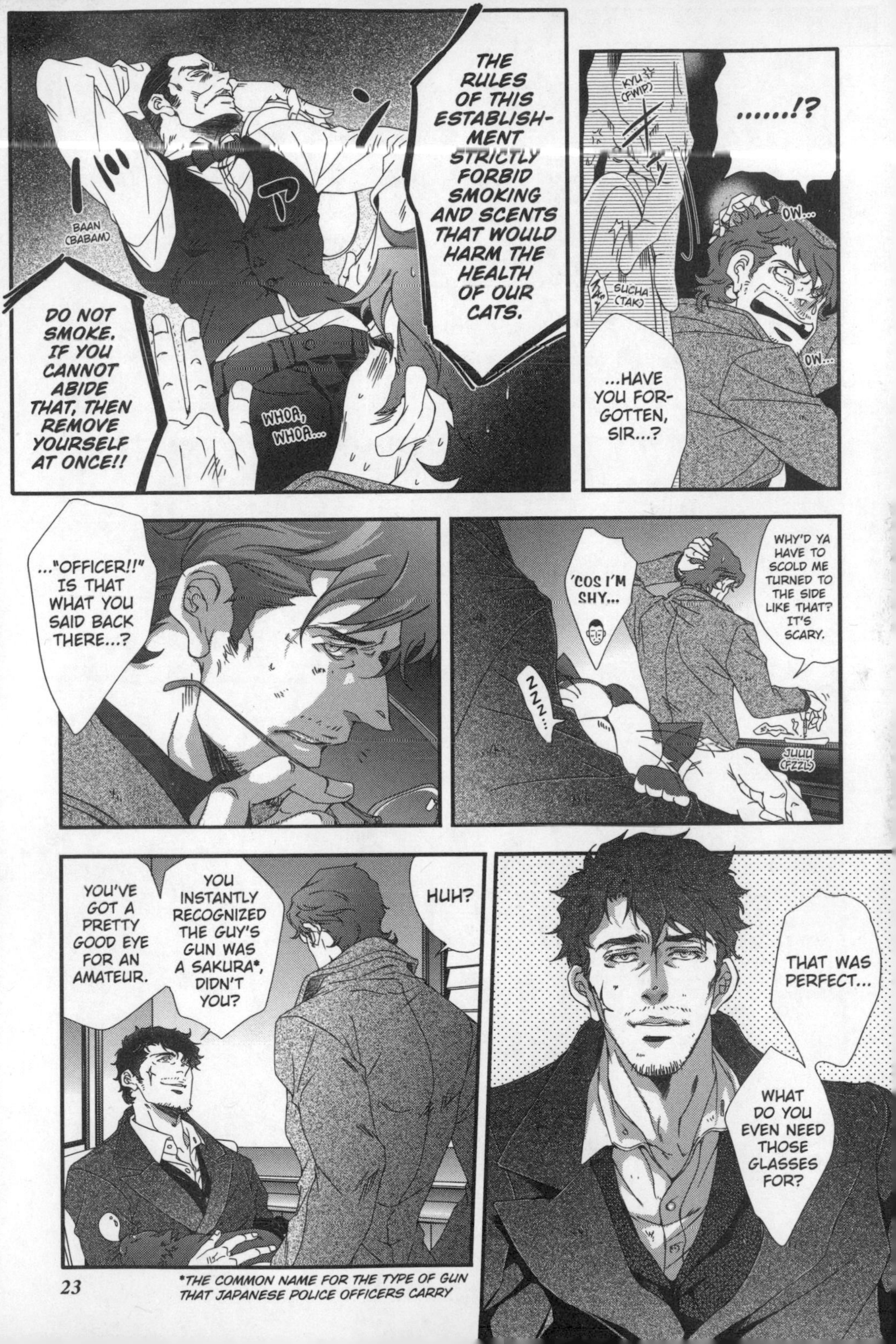
......!?
KYU (FWIP)
OW...
SUCHA (TAK)
OW...
...HAVE YOU FORGOTTEN, SIR...?
BAAN (BABAM)
THE RULES OF THIS ESTABLISHMENT STRICTLY FORBID SMOKING AND SCENTS THAT WOULD HARM THE HEALTH OF OUR CATS.
DO NOT SMOKE. IF YOU CANNOT ABIDE THAT, THEN REMOVE YOURSELF AT ONCE!!
WHOA, WHOA...
WHY'D YA HAVE TO SCOLD ME TURNED TO THE SIDE LIKE THAT? IT'S SCARY.
'COS I'M SHY...
ZZZ...
JUUU (FZZL)
..."OFFICER!!" IS THAT WHAT YOU SAID BACK THERE...?
THAT WAS PERFECT...
WHAT DO YOU EVEN NEED THOSE GLASSES FOR?
HUH?
YOU INSTANTLY RECOGNIZED THE GUY'S GUN WAS A SAKURA*, DIDN'T YOU?
YOU'VE GOT A PRETTY GOOD EYE FOR AN AMATEUR.

*THE COMMON NAME FOR THE TYPE OF GUN THAT JAPANESE POLICE OFFICERS CARRY

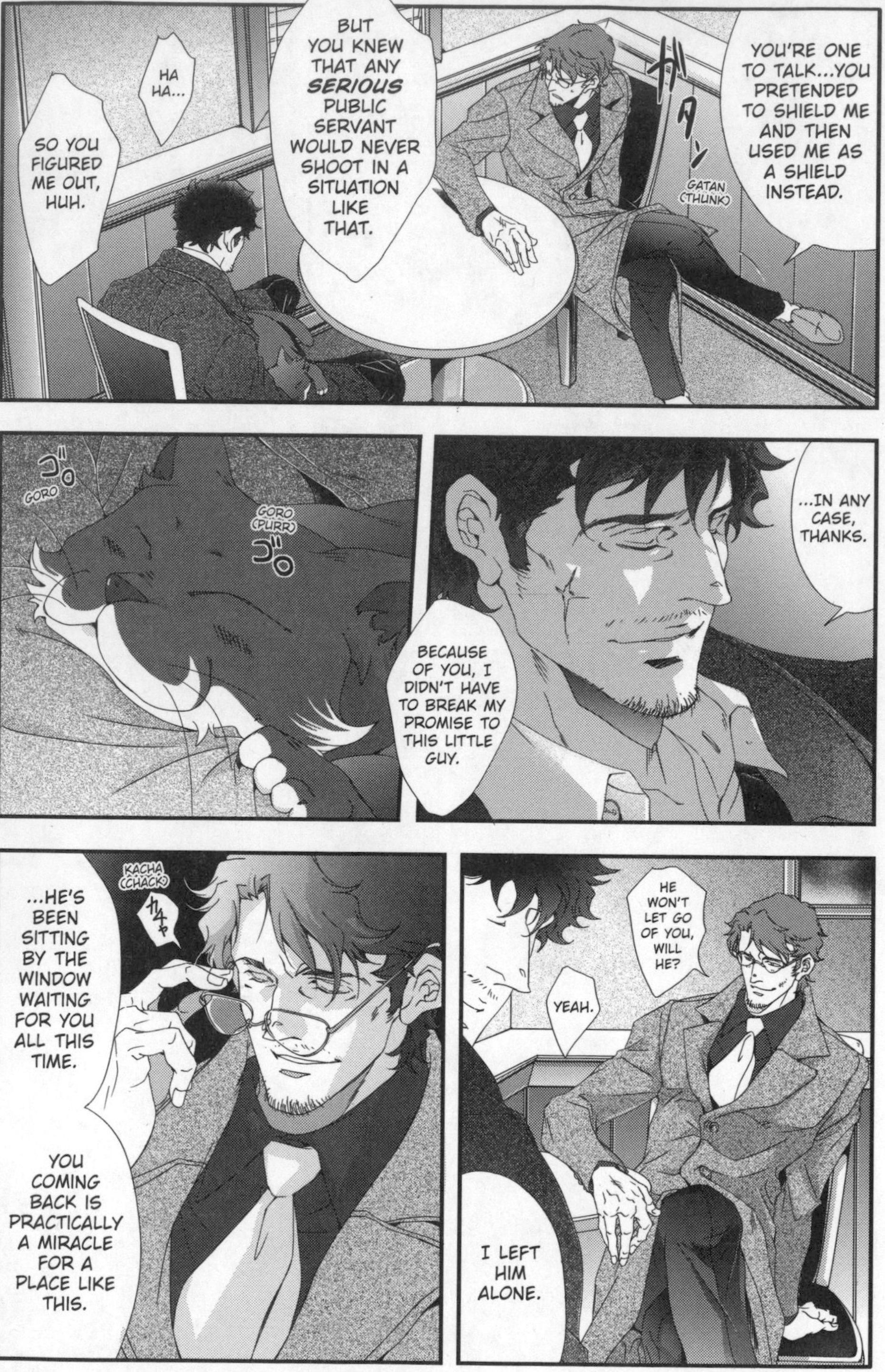
YOU'RE ONE TO TALK...YOU PRETENDED TO SHIELD ME AND THEN USED ME AS A SHIELD INSTEAD.
GATAN (THUNK)
BUT YOU KNEW THAT ANY SERIOUS PUBLIC SERVANT WOULD NEVER SHOOT IN A SITUATION LIKE THAT.
HA HA...
SO YOU FIGURED ME OUT, HUH.
...IN ANY CASE, THANKS.
BECAUSE OF YOU, I DIDN'T HAVE TO BREAK MY PROMISE TO THIS LITTLE GUY.
GORO (PURR)
GORO
HE WON'T LET GO OF YOU, WILL HE?
YEAH.
I LEFT HIM ALONE.
KACHA (CHACK)
...HE'S BEEN SITTING BY THE WINDOW WAITING FOR YOU ALL THIS TIME.
YOU COMING BACK IS PRACTICALLY A MIRACLE FOR A PLACE LIKE THIS.

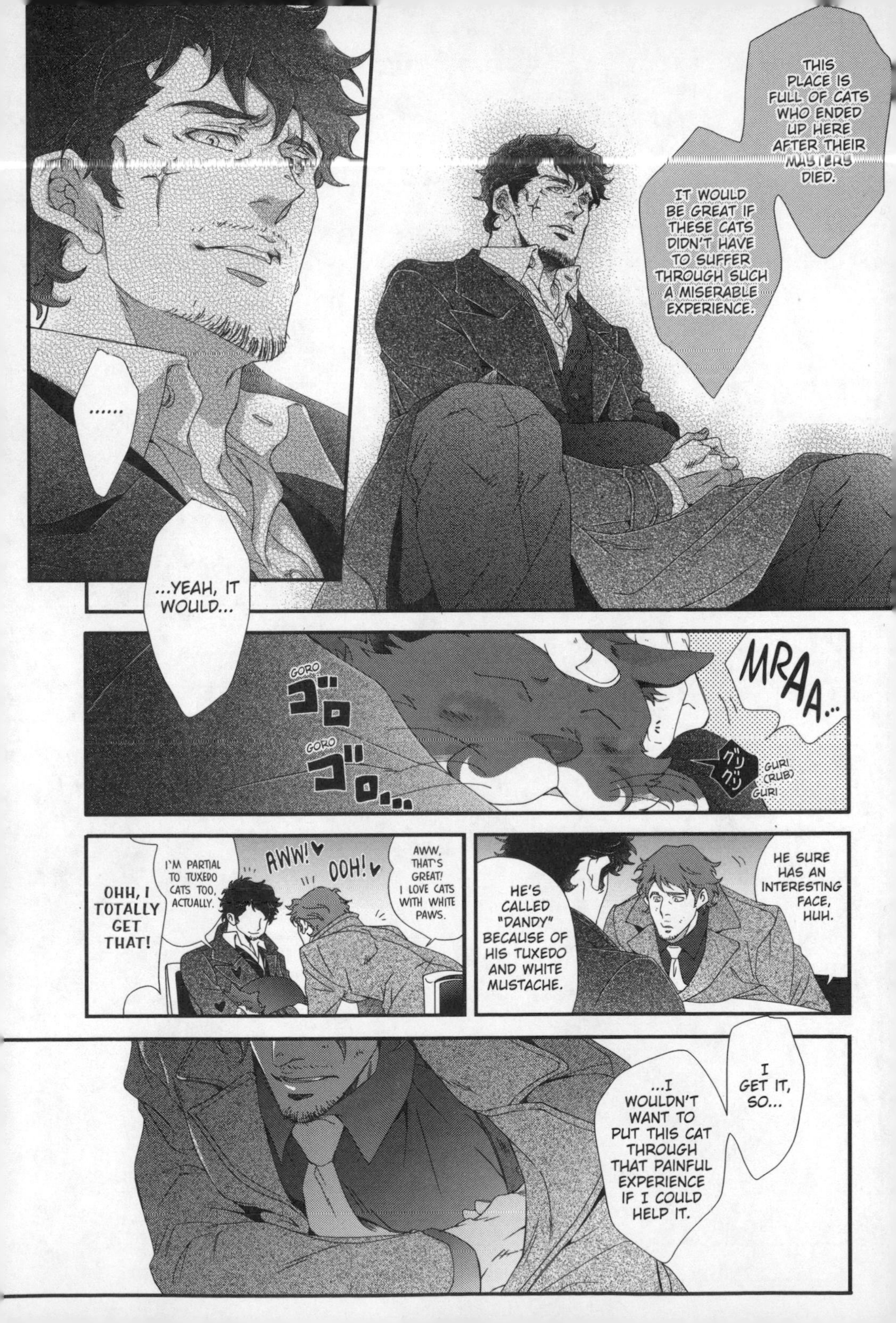
THIS PLACE IS FULL OF CATS WHO ENDED UP HERE AFTER THEIR MASTERS DIED.
IT WOULD BE GREAT IF THESE CATS DIDN'T HAVE TO SUFFER THROUGH SUCH A MISERABLE EXPERIENCE.
......
...YEAH, IT WOULD...
MRAA...
グリグリ GURI (RUB) GURI
ゴロ GORO
ゴロ... GORO
HE SURE HAS AN INTERESTING FACE, HUH.
HE'S CALLED "DANDY" BECAUSE OF HIS TUXEDO AND WHITE MUSTACHE.
AWW, THAT'S GREAT! I LOVE CATS WITH WHITE PAWS.
OOH!
AWW!
I'M PARTIAL TO TUXEDO CATS TOO, ACTUALLY.
OHH, I TOTALLY GET THAT!
I GET IT, SO...
...I WOULDN'T WANT TO PUT THIS CAT THROUGH THAT PAINFUL EXPERIENCE IF I COULD HELP IT.

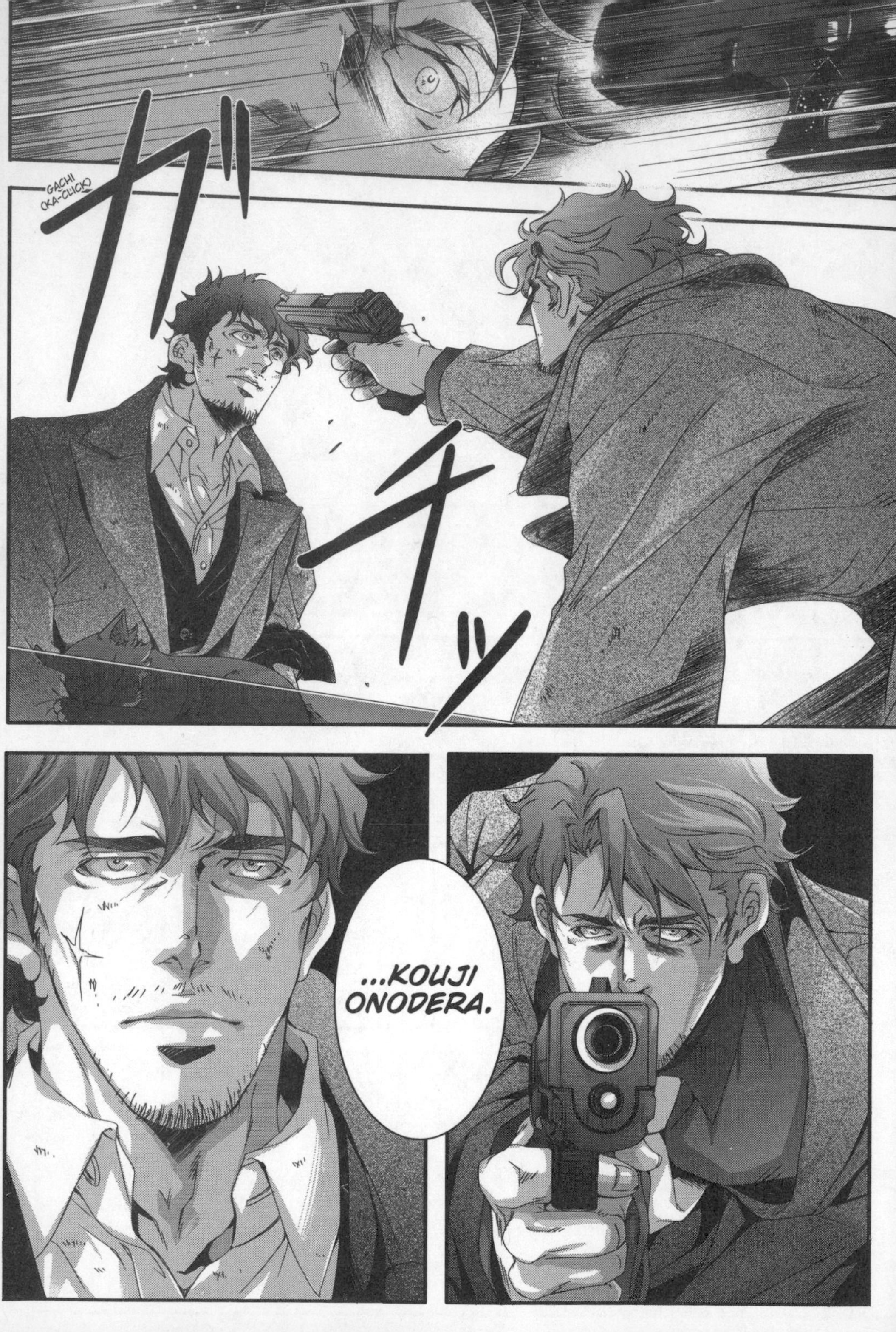
ガチッ
GACHI (KA-CLICK)
...KOUJI ONODERA.

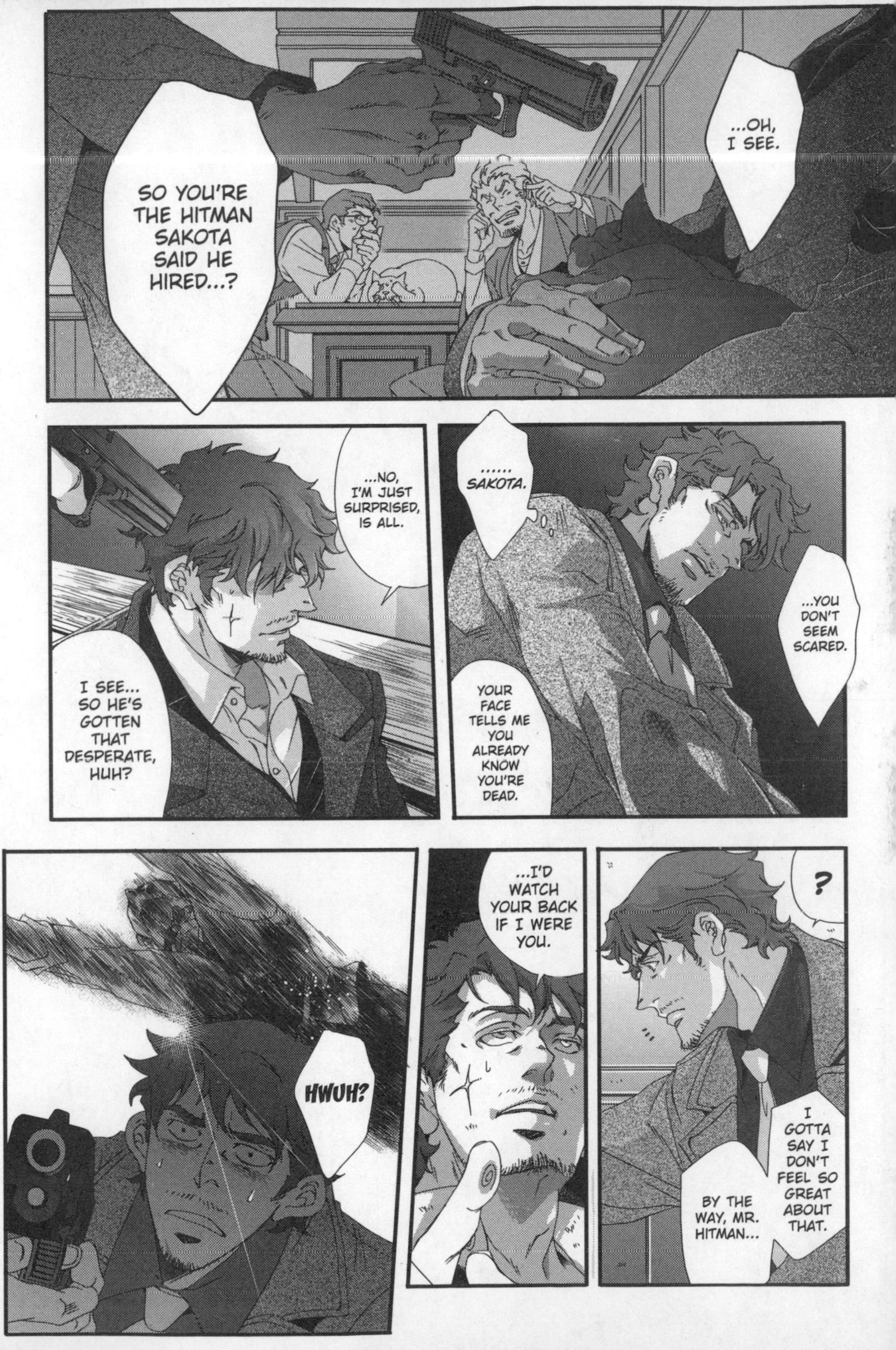
...OH, I SEE.
SO YOU'RE THE HITMAN SAKOTA SAID HE HIRED...?
...... SAKOTA.
...YOU DON'T SEEM SCARED.
YOUR FACE TELLS ME YOU ALREADY KNOW YOU'RE DEAD.
...NO, I'M JUST SURPRISED, IS ALL.
I SEE... SO HE'S GOTTEN THAT DESPERATE, HUH?
?
I GOTTA SAY I DON'T FEEL SO GREAT ABOUT THAT.
BY THE WAY, MR. HITMAN...
...I'D WATCH YOUR BACK IF I WERE YOU.
HWUH?

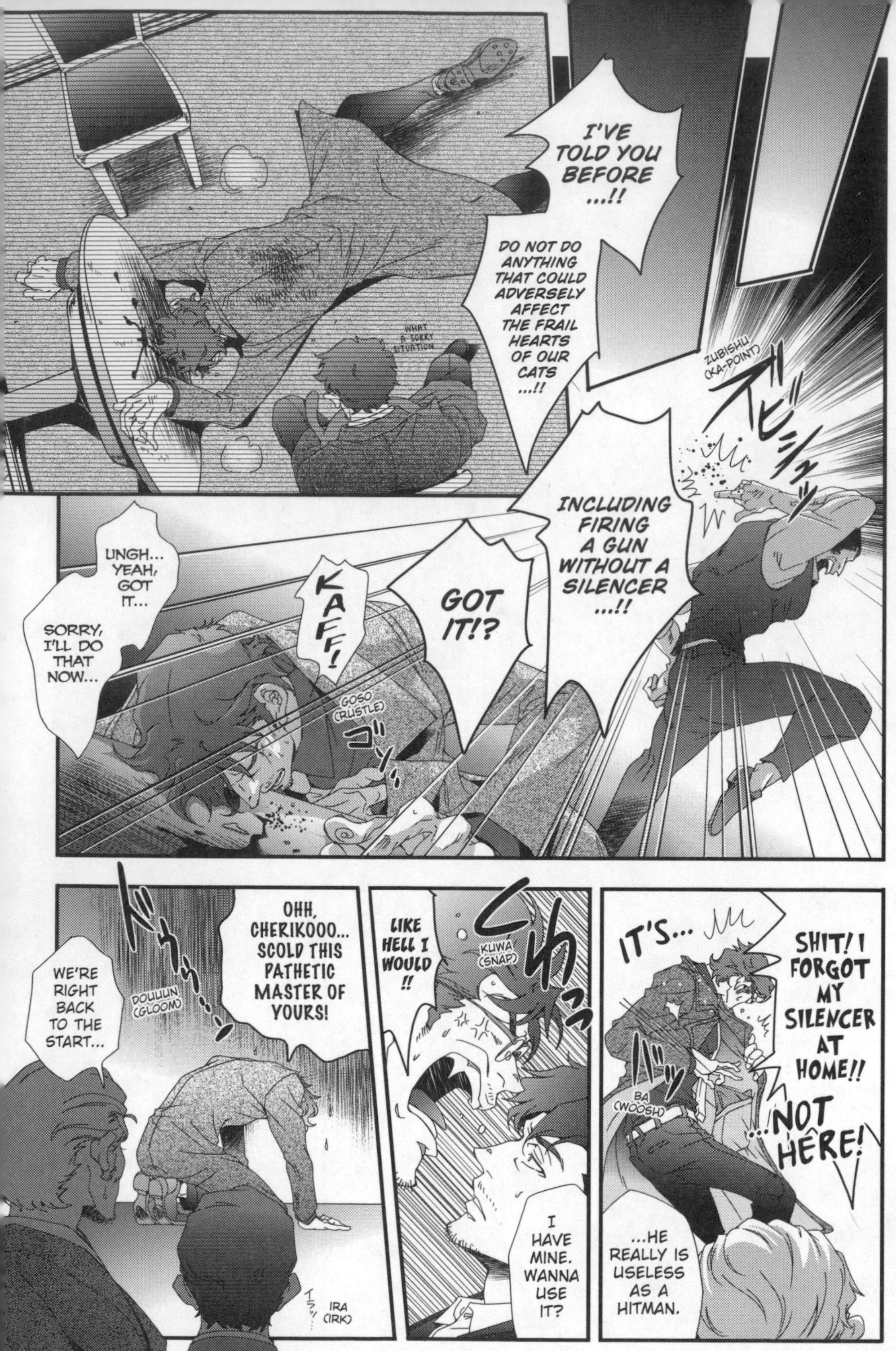
I'VE TOLD YOU BEFORE ...!!
DO NOT DO ANYTHING THAT COULD ADVERSELY AFFECT THE FRAIL HEARTS OF OUR CATS ...!!
WHAT A SORRY SITUATION
ZUBISHU (KA-POINT)
INCLUDING FIRING A GUN WITHOUT A SILENCER ...!!
GOT IT!?
KAFF!
GOSO (RUSTLE)
UNGH... YEAH, GOT IT...
SORRY, I'LL DO THAT NOW...
IT'S...
SHIT! I FORGOT MY SILENCER AT HOME!!
BA (WOOSH)
...NOT HERE!
...HE REALLY IS USELESS AS A HITMAN.
KUWA (SNAP)
I HAVE MINE. WANNA USE IT?
LIKE HELL I WOULD !!
OHH, CHERIKOOO... SCOLD THIS PATHETIC MASTER OF YOURS!
DOUUUN (GLOOM)
WE'RE RIGHT BACK TO THE START...
IRA (IRK)

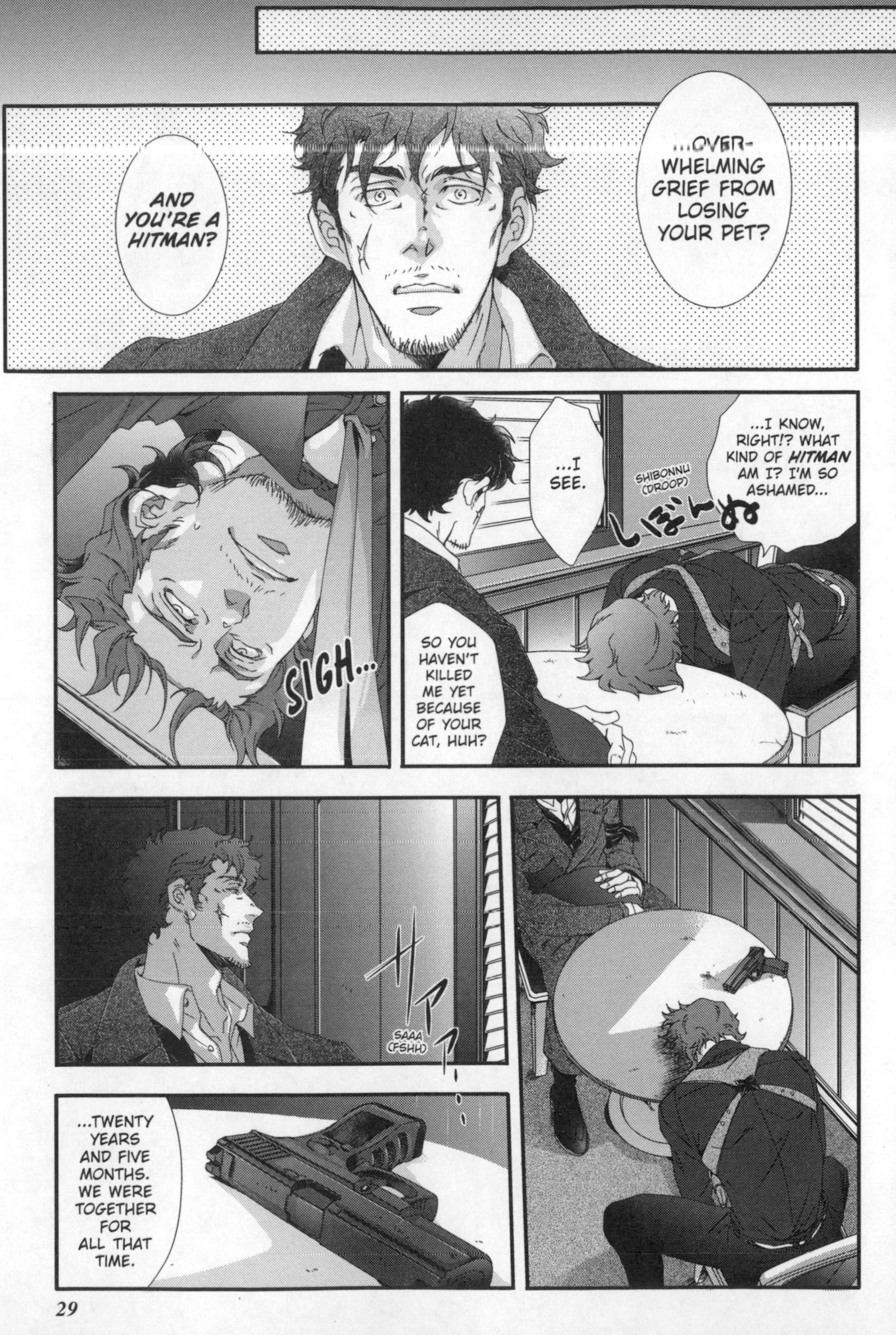
...OVER-WHELMING GRIEF FROM LOSING YOUR PET?
AND YOU'RE A HITMAN?
...I KNOW, RIGHT!? WHAT KIND OF HITMAN AM I? I'M SO ASHAMED...
しぼんぬ
SHIBONNU (DROOP)
...I SEE.
SO YOU HAVEN'T KILLED ME YET BECAUSE OF YOUR CAT, HUH?
SIGH...
ザァア
SAAA (FSHH)
...TWENTY YEARS AND FIVE MONTHS. WE WERE TOGETHER FOR ALL THAT TIME.

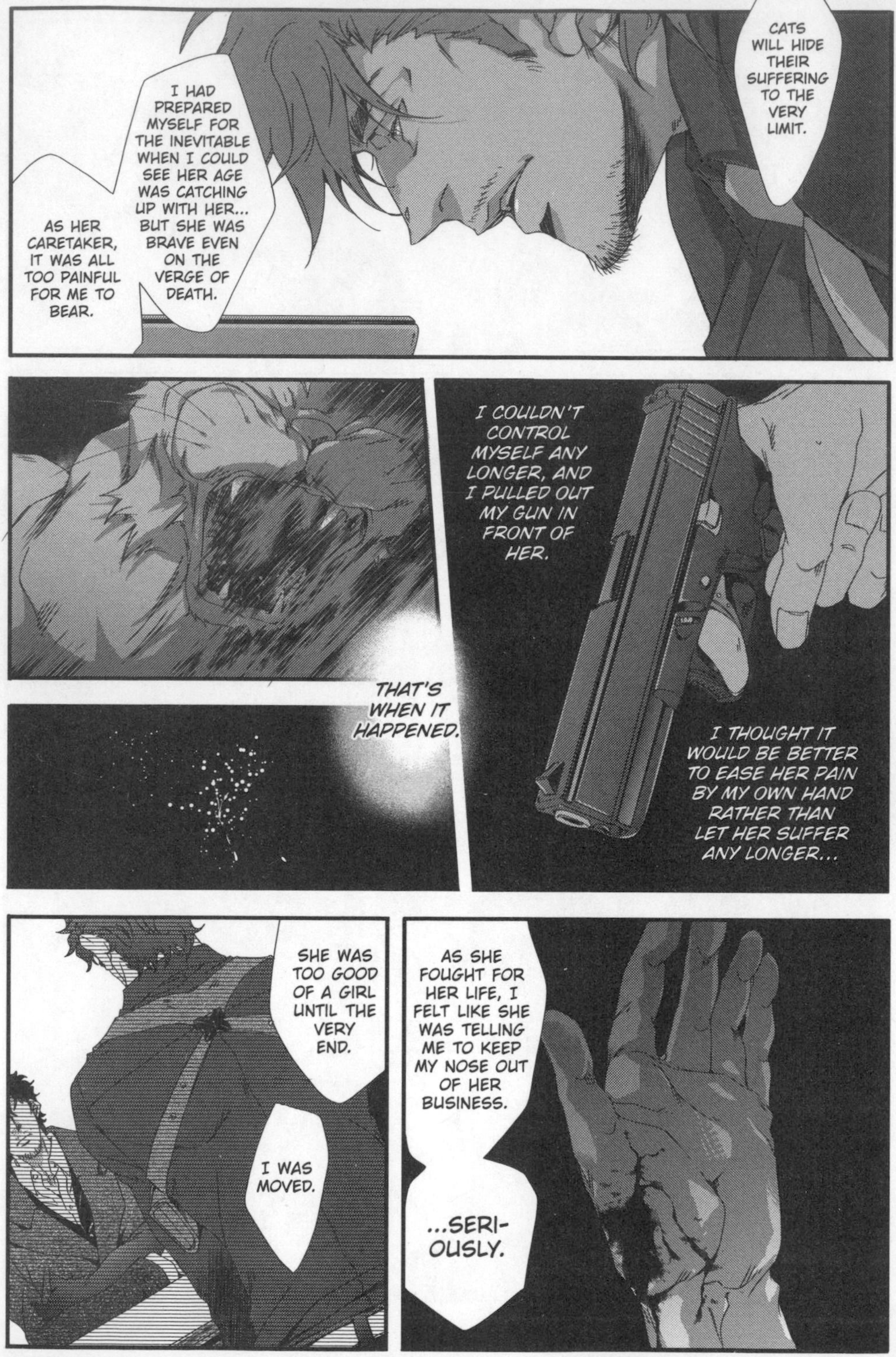
CATS WILL HIDE THEIR SUFFERING TO THE VERY LIMIT.
I HAD PREPARED MYSELF FOR THE INEVITABLE WHEN I COULD SEE HER AGE WAS CATCHING UP WITH HER... BUT SHE WAS BRAVE EVEN ON THE VERGE OF DEATH.
AS HER CARETAKER, IT WAS ALL TOO PAINFUL FOR ME TO BEAR.
I COULDN'T CONTROL MYSELF ANY LONGER, AND I PULLED OUT MY GUN IN FRONT OF HER.
I THOUGHT IT WOULD BE BETTER TO EASE HER PAIN BY MY OWN HAND RATHER THAN LET HER SUFFER ANY LONGER...
THAT'S WHEN IT HAPPENED.
AS SHE FOUGHT FOR HER LIFE, I FELT LIKE SHE WAS TELLING ME TO KEEP MY NOSE OUT OF HER BUSINESS.
...SERI-OUSLY.
SHE WAS TOO GOOD OF A GIRL UNTIL THE VERY END.
I WAS MOVED.

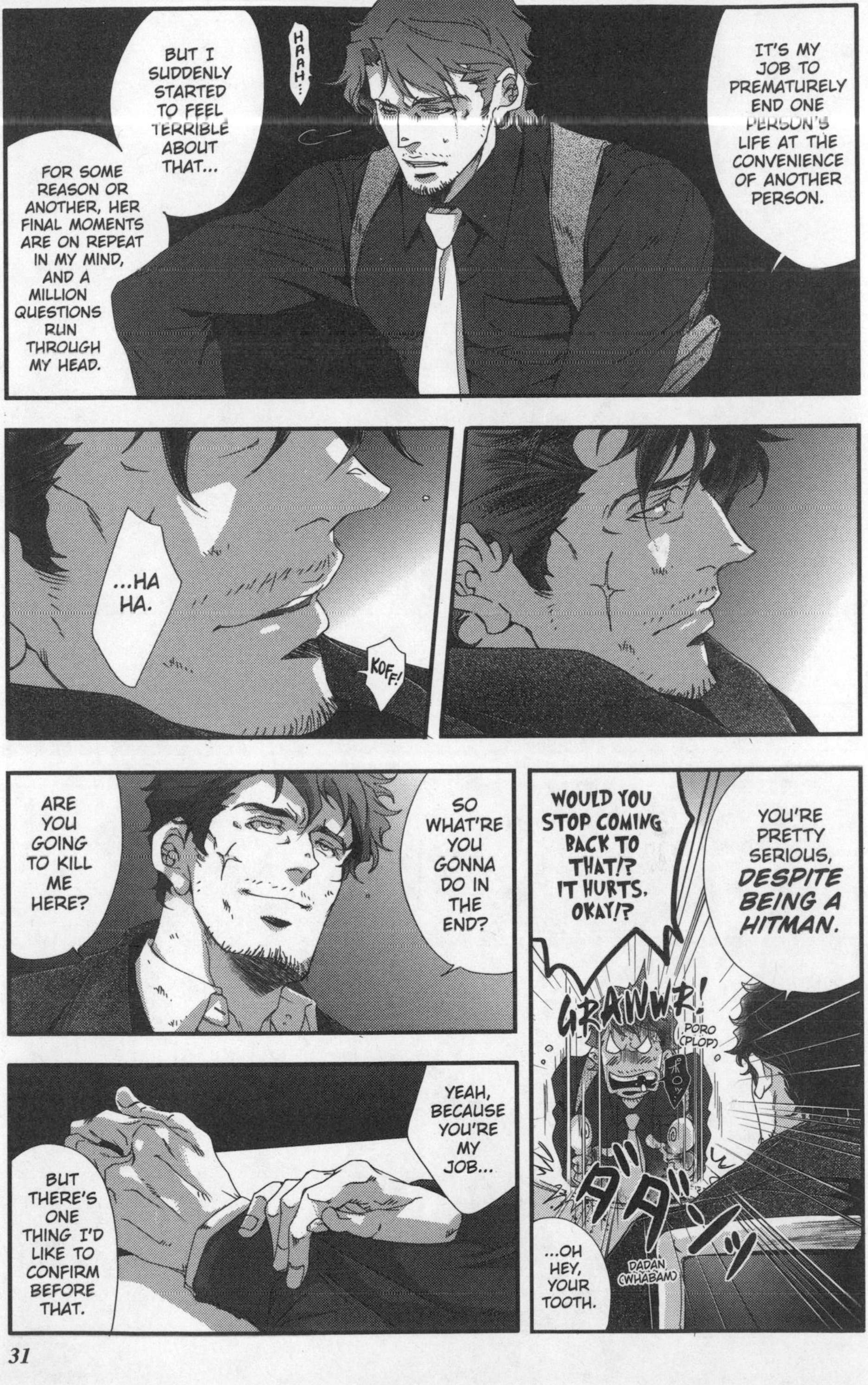
IT'S MY JOB TO PREMATURELY END ONE PERSON'S LIFE AT THE CONVENIENCE OF ANOTHER PERSON.
HAAH...
BUT I SUDDENLY STARTED TO FEEL TERRIBLE ABOUT THAT...
FOR SOME REASON OR ANOTHER, HER FINAL MOMENTS ARE ON REPEAT IN MY MIND, AND A MILLION QUESTIONS RUN THROUGH MY HEAD.
...HA HA.
KOFF!
YOU'RE PRETTY SERIOUS, DESPITE BEING A HITMAN.
WOULD YOU STOP COMING BACK TO THAT!? IT HURTS. OKAY!?
GRAWWR!
PORO (PLOP)
...OH HEY, YOUR TOOTH.
DADAN (WHABAM)
SO WHAT'RE YOU GONNA DO IN THE END?
ARE YOU GOING TO KILL ME HERE?
YEAH, BECAUSE YOU'RE MY JOB...
BUT THERE'S ONE THING I'D LIKE TO CONFIRM BEFORE THAT.

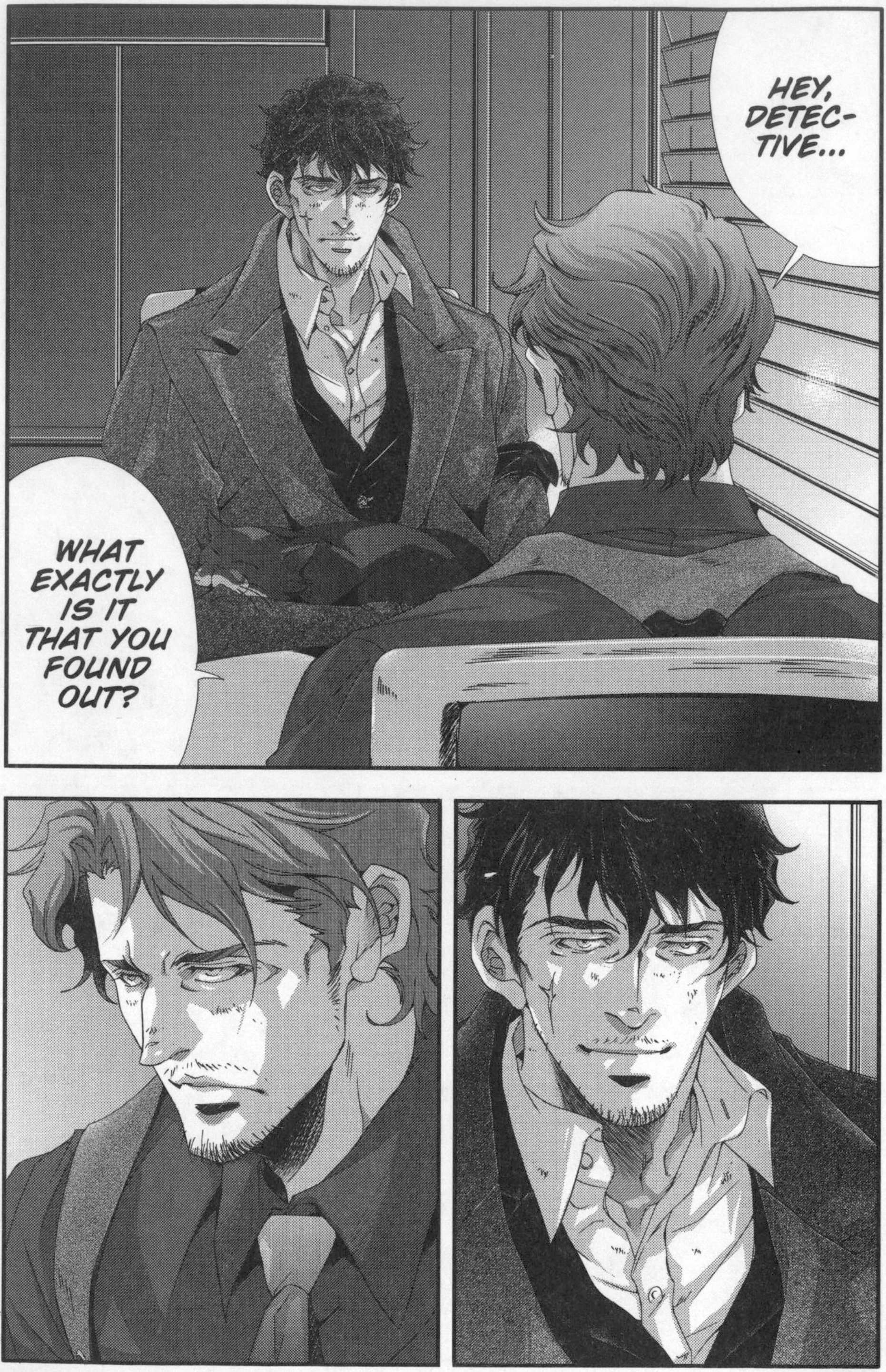
HEY, DETECTIVE...
WHAT EXACTLY IS IT THAT YOU FOUND OUT?

END

CHAPTER 2
Retaliation

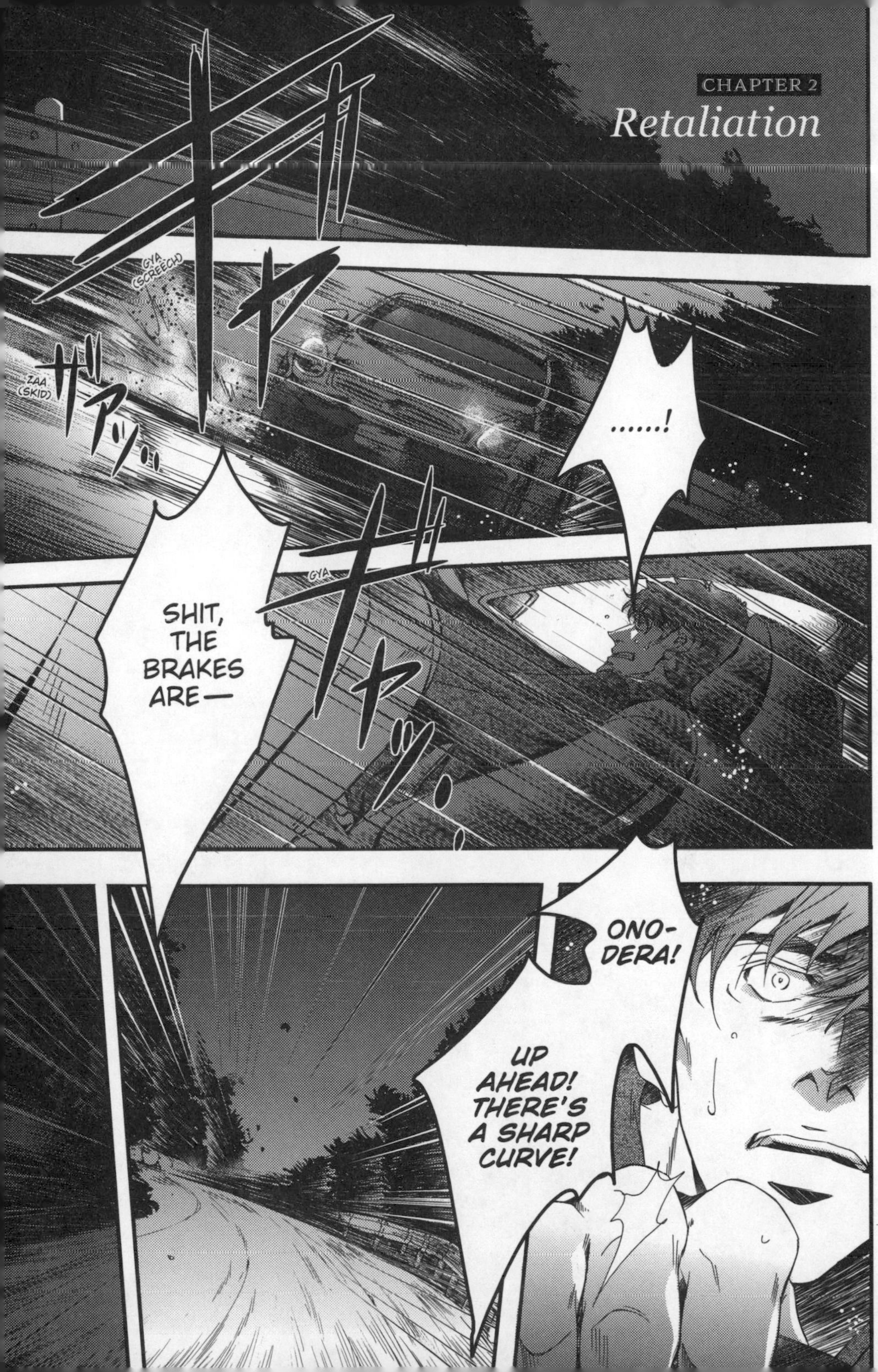
GYA (SCREECH)
......!
ZAA (SKID)
SHIT, THE BRAKES ARE—
GYA
ONO-DERA!
UP AHEAD! THERE'S A SHARP CURVE!

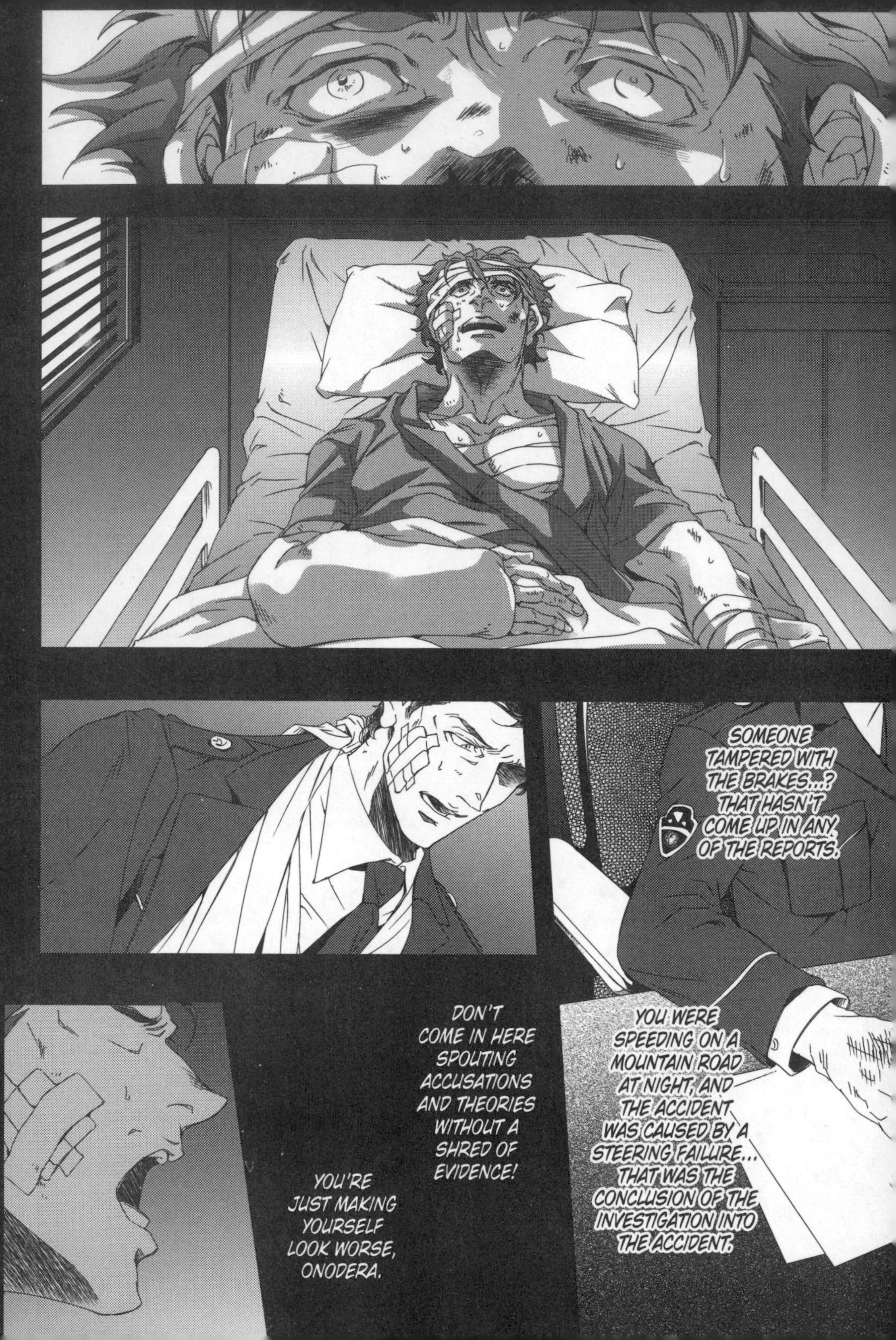
SOMEONE TAMPERED WITH THE BRAKES...? THAT HASN'T COME UP IN ANY OF THE REPORTS.
YOU WERE SPEEDING ON A MOUNTAIN ROAD AT NIGHT, AND THE ACCIDENT WAS CAUSED BY A STEERING FAILURE... THAT WAS THE CONCLUSION OF THE INVESTIGATION INTO THE ACCIDENT.
DON'T COME IN HERE SPOUTING ACCUSATIONS AND THEORIES WITHOUT A SHRED OF EVIDENCE!
YOU'RE JUST MAKING YOURSELF LOOK WORSE, ONODERA.

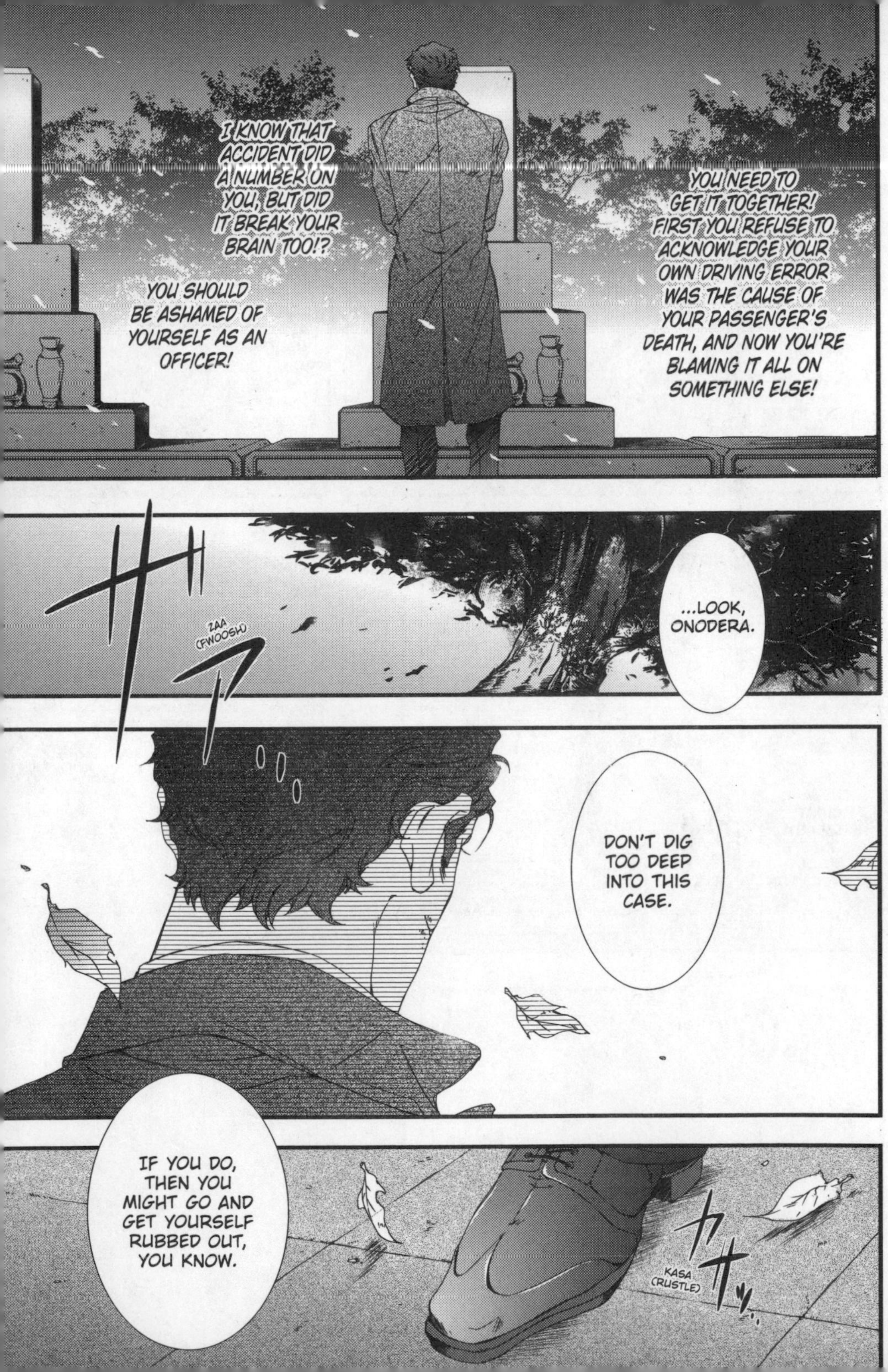
YOU NEED TO GET IT TOGETHER! FIRST YOU REFUSE TO ACKNOWLEDGE YOUR OWN DRIVING ERROR WAS THE CAUSE OF YOUR PASSENGER'S DEATH, AND NOW YOU'RE BLAMING IT ALL ON SOMETHING ELSE!
I KNOW THAT ACCIDENT DID A NUMBER ON YOU, BUT DID IT BREAK YOUR BRAIN TOO!?
YOU SHOULD BE ASHAMED OF YOURSELF AS AN OFFICER!
...LOOK, ONODERA.
ZAA (FWOOSH)
DON'T DIG TOO DEEP INTO THIS CASE.
KASA (RUSTLE)
IF YOU DO, THEN YOU MIGHT GO AND GET YOURSELF RUBBED OUT, YOU KNOW.

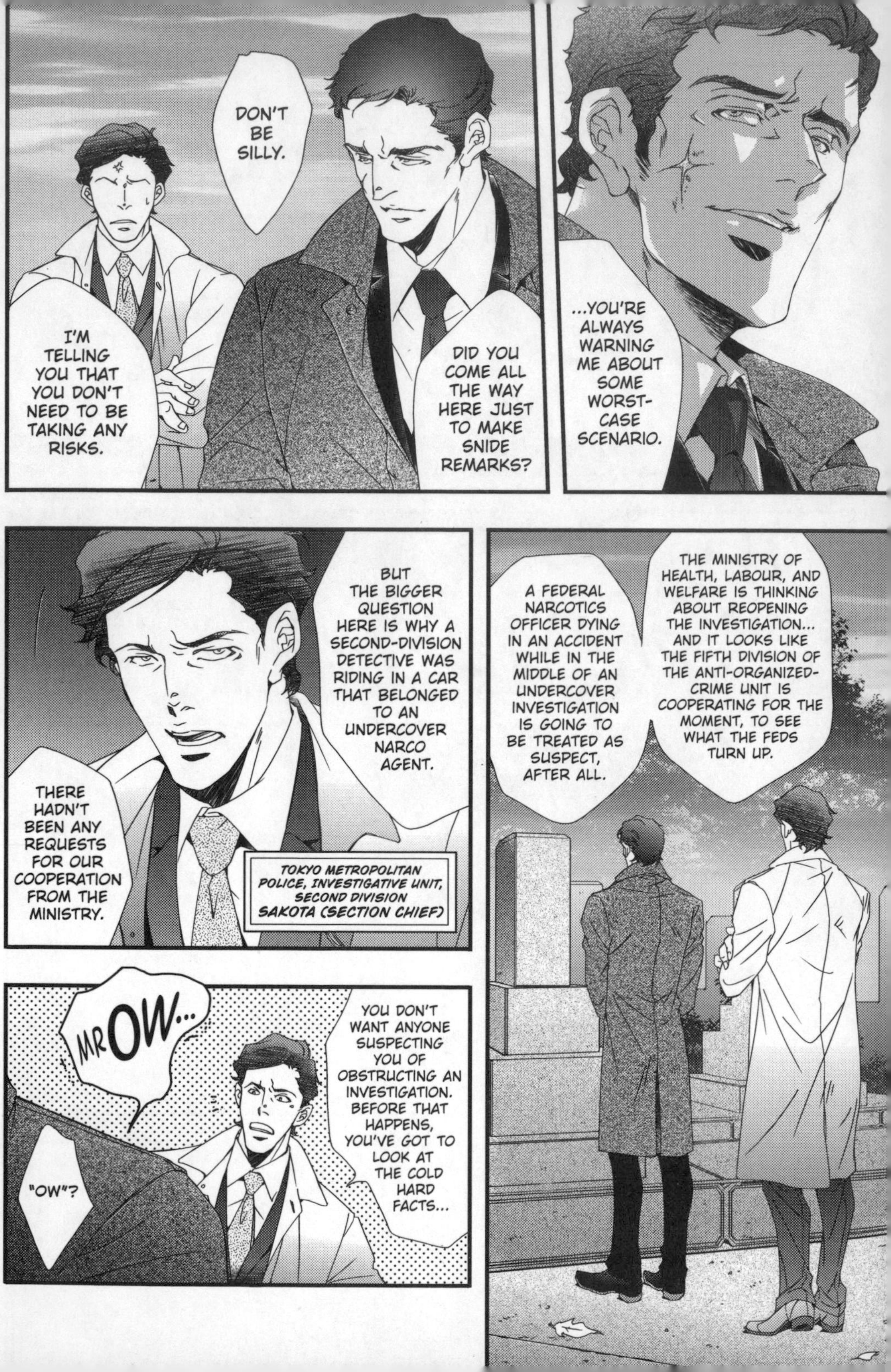
...YOU'RE ALWAYS WARNING ME ABOUT SOME WORST-CASE SCENARIO.
DID YOU COME ALL THE WAY HERE JUST TO MAKE SNIDE REMARKS?
DON'T BE SILLY.
I'M TELLING YOU THAT YOU DON'T NEED TO BE TAKING ANY RISKS.
THE MINISTRY OF HEALTH, LABOUR, AND WELFARE IS THINKING ABOUT REOPENING THE INVESTIGATION... AND IT LOOKS LIKE THE FIFTH DIVISION OF THE ANTI-ORGANIZED-CRIME UNIT IS COOPERATING FOR THE MOMENT, TO SEE WHAT THE FEDS TURN UP.
A FEDERAL NARCOTICS OFFICER DYING IN AN ACCIDENT WHILE IN THE MIDDLE OF AN UNDERCOVER INVESTIGATION IS GOING TO BE TREATED AS SUSPECT, AFTER ALL.
BUT THE BIGGER QUESTION HERE IS WHY A SECOND-DIVISION DETECTIVE WAS RIDING IN A CAR THAT BELONGED TO AN UNDERCOVER NARCO AGENT.
THERE HADN'T BEEN ANY REQUESTS FOR OUR COOPERATION FROM THE MINISTRY.
TOKYO METROPOLITAN POLICE, INVESTIGATIVE UNIT, SECOND DIVISION SAKOTA (SECTION CHIEF)
YOU DON'T WANT ANYONE SUSPECTING YOU OF OBSTRUCTING AN INVESTIGATION. BEFORE THAT HAPPENS, YOU'VE GOT TO LOOK AT THE COLD HARD FACTS...
MROW...
"OW"?

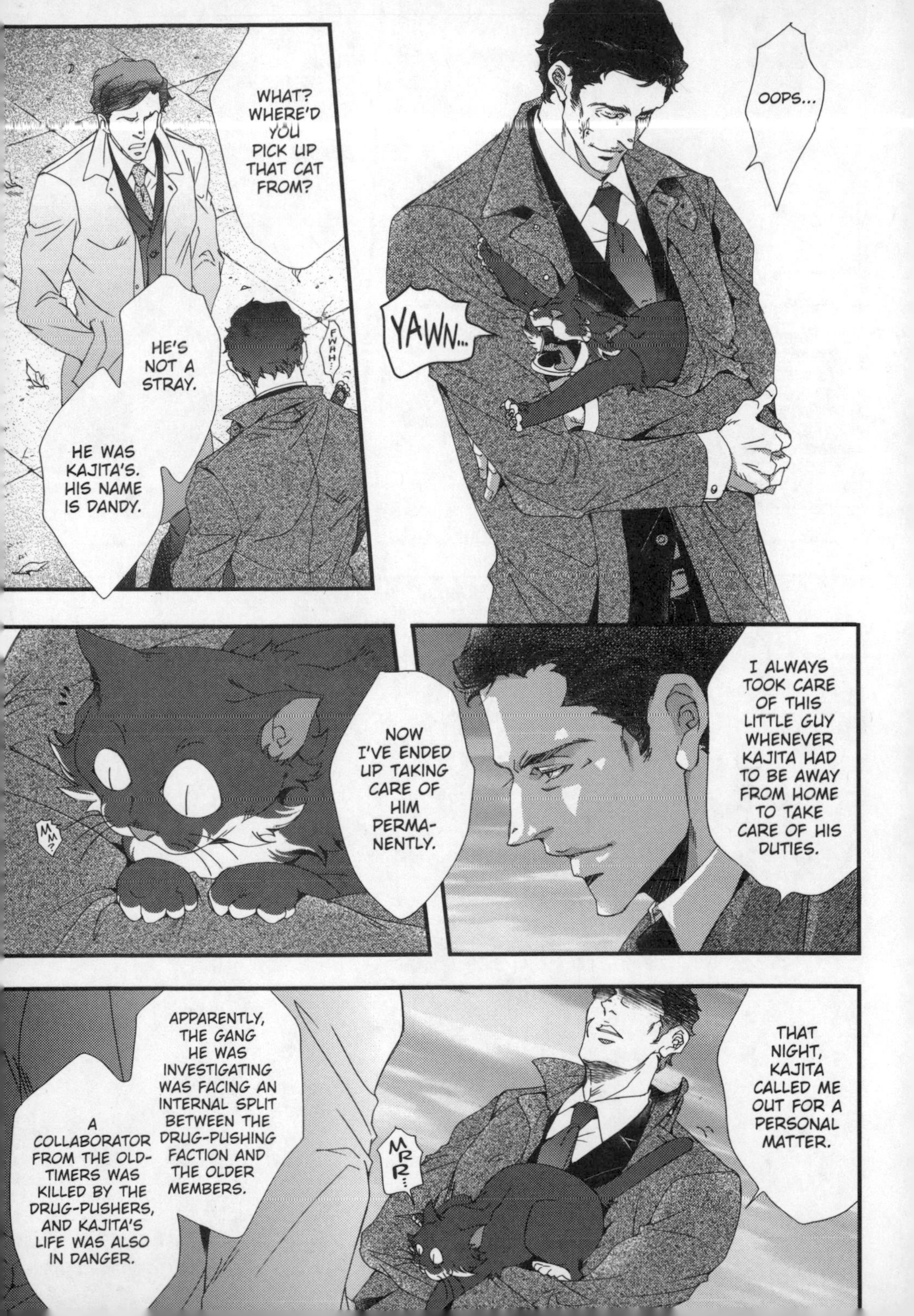
OOPS...
YAWN...
WHAT? WHERE'D YOU PICK UP THAT CAT FROM?
HE'S NOT A STRAY.
HE WAS KAJITA'S. HIS NAME IS DANDY.
I ALWAYS TOOK CARE OF THIS LITTLE GUY WHENEVER KAJITA HAD TO BE AWAY FROM HOME TO TAKE CARE OF HIS DUTIES.
NOW I'VE ENDED UP TAKING CARE OF HIM PERMA-NENTLY.
MM?
THAT NIGHT, KAJITA CALLED ME OUT FOR A PERSONAL MATTER.
MRR...
APPARENTLY, THE GANG HE WAS INVESTIGATING WAS FACING AN INTERNAL SPLIT BETWEEN THE DRUG-PUSHING FACTION AND THE OLDER MEMBERS.
A COLLABORATOR FROM THE OLD-TIMERS WAS KILLED BY THE DRUG-PUSHERS, AND KAJITA'S LIFE WAS ALSO IN DANGER.

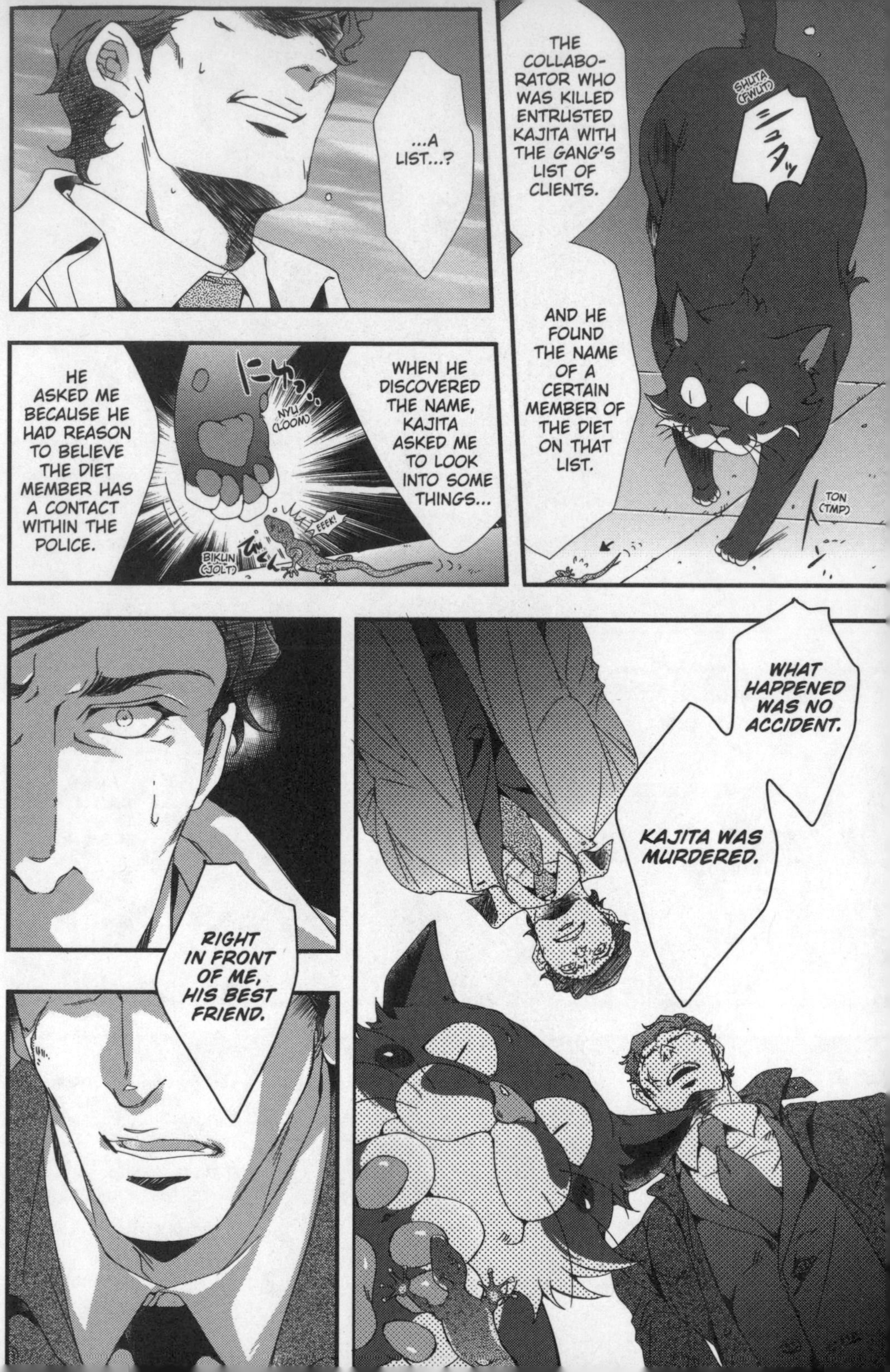
THE COLLABORATOR WHO WAS KILLED ENTRUSTED KAJITA WITH THE GANG'S LIST OF CLIENTS.
SHUTA (FWUT)
AND HE FOUND THE NAME OF A CERTAIN MEMBER OF THE DIET ON THAT LIST.
TON (TMP)
...A LIST...?
WHEN HE DISCOVERED THE NAME, KAJITA ASKED ME TO LOOK INTO SOME THINGS...
NYU (LOOM)
EEEK!
BIKUN (JOLT)
HE ASKED ME BECAUSE HE HAD REASON TO BELIEVE THE DIET MEMBER HAS A CONTACT WITHIN THE POLICE.
WHAT HAPPENED WAS NO ACCIDENT.
KAJITA WAS MURDERED.
RIGHT IN FRONT OF ME, HIS BEST FRIEND.

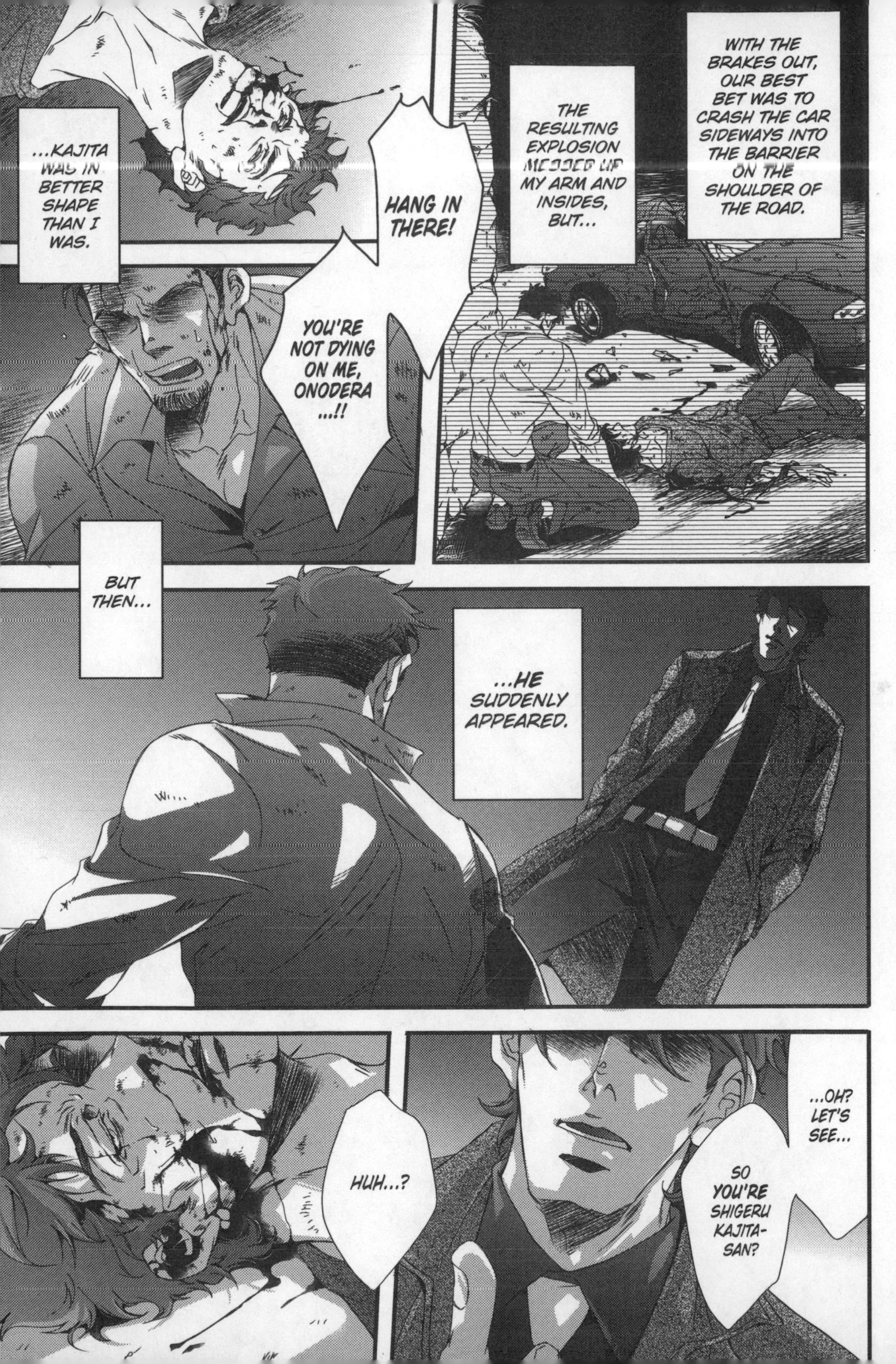
WITH THE BRAKES OUT, OUR BEST BET WAS TO CRASH THE CAR SIDEWAYS INTO THE BARRIER ON THE SHOULDER OF THE ROAD.
THE RESULTING EXPLOSION MESSED UP MY ARM AND INSIDES, BUT...
...KAJITA WAS IN BETTER SHAPE THAN I WAS.
HANG IN THERE!
YOU'RE NOT DYING ON ME, ONODERA ...!!
BUT THEN...
...HE SUDDENLY APPEARED.
...OH? LET'S SEE...
SO YOU'RE SHIGERU KAJITA-SAN?
HUH...?

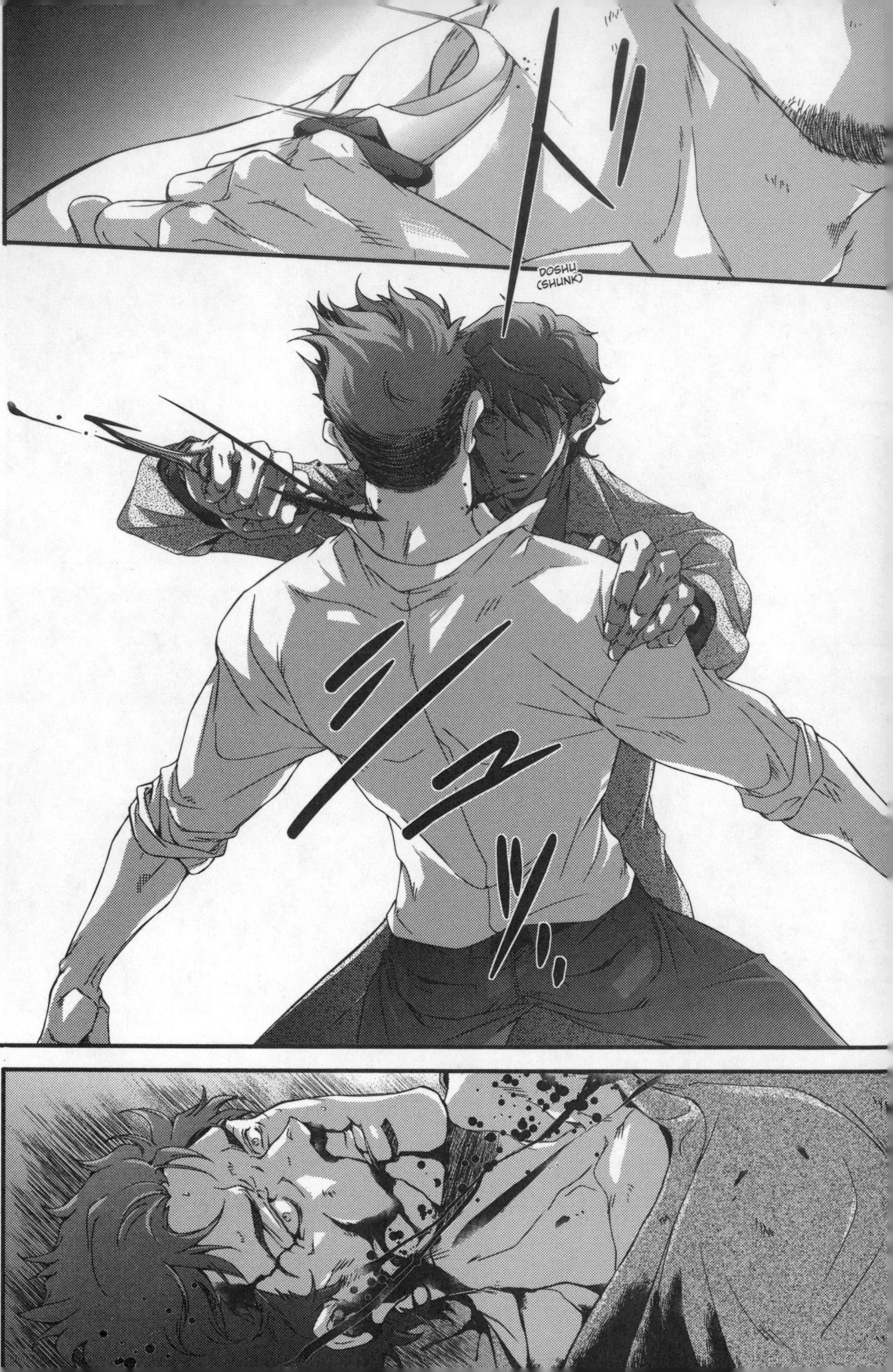
DOSHU
(SHUNK)

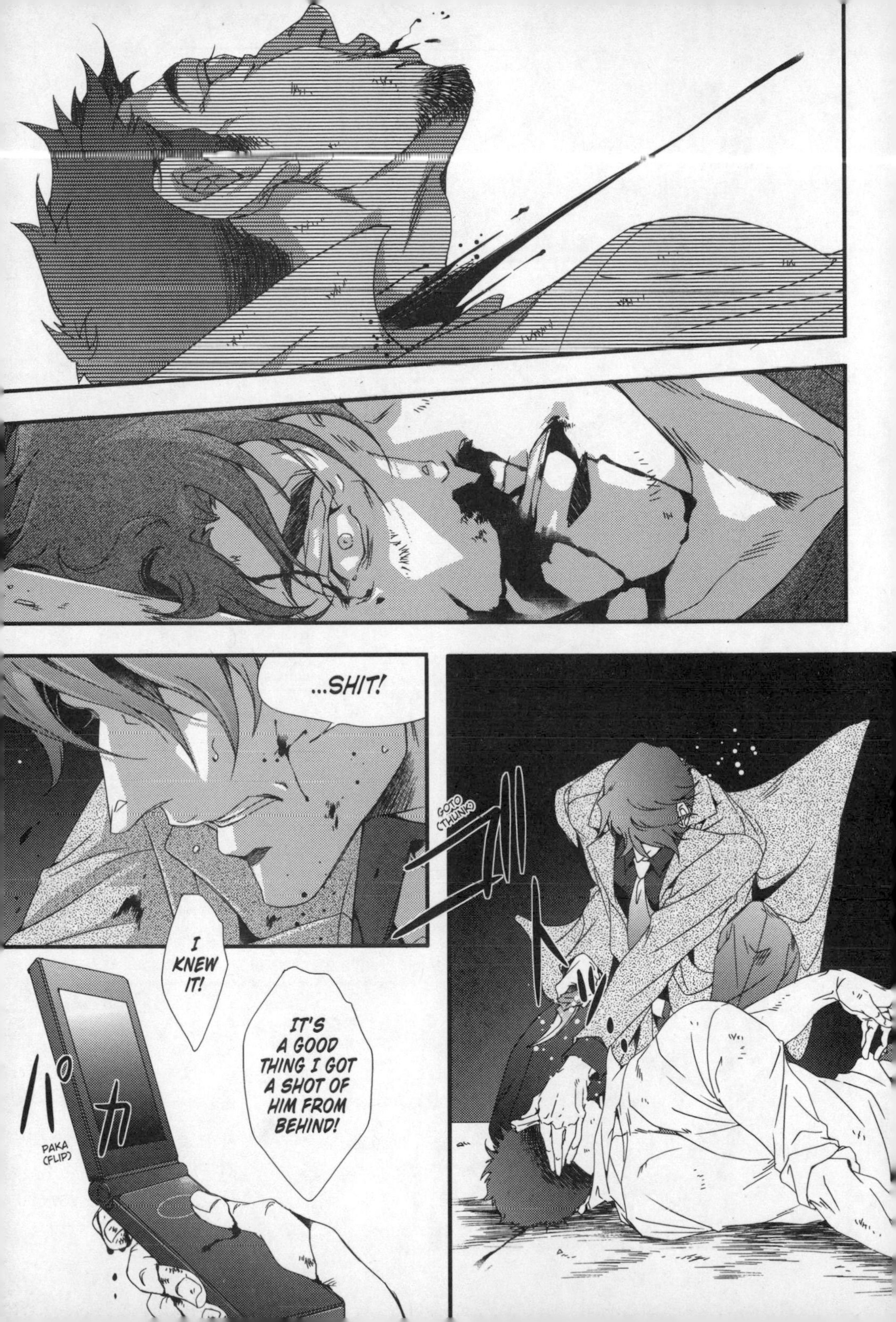
GOTO (THUNK)
...SHIT!
I KNEW IT!
IT'S A GOOD THING I GOT A SHOT OF HIM FROM BEHIND!
パカ
PAKA (FLIP)

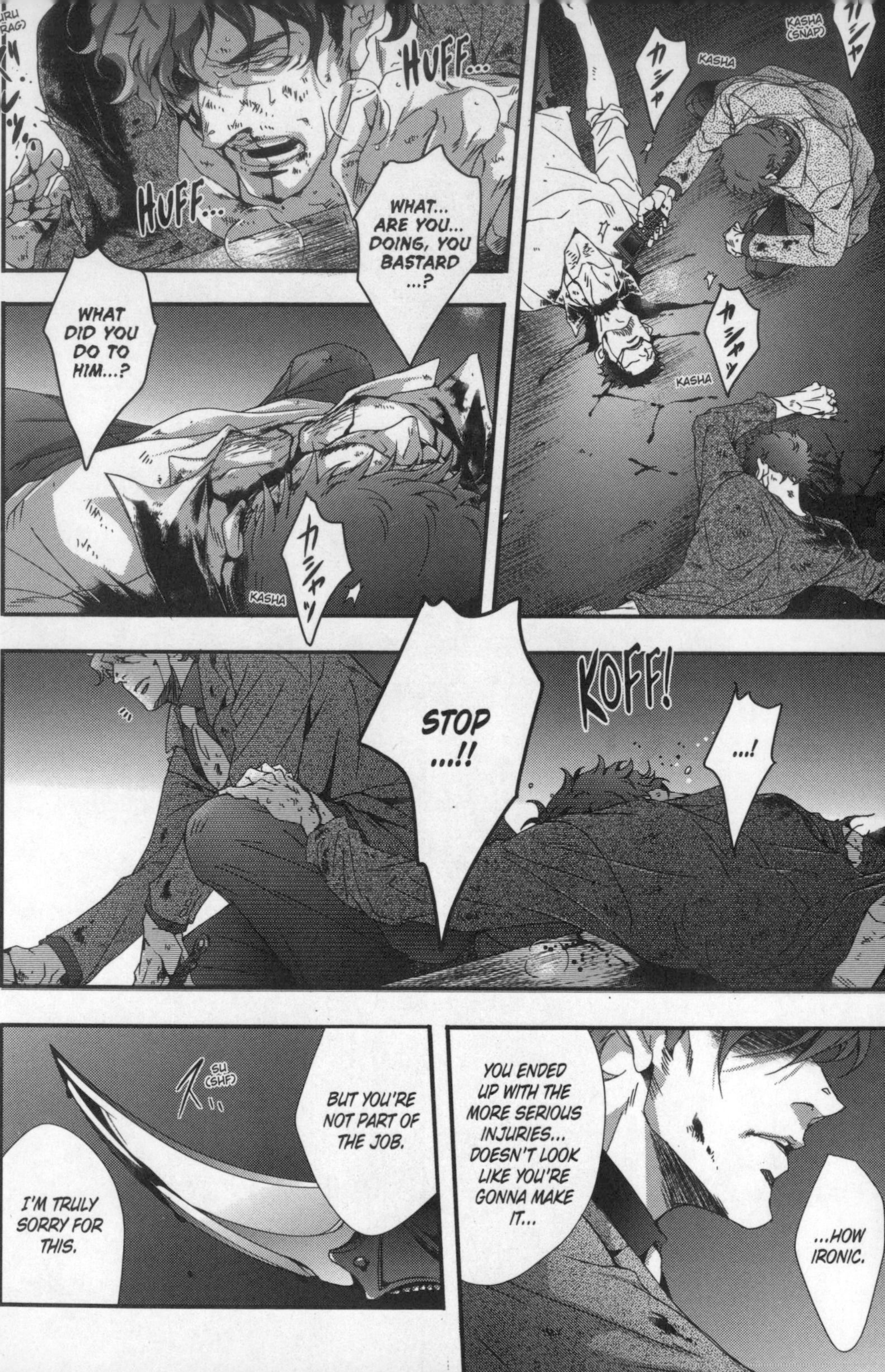

ガシャ
KASHA (SNAP)
カシャ
KASHA
カシャッ
KASHA
ズルッ
ZURU (DRAG)
HUFF...
HUFF...
WHAT... ARE YOU... DOING, YOU BASTARD ...?
WHAT DID YOU DO TO HIM...?
カシャッ
KASHA
KOFF!
...!
STOP ...!!
YOU ENDED UP WITH THE MORE SERIOUS INJURIES... DOESN'T LOOK LIKE YOU'RE GONNA MAKE IT...
...HOW IRONIC.
BUT YOU'RE NOT PART OF THE JOB.
ス
SU (SHF)
I'M TRULY SORRY FOR THIS.

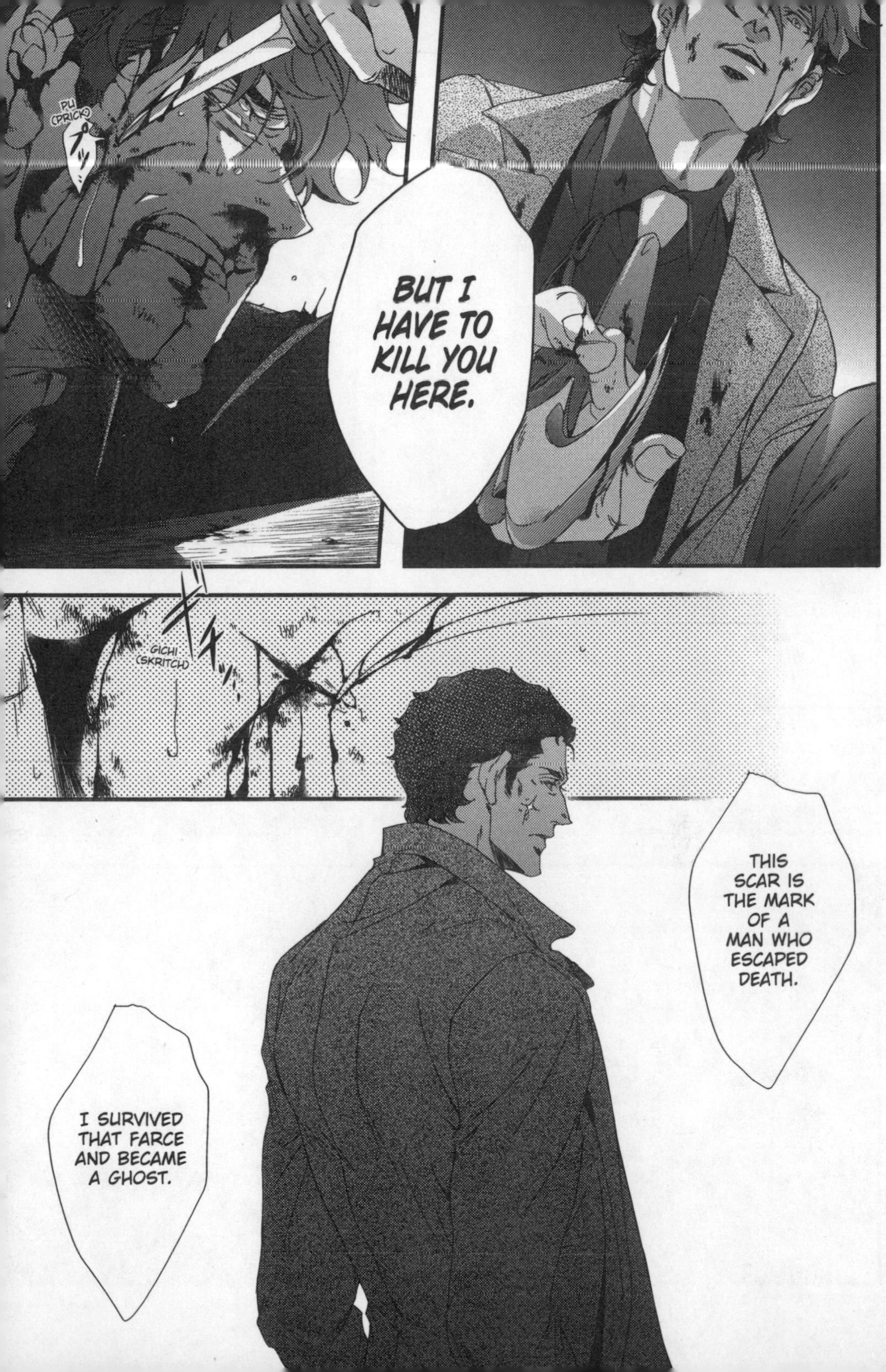
BUT I HAVE TO KILL YOU HERE.
PU (PRICK)
GICHI (SKRITCH)
THIS SCAR IS THE MARK OF A MAN WHO ESCAPED DEATH.
I SURVIVED THAT FARCE AND BECAME A GHOST.

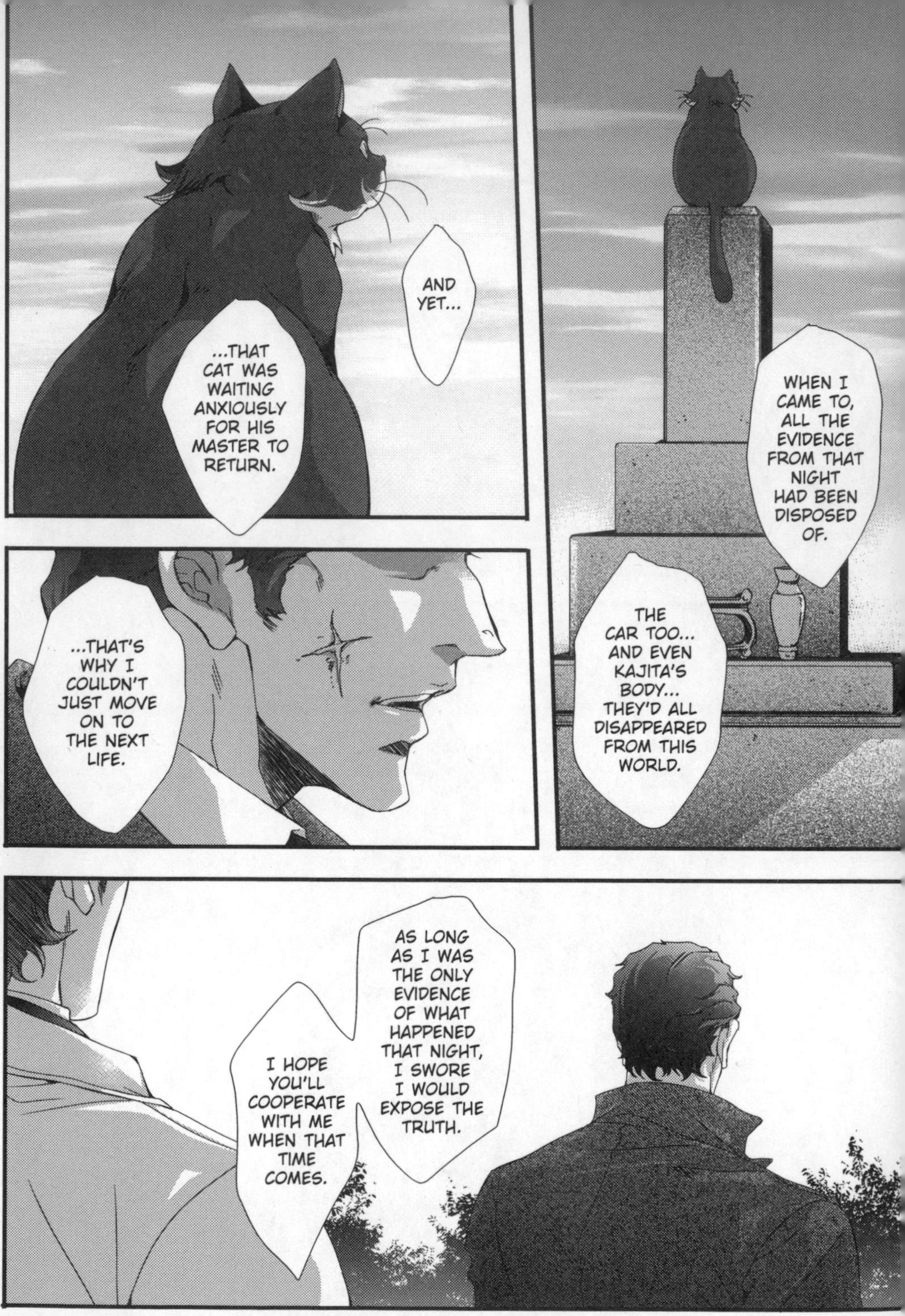
WHEN I CAME TO, ALL THE EVIDENCE FROM THAT NIGHT HAD BEEN DISPOSED OF.
THE CAR TOO... AND EVEN KAJITA'S BODY... THEY'D ALL DISAPPEARED FROM THIS WORLD.
AND YET...
...THAT CAT WAS WAITING ANXIOUSLY FOR HIS MASTER TO RETURN.
...THAT'S WHY I COULDN'T JUST MOVE ON TO THE NEXT LIFE.
AS LONG AS I WAS THE ONLY EVIDENCE OF WHAT HAPPENED THAT NIGHT, I SWORE I WOULD EXPOSE THE TRUTH.
I HOPE YOU'LL COOPERATE WITH ME WHEN THAT TIME COMES.

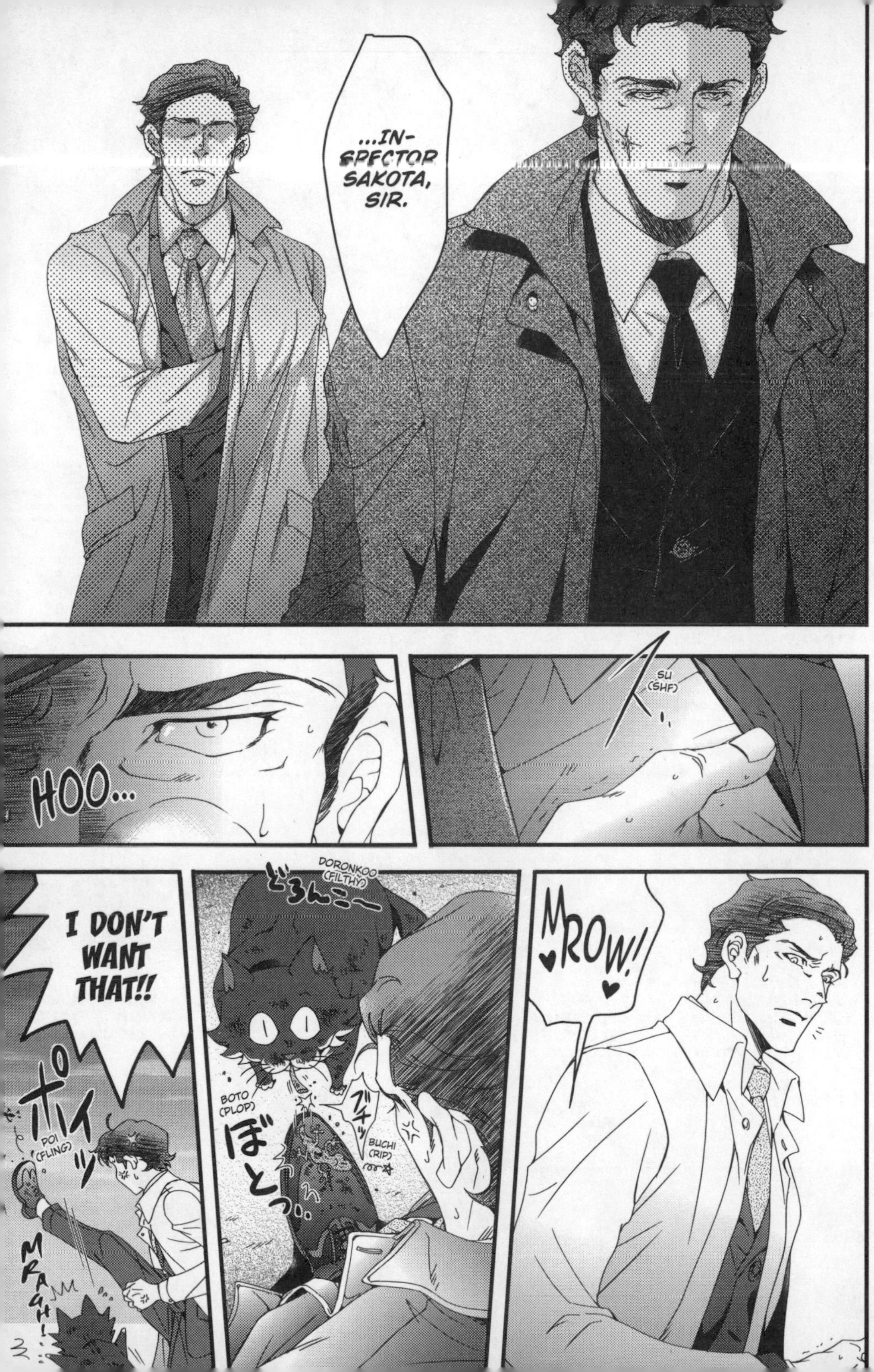
...IN-SPECTOR SAKOTA, SIR.
SU (SHF)
HOO...
MROW!
DORONKOO (FILTHY)
どろんこ〜〜
BOTO (PLOP)
ぼとっ
BUCHI (RIP)
ブチッ
I DON'T WANT THAT!!
POI (FLING)
ポイッ
MRAGH!...

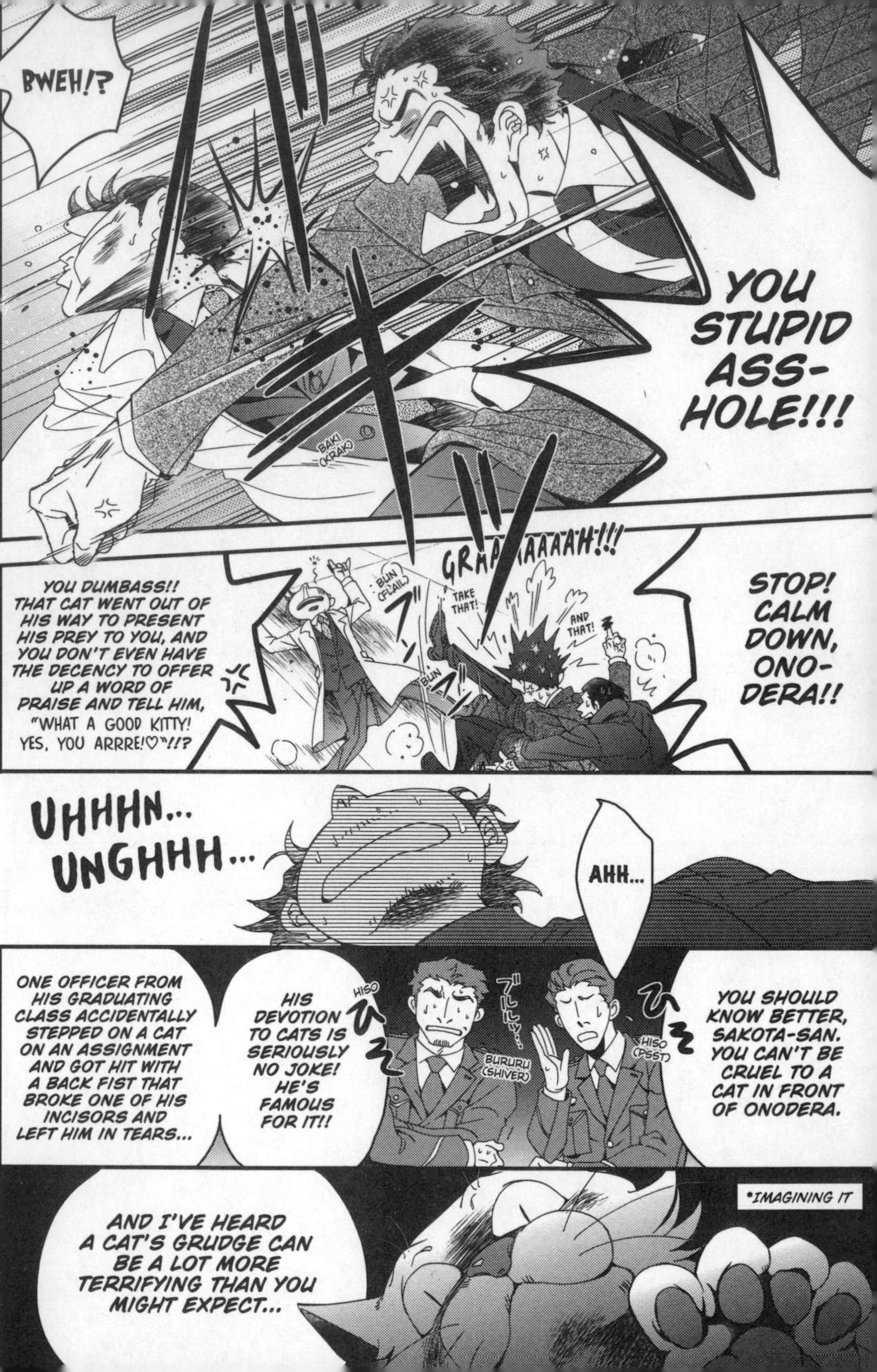
YOU STUPID ASS-HOLE!!!
BAKI (KRAK)
BWEH!?
STOP! CALM DOWN, ONO-DERA!!
GRAAAAAAH!!!
AND THAT!
TAKE THAT!
BUN (FLAIL)
BUN
YOU DUMBASS!! THAT CAT WENT OUT OF HIS WAY TO PRESENT HIS PREY TO YOU, AND YOU DON'T EVEN HAVE THE DECENCY TO OFFER UP A WORD OF PRAISE AND TELL HIM, "WHAT A GOOD KITTY! YES, YOU ARRRE!♡"!!?
AHH...
UHHHN... UNGHHH...
YOU SHOULD KNOW BETTER, SAKOTA-SAN. YOU CAN'T BE CRUEL TO A CAT IN FRONT OF ONODERA.
HISO (PSST)
BURURU (SHIVER)
HIS DEVOTION TO CATS IS SERIOUSLY NO JOKE! HE'S FAMOUS FOR IT!!
HISO
ONE OFFICER FROM HIS GRADUATING CLASS ACCIDENTALLY STEPPED ON A CAT ON AN ASSIGNMENT AND GOT HIT WITH A BACK FIST THAT BROKE ONE OF HIS INCISORS AND LEFT HIM IN TEARS...
*IMAGINING IT
AND I'VE HEARD A CAT'S GRUDGE CAN BE A LOT MORE TERRIFYING THAN YOU MIGHT EXPECT...

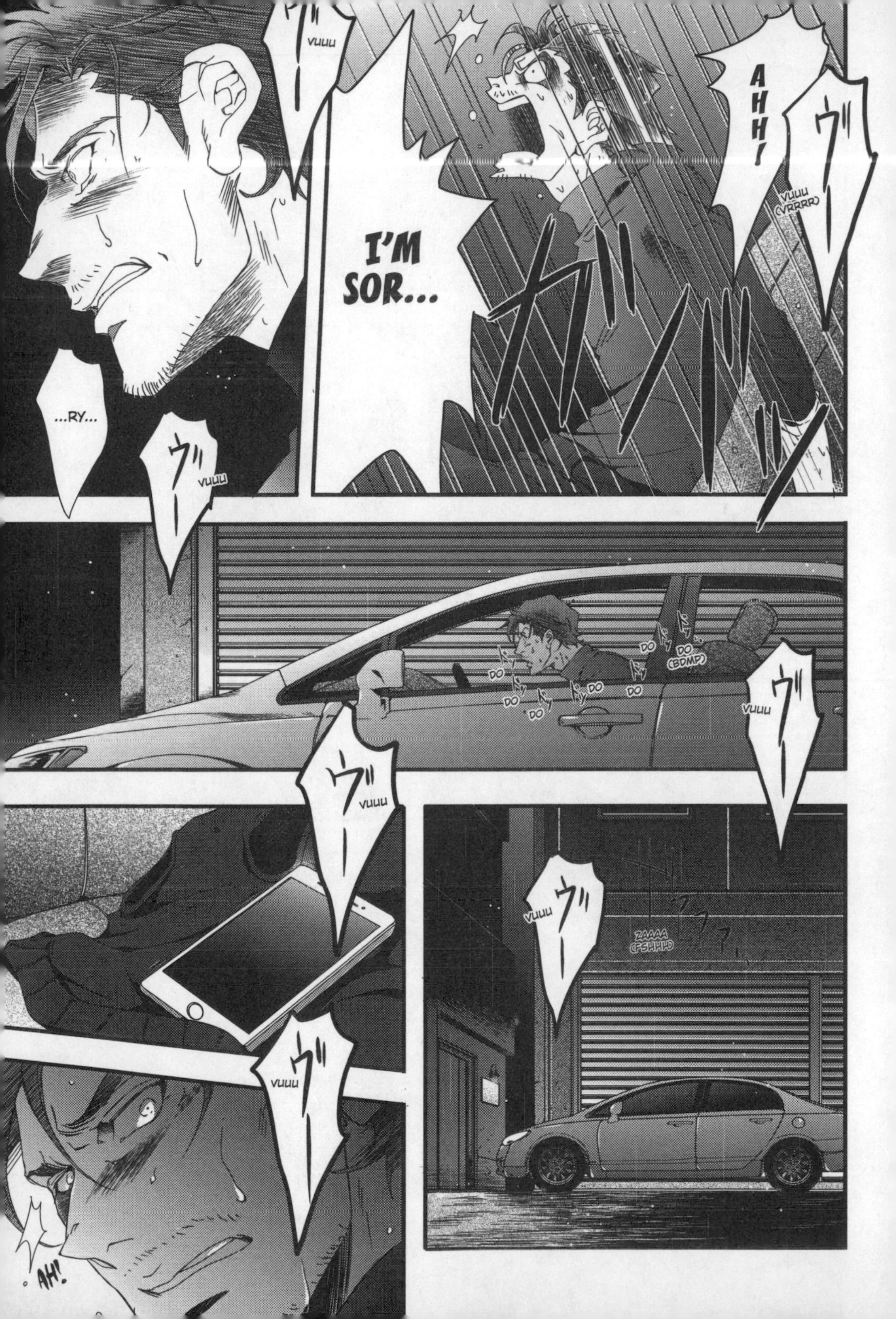

AHH!
VUUU (VRRRR)
vuuu
I'M SOR...
...RY...
vuuu
DO DO (BDMP)
DO
DO
DO
DO
DO
DO
vuuu
vuuu
ZAAAA (FSHHH)
vuuu
vuuu
AH!

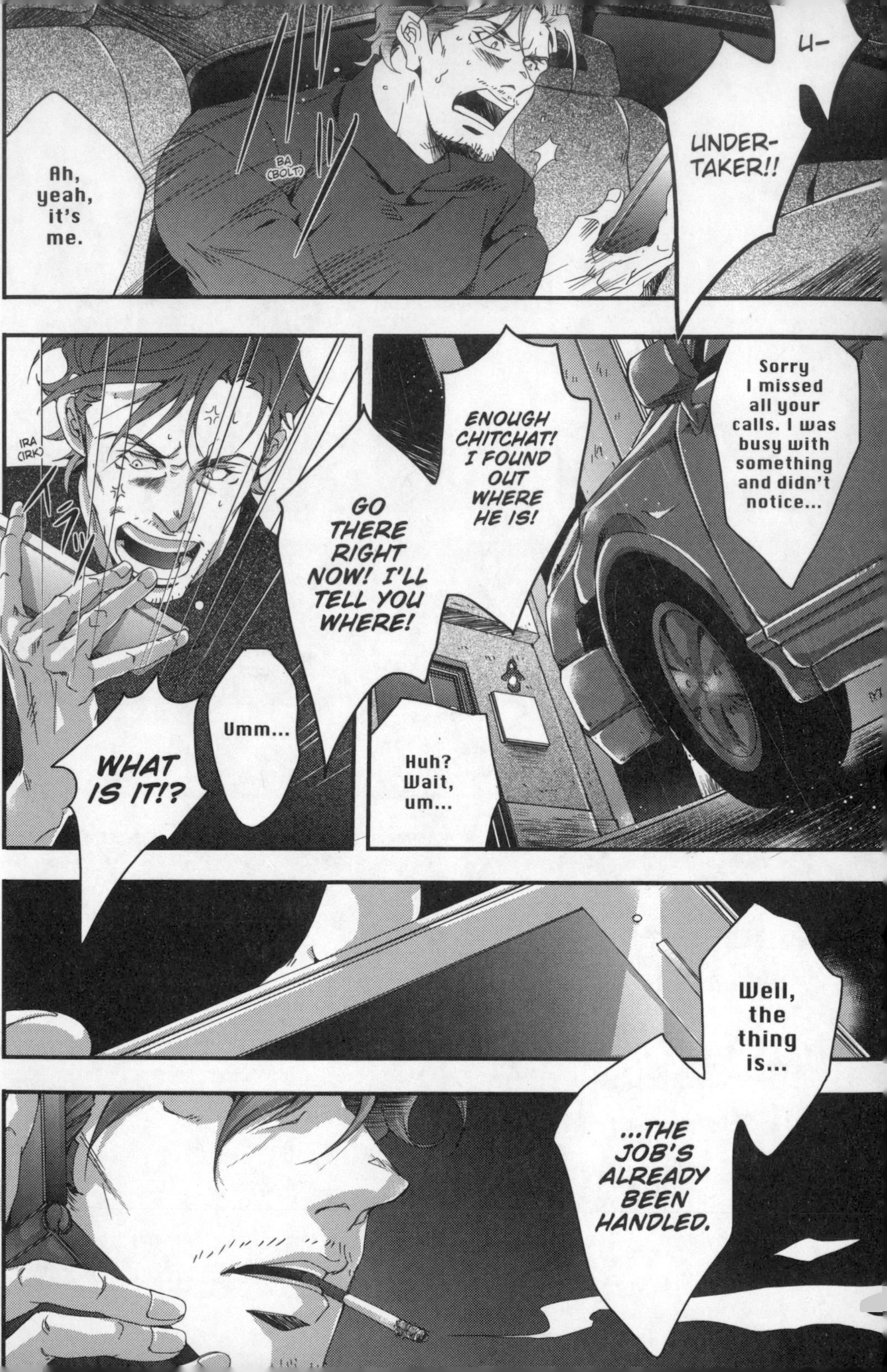
U-
UNDER-TAKER!!
BA (BOLT)
Ah, yeah, it's me.
Sorry I missed all your calls. I was busy with something and didn't notice...
ENOUGH CHITCHAT! I FOUND OUT WHERE HE IS!
GO THERE RIGHT NOW! I'LL TELL YOU WHERE!
Huh? Wait, um...
IRA (IRK)
Umm...
WHAT IS IT!?
Well, the thing is...
...THE JOB'S ALREADY BEEN HANDLED.

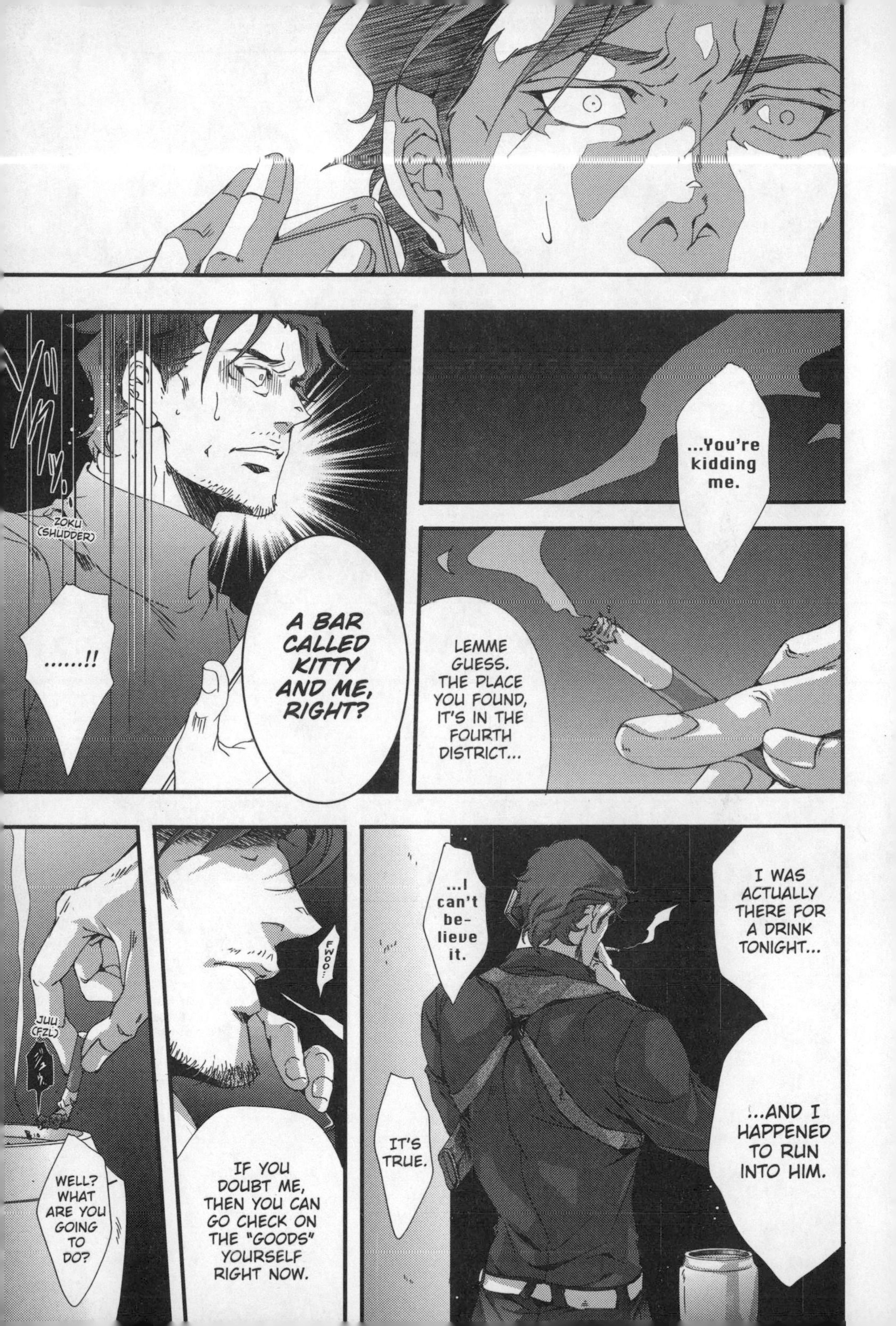
...You're kidding me.
LEMME GUESS. THE PLACE YOU FOUND, IT'S IN THE FOURTH DISTRICT...
A BAR CALLED KITTY AND ME, RIGHT?
ZOKU (SHUDDER)
......!!
I WAS ACTUALLY THERE FOR A DRINK TONIGHT...
...I can't be-lieve it.
...AND I HAPPENED TO RUN INTO HIM.
IT'S TRUE.
FWOO...
IF YOU DOUBT ME, THEN YOU CAN GO CHECK ON THE "GOODS" YOURSELF RIGHT NOW.
JUU (FZL)
WELL? WHAT ARE YOU GOING TO DO?

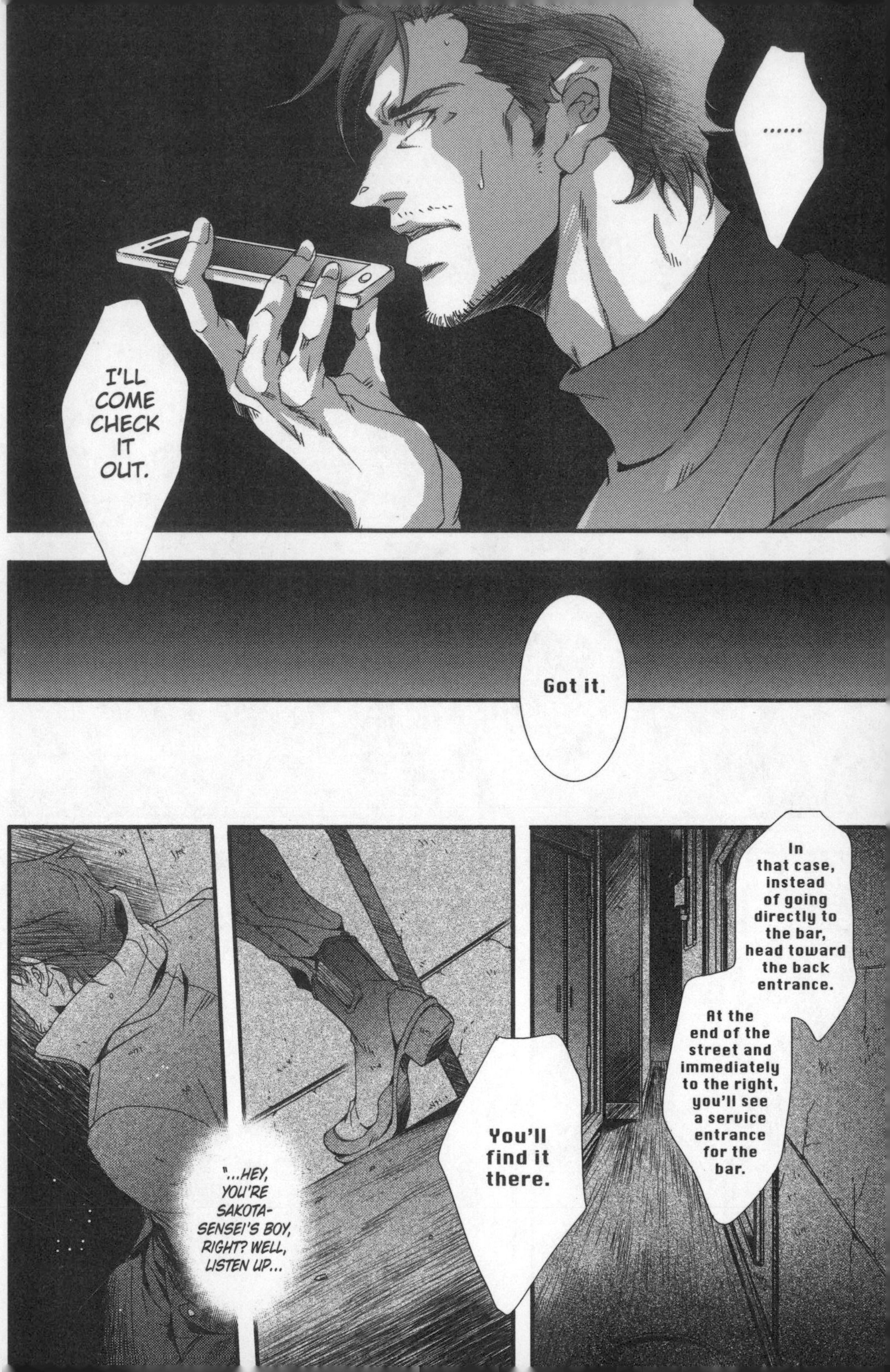
......
I'LL COME CHECK IT OUT.
Got it.
In that case, instead of going directly to the bar, head toward the back entrance.
At the end of the street and immediately to the right, you'll see a service entrance for the bar.
You'll find it there.
"...HEY, YOU'RE SAKOTA-SENSEI'S BOY, RIGHT? WELL, LISTEN UP...

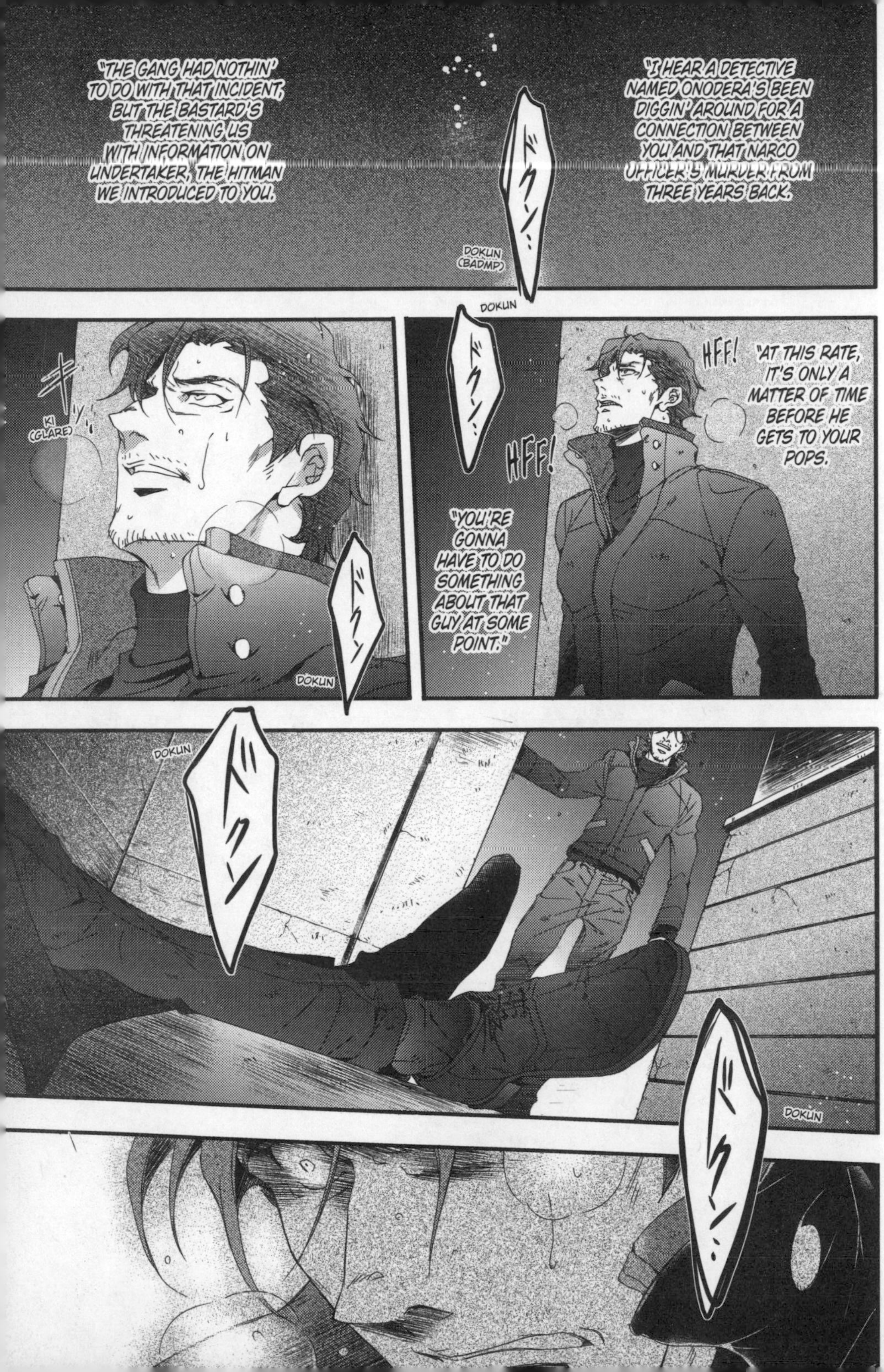
"I HEAR A DETECTIVE NAMED ONODERA'S BEEN DIGGIN' AROUND FOR A CONNECTION BETWEEN YOU AND THAT NARCO OFFICER'S MURDER FROM THREE YEARS BACK.
ドクン
DOKUN (BADMP)
"THE GANG HAD NOTHIN' TO DO WITH THAT INCIDENT, BUT THE BASTARD'S THREATENING US WITH INFORMATION ON UNDERTAKER, THE HITMAN WE INTRODUCED TO YOU.
ドクン
DOKUN
"AT THIS RATE, IT'S ONLY A MATTER OF TIME BEFORE HE GETS TO YOUR POPS.
HFF!
HFF!
"YOU'RE GONNA HAVE TO DO SOMETHING ABOUT THAT GUY AT SOME POINT."
ギ
KI (GLARE)
ドクン
DOKUN
ドクン
DOKUN
ドクン
DOKUN

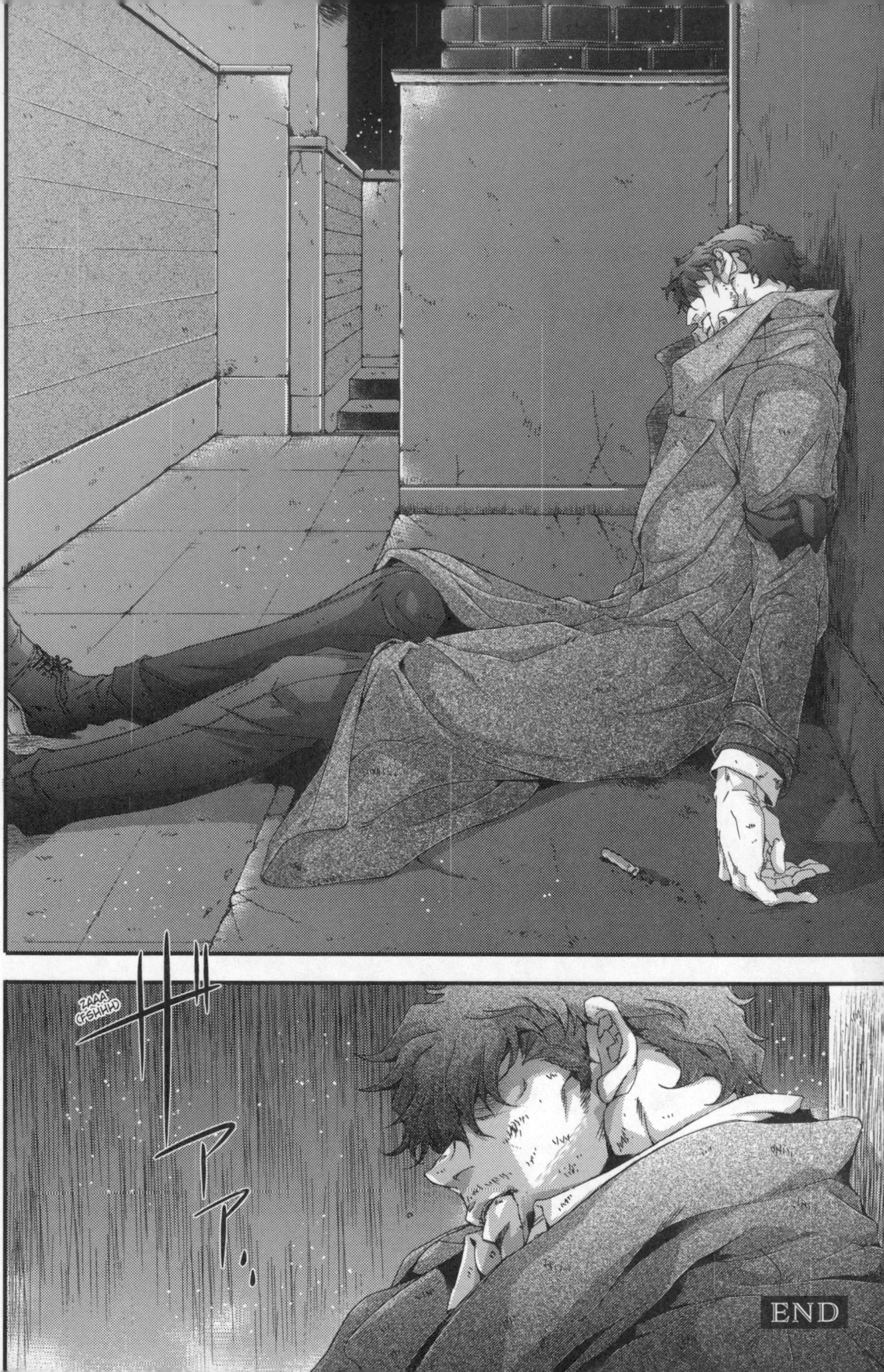
ザーァ…
ZAAA (FSHHH)
END

CHAPTER 3

Cats

ジリ
JIRI
CSKSKJ

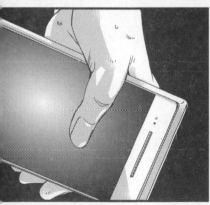

HAAH...

HFF...

Those're the "goods" you ordered.

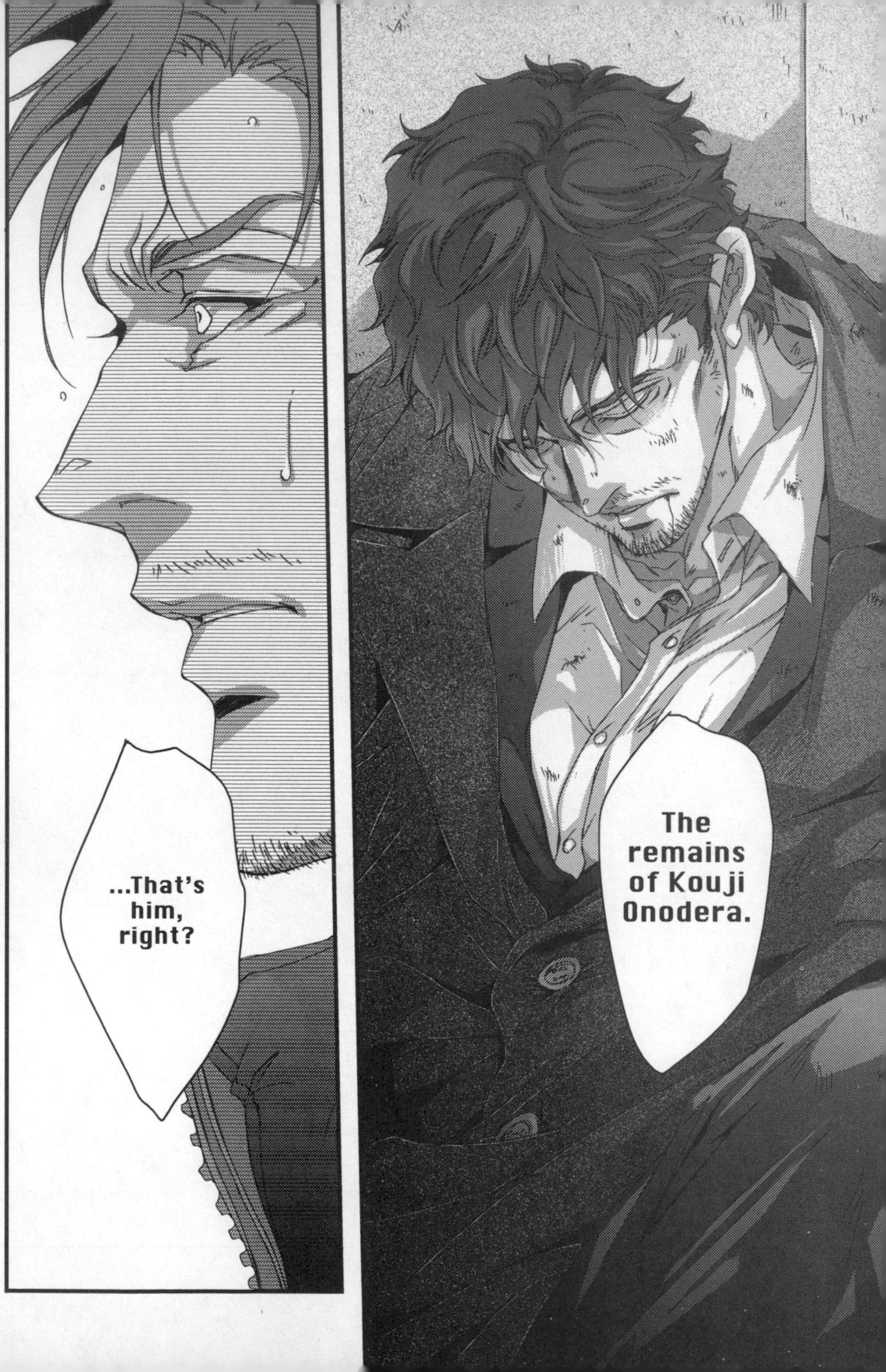
The remains of Kouji Onodera.
...That's him, right?

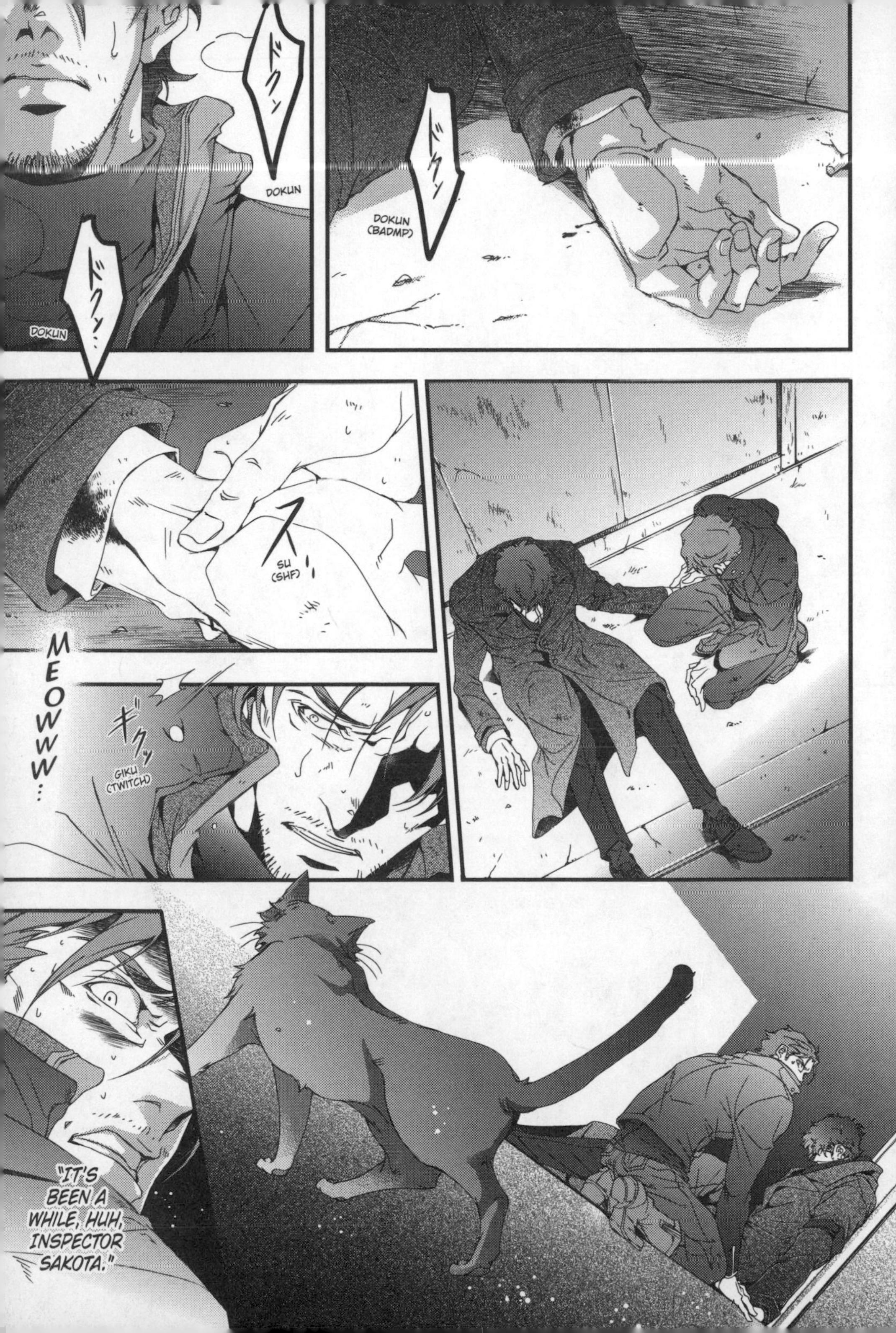
ドクン
DOKUN (BADMP)
ドクン
DOKUN
ドクン…
DOKUN
ス
SU (SHF)
ギクッ
GIKU (TWITCH)
MEOWWW…
"IT'S BEEN A WHILE, HUH, INSPECTOR SAKOTA."

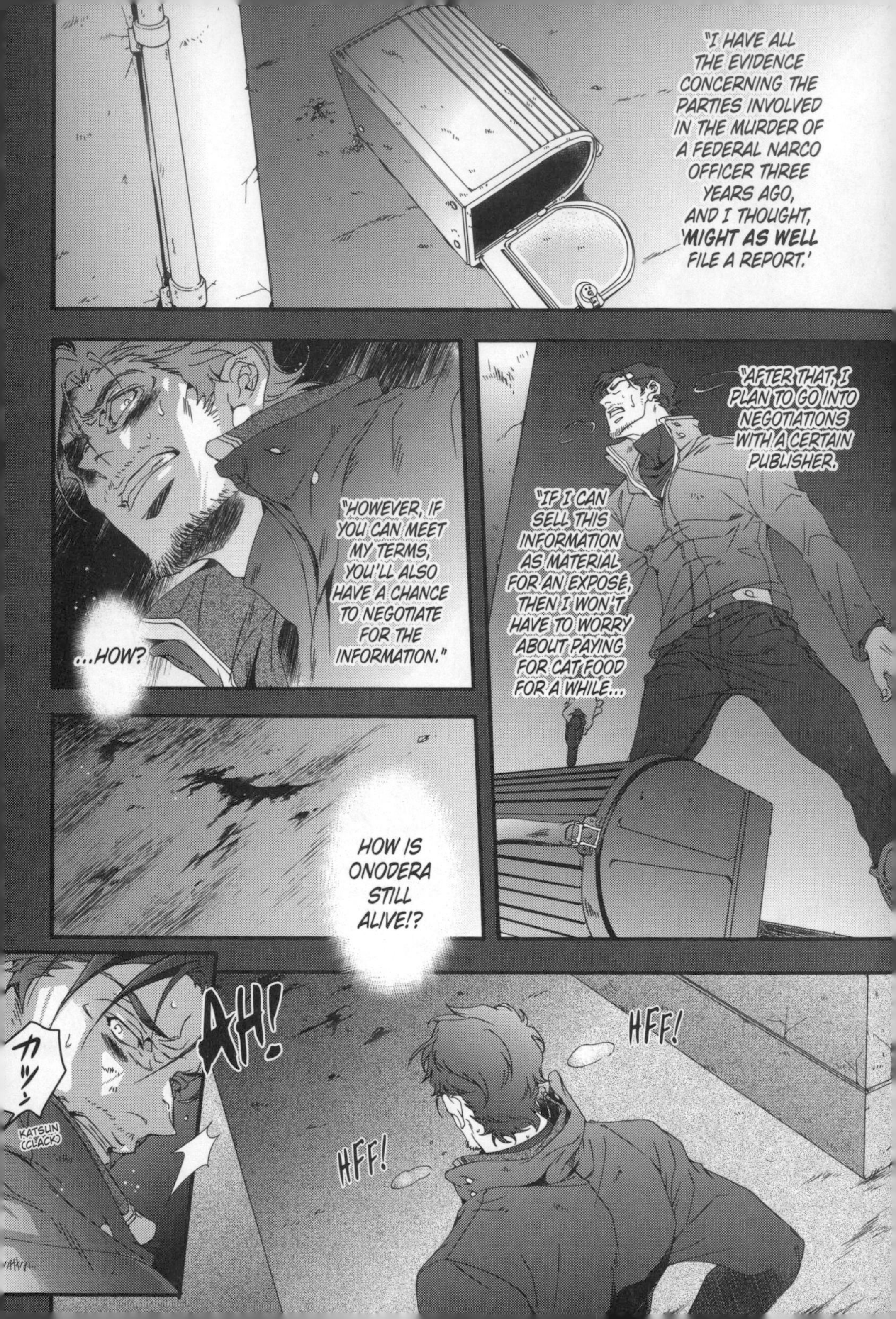
"I HAVE ALL THE EVIDENCE CONCERNING THE PARTIES INVOLVED IN THE MURDER OF A FEDERAL NARCO OFFICER THREE YEARS AGO, AND I THOUGHT, '**MIGHT AS WELL** FILE A REPORT.'
"AFTER THAT, I PLAN TO GO INTO NEGOTIATIONS WITH A CERTAIN PUBLISHER.
"IF I CAN SELL THIS INFORMATION AS MATERIAL FOR AN EXPOSÉ, THEN I WON'T HAVE TO WORRY ABOUT PAYING FOR CAT FOOD FOR A WHILE...
"HOWEVER, IF YOU CAN MEET MY TERMS, YOU'LL ALSO HAVE A CHANCE TO NEGOTIATE FOR THE INFORMATION."
...HOW?
HOW IS ONODERA STILL ALIVE!?
HFF!
AH!
カッ
KATSUN (CLACK)
HFF!

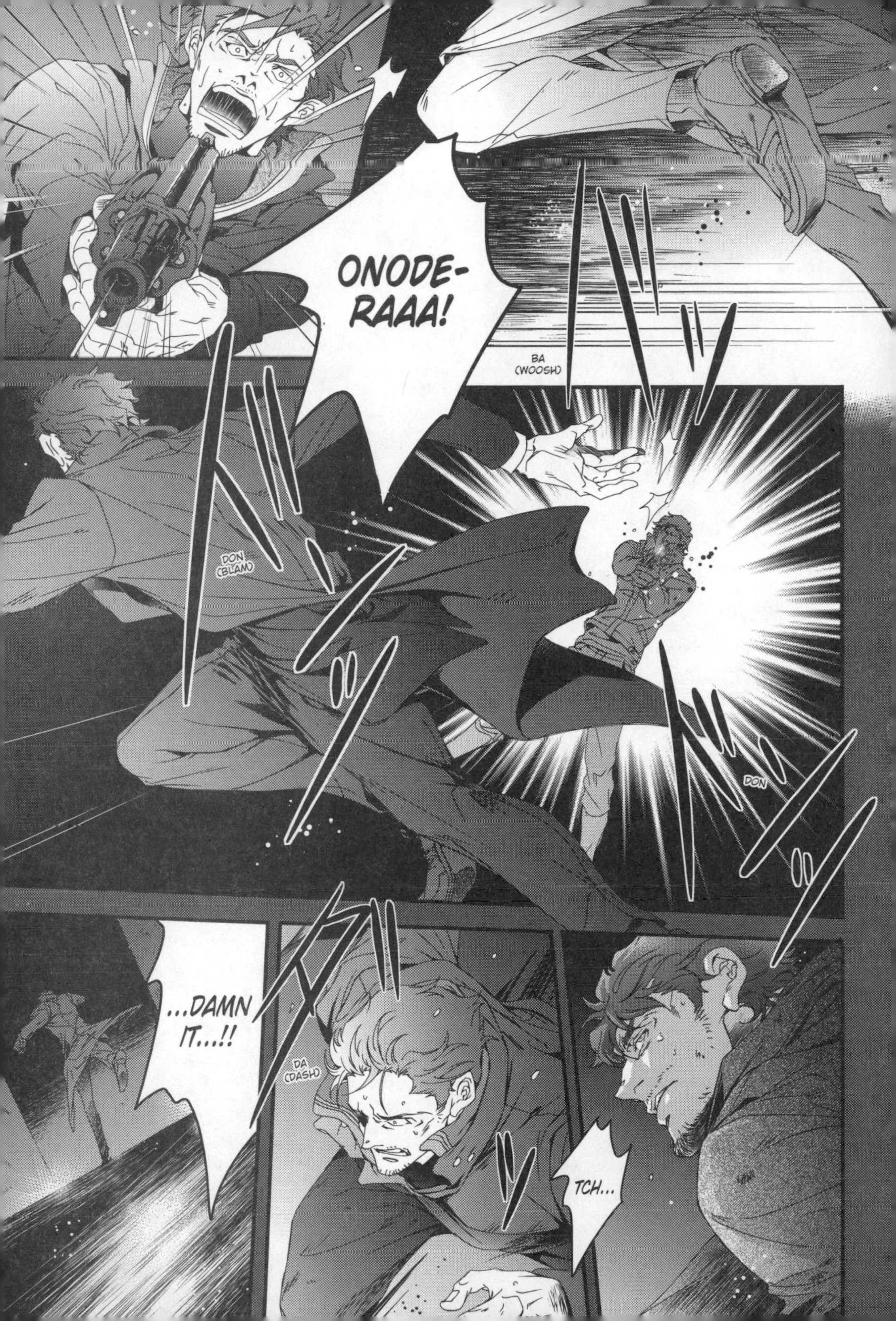
ONODE-RAAA!
BA (WOOSH)
DON
DON (BLAM)
TCH...
DA (DASH)
...DAMN IT...!!

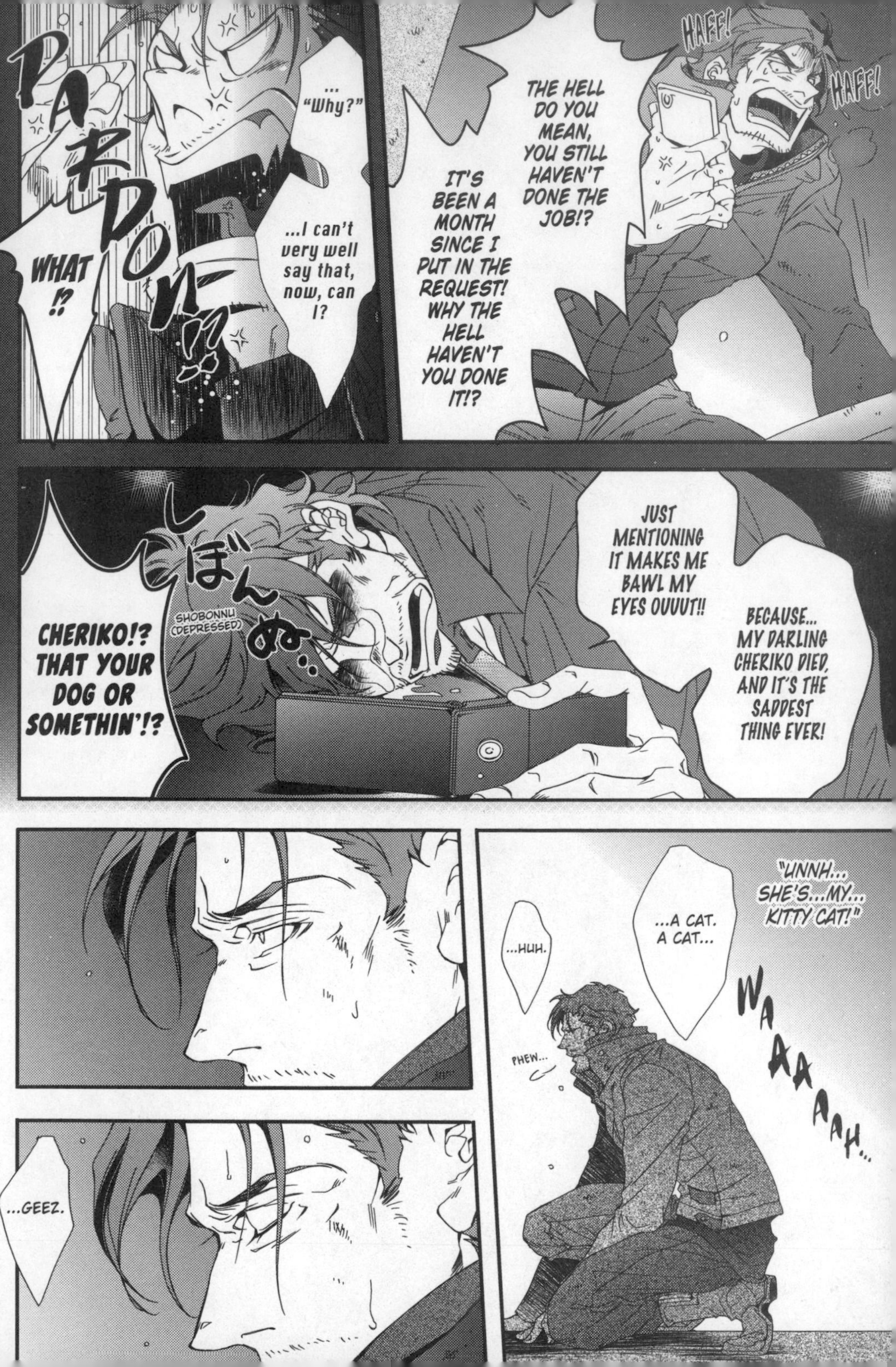
HAFF!
HAFF!
THE HELL DO YOU MEAN, YOU STILL HAVEN'T DONE THE JOB!?
IT'S BEEN A MONTH SINCE I PUT IN THE REQUEST! WHY THE HELL HAVEN'T YOU DONE IT!?
... "Why?"
...I can't very well say that, now, can I?
PARDON!?
WHAT!?
JUST MENTIONING IT MAKES ME BAWL MY EYES OUUUT!!
BECAUSE... MY DARLING CHERIKO DIED, AND IT'S THE SADDEST THING EVER!
しぼんぬ..
SHOBONNU (DEPRESSED)
CHERIKO!? THAT YOUR DOG OR SOMETHIN'!?
"UNNH... SHE'S...MY... KITTY CAT!"
WAAAAAAH...
...A CAT. A CAT...
...HUH.
PHEW...
...GEEZ.

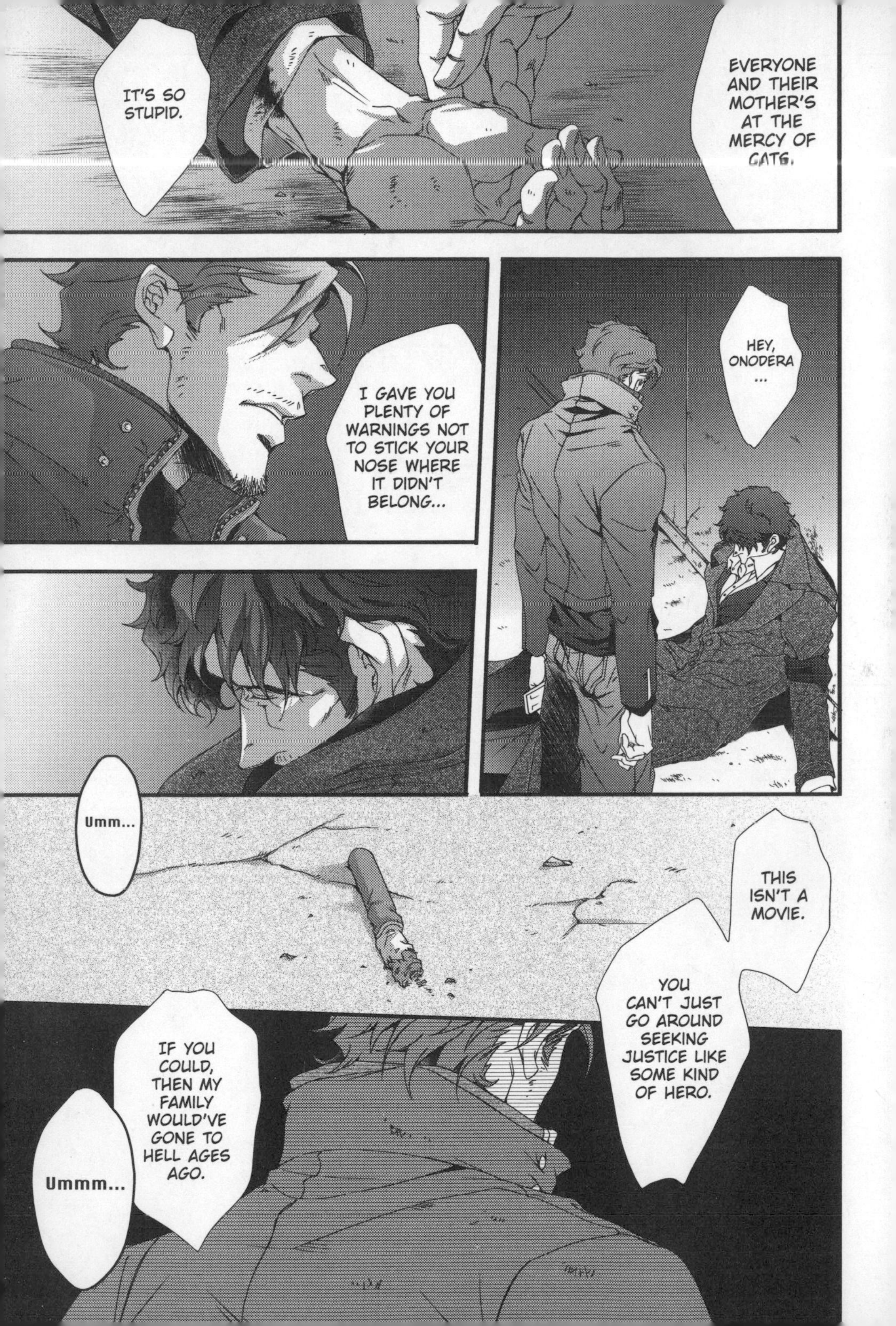
EVERYONE AND THEIR MOTHER'S AT THE MERCY OF CATS.
IT'S SO STUPID.
HEY, ONODERA...
I GAVE YOU PLENTY OF WARNINGS NOT TO STICK YOUR NOSE WHERE IT DIDN'T BELONG...
THIS ISN'T A MOVIE.
Umm...
YOU CAN'T JUST GO AROUND SEEKING JUSTICE LIKE SOME KIND OF HERO.
IF YOU COULD, THEN MY FAMILY WOULD'VE GONE TO HELL AGES AGO.
Ummm...

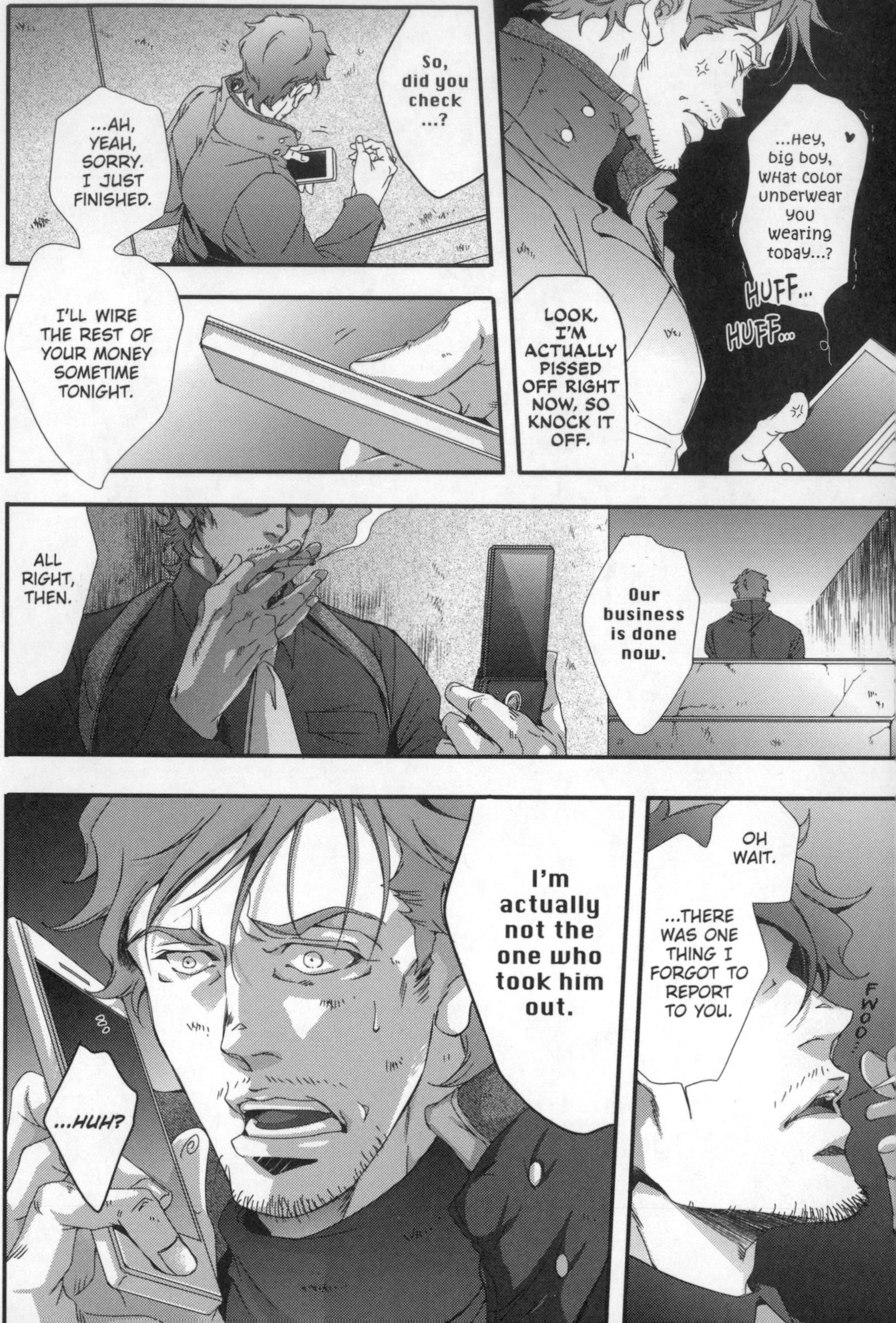
...Hey, big boy, What color underwear you wearing today...?
HUFF... HUFF...
LOOK, I'M ACTUALLY PISSED OFF RIGHT NOW, SO KNOCK IT OFF.
So, did you check ...?
...AH, YEAH, SORRY. I JUST FINISHED.
I'LL WIRE THE REST OF YOUR MONEY SOMETIME TONIGHT.
Our business is done now.
ALL RIGHT, THEN.
OH WAIT.
...THERE WAS ONE THING I FORGOT TO REPORT TO YOU.
FWOO...
I'm actually not the one who took him out.
...HUH?

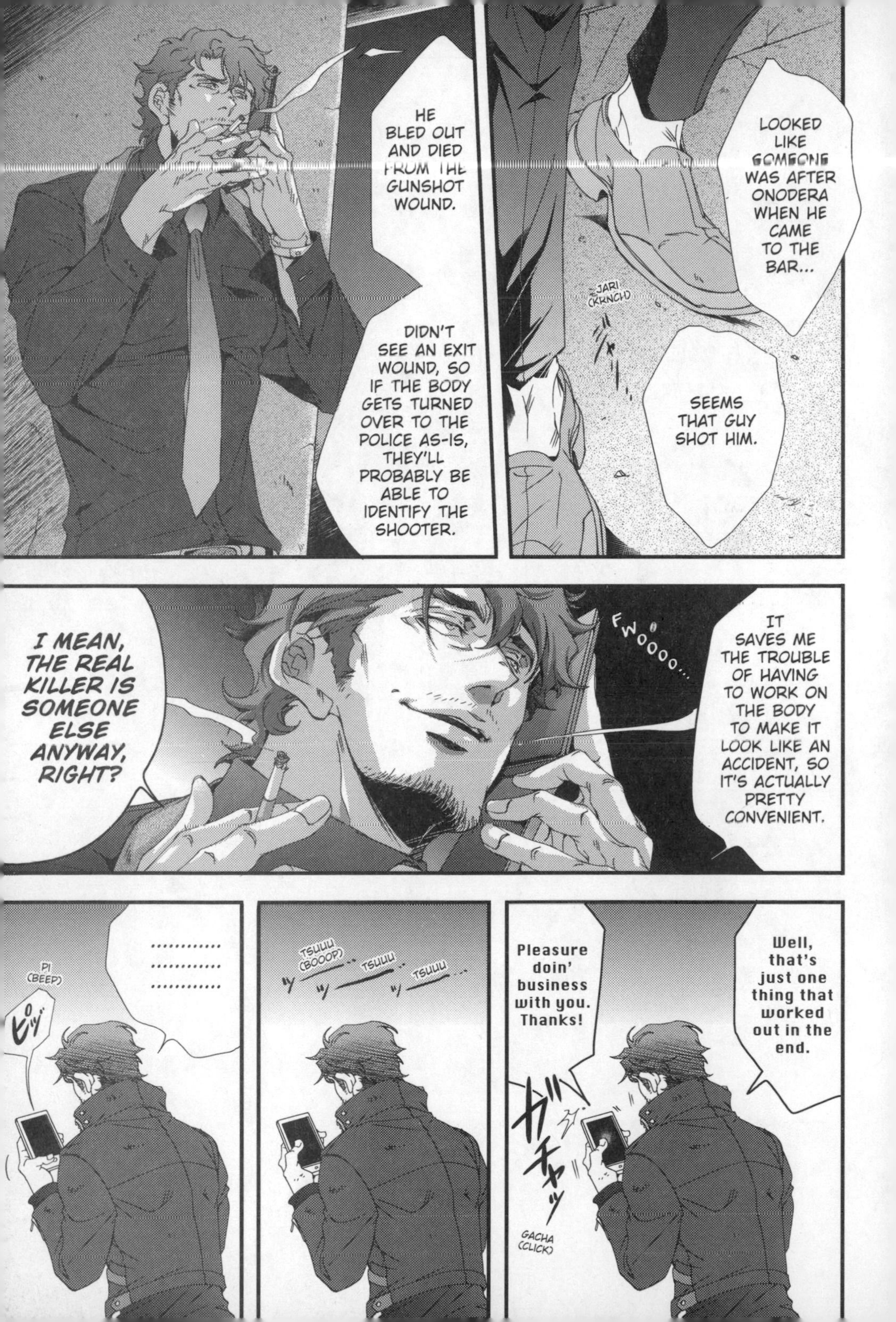
LOOKED LIKE SOMEONE WAS AFTER ONODERA WHEN HE CAME TO THE BAR...
JARI (KRNCH)
SEEMS THAT GUY SHOT HIM.
HE BLED OUT AND DIED FROM THE GUNSHOT WOUND.
DIDN'T SEE AN EXIT WOUND, SO IF THE BODY GETS TURNED OVER TO THE POLICE AS-IS, THEY'LL PROBABLY BE ABLE TO IDENTIFY THE SHOOTER.
FWOOOO...
IT SAVES ME THE TROUBLE OF HAVING TO WORK ON THE BODY TO MAKE IT LOOK LIKE AN ACCIDENT, SO IT'S ACTUALLY PRETTY CONVENIENT.
I MEAN, THE REAL KILLER IS SOMEONE ELSE ANYWAY, RIGHT?
Well, that's just one thing that worked out in the end.
Pleasure doin' business with you. Thanks!
GACHA (CLICK)
TSUUU (BOOOP)
TSUUU
TSUUU
....
....
....
PI (BEEP)

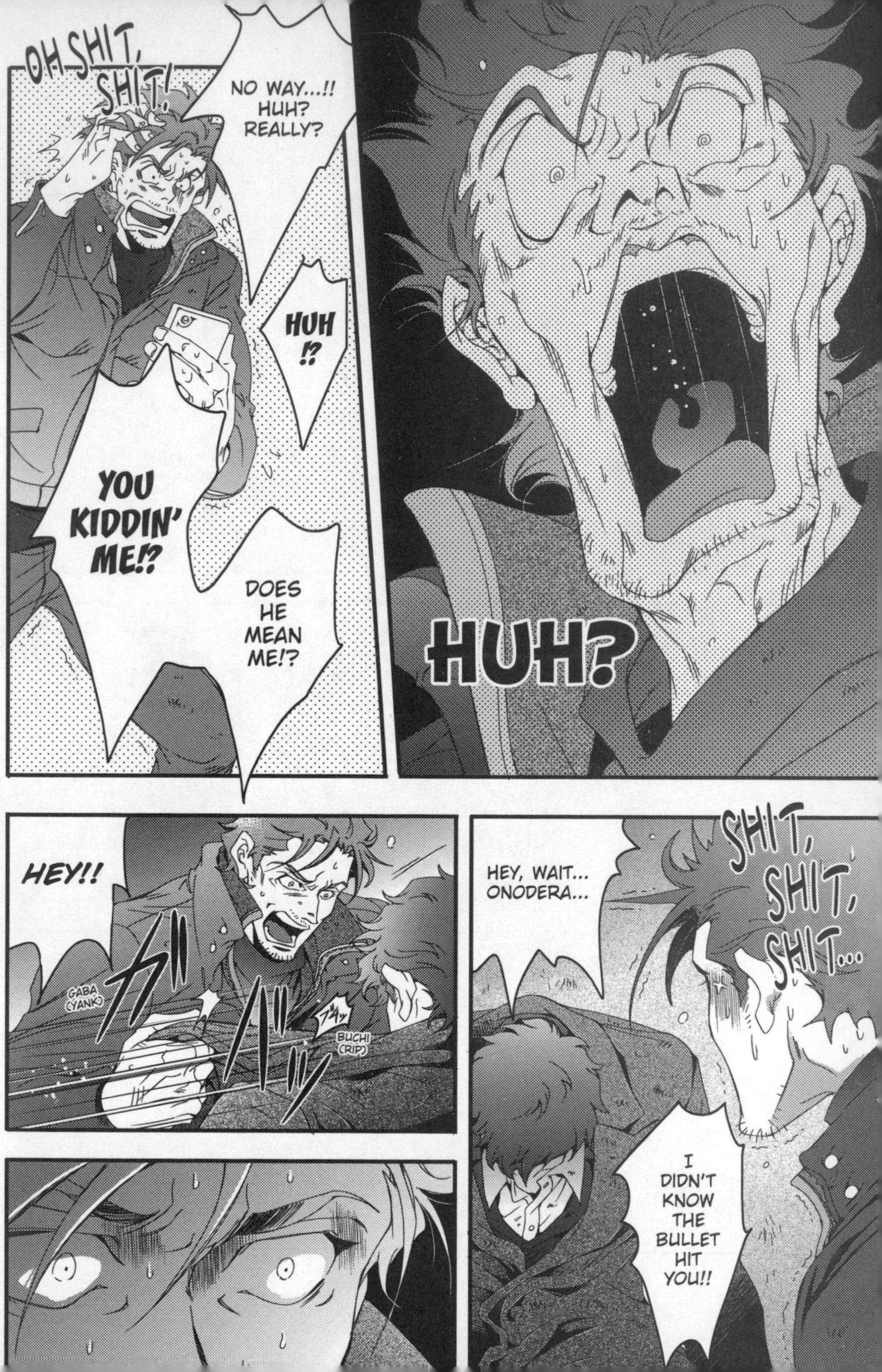
HUH?
NO WAY...!! HUH? REALLY?
OH SHIT, SHIT!
HUH!?
YOU KIDDIN' ME!?
DOES HE MEAN ME!?
SHIT, SHIT, SHIT...
HEY, WAIT... ONODERA...
I DIDN'T KNOW THE BULLET HIT YOU!!
HEY!!
BUCHI (RIP)
GABA (YANK)

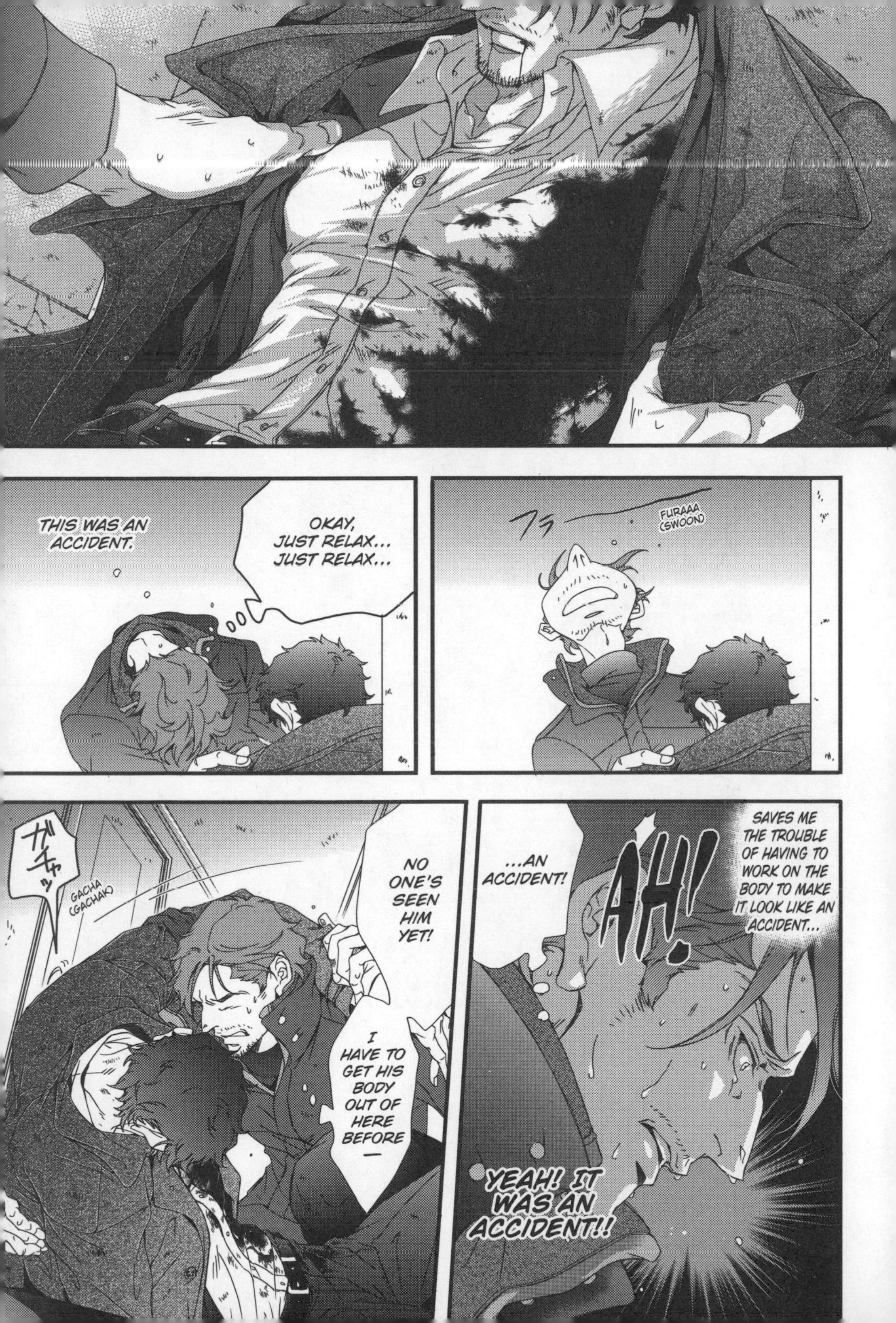
FURAAA (SWOON)
OKAY, JUST RELAX... JUST RELAX...
THIS WAS AN ACCIDENT.
SAVES ME THE TROUBLE OF HAVING TO WORK ON THE BODY TO MAKE IT LOOK LIKE AN ACCIDENT...
...AN ACCIDENT!
AH!
YEAH! IT WAS AN ACCIDENT!!
NO ONE'S SEEN HIM YET!
I HAVE TO GET HIS BODY OUT OF HERE BEFORE—
GACHA (GACHAK)

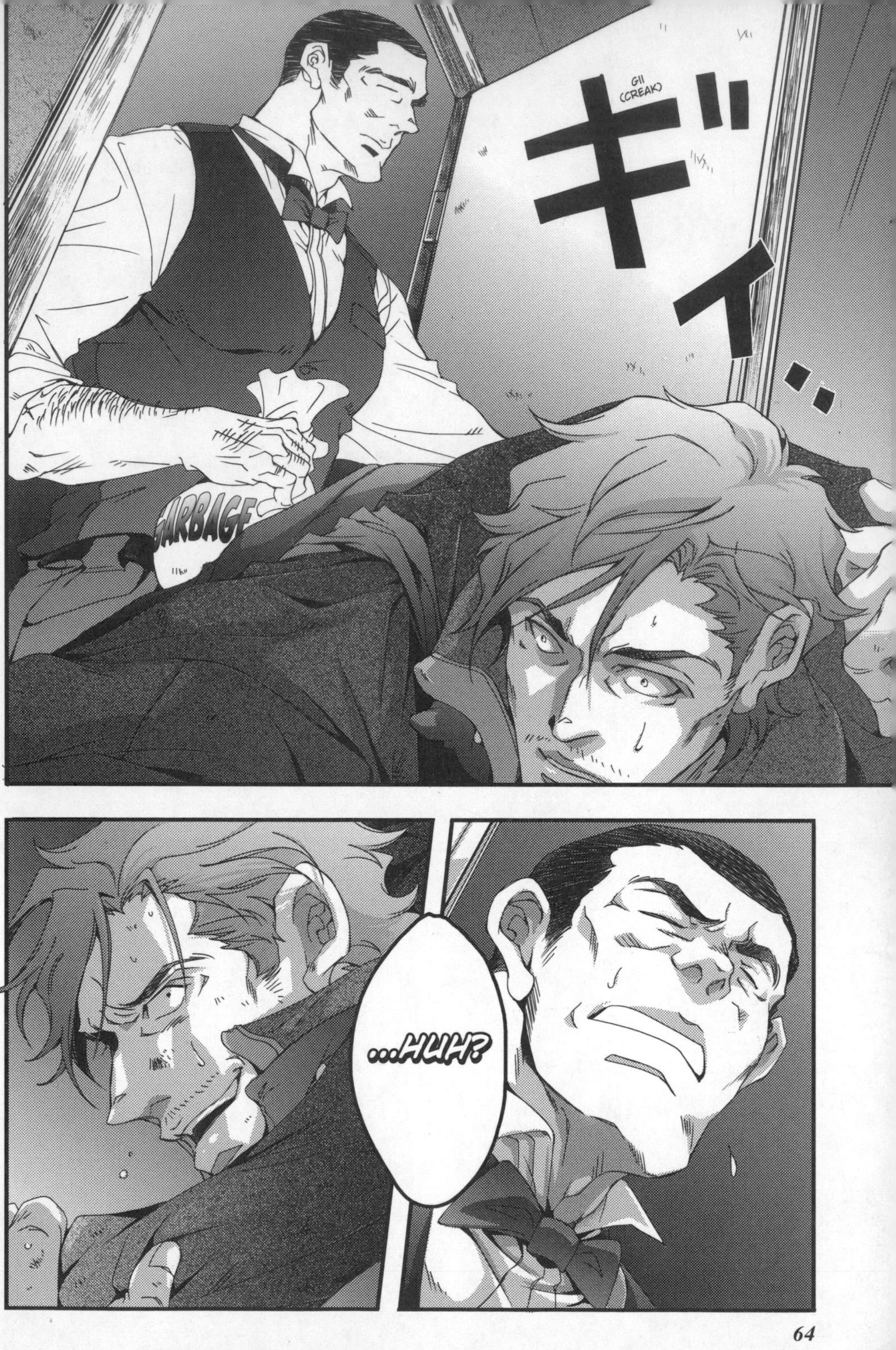

GII (CREAK)
ギイ..
GARBAGE
...HUH?

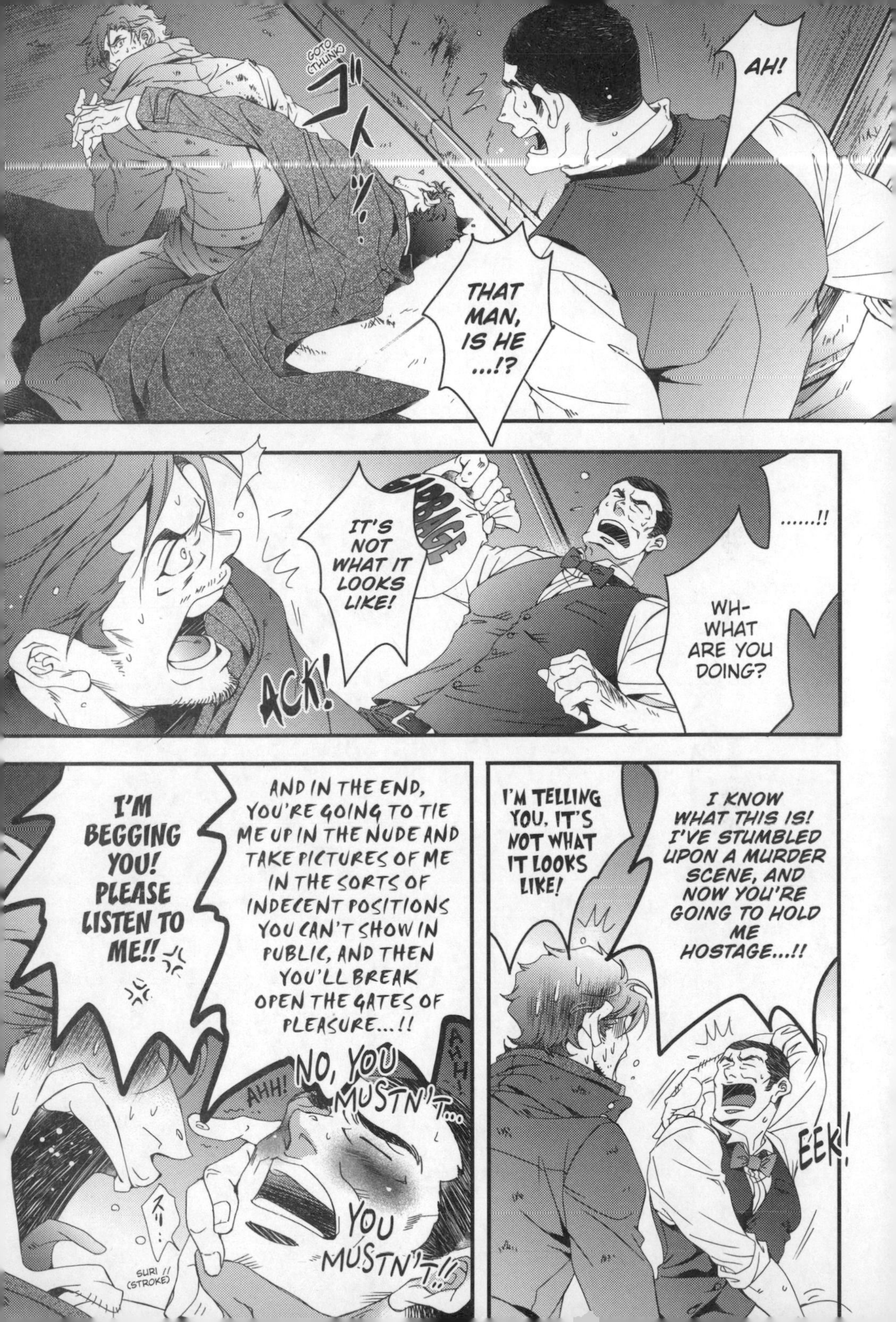
AH!
GOTO (THUNK)
THAT MAN, IS HE ...!?
......!!
WH- WHAT ARE YOU DOING?
IT'S NOT WHAT IT LOOKS LIKE!
ACK!
I KNOW WHAT THIS IS! I'VE STUMBLED UPON A MURDER SCENE, AND NOW YOU'RE GOING TO HOLD ME HOSTAGE...!!
I'M TELLING YOU, IT'S NOT WHAT IT LOOKS LIKE!
EEK!
AND IN THE END, YOU'RE GOING TO TIE ME UP IN THE NUDE AND TAKE PICTURES OF ME IN THE SORTS OF INDECENT POSITIONS YOU CAN'T SHOW IN PUBLIC, AND THEN YOU'LL BREAK OPEN THE GATES OF PLEASURE...!!
I'M BEGGING YOU! PLEASE LISTEN TO ME!!
AHH!
NO, YOU MUSTN'T...
YOU MUSTN'T!!
SURI (STROKE)

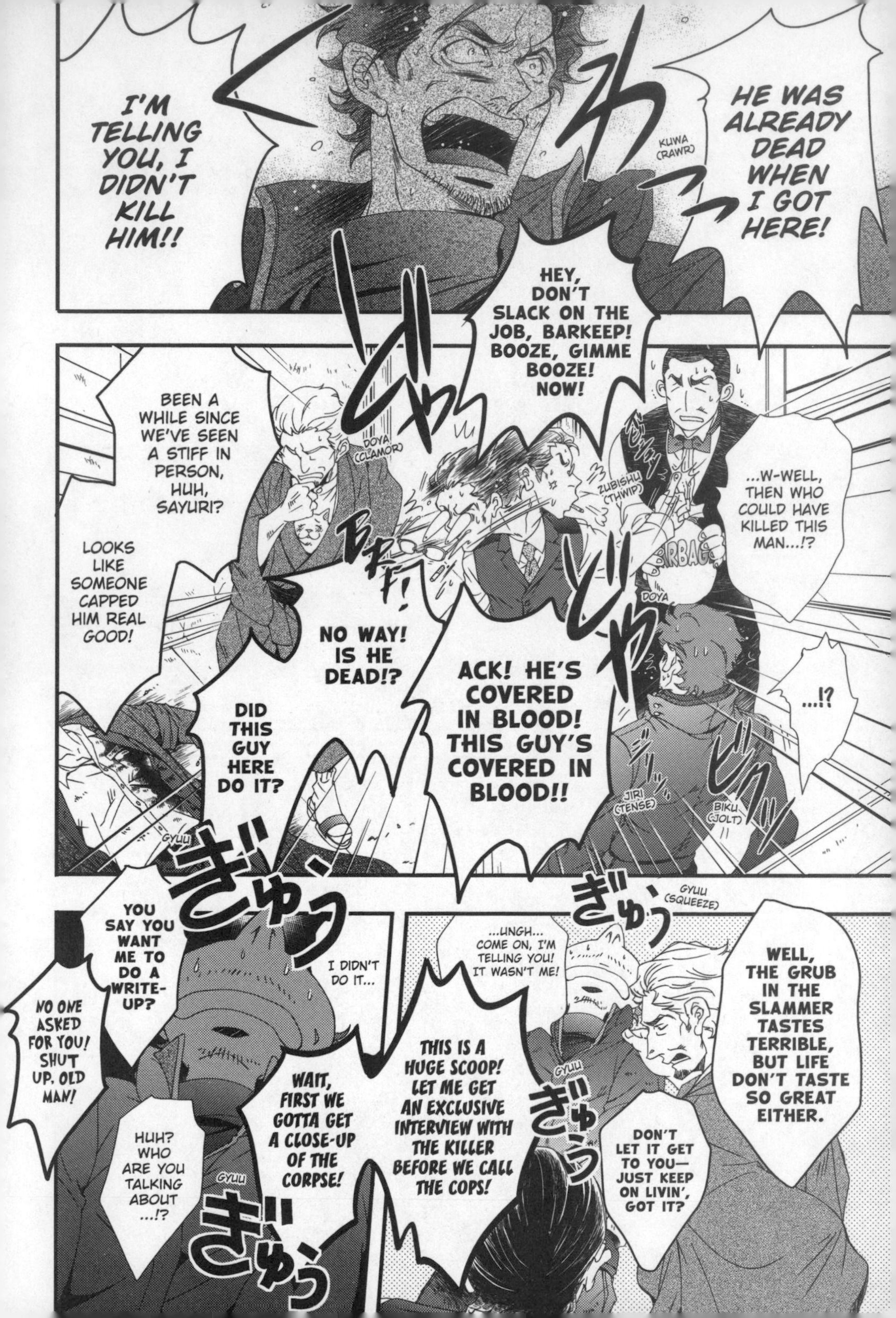
HE WAS ALREADY DEAD WHEN I GOT HERE!
KUWA (RAWR)
I'M TELLING YOU, I DIDN'T KILL HIM!!
HEY, DON'T SLACK ON THE JOB, BARKEEP! BOOZE, GIMME BOOZE! NOW!
...W-WELL, THEN WHO COULD HAVE KILLED THIS MAN...!?
ZUBISHU (THWIP)
DOYA (CLAMOR)
BEEN A WHILE SINCE WE'VE SEEN A STIFF IN PERSON, HUH, SAYURI?
LOOKS LIKE SOMEONE CAPPED HIM REAL GOOD!
DOYA
...!?
ACK! HE'S COVERED IN BLOOD! THIS GUY'S COVERED IN BLOOD!!
NO WAY! IS HE DEAD!?
DID THIS GUY HERE DO IT?
BIKU (JOLT)
JIRI (TENSE)
GYUU
GYUU (SQUEEZE)
WELL, THE GRUB IN THE SLAMMER TASTES TERRIBLE, BUT LIFE DON'T TASTE SO GREAT EITHER.
...UNGH... COME ON, I'M TELLING YOU! IT WASN'T ME!
DON'T LET IT GET TO YOU—JUST KEEP ON LIVIN', GOT IT?
GYUU
THIS IS A HUGE SCOOP! LET ME GET AN EXCLUSIVE INTERVIEW WITH THE KILLER BEFORE WE CALL THE COPS!
WAIT, FIRST WE GOTTA GET A CLOSE-UP OF THE CORPSE!
I DIDN'T DO IT...
YOU SAY YOU WANT ME TO DO A WRITE-UP?
NO ONE ASKED FOR YOU! SHUT UP, OLD MAN!
HUH? WHO ARE YOU TALKING ABOUT ...!?
GYUU

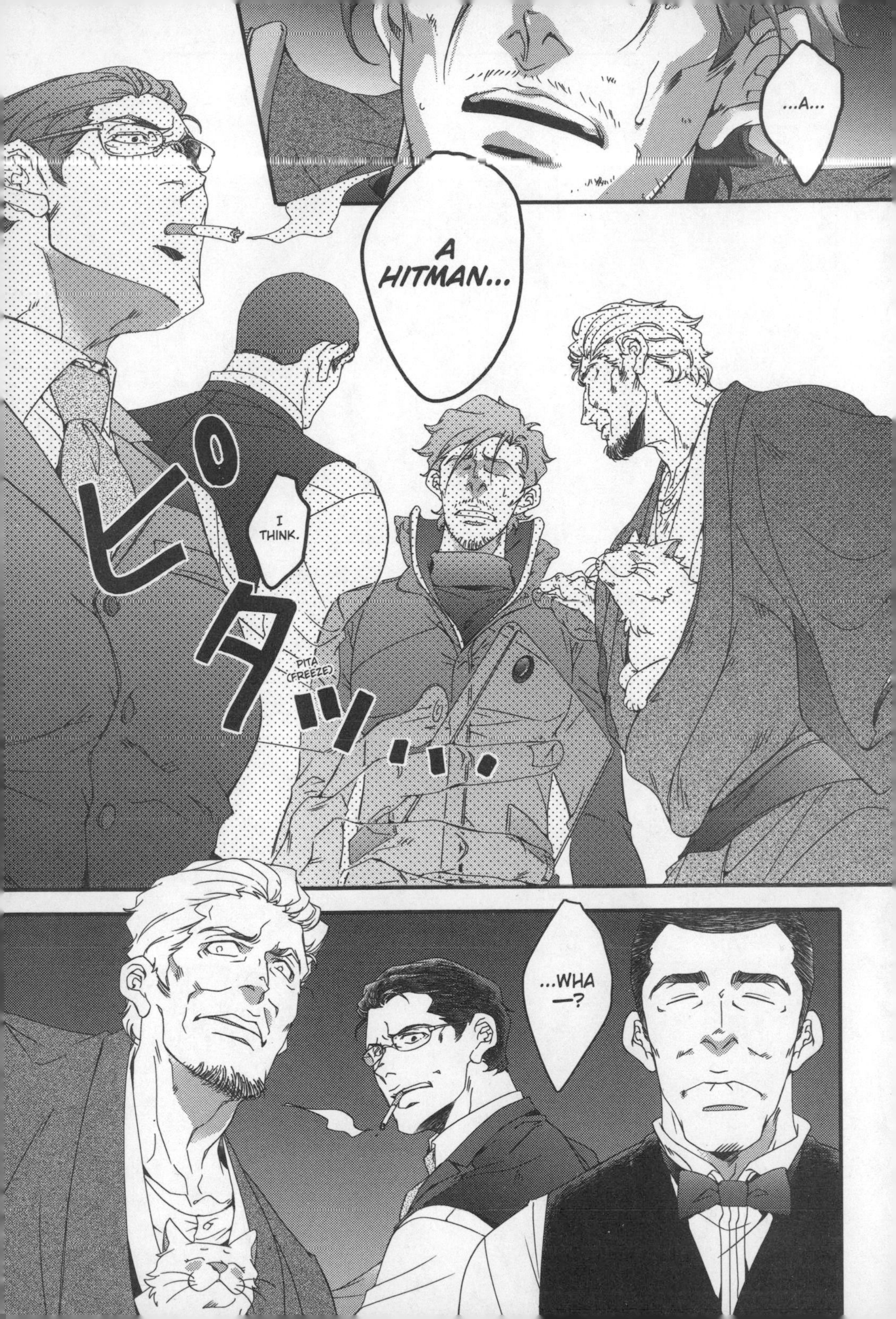
...A...
A HITMAN...
I THINK.
ピタッ...
PITA (FREEZE)
...WHA—?

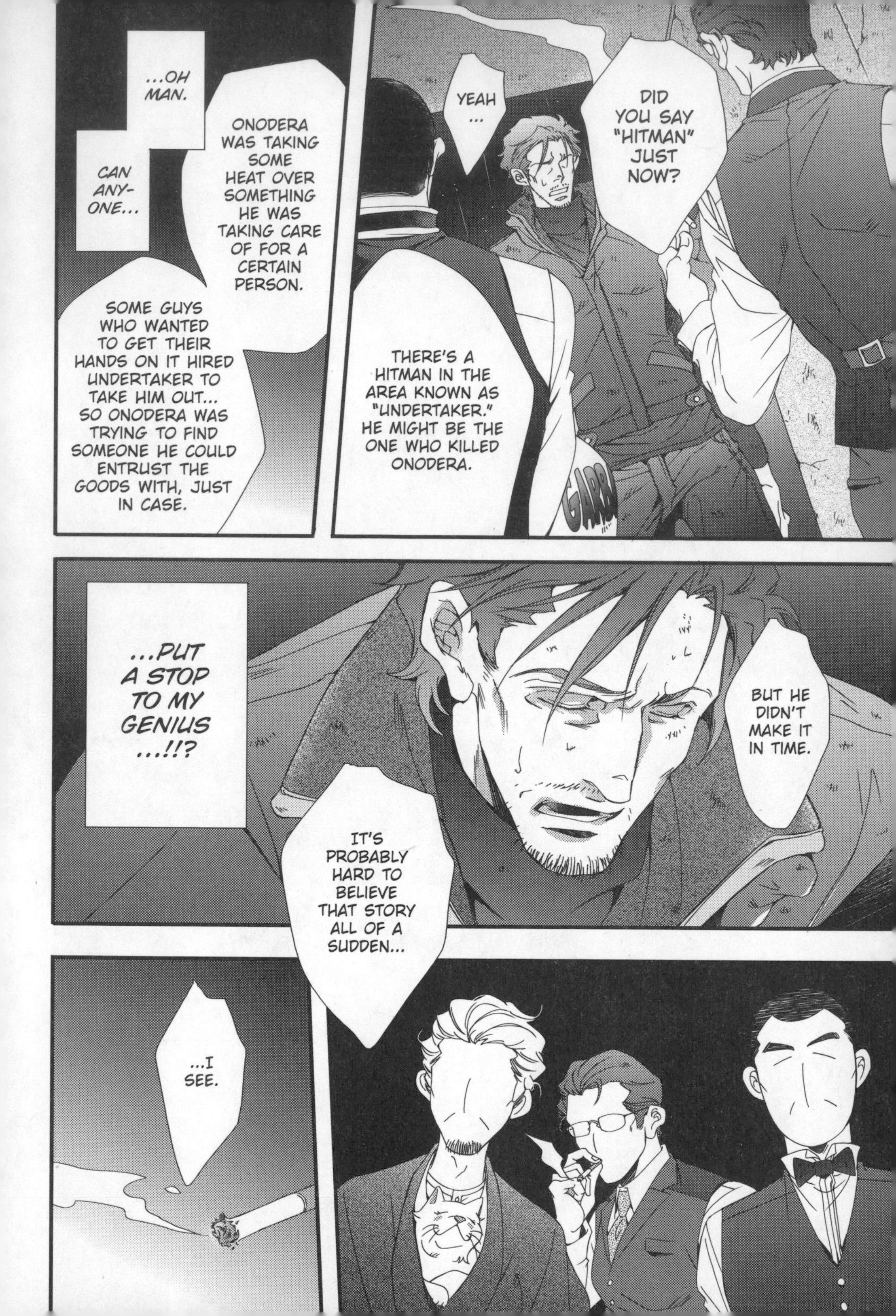
DID YOU SAY "HITMAN" JUST NOW?
YEAH...
THERE'S A HITMAN IN THE AREA KNOWN AS "UNDERTAKER." HE MIGHT BE THE ONE WHO KILLED ONODERA.
ONODERA WAS TAKING SOME HEAT OVER SOMETHING HE WAS TAKING CARE OF FOR A CERTAIN PERSON.
...OH MAN.
CAN ANYONE...
SOME GUYS WHO WANTED TO GET THEIR HANDS ON IT HIRED UNDERTAKER TO TAKE HIM OUT... SO ONODERA WAS TRYING TO FIND SOMEONE HE COULD ENTRUST THE GOODS WITH, JUST IN CASE.
BUT HE DIDN'T MAKE IT IN TIME.
...PUT A STOP TO MY GENIUS ...!!?
IT'S PROBABLY HARD TO BELIEVE THAT STORY ALL OF A SUDDEN...
...I SEE.

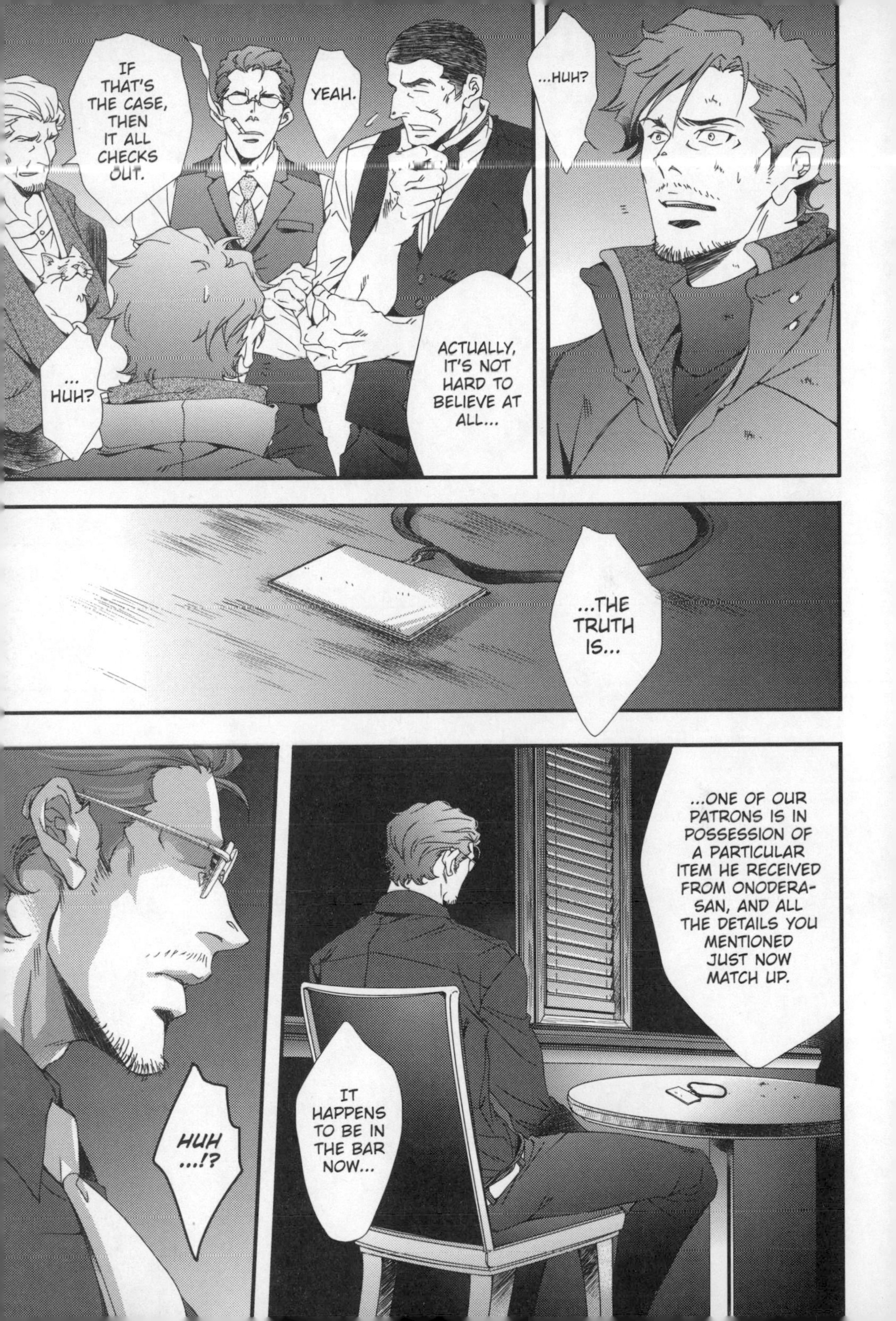
...HUH?
YEAH.
IF THAT'S THE CASE, THEN IT ALL CHECKS OUT.
ACTUALLY, IT'S NOT HARD TO BELIEVE AT ALL...
...HUH?
...THE TRUTH IS...
...ONE OF OUR PATRONS IS IN POSSESSION OF A PARTICULAR ITEM HE RECEIVED FROM ONODERA-SAN, AND ALL THE DETAILS YOU MENTIONED JUST NOW MATCH UP.
IT HAPPENS TO BE IN THE BAR NOW...
HUH...!?

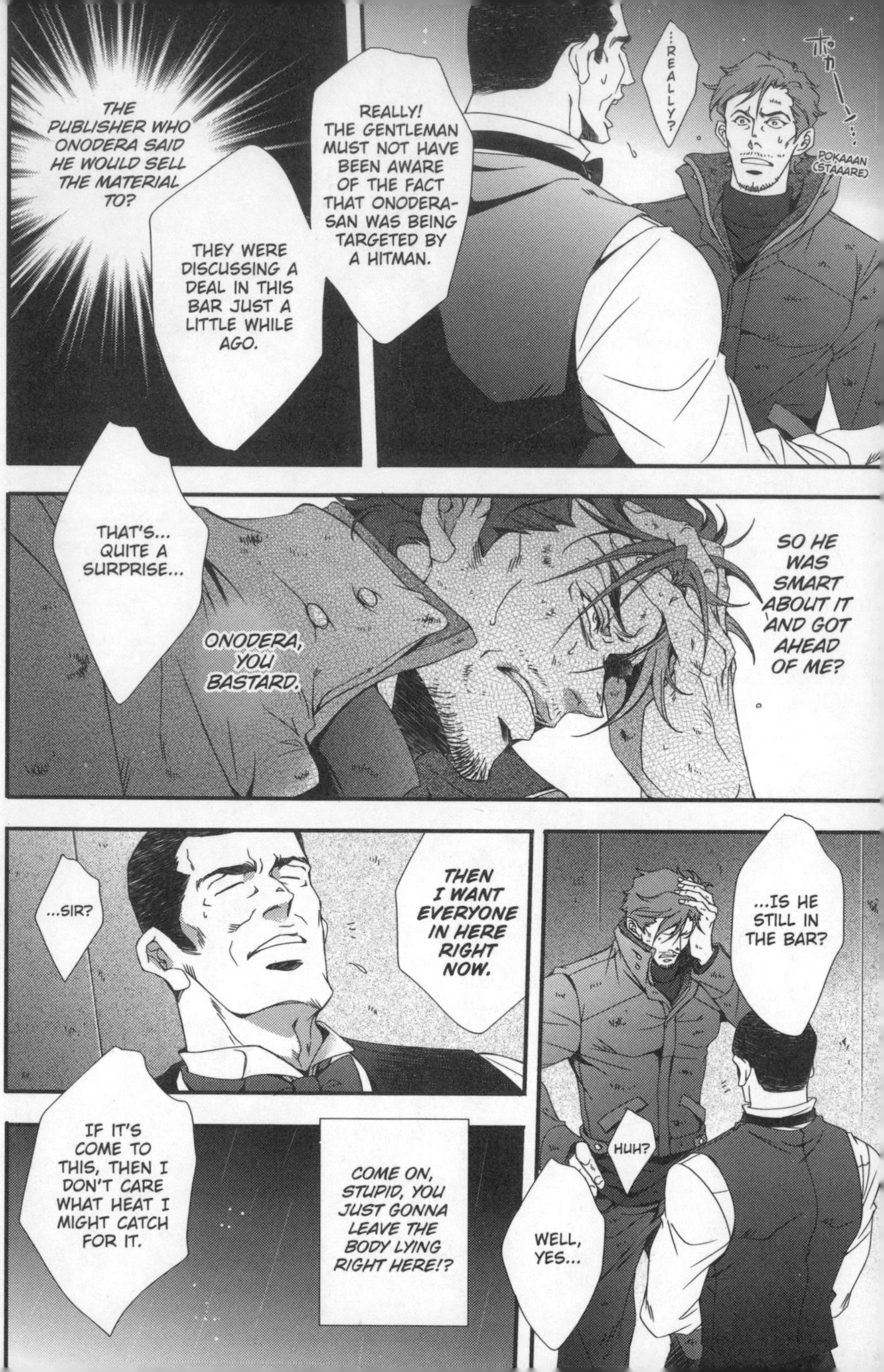
ポカーーン
POKAAAN (STAAARE)
...REALLY?
REALLY! THE GENTLEMAN MUST NOT HAVE BEEN AWARE OF THE FACT THAT ONODERA-SAN WAS BEING TARGETED BY A HITMAN.
THEY WERE DISCUSSING A DEAL IN THIS BAR JUST A LITTLE WHILE AGO.
THE PUBLISHER WHO ONODERA SAID HE WOULD SELL THE MATERIAL TO?
SO HE WAS SMART ABOUT IT AND GOT AHEAD OF ME?
THAT'S... QUITE A SURPRISE...
ONODERA, YOU BASTARD.
...IS HE STILL IN THE BAR?
HUH?
WELL, YES...
THEN I WANT EVERYONE IN HERE RIGHT NOW.
...SIR?
COME ON, STUPID, YOU JUST GONNA LEAVE THE BODY LYING RIGHT HERE!?
IF IT'S COME TO THIS, THEN I DON'T CARE WHAT HEAT I MIGHT CATCH FOR IT.

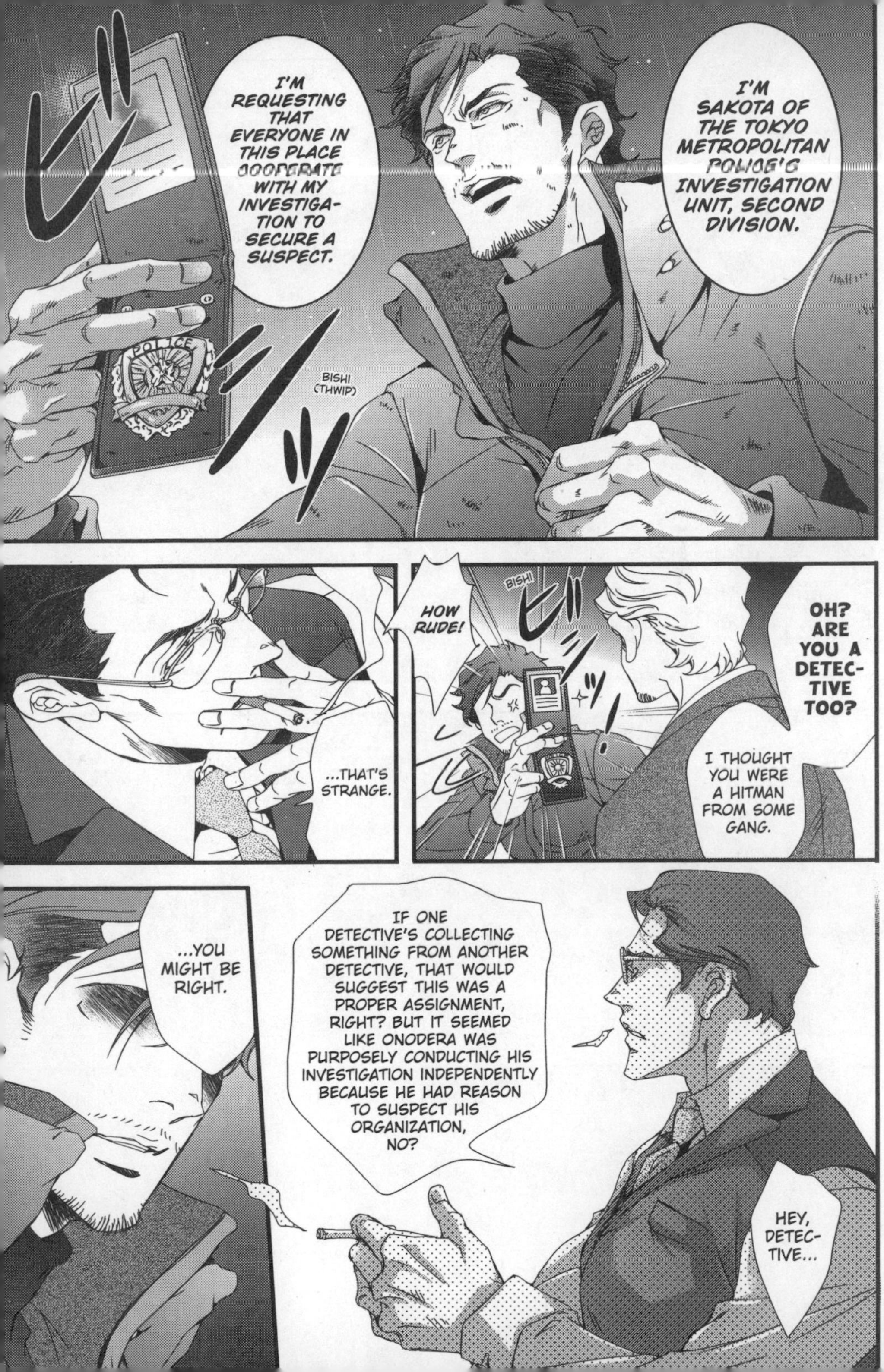
I'M SAKOTA OF THE TOKYO METROPOLITAN POLICE'S INVESTIGATION UNIT, SECOND DIVISION.
I'M REQUESTING THAT EVERYONE IN THIS PLACE COOPERATE WITH MY INVESTIGATION TO SECURE A SUSPECT.
BISHI (THWIP)
OH? ARE YOU A DETECTIVE TOO?
I THOUGHT YOU WERE A HITMAN FROM SOME GANG.
BISHI
HOW RUDE!
...THAT'S STRANGE.
IF ONE DETECTIVE'S COLLECTING SOMETHING FROM ANOTHER DETECTIVE, THAT WOULD SUGGEST THIS WAS A PROPER ASSIGNMENT, RIGHT? BUT IT SEEMED LIKE ONODERA WAS PURPOSELY CONDUCTING HIS INVESTIGATION INDEPENDENTLY BECAUSE HE HAD REASON TO SUSPECT HIS ORGANIZATION, NO?
HEY, DETECTIVE...
...YOU MIGHT BE RIGHT.

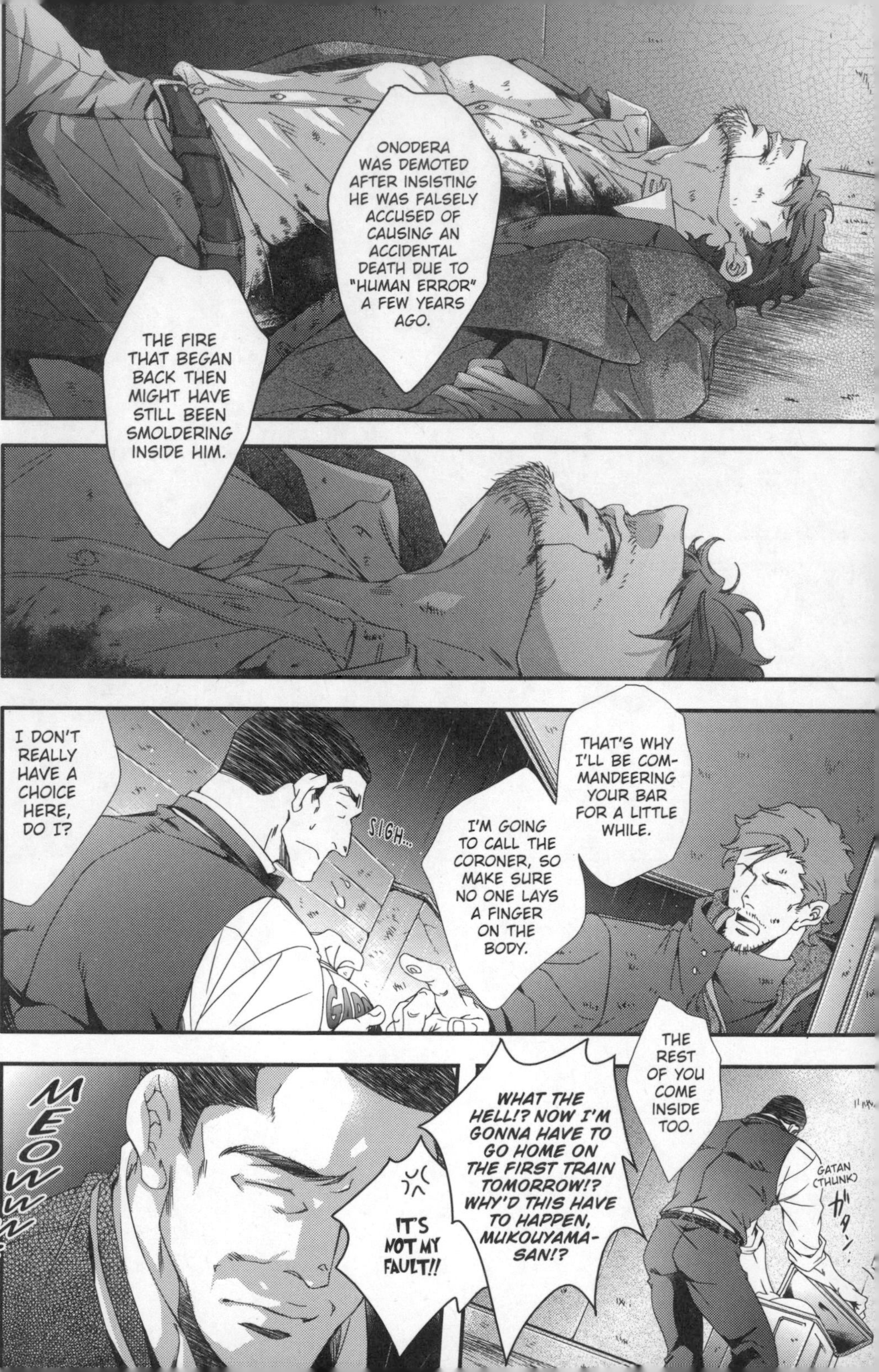

ONODERA WAS DEMOTED AFTER INSISTING HE WAS FALSELY ACCUSED OF CAUSING AN ACCIDENTAL DEATH DUE TO "HUMAN ERROR" A FEW YEARS AGO.
THE FIRE THAT BEGAN BACK THEN MIGHT HAVE STILL BEEN SMOLDERING INSIDE HIM.
THAT'S WHY I'LL BE COM-MANDEERING YOUR BAR FOR A LITTLE WHILE.
I'M GOING TO CALL THE CORONER, SO MAKE SURE NO ONE LAYS A FINGER ON THE BODY.
SIGH...
I DON'T REALLY HAVE A CHOICE HERE, DO I?
THE REST OF YOU COME INSIDE TOO.
GATAN (THUNK)
WHAT THE HELL!? NOW I'M GONNA HAVE TO GO HOME ON THE FIRST TRAIN TOMORROW!? WHY'D THIS HAVE TO HAPPEN, MUKOUYAMA-SAN!?
IT'S NOT MY FAULT!!
MEOWWW...

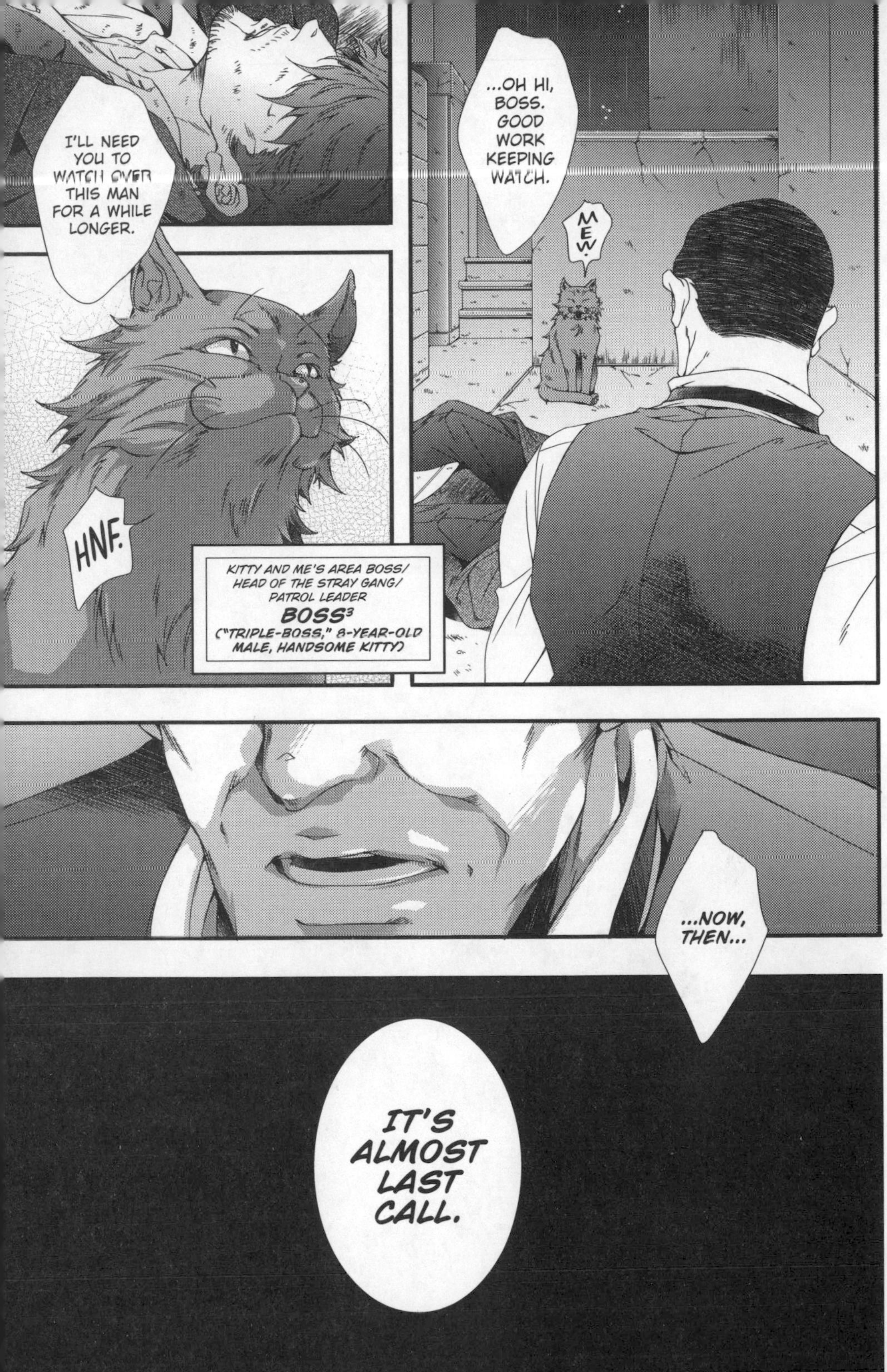
...OH HI, BOSS. GOOD WORK KEEPING WATCH.
MEW.
I'LL NEED YOU TO WATCH OVER THIS MAN FOR A WHILE LONGER.
HNF.
KITTY AND ME'S AREA BOSS/ HEAD OF THE STRAY GANG/ PATROL LEADER
BOSS^3
("TRIPLE-BOSS," 8-YEAR-OLD MALE, HANDSOME KITTY)
...NOW, THEN...
IT'S ALMOST LAST CALL.

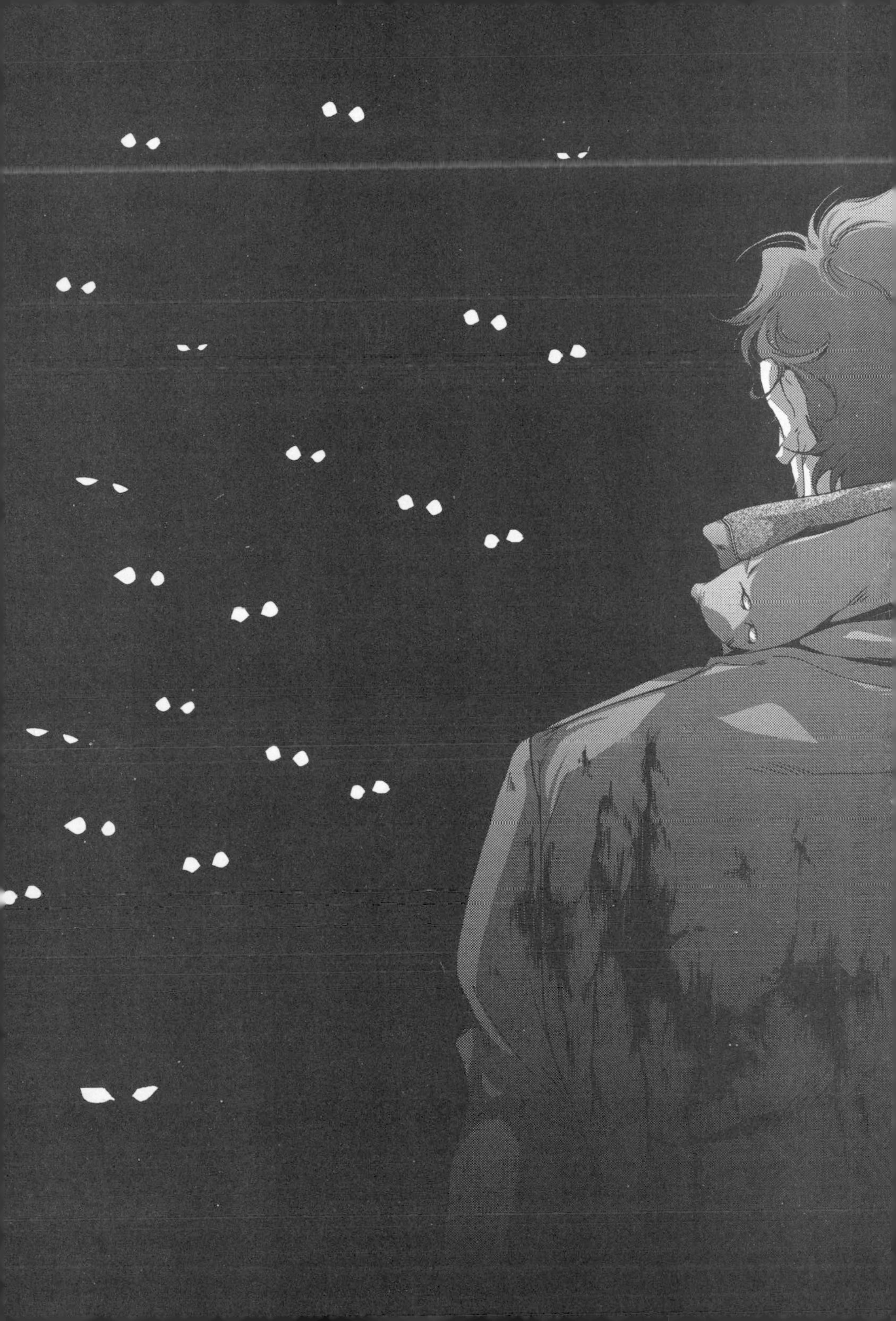

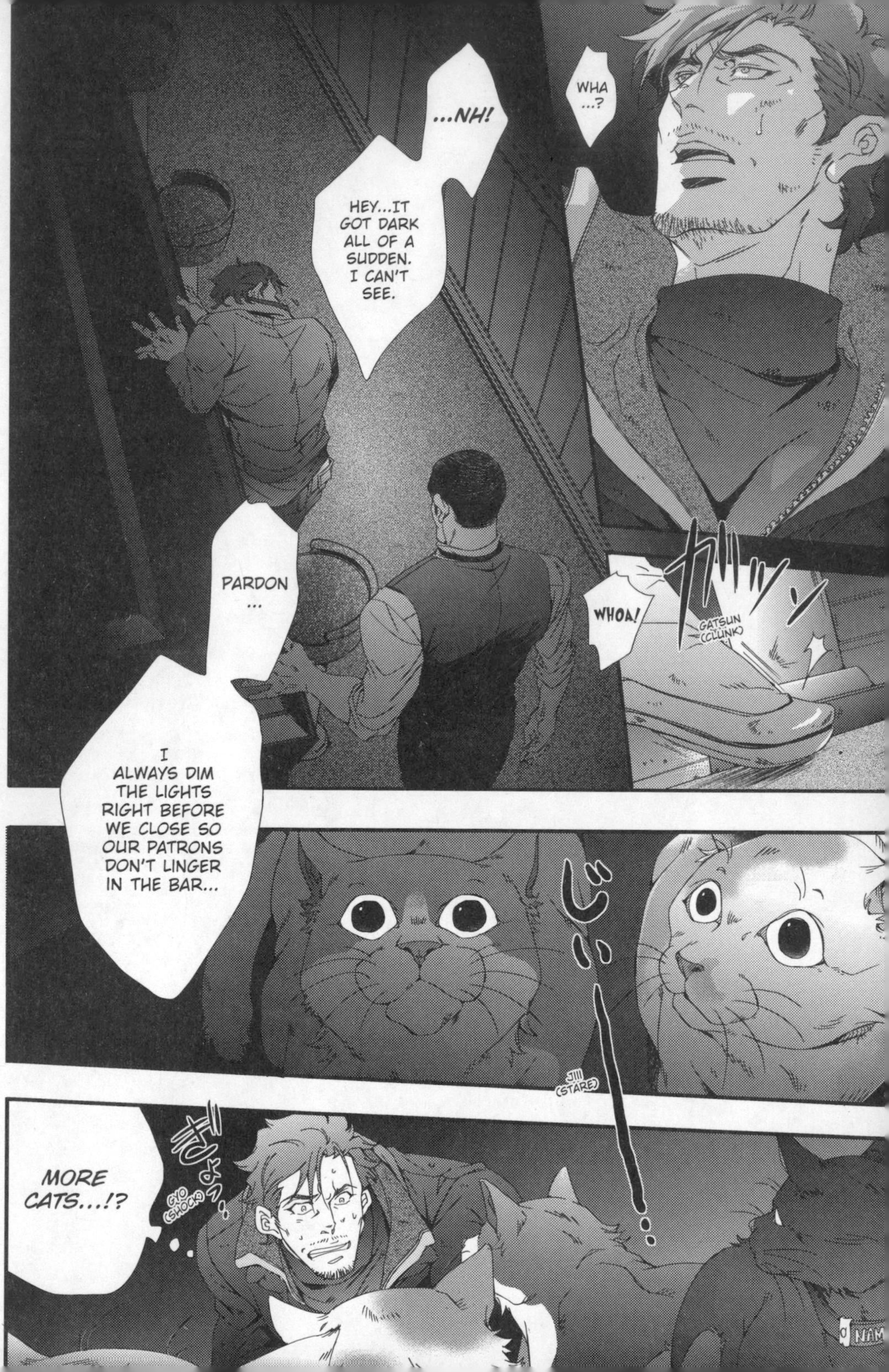
WHA...?
...NH!
HEY...IT GOT DARK ALL OF A SUDDEN. I CAN'T SEE.
WHOA!
GATSUN (CLUNK)
PARDON...
I ALWAYS DIM THE LIGHTS RIGHT BEFORE WE CLOSE SO OUR PATRONS DON'T LINGER IN THE BAR...
JIII (STARE)
MORE CATS...!?
GYO (SHOCK)

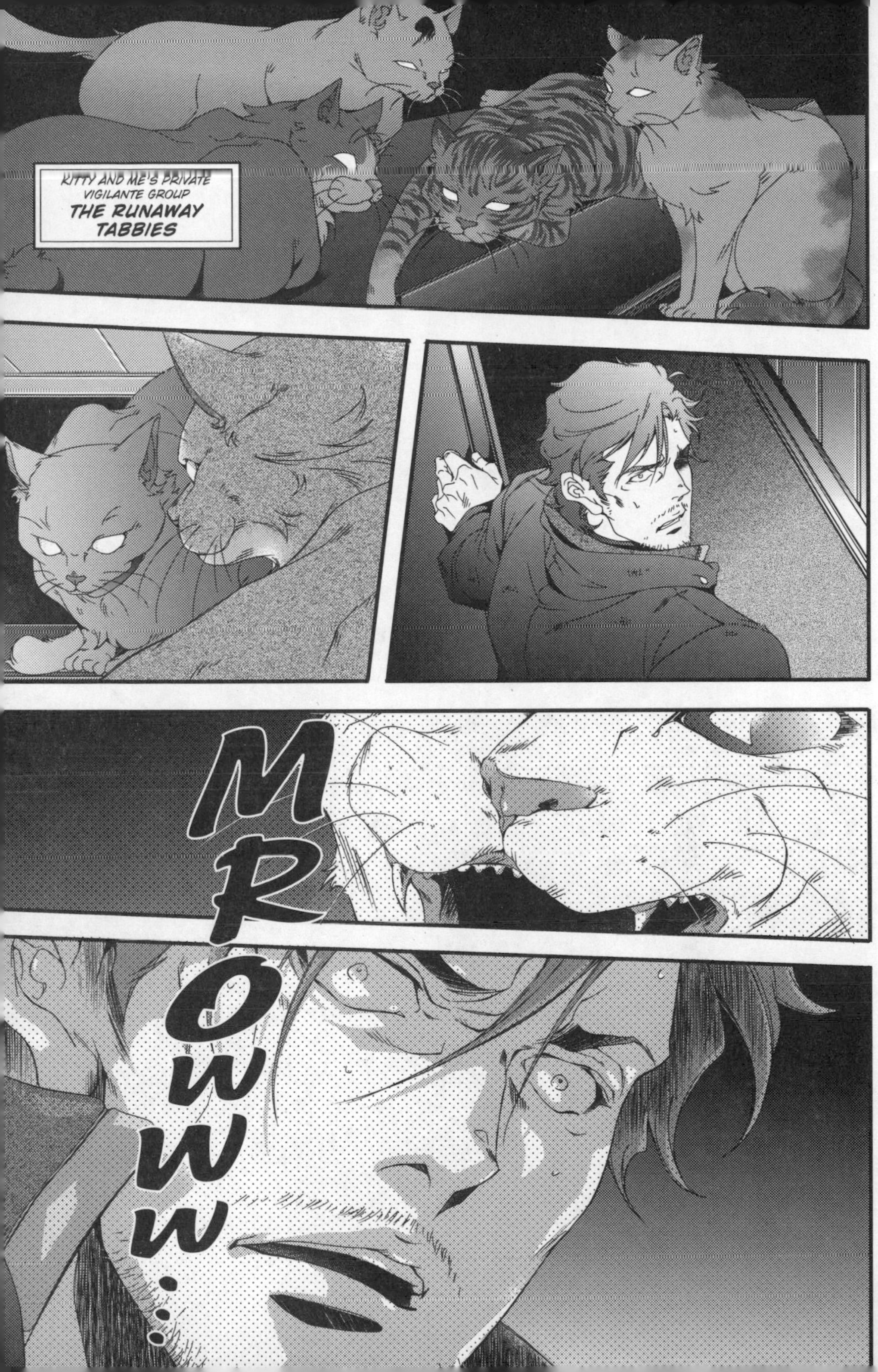
KITTY AND ME'S PRIVATE VIGILANTE GROUP
THE RUNAWAY TABBIES
MROWWW...

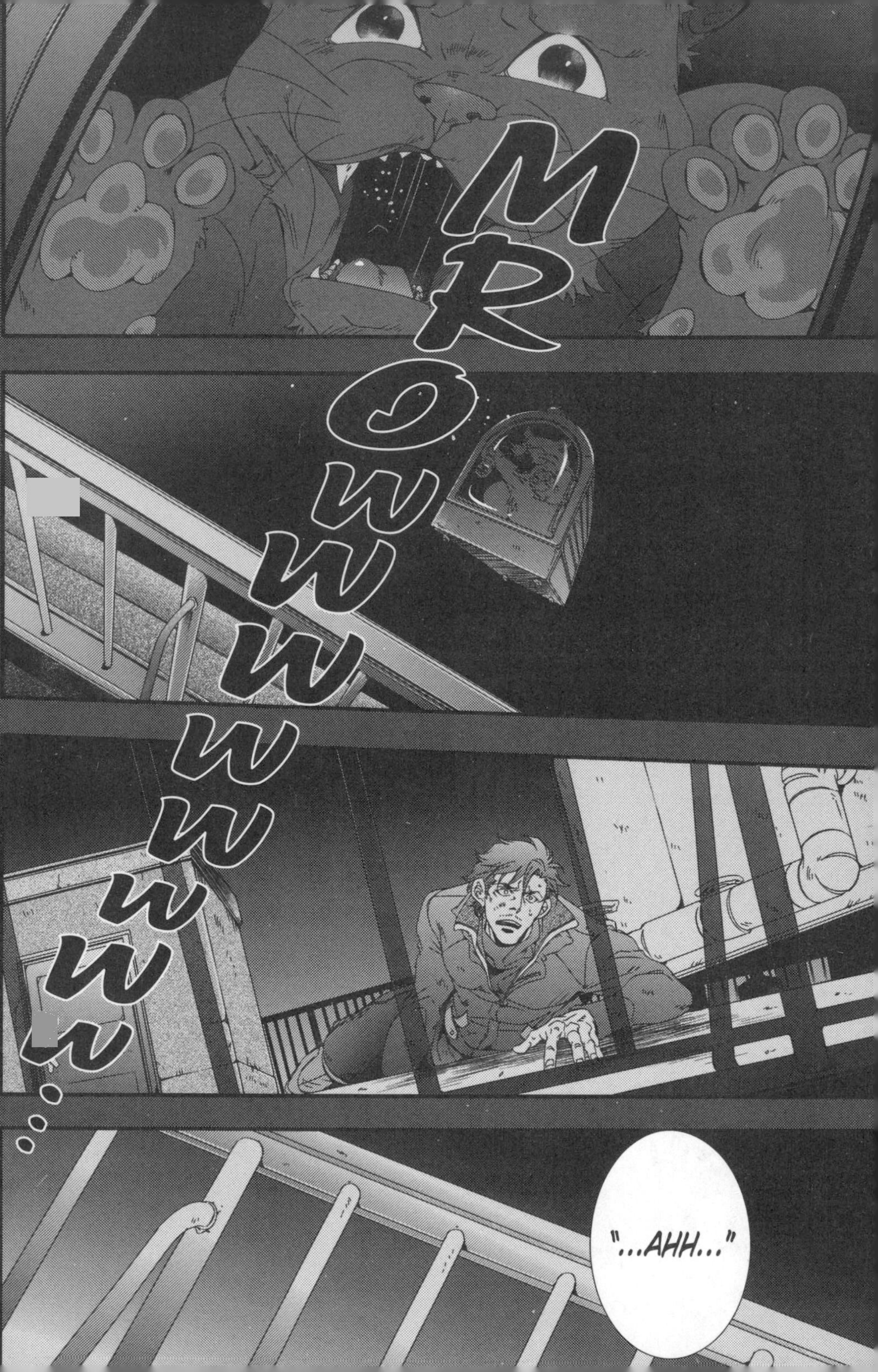
MROWWWWWWWW...
"...AHH..."

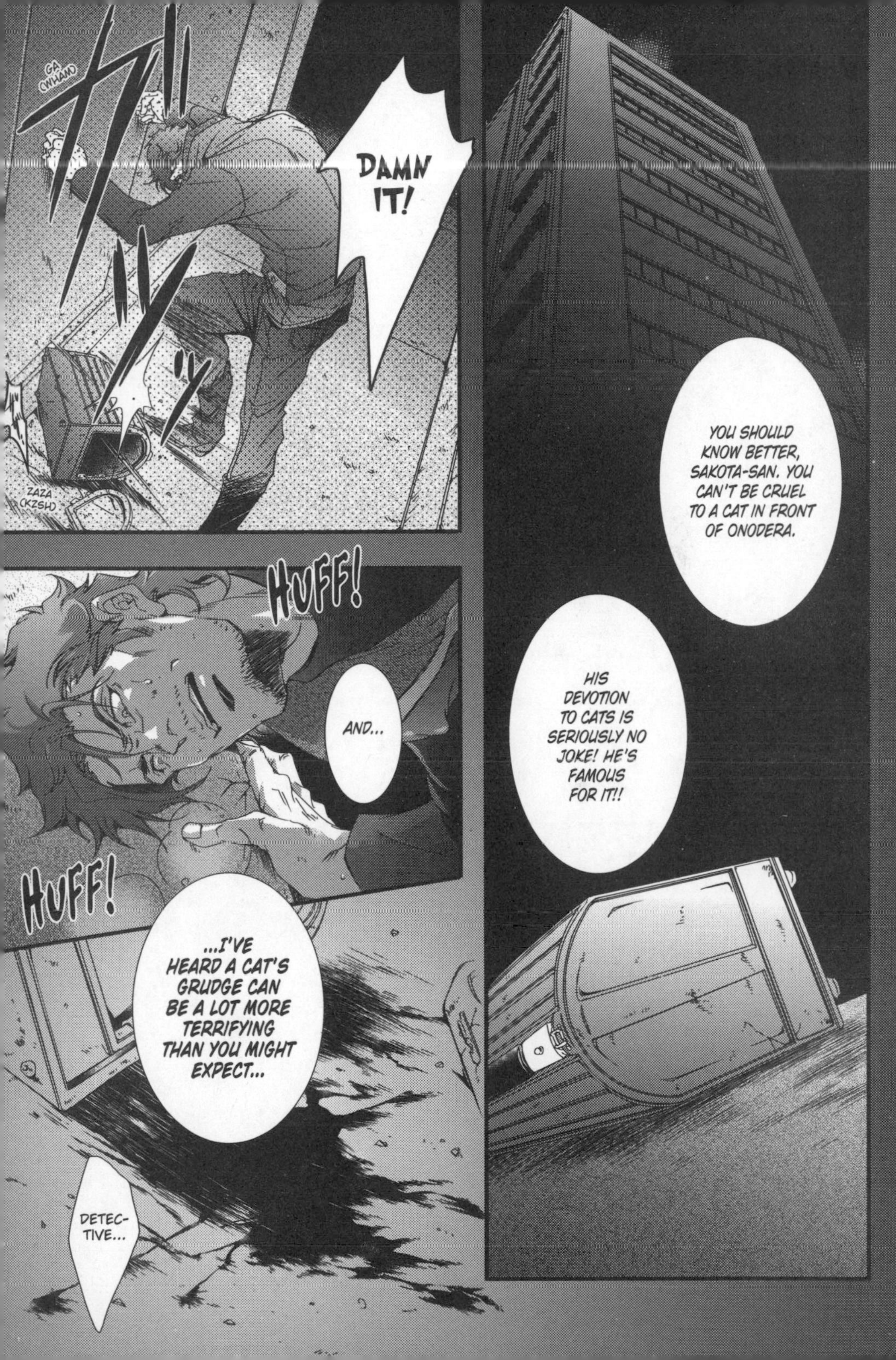
YOU SHOULD KNOW BETTER, SAKOTA-SAN. YOU CAN'T BE CRUEL TO A CAT IN FRONT OF ONODERA.
HIS DEVOTION TO CATS IS SERIOUSLY NO JOKE! HE'S FAMOUS FOR IT!!
GA (WHAM)
DAMN IT!
ZAZA (KZSH)
HUFF!
AND...
HUFF!
...I'VE HEARD A CAT'S GRUDGE CAN BE A LOT MORE TERRIFYING THAN YOU MIGHT EXPECT...
DETEC-TIVE...

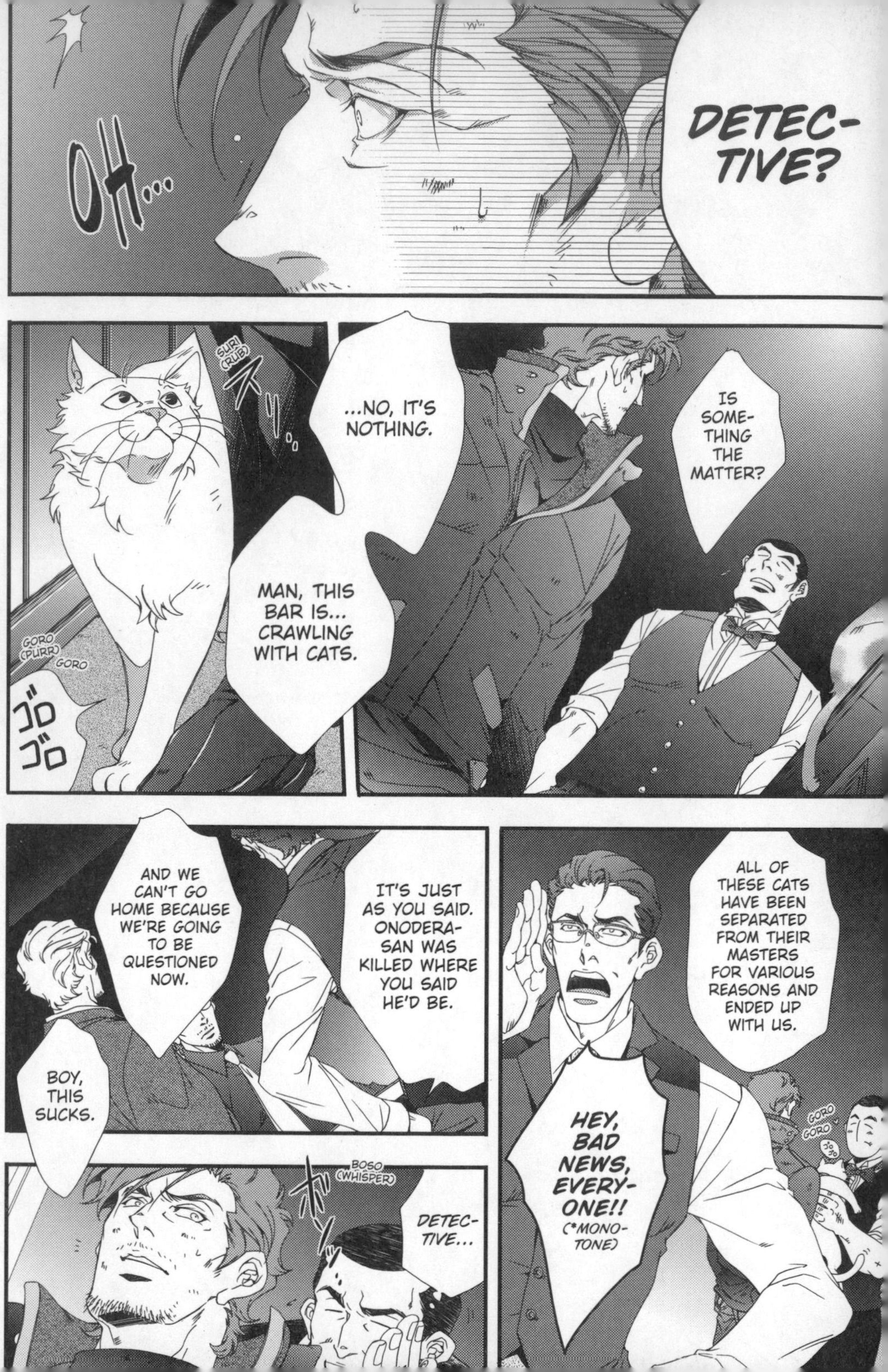
DETEC-TIVE?
OH...
IS SOMETHING THE MATTER?
...NO, IT'S NOTHING.
MAN, THIS BAR IS... CRAWLING WITH CATS.
SURI (RUB)
GORO (PURR) GORO
ゴロゴロ
ALL OF THESE CATS HAVE BEEN SEPARATED FROM THEIR MASTERS FOR VARIOUS REASONS AND ENDED UP WITH US.
HEY, BAD NEWS, EVERYONE!! (*MONOTONE)
GORO GORO
IT'S JUST AS YOU SAID. ONODERA-SAN WAS KILLED WHERE YOU SAID HE'D BE.
AND WE CAN'T GO HOME BECAUSE WE'RE GOING TO BE QUESTIONED NOW.
BOY, THIS SUCKS.
BOSO (WHISPER)
DETEC-TIVE...

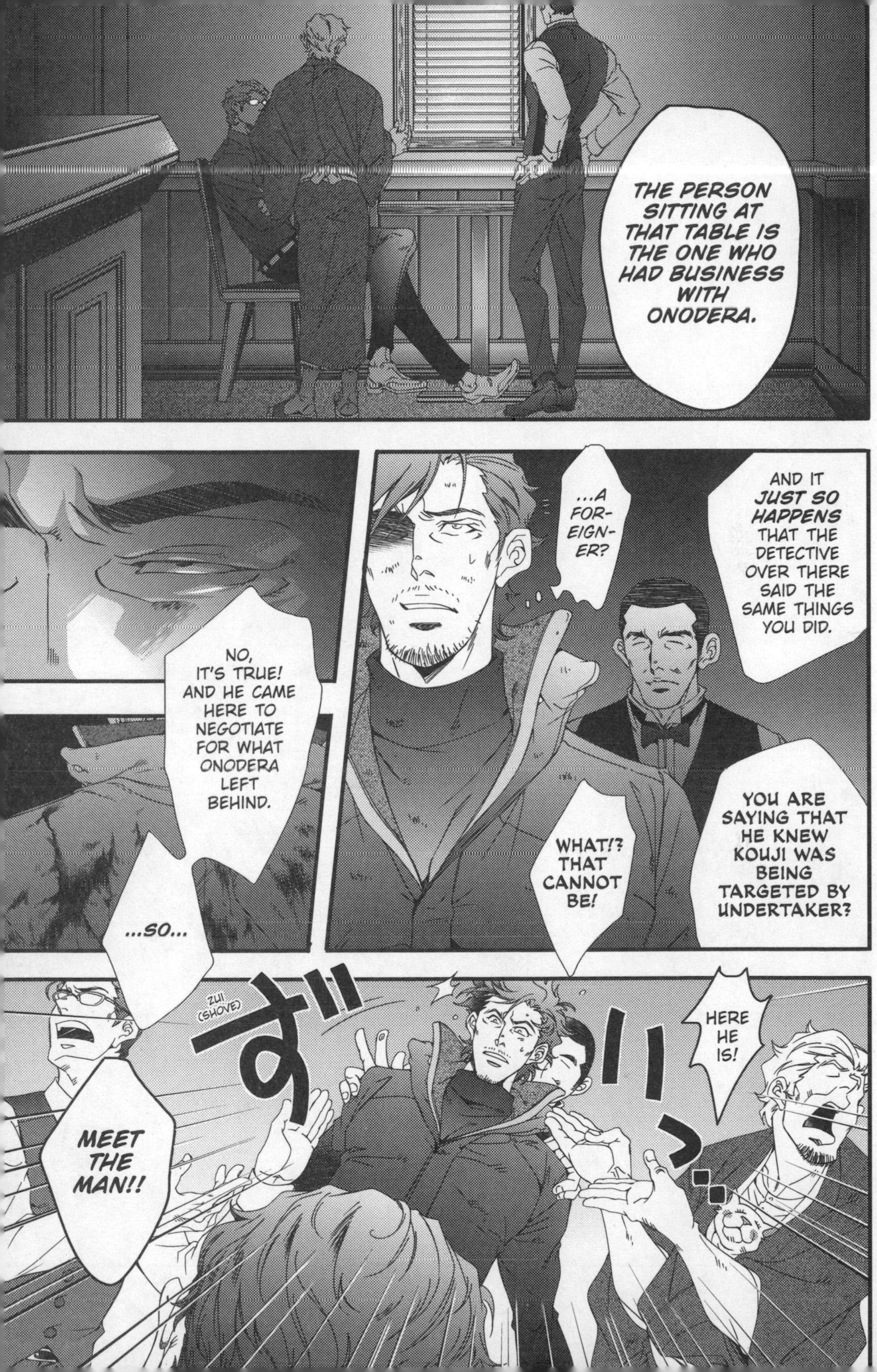
THE PERSON SITTING AT THAT TABLE IS THE ONE WHO HAD BUSINESS WITH ONODERA.
AND IT JUST SO HAPPENS THAT THE DETECTIVE OVER THERE SAID THE SAME THINGS YOU DID.
...A FOREIGNER?
YOU ARE SAYING THAT HE KNEW KOUJI WAS BEING TARGETED BY UNDERTAKER?
WHAT!? THAT CANNOT BE!
NO, IT'S TRUE! AND HE CAME HERE TO NEGOTIATE FOR WHAT ONODERA LEFT BEHIND.
...SO...
HERE HE IS!
ZUI (SHOVE)
MEET THE MAN!!

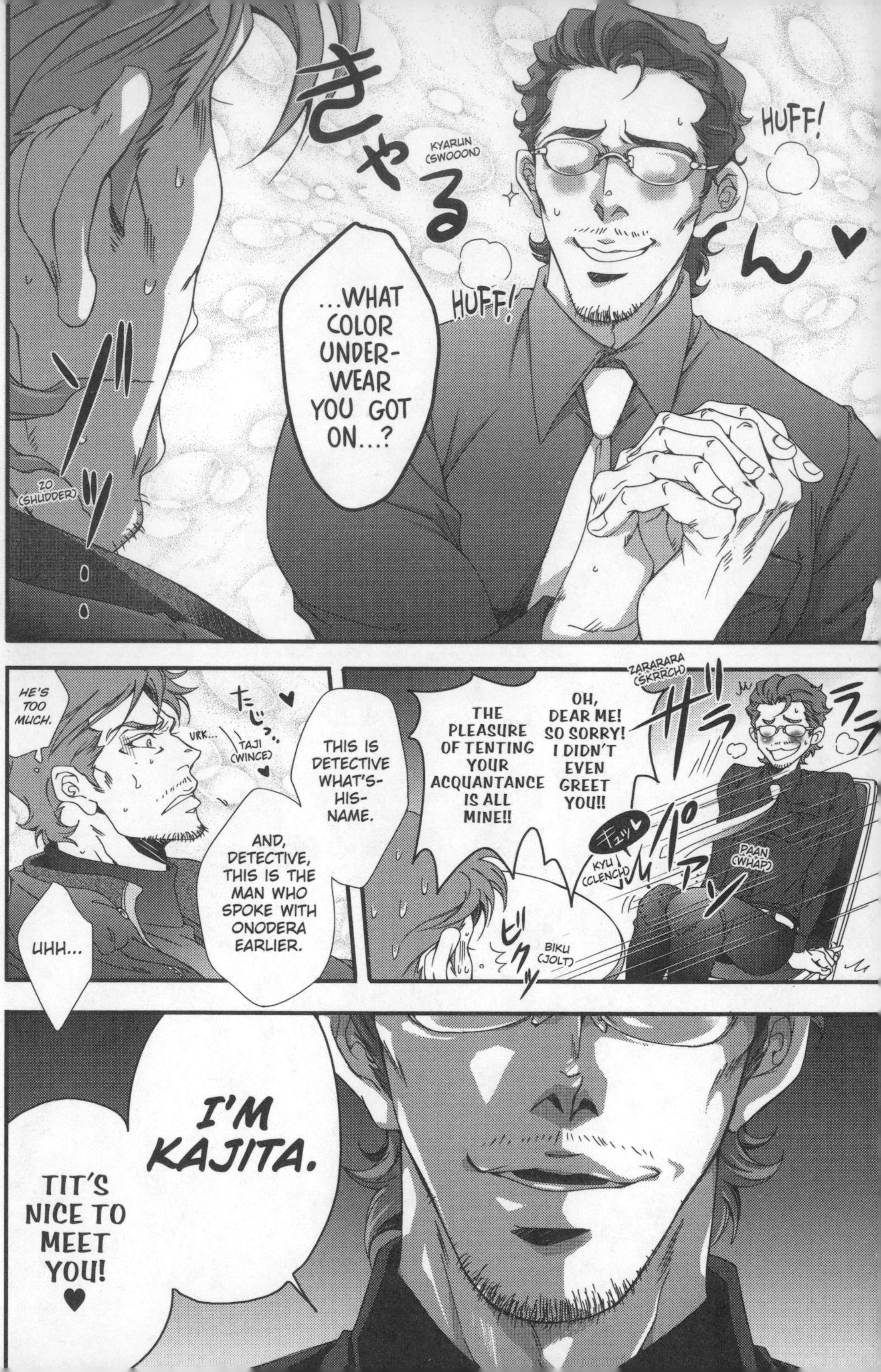
きゃるん♥
KYARUN (SWOOON)
HUFF!
HUFF!
...WHAT COLOR UNDER-WEAR YOU GOT ON...?
ZO (SHUDDER)
ZARARARA (SKRRCH)
OH, DEAR ME! SO SORRY! I DIDN'T EVEN GREET YOU!!
THE PLEASURE OF TENTING YOUR ACQUANTANCE IS ALL MINE!!
KYU (CLENCH)
PAAN (WHAP)
BIKU (JOLT)
THIS IS DETECTIVE WHAT'S-HIS-NAME.
TAJI (WINCE)
URK...
HE'S TOO MUCH.
AND, DETECTIVE, THIS IS THE MAN WHO SPOKE WITH ONODERA EARLIER.
UHH...
I'M KAJITA.
TIT'S NICE TO MEET YOU! ♥

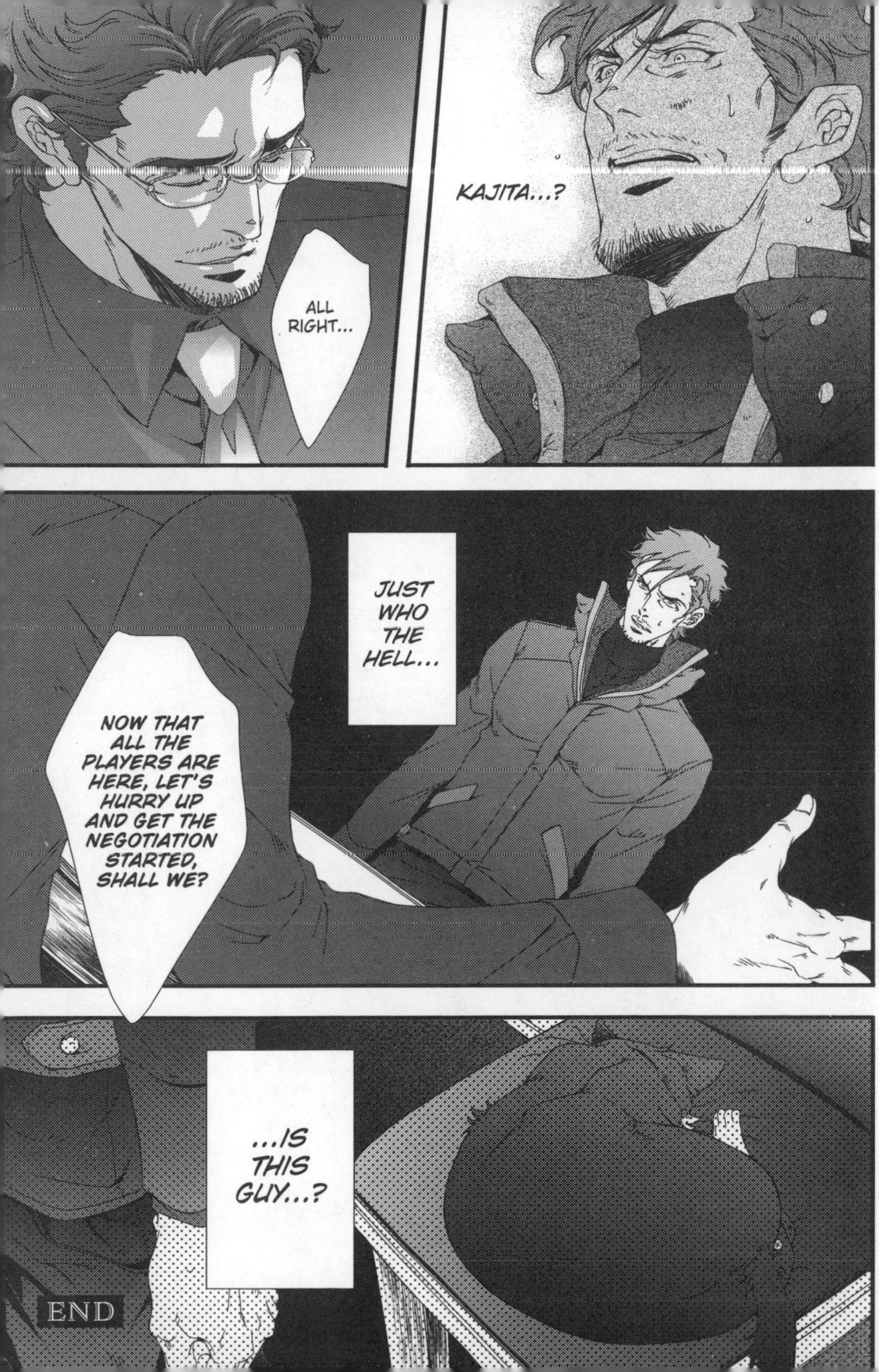
KAJITA...?
ALL RIGHT...
JUST WHO THE HELL...
NOW THAT ALL THE PLAYERS ARE HERE, LET'S HURRY UP AND GET THE NEGOTIATION STARTED, SHALL WE?
...IS THIS GUY...?
END

Hard-
Boiled
Stories
FROM THE
CAT BAR

CHAPTER 4
Behind the Smile

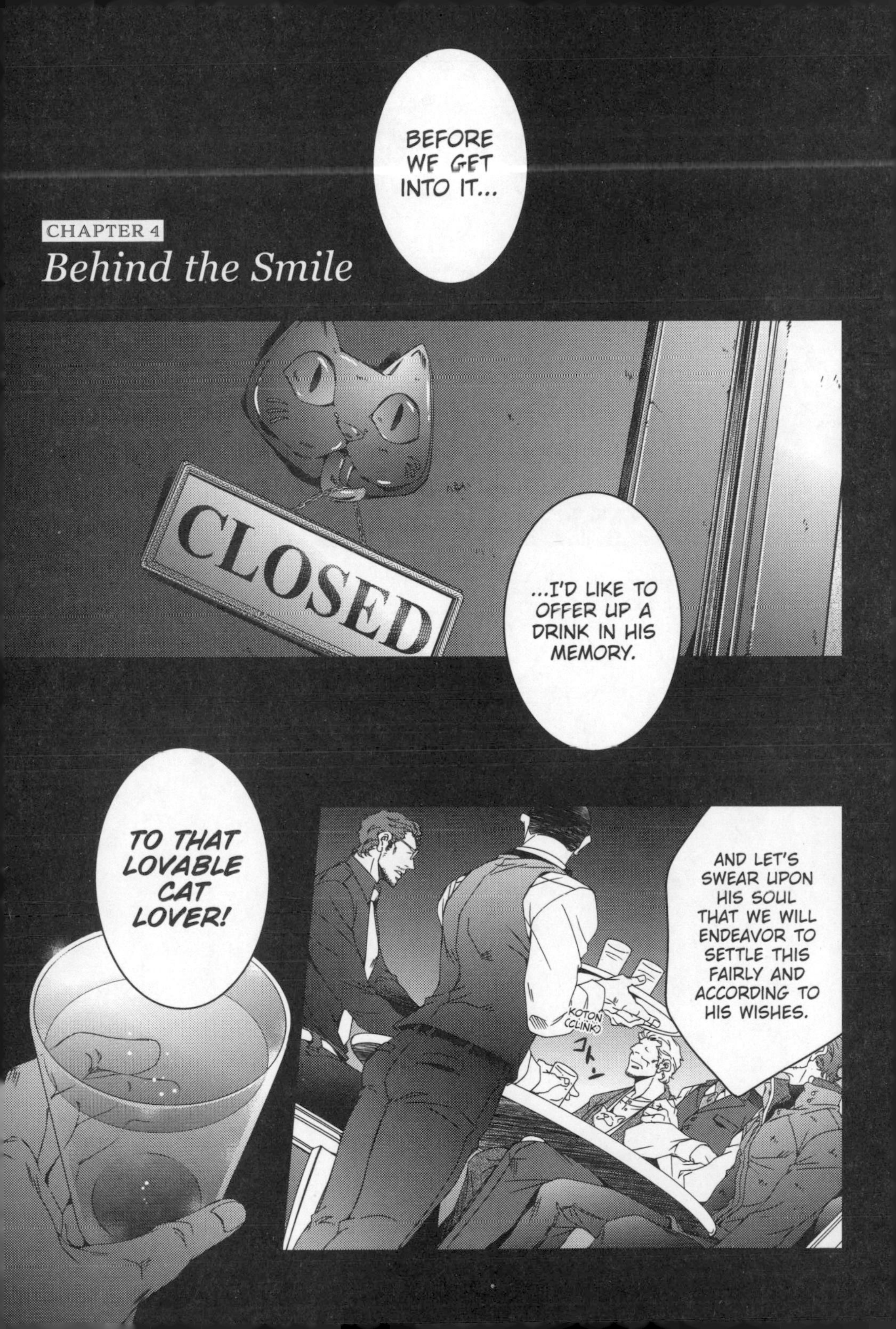
BEFORE WE GET INTO IT...
CLOSED
...I'D LIKE TO OFFER UP A DRINK IN HIS MEMORY.
AND LET'S SWEAR UPON HIS SOUL THAT WE WILL ENDEAVOR TO SETTLE THIS FAIRLY AND ACCORDING TO HIS WISHES.
KOTON (CLINK)
TO THAT LOVABLE CAT LOVER!

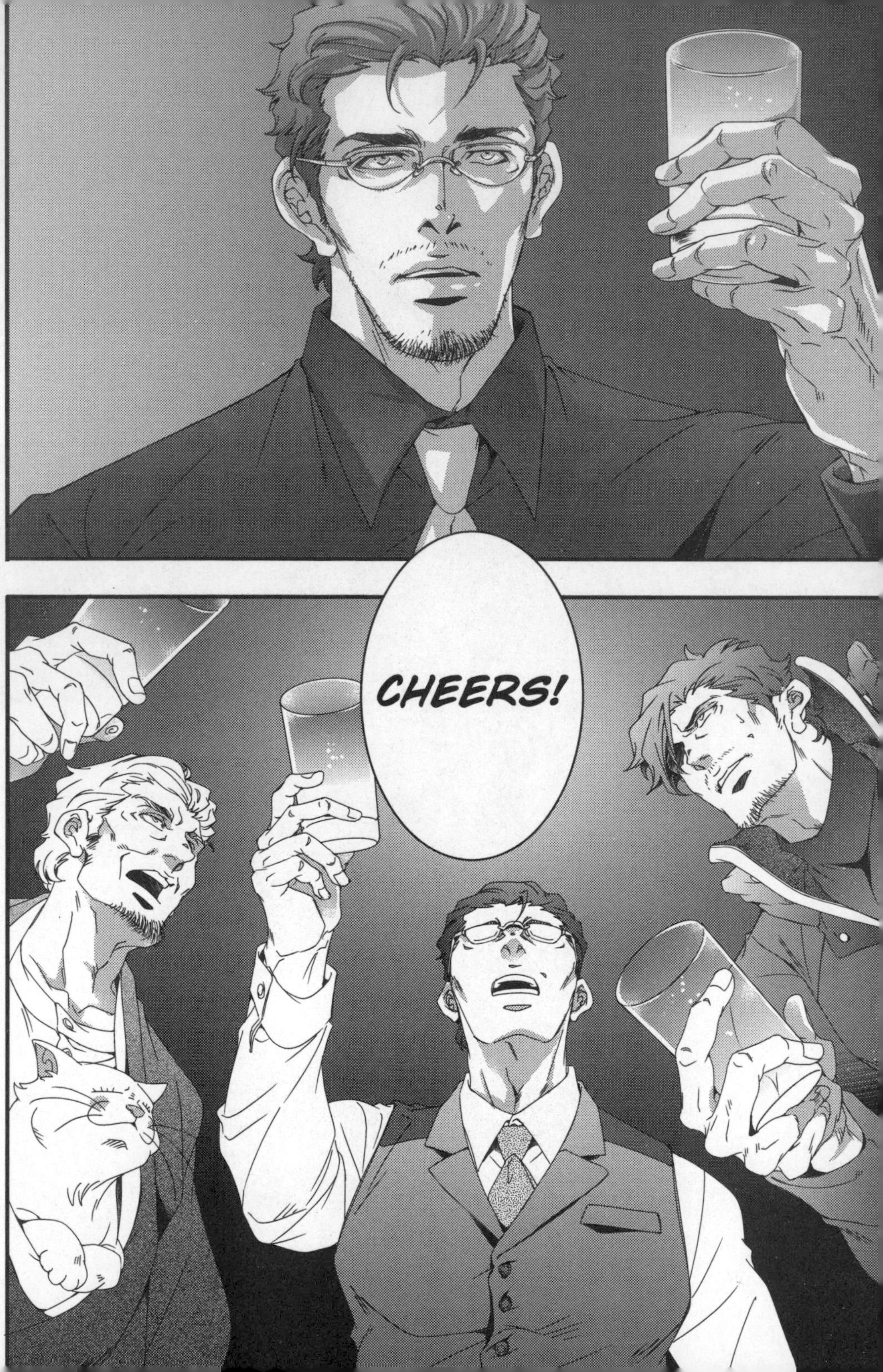
CHEERS!

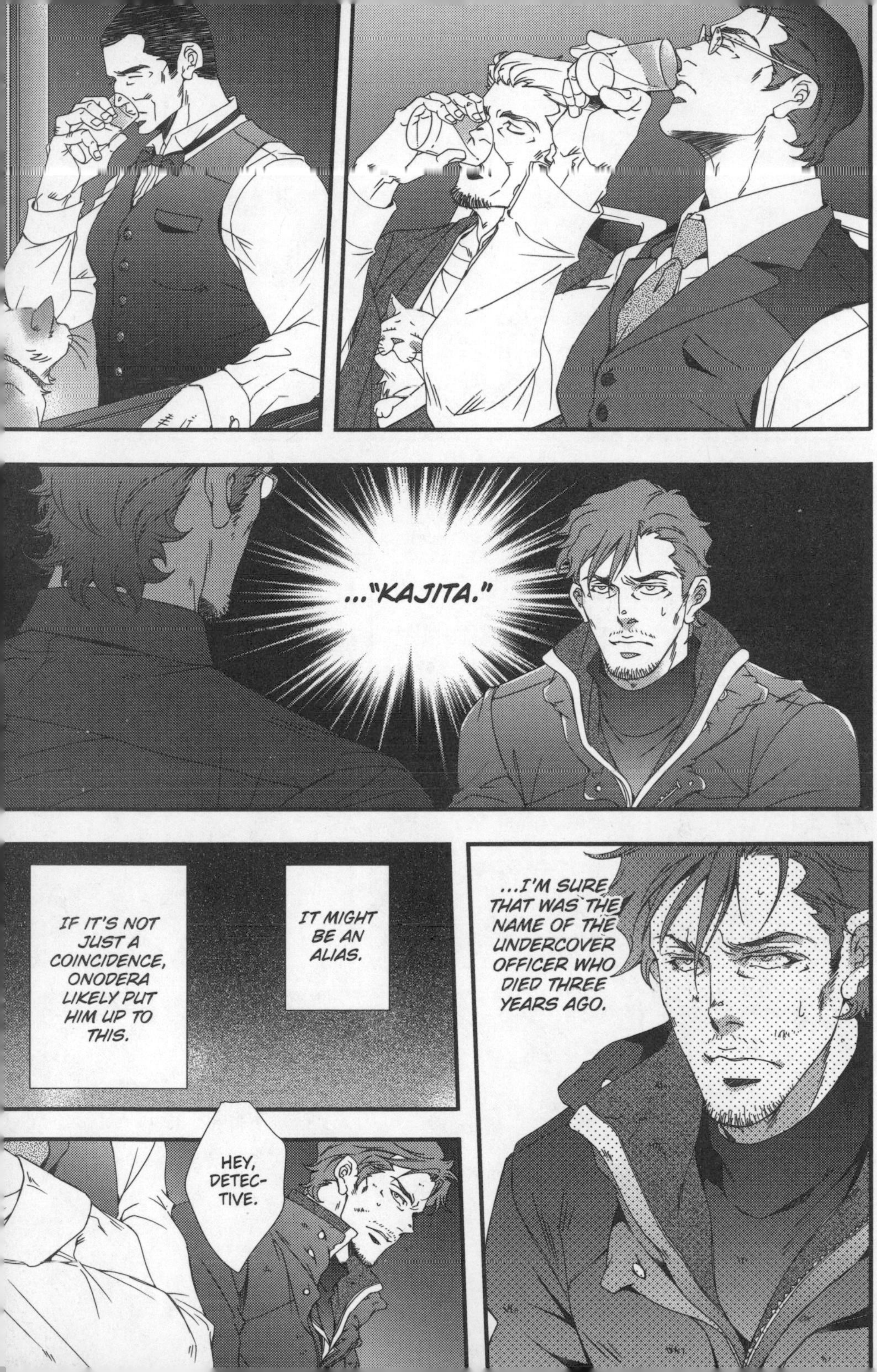
..."KAJITA."
...I'M SURE THAT WAS THE NAME OF THE UNDERCOVER OFFICER WHO DIED THREE YEARS AGO.
IT MIGHT BE AN ALIAS.
IF IT'S NOT JUST A COINCIDENCE, ONODERA LIKELY PUT HIM UP TO THIS.
HEY, DETEC-TIVE.

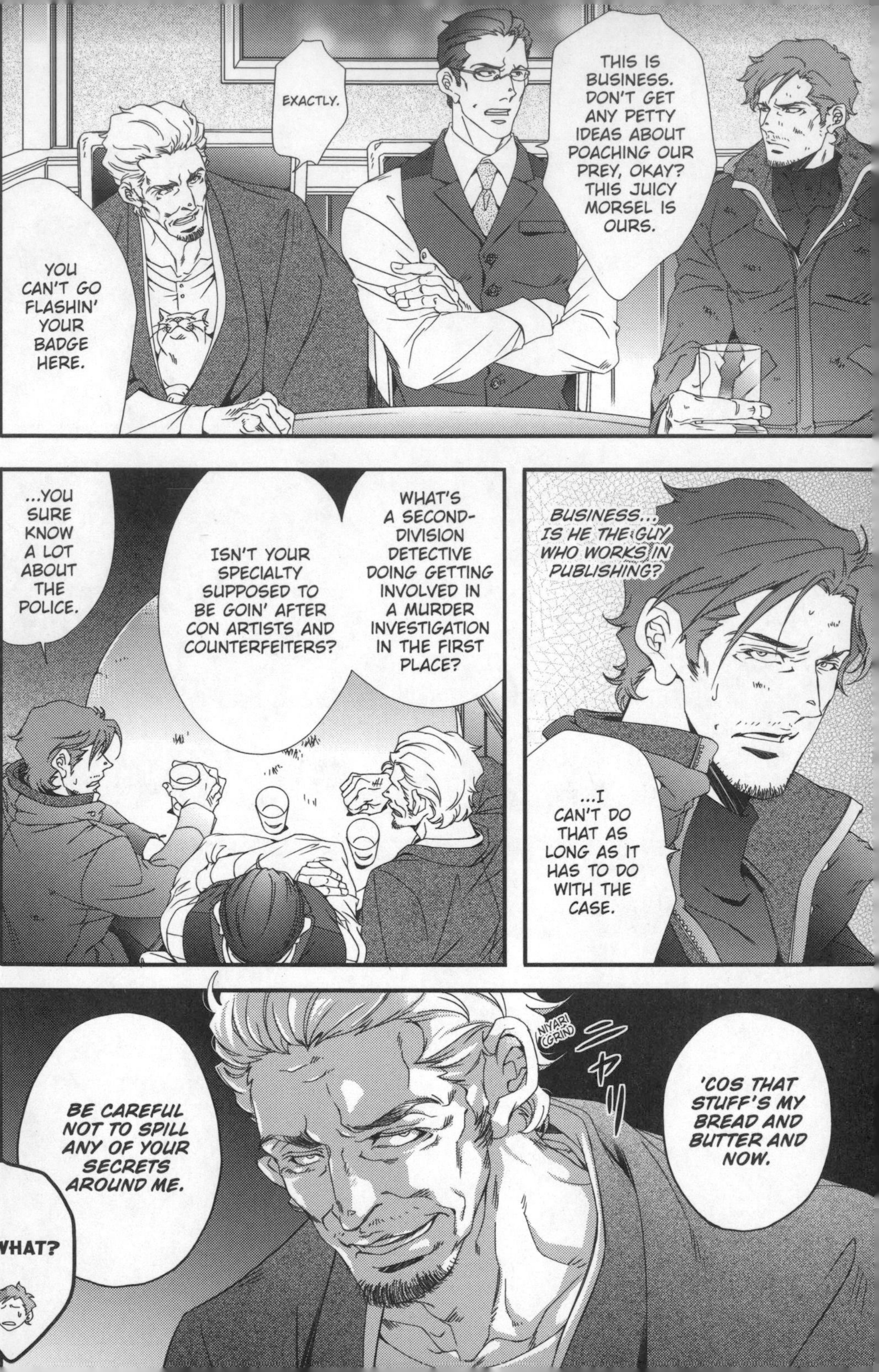
THIS IS BUSINESS. DON'T GET ANY PETTY IDEAS ABOUT POACHING OUR PREY, OKAY? THIS JUICY MORSEL IS OURS.
EXACTLY.
YOU CAN'T GO FLASHIN' YOUR BADGE HERE.
BUSINESS... IS HE THE GUY WHO WORKS IN PUBLISHING?
...I CAN'T DO THAT AS LONG AS IT HAS TO DO WITH THE CASE.
WHAT'S A SECOND-DIVISION DETECTIVE DOING GETTING INVOLVED IN A MURDER INVESTIGATION IN THE FIRST PLACE?
ISN'T YOUR SPECIALTY SUPPOSED TO BE GOIN' AFTER CON ARTISTS AND COUNTERFEITERS?
...YOU SURE KNOW A LOT ABOUT THE POLICE.
'COS THAT STUFF'S MY BREAD AND BUTTER AND NOW.
NIYARI (GRIN)
BE CAREFUL NOT TO SPILL ANY OF YOUR SECRETS AROUND ME.
...WHAT?

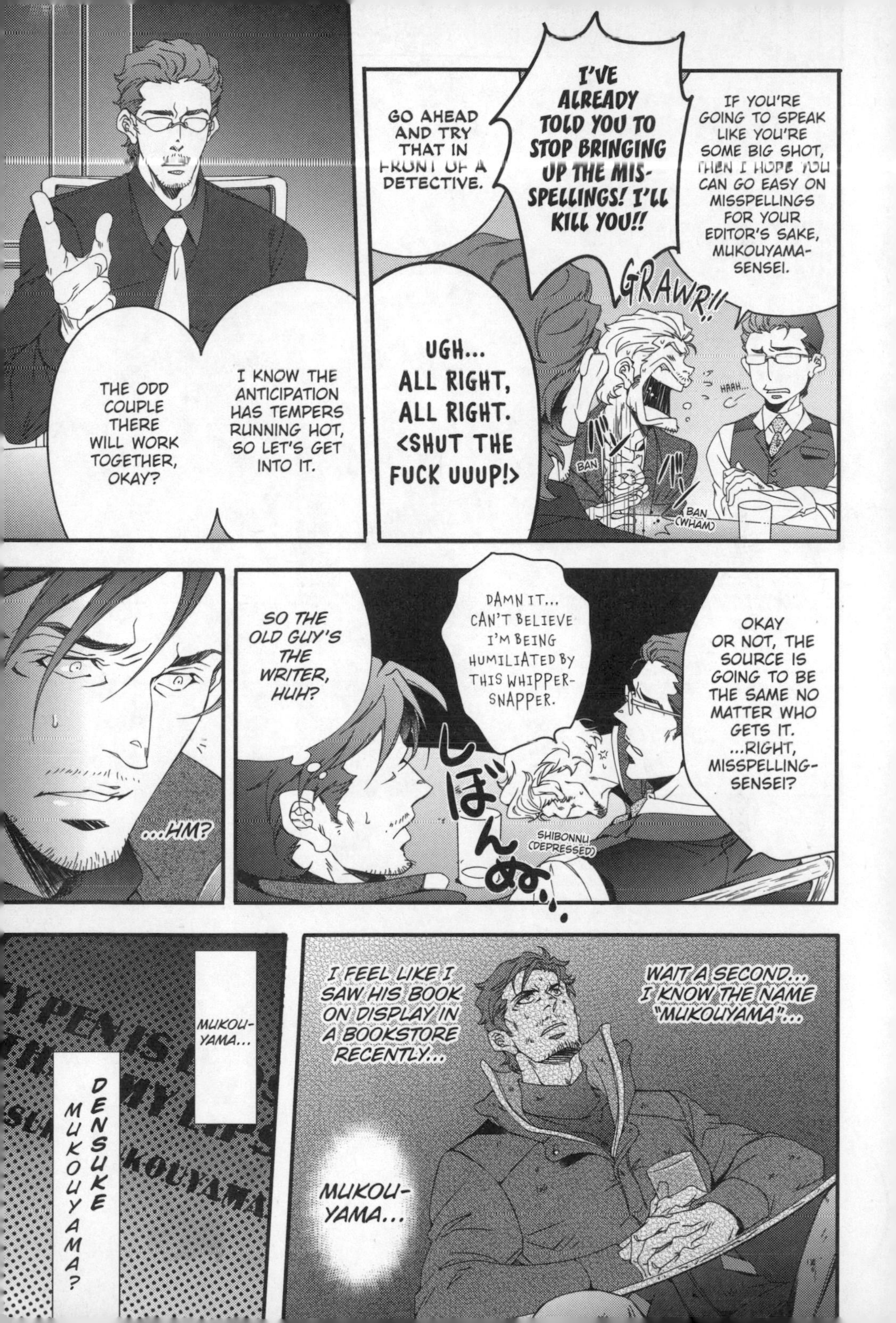
IF YOU'RE GOING TO SPEAK LIKE YOU'RE SOME BIG SHOT, THEN I HOPE YOU CAN GO EASY ON MISSPELLINGS FOR YOUR EDITOR'S SAKE, MUKOUYAMA-SENSEI.
I'VE ALREADY TOLD YOU TO STOP BRINGING UP THE MIS-SPELLINGS! I'LL KILL YOU!!
GRAWR!!
GO AHEAD AND TRY THAT IN FRONT OF A DETECTIVE.
HAAH...
BAN
BAN (WHAM)
UGH... ALL RIGHT, ALL RIGHT. <SHUT THE FUCK UUUP!>
I KNOW THE ANTICIPATION HAS TEMPERS RUNNING HOT, SO LET'S GET INTO IT.
THE ODD COUPLE THERE WILL WORK TOGETHER, OKAY?
OKAY OR NOT, THE SOURCE IS GOING TO BE THE SAME NO MATTER WHO GETS IT. ...RIGHT, MISSPELLING-SENSEI?
DAMN IT... CAN'T BELIEVE I'M BEING HUMILIATED BY THIS WHIPPER-SNAPPER.
SO THE OLD GUY'S THE WRITER, HUH?
しぼんぬ…
SHIBONNU (DEPRESSED)
...HM?
WAIT A SECOND... I KNOW THE NAME "MUKOUYAMA"...
I FEEL LIKE I SAW HIS BOOK ON DISPLAY IN A BOOKSTORE RECENTLY...
MUKOU-YAMA...
MUKOU-YAMA...
DENSUKE MUKOUYAMA?

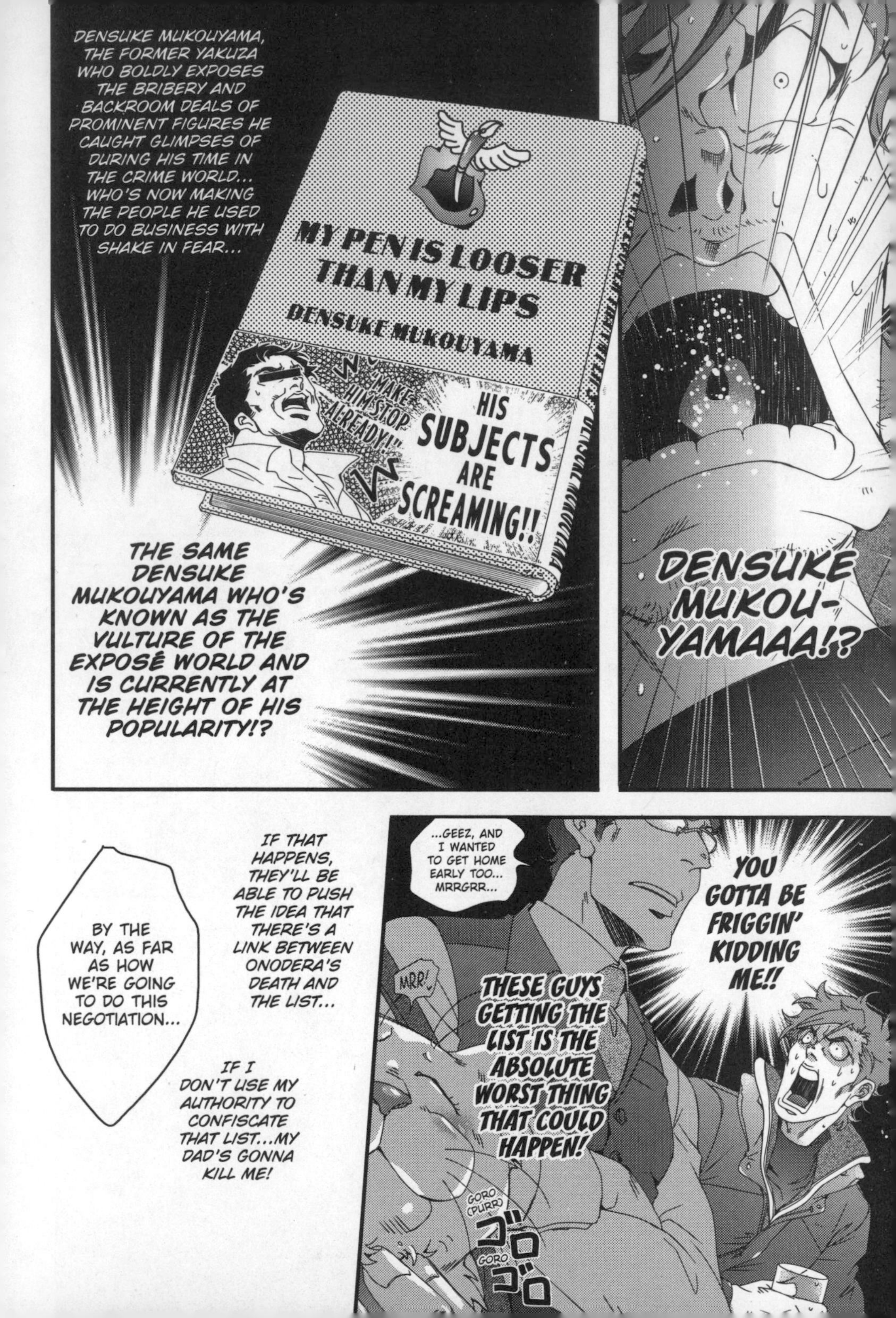
DENSUKE MUKOU-YAMAAA!?
DENSUKE MUKOUYAMA, THE FORMER YAKUZA WHO BOLDLY EXPOSES THE BRIBERY AND BACKROOM DEALS OF PROMINENT FIGURES HE CAUGHT GLIMPSES OF DURING HIS TIME IN THE CRIME WORLD... WHO'S NOW MAKING THE PEOPLE HE USED TO DO BUSINESS WITH SHAKE IN FEAR...
MY PEN IS LOOSER THAN MY LIPS
DENSUKE MUKOUYAMA
"MAKE HIM STOP ALREADY!!"
HIS SUBJECTS ARE SCREAMING!!
THE SAME DENSUKE MUKOUYAMA WHO'S KNOWN AS THE VULTURE OF THE EXPOSÊ WORLD AND IS CURRENTLY AT THE HEIGHT OF HIS POPULARITY!?
...GEEZ, AND I WANTED TO GET HOME EARLY TOO... MRRGRR...
YOU GOTTA BE FRIGGIN' KIDDING ME!!
MRR!
THESE GUYS GETTING THE LIST IS THE ABSOLUTE WORST THING THAT COULD HAPPEN!
GORO (PURR) ゴロ
GORO ゴロ
IF THAT HAPPENS, THEY'LL BE ABLE TO PUSH THE IDEA THAT THERE'S A LINK BETWEEN ONODERA'S DEATH AND THE LIST...
BY THE WAY, AS FAR AS HOW WE'RE GOING TO DO THIS NEGOTIATION...
IF I DON'T USE MY AUTHORITY TO CONFISCATE THAT LIST...MY DAD'S GONNA KILL ME!

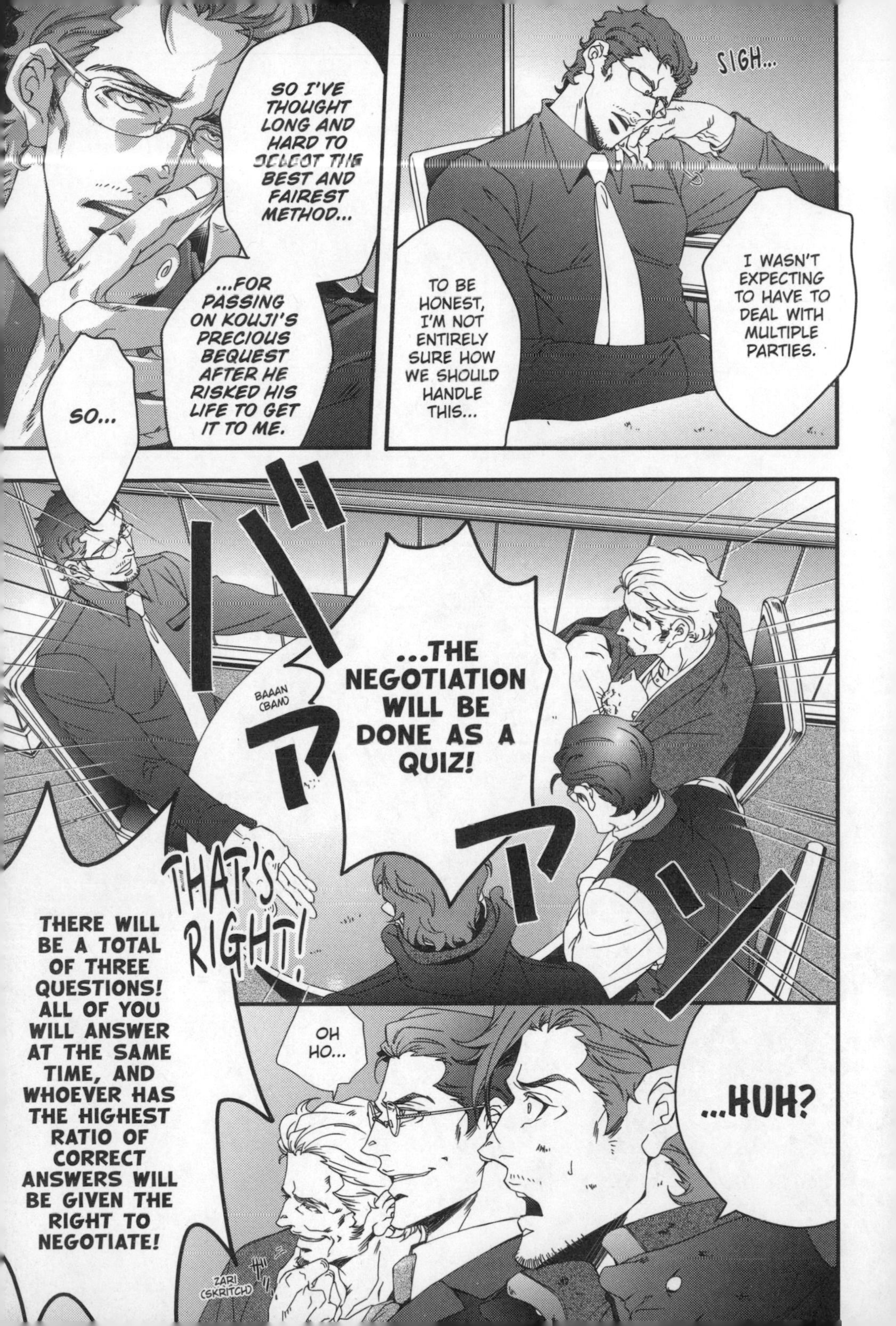
SIGH...
I WASN'T EXPECTING TO HAVE TO DEAL WITH MULTIPLE PARTIES.
TO BE HONEST, I'M NOT ENTIRELY SURE HOW WE SHOULD HANDLE THIS...
SO I'VE THOUGHT LONG AND HARD TO SELECT THE BEST AND FAIREST METHOD...
...FOR PASSING ON KOUJI'S PRECIOUS BEQUEST AFTER HE RISKED HIS LIFE TO GET IT TO ME.
SO...
...THE NEGOTIATION WILL BE DONE AS A QUIZ!
バァァン
BAAAN (BAM)
THAT'S RIGHT!
THERE WILL BE A TOTAL OF THREE QUESTIONS! ALL OF YOU WILL ANSWER AT THE SAME TIME, AND WHOEVER HAS THE HIGHEST RATIO OF CORRECT ANSWERS WILL BE GIVEN THE RIGHT TO NEGOTIATE!
...HUH?
OH HO...
ザリ
ZARI (SKRITCH)

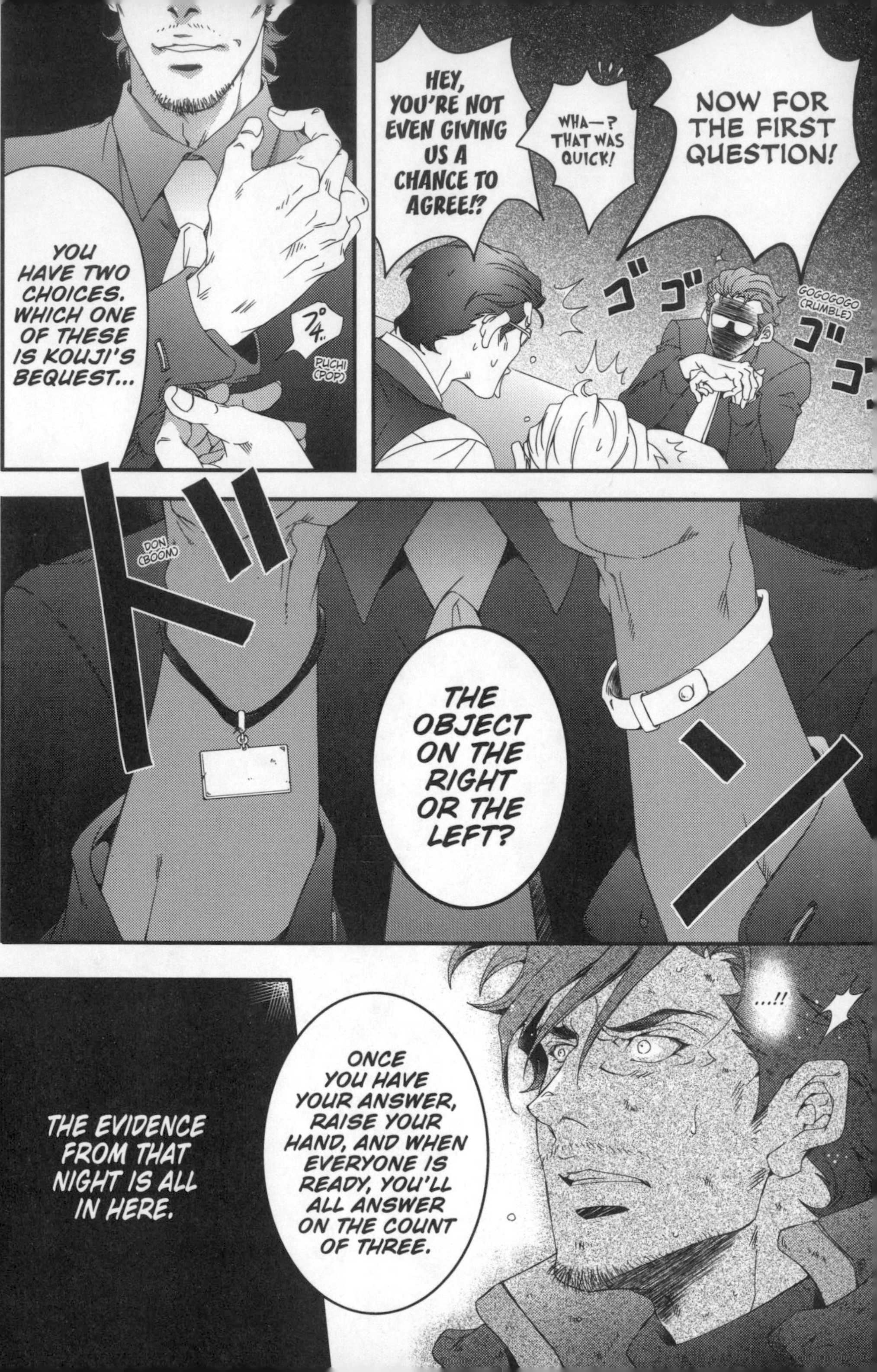
NOW FOR THE FIRST QUESTION!
WHA—? THAT WAS QUICK!
HEY, YOU'RE NOT EVEN GIVING US A CHANCE TO AGREE!?
ゴゴ
GOGOGOGO (RUMBLE)
ゴゴ
YOU HAVE TWO CHOICES. WHICH ONE OF THESE IS KOUJI'S BEQUEST...
プチ
PUCHI (POP)
ド
DON (BOOM)
THE OBJECT ON THE RIGHT OR THE LEFT?
ン
...!!
ONCE YOU HAVE YOUR ANSWER, RAISE YOUR HAND, AND WHEN EVERYONE IS READY, YOU'LL ALL ANSWER ON THE COUNT OF THREE.
THE EVIDENCE FROM THAT NIGHT IS ALL IN HERE.

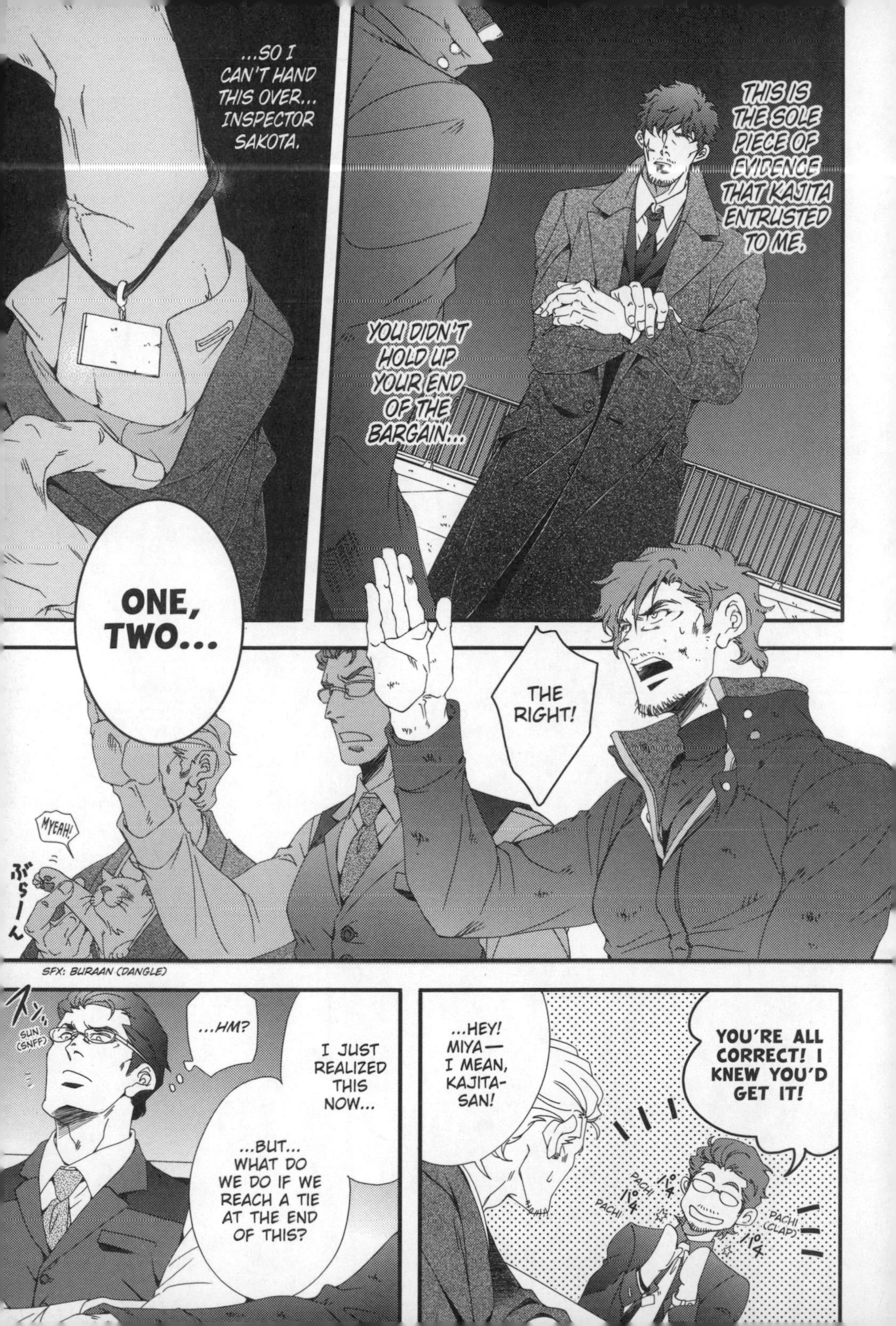
THIS IS THE SOLE PIECE OF EVIDENCE THAT KAJITA ENTRUSTED TO ME.
YOU DIDN'T HOLD UP YOUR END OF THE BARGAIN...
...SO I CAN'T HAND THIS OVER... INSPECTOR SAKOTA.
ONE, TWO...
THE RIGHT!
MYEAH!
ぶらーん
SFX: BURAAN (DANGLE)
YOU'RE ALL CORRECT! I KNEW YOU'D GET IT!
パチ PACHI
パチ PACHI
パチ PACHI (CLAP)
...HEY! MIYA— I MEAN, KAJITA-SAN!
スン SUN (SNFF)
...HM?
I JUST REALIZED THIS NOW...
...BUT... WHAT DO WE DO IF WE REACH A TIE AT THE END OF THIS?

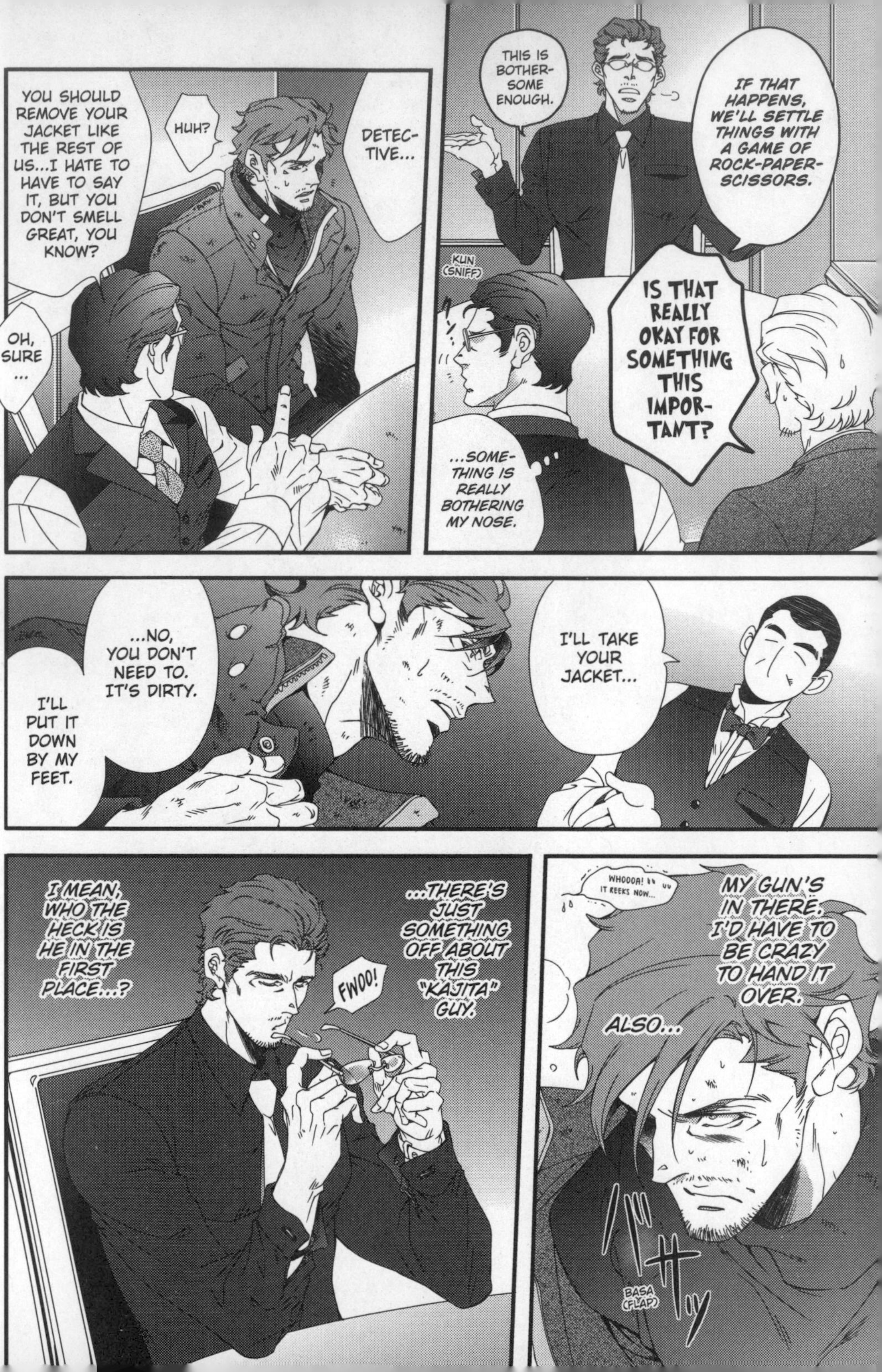
IF THAT HAPPENS, WE'LL SETTLE THINGS WITH A GAME OF ROCK-PAPER-SCISSORS.
THIS IS BOTHER-SOME ENOUGH.
IS THAT REALLY OKAY FOR SOMETHING THIS IMPOR-TANT?
KUN (SNIFF)
...SOME-THING IS REALLY BOTHERING MY NOSE.
DETEC-TIVE...
HUH?
YOU SHOULD REMOVE YOUR JACKET LIKE THE REST OF US...I HATE TO HAVE TO SAY IT, BUT YOU DON'T SMELL GREAT, YOU KNOW?
OH, SURE ...
I'LL TAKE YOUR JACKET...
...NO, YOU DON'T NEED TO. IT'S DIRTY.
I'LL PUT IT DOWN BY MY FEET.
MY GUN'S IN THERE. I'D HAVE TO BE CRAZY TO HAND IT OVER.
WHOOOA! IT REEKS NOW...
ALSO...
BASA (FLAP)
...THERE'S JUST SOMETHING OFF ABOUT THIS "KAJITA" GUY.
FWOO!
I MEAN, WHO THE HECK IS HE IN THE FIRST PLACE...?

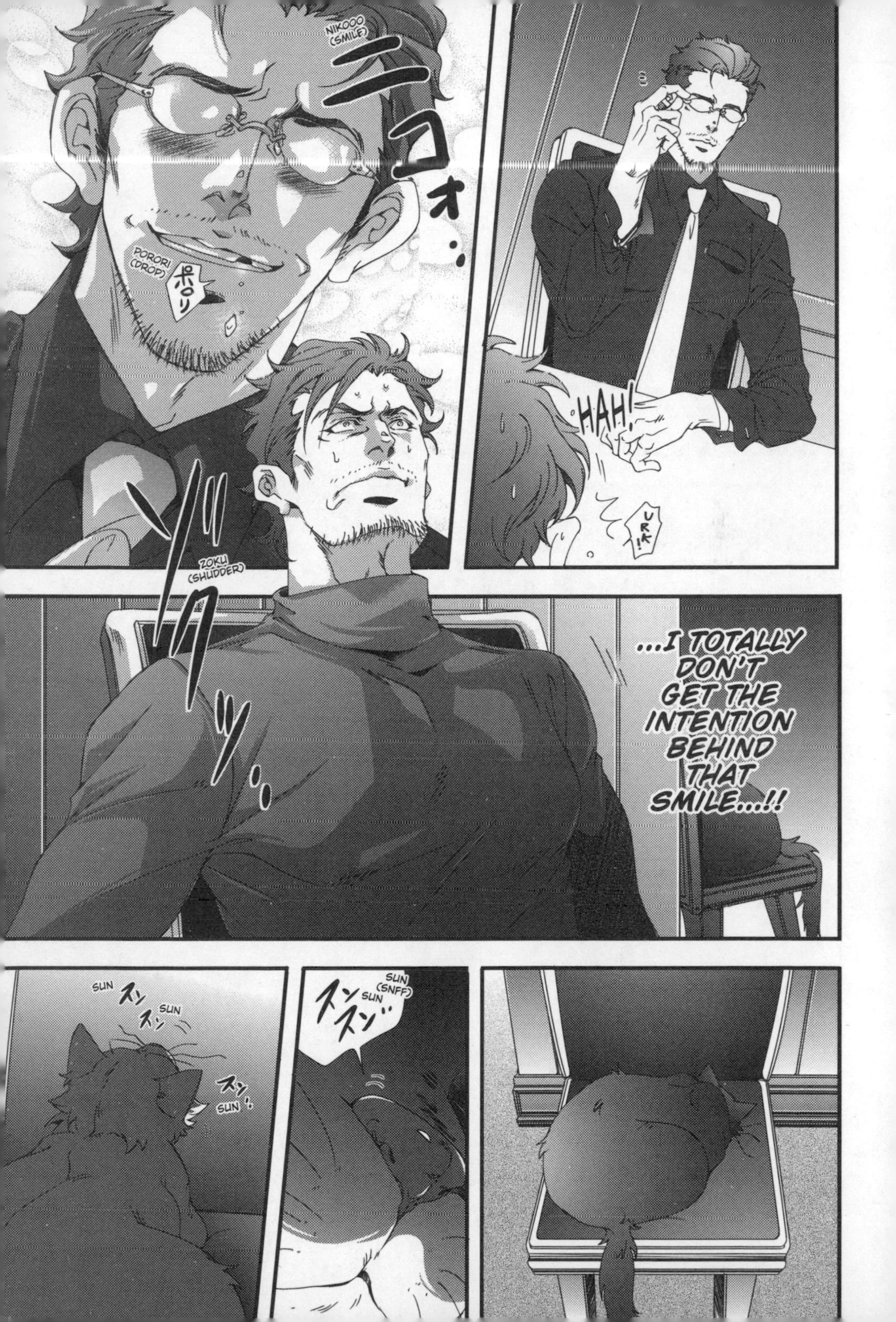
HAH!
URK!
NIKOOO (SMILE)
ニコォ‥
PORORI (DROP)
ポロリ
ZOKU (SHUDDER)
ゾクッ‥
...I TOTALLY DON'T GET THE INTENTION BEHIND THAT SMILE...!!
SUN (SNFF) SUN
スンスン
SUN
SUN
SUN

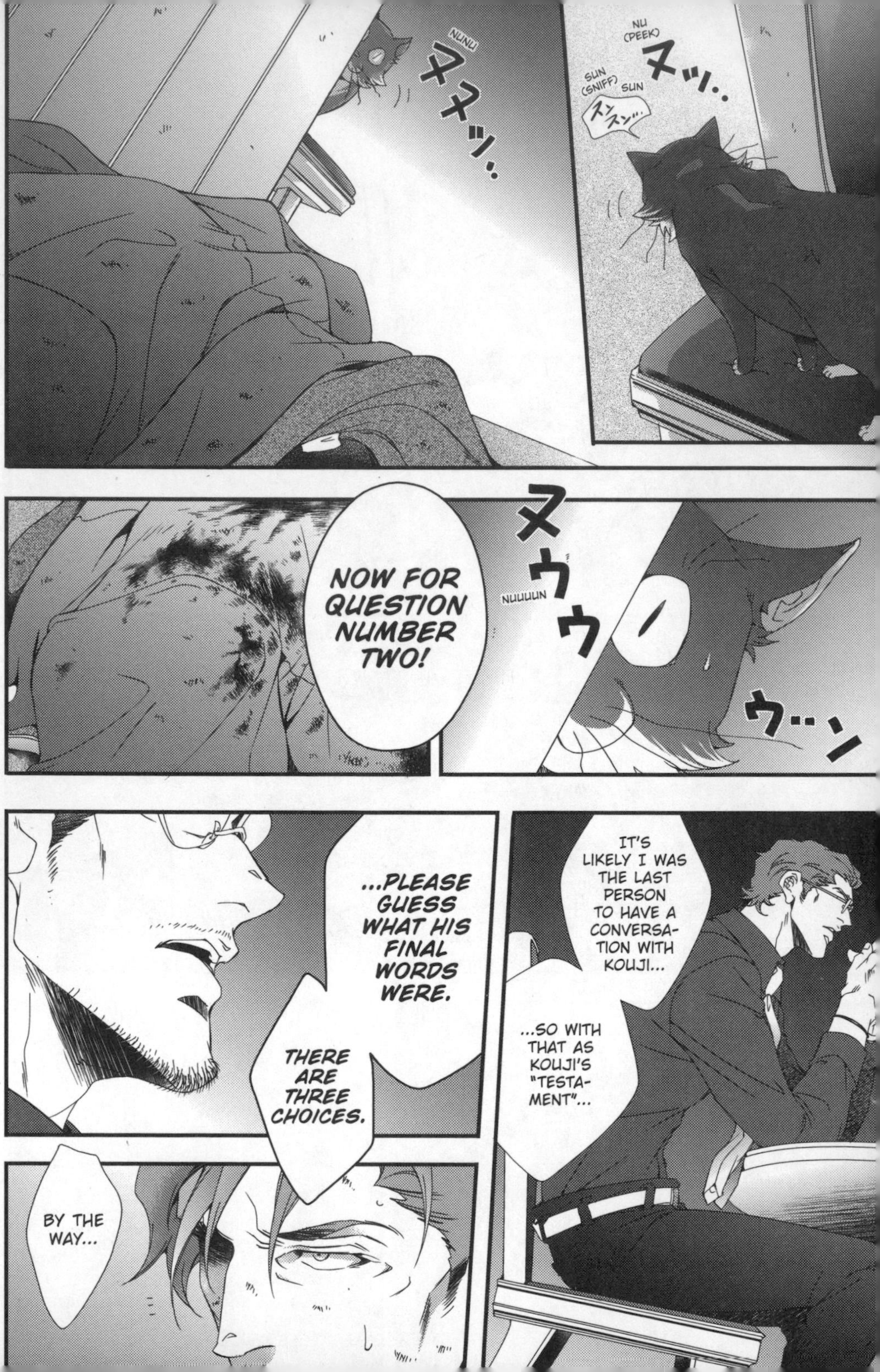
NU (PEEK)
ヌッ‥
SUN (SNIFF) SUN
スンスン…
NUNU
ヌヌッ‥
NUUUUN
ヌウウ
ウ゛ーン
NOW FOR QUESTION NUMBER TWO!
IT'S LIKELY I WAS THE LAST PERSON TO HAVE A CONVERSATION WITH KOUJI...
...SO WITH THAT AS KOUJI'S "TESTAMENT"...
...PLEASE GUESS WHAT HIS FINAL WORDS WERE.
THERE ARE THREE CHOICES.
BY THE WAY...

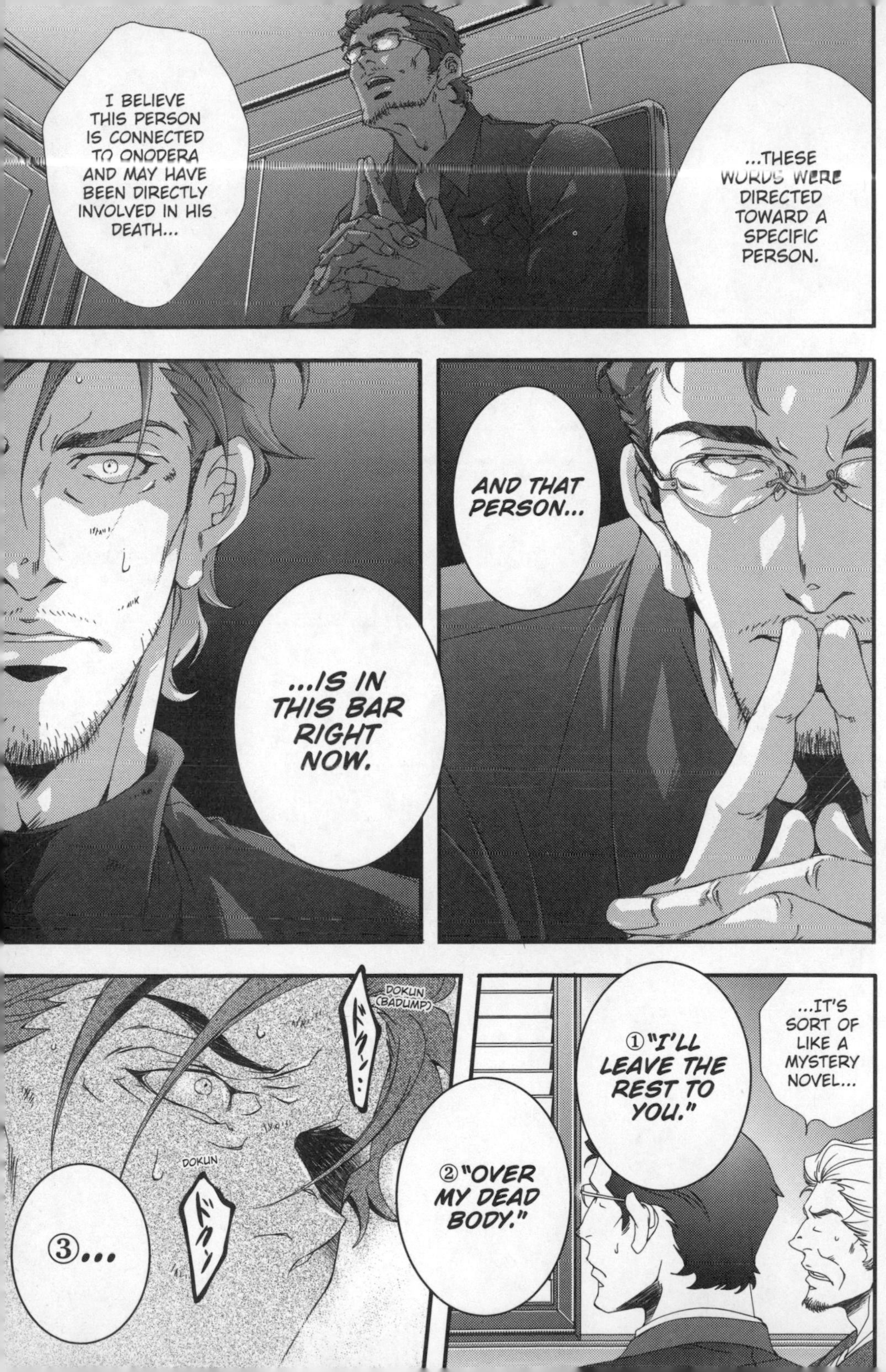
...THESE WORDS WERE DIRECTED TOWARD A SPECIFIC PERSON.
I BELIEVE THIS PERSON IS CONNECTED TO ONODERA AND MAY HAVE BEEN DIRECTLY INVOLVED IN HIS DEATH...
AND THAT PERSON...
...IS IN THIS BAR RIGHT NOW.
...IT'S SORT OF LIKE A MYSTERY NOVEL...
①"I'LL LEAVE THE REST TO YOU."
②"OVER MY DEAD BODY."
DOKUN (BADUMP)
ドクン…
DOKUN
ドクン
③...

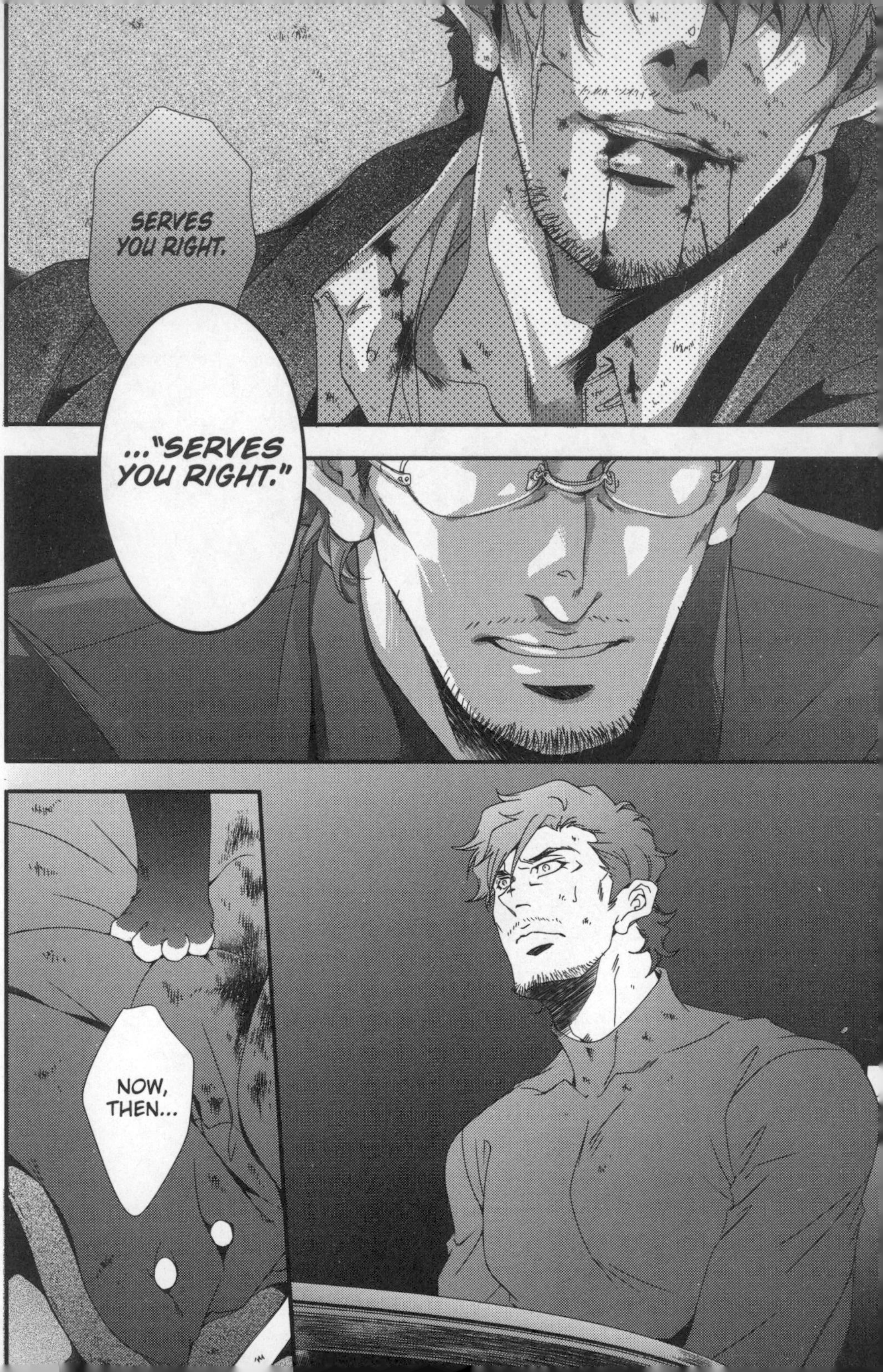
SERVES YOU RIGHT.
..."SERVES YOU RIGHT."
NOW, THEN...

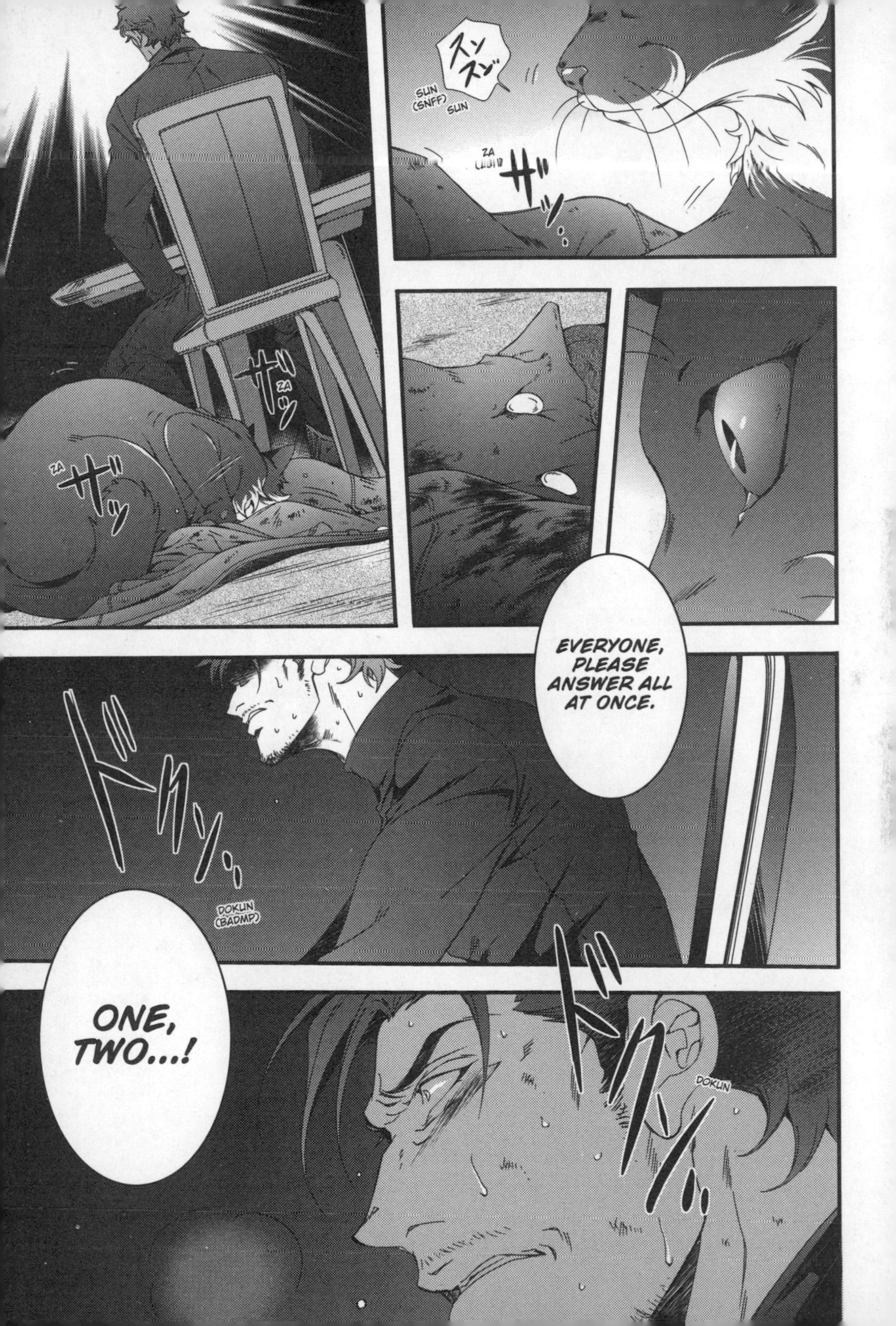
スンスン
SUN (SNFF) SUN
ザッ
ZA
ザッ
ZA
ザッ
ZA
EVERYONE, PLEASE ANSWER ALL AT ONCE.
ドクン
DOKUN (BADMP)
ONE, TWO...!
ドクン
DOKUN

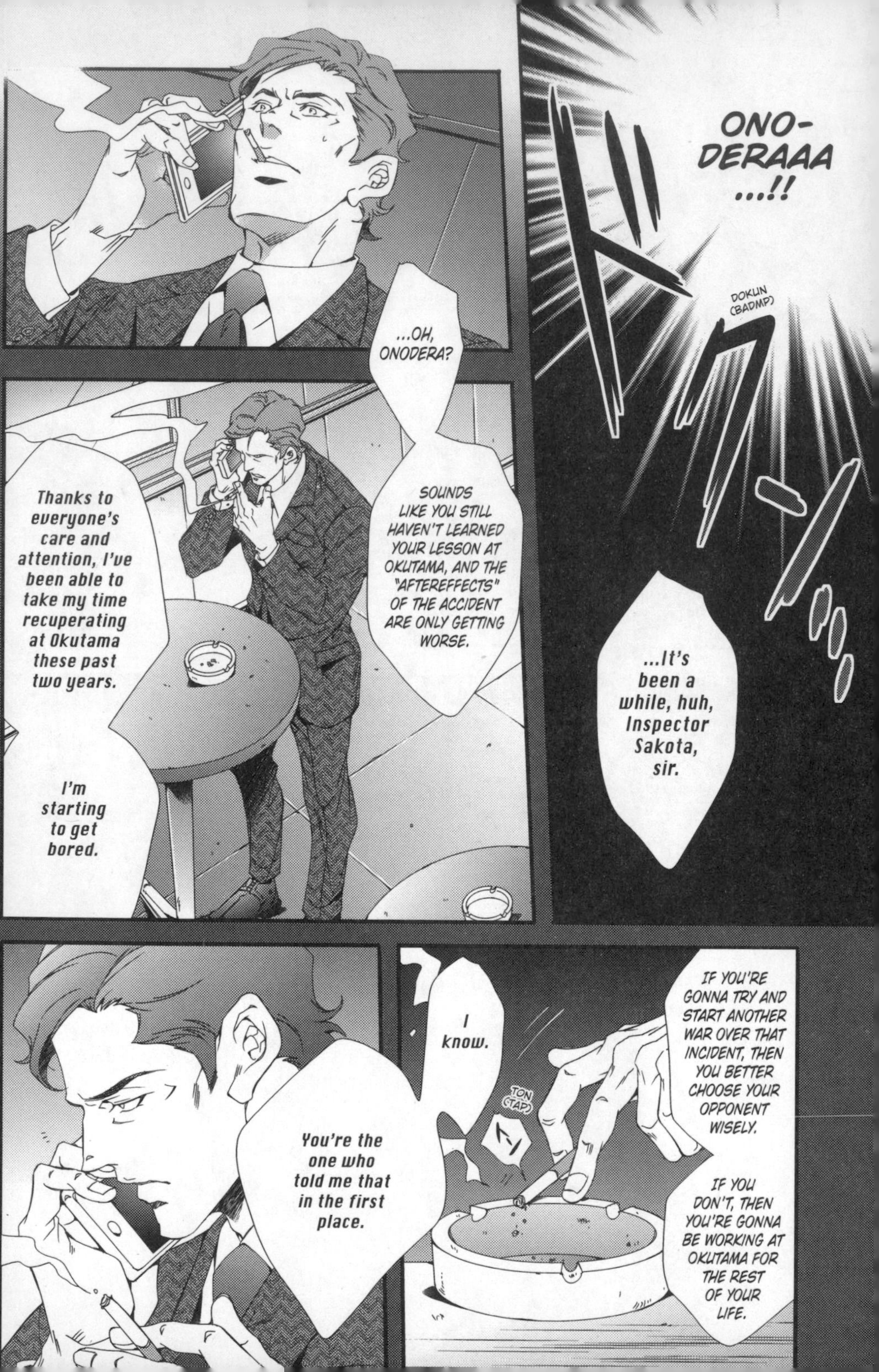
ONO-DERAAA ...!!
DOKUN (BADMP)
...It's been a while, huh, Inspector Sakota, sir.
...OH, ONODERA?
SOUNDS LIKE YOU STILL HAVEN'T LEARNED YOUR LESSON AT OKUTAMA, AND THE "AFTEREFFECTS" OF THE ACCIDENT ARE ONLY GETTING WORSE.
Thanks to everyone's care and attention, I've been able to take my time recuperating at Okutama these past two years.
I'm starting to get bored.
IF YOU'RE GONNA TRY AND START ANOTHER WAR OVER THAT INCIDENT, THEN YOU BETTER CHOOSE YOUR OPPONENT WISELY.
TON (TAP)
IF YOU DON'T, THEN YOU'RE GONNA BE WORKING AT OKUTAMA FOR THE REST OF YOUR LIFE.
I know.
You're the one who told me that in the first place.

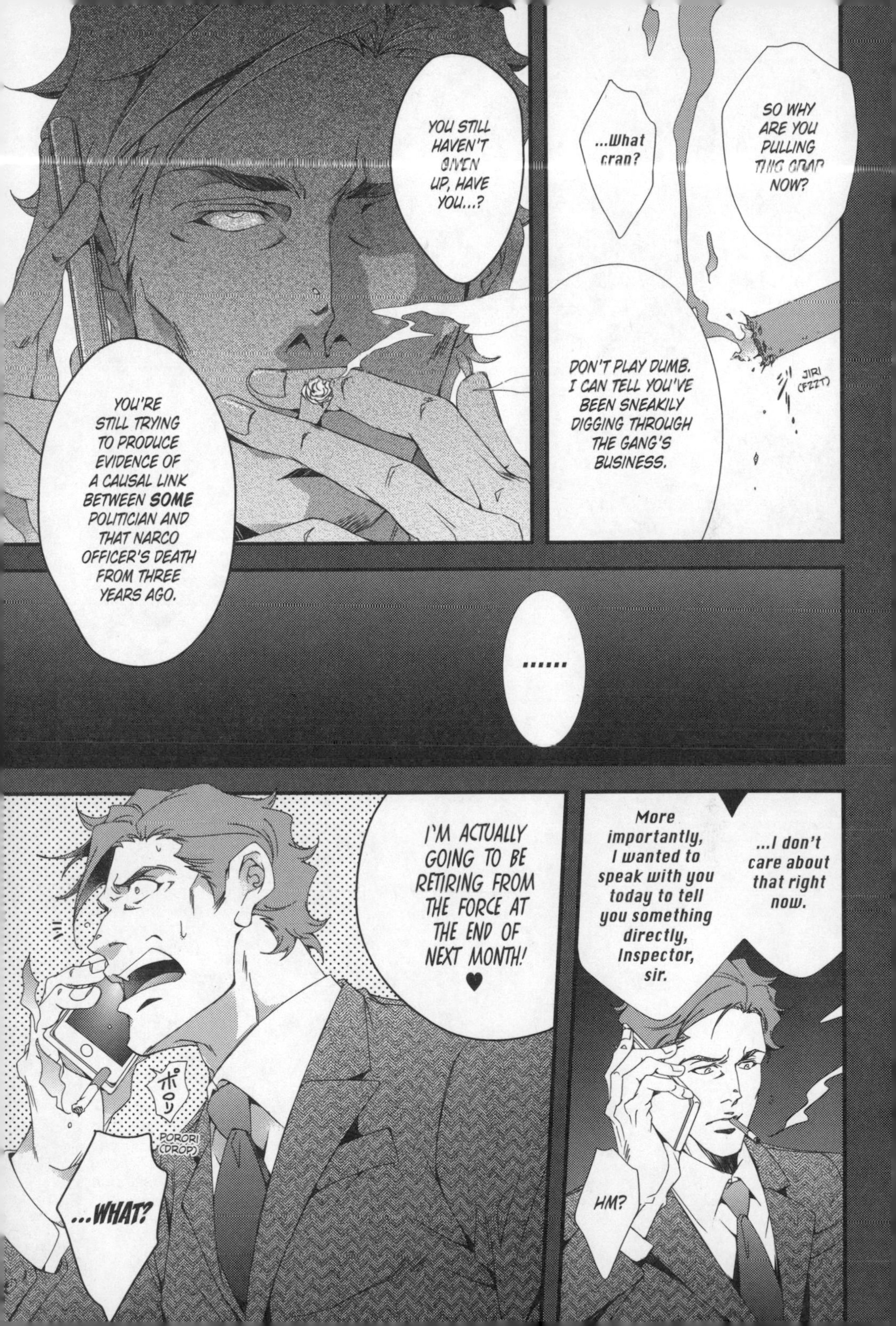
SO WHY ARE YOU PULLING THIS CRAP NOW?
...What crap?
DON'T PLAY DUMB. I CAN TELL YOU'VE BEEN SNEAKILY DIGGING THROUGH THE GANG'S BUSINESS.
JIRI (FZZT)
YOU STILL HAVEN'T GIVEN UP, HAVE YOU...?
YOU'RE STILL TRYING TO PRODUCE EVIDENCE OF A CAUSAL LINK BETWEEN **SOME** POLITICIAN AND THAT NARCO OFFICER'S DEATH FROM THREE YEARS AGO.
......
...I don't care about that right now.
More importantly, I wanted to speak with you today to tell you something directly, Inspector, sir.
HM?
I'M ACTUALLY GOING TO BE RETIRING FROM THE FORCE AT THE END OF NEXT MONTH! ♥
ポロリ
PORORI (DROP)
...WHAT?

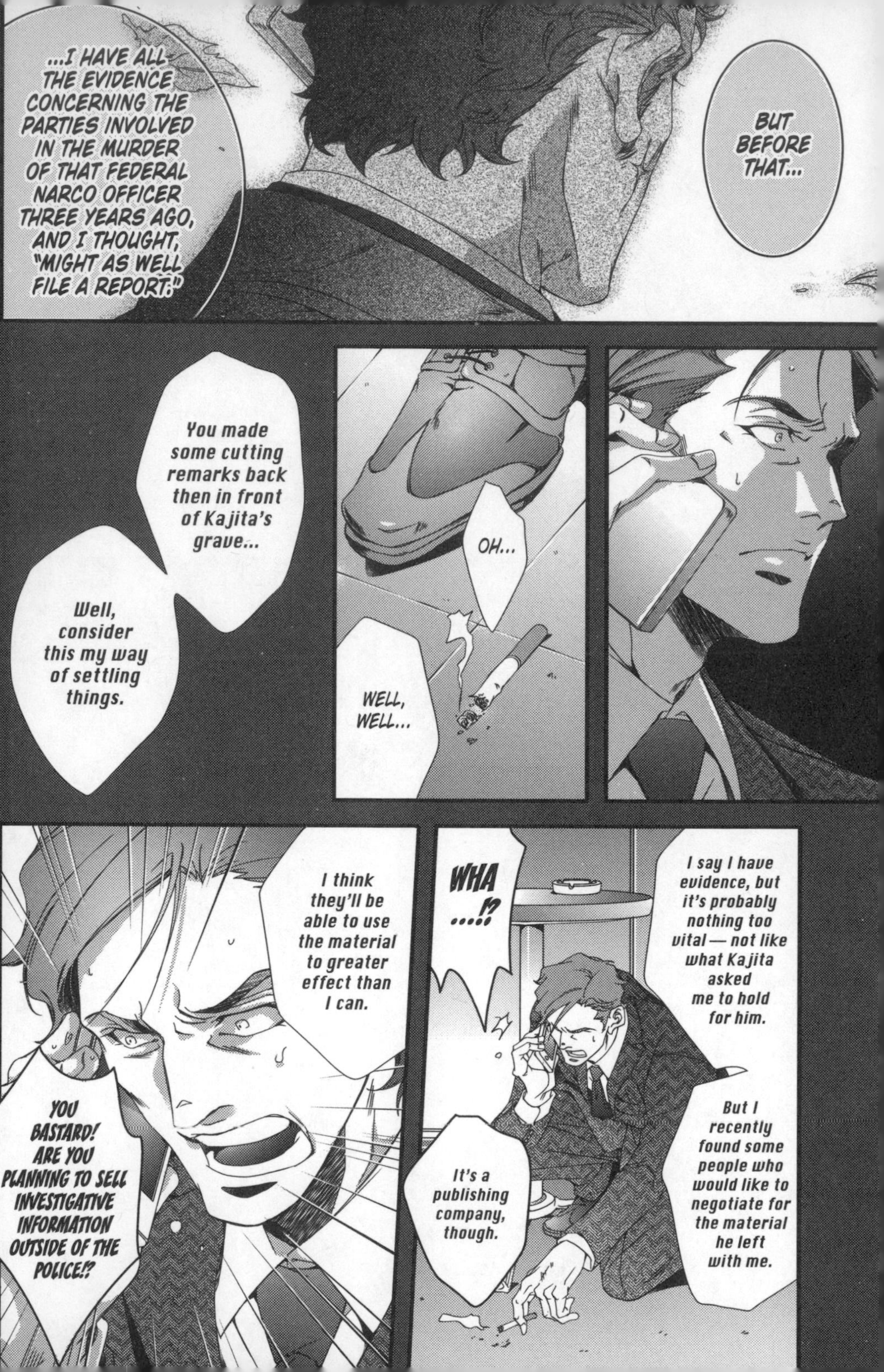
...I HAVE ALL THE EVIDENCE CONCERNING THE PARTIES INVOLVED IN THE MURDER OF THAT FEDERAL NARCO OFFICER THREE YEARS AGO, AND I THOUGHT, "MIGHT AS WELL FILE A REPORT."
BUT BEFORE THAT...
OH...
WELL, WELL...
You made some cutting remarks back then in front of Kajita's grave...
Well, consider this my way of settling things.
I say I have evidence, but it's probably nothing too vital — not like what Kajita asked me to hold for him.
WHA ...!?
But I recently found some people who would like to negotiate for the material he left with me.
It's a publishing company, though.
I think they'll be able to use the material to greater effect than I can.
YOU BASTARD! ARE YOU PLANNING TO SELL INVESTIGATIVE INFORMATION OUTSIDE OF THE POLICE!?

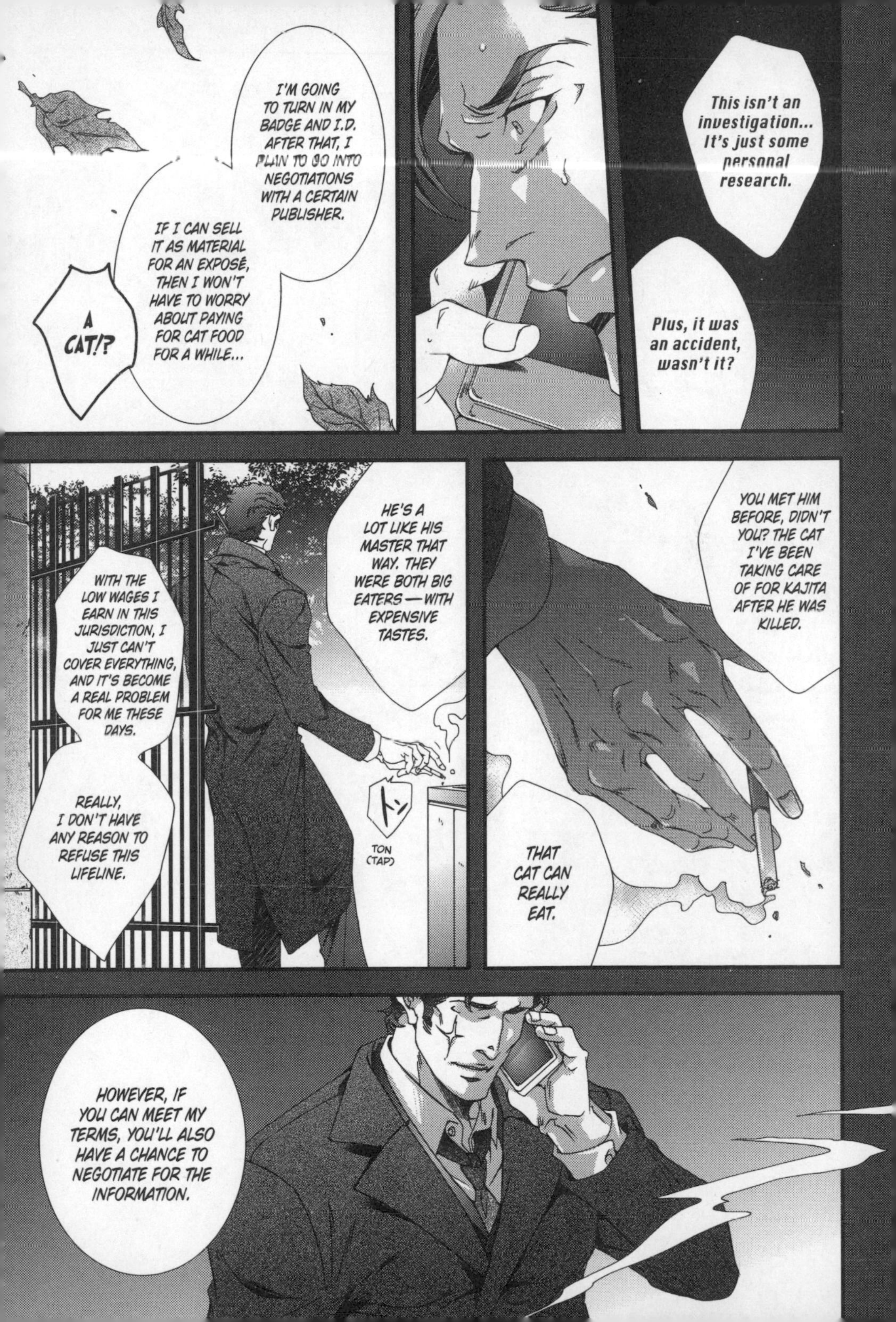
This isn't an investigation... It's just some personal research.
Plus, it was an accident, wasn't it?
I'M GOING TO TURN IN MY BADGE AND I.D. AFTER THAT, I PLAN TO GO INTO NEGOTIATIONS WITH A CERTAIN PUBLISHER.
IF I CAN SELL IT AS MATERIAL FOR AN EXPOSÉ, THEN I WON'T HAVE TO WORRY ABOUT PAYING FOR CAT FOOD FOR A WHILE...
A CAT!?
YOU MET HIM BEFORE, DIDN'T YOU? THE CAT I'VE BEEN TAKING CARE OF FOR KAJITA AFTER HE WAS KILLED.
THAT CAT CAN REALLY EAT.
HE'S A LOT LIKE HIS MASTER THAT WAY. THEY WERE BOTH BIG EATERS — WITH EXPENSIVE TASTES.
WITH THE LOW WAGES I EARN IN THIS JURISDICTION, I JUST CAN'T COVER EVERYTHING, AND IT'S BECOME A REAL PROBLEM FOR ME THESE DAYS.
トン
TON (TAP)
REALLY, I DON'T HAVE ANY REASON TO REFUSE THIS LIFELINE.
HOWEVER, IF YOU CAN MEET MY TERMS, YOU'LL ALSO HAVE A CHANCE TO NEGOTIATE FOR THE INFORMATION.

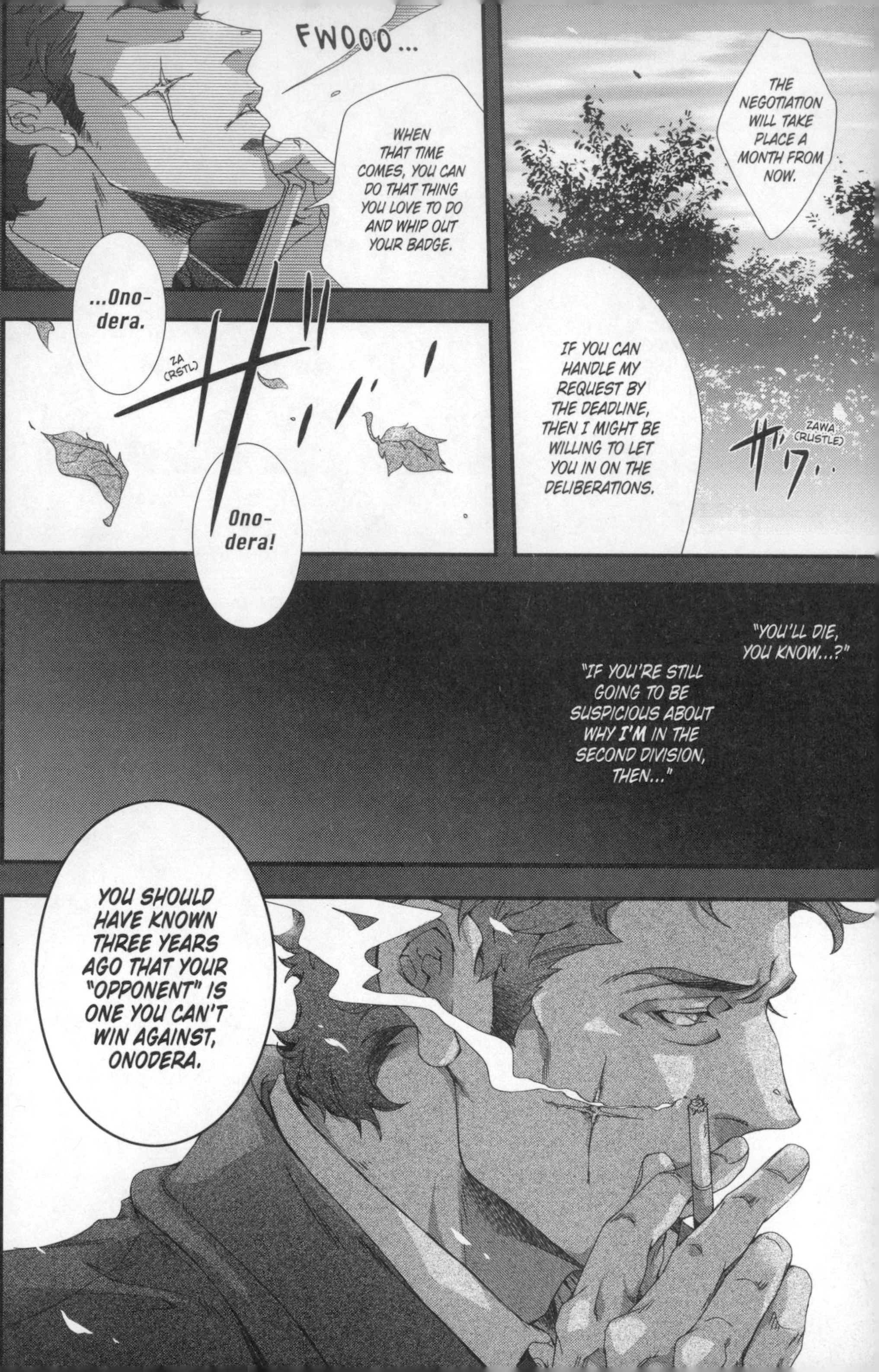
THE NEGOTIATION WILL TAKE PLACE A MONTH FROM NOW.
IF YOU CAN HANDLE MY REQUEST BY THE DEADLINE, THEN I MIGHT BE WILLING TO LET YOU IN ON THE DELIBERATIONS.
ZAWA (RUSTLE)
FWOOO...
WHEN THAT TIME COMES, YOU CAN DO THAT THING YOU LOVE TO DO AND WHIP OUT YOUR BADGE.
...Onodera.
ZA (RSTL)
Onodera!
"YOU'LL DIE, YOU KNOW...?"
"IF YOU'RE STILL GOING TO BE SUSPICIOUS ABOUT WHY I'M IN THE SECOND DIVISION, THEN..."
YOU SHOULD HAVE KNOWN THREE YEARS AGO THAT YOUR "OPPONENT" IS ONE YOU CAN'T WIN AGAINST, ONODERA.

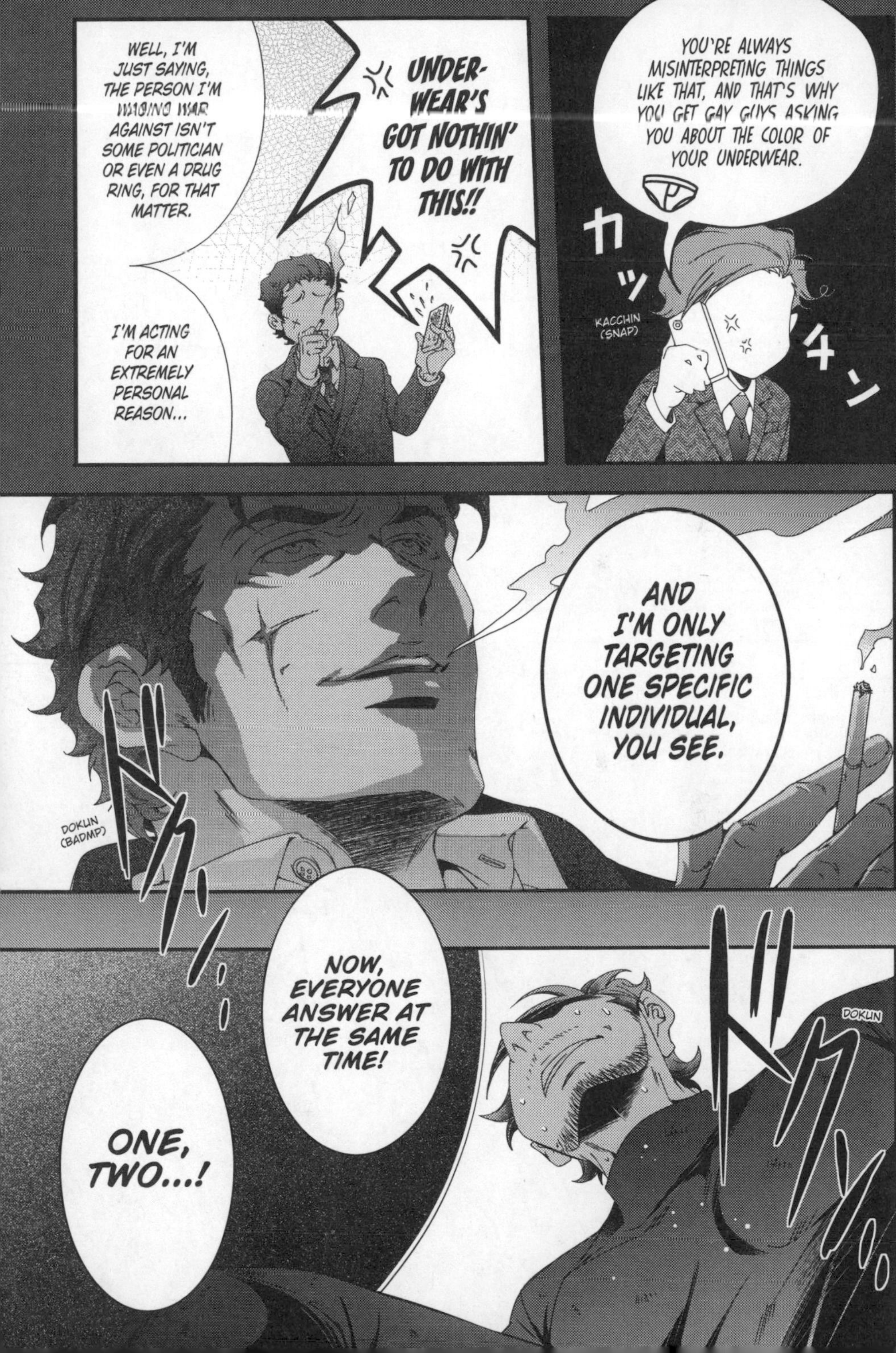
YOU'RE ALWAYS MISINTERPRETING THINGS LIKE THAT, AND THAT'S WHY YOU GET GAY GUYS ASKING YOU ABOUT THE COLOR OF YOUR UNDERWEAR.
KACCHIN (SNAP)
UNDER-WEAR'S GOT NOTHIN' TO DO WITH THIS!!
WELL, I'M JUST SAYING, THE PERSON I'M WAGING WAR AGAINST ISN'T SOME POLITICIAN OR EVEN A DRUG RING, FOR THAT MATTER.
I'M ACTING FOR AN EXTREMELY PERSONAL REASON...
AND I'M ONLY TARGETING ONE SPECIFIC INDIVIDUAL, YOU SEE.
DOKUN (BADMP)
DOKUN
NOW, EVERYONE ANSWER AT THE SAME TIME!
ONE, TWO...!

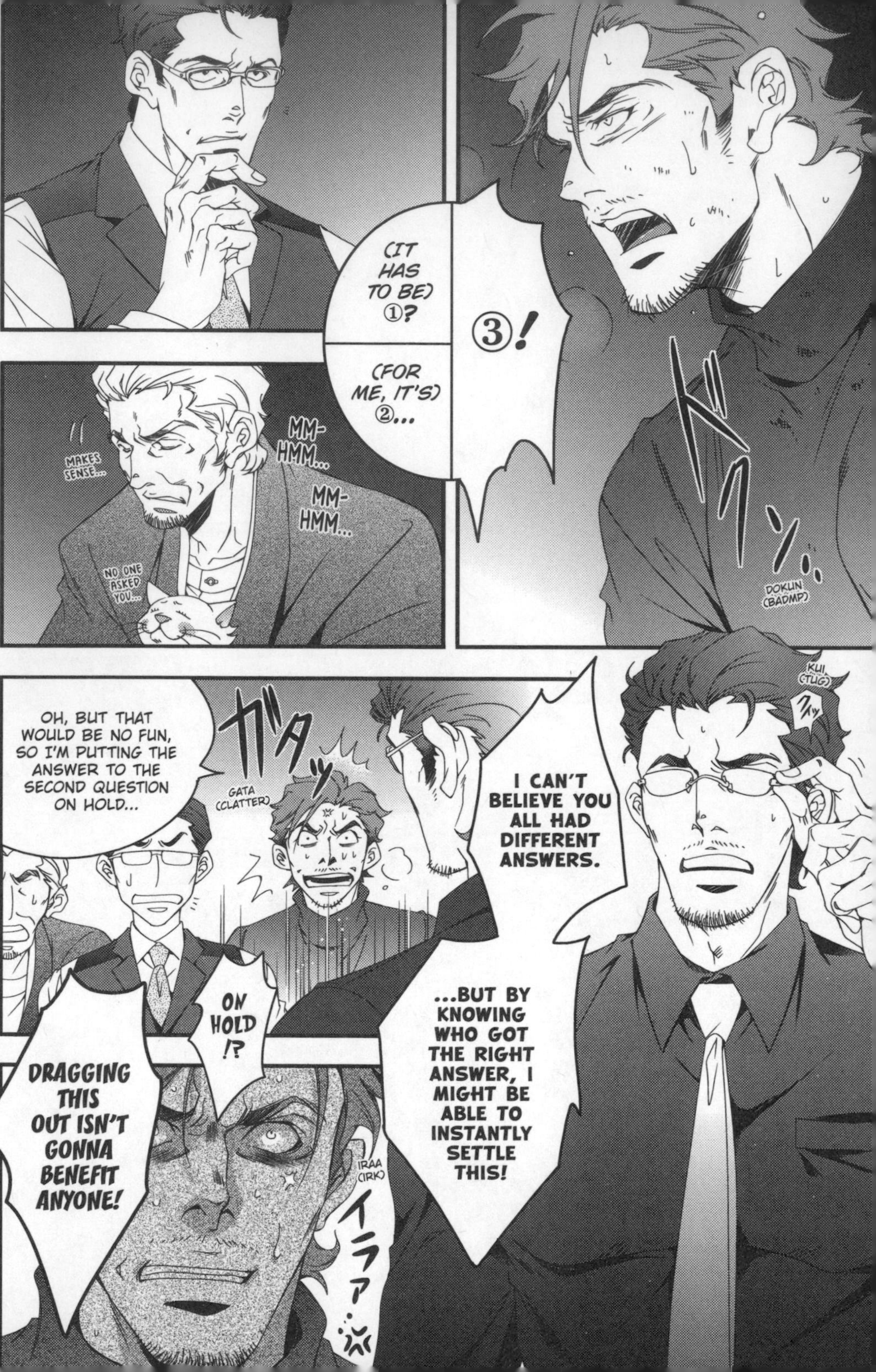
③!
DOKUN (BADMP)
(IT HAS TO BE) ①?
(FOR ME, IT'S) ②...
MM-HMM...
MAKES SENSE...
MM-HMM...
NO ONE ASKED YOU...
KUI (TUG)
I CAN'T BELIEVE YOU ALL HAD DIFFERENT ANSWERS.
...BUT BY KNOWING WHO GOT THE RIGHT ANSWER, I MIGHT BE ABLE TO INSTANTLY SETTLE THIS!
OH, BUT THAT WOULD BE NO FUN, SO I'M PUTTING THE ANSWER TO THE SECOND QUESTION ON HOLD...
GATA (CLATTER)
ON HOLD!?
DRAGGING THIS OUT ISN'T GONNA BENEFIT ANYONE!
IRAA (IRK)

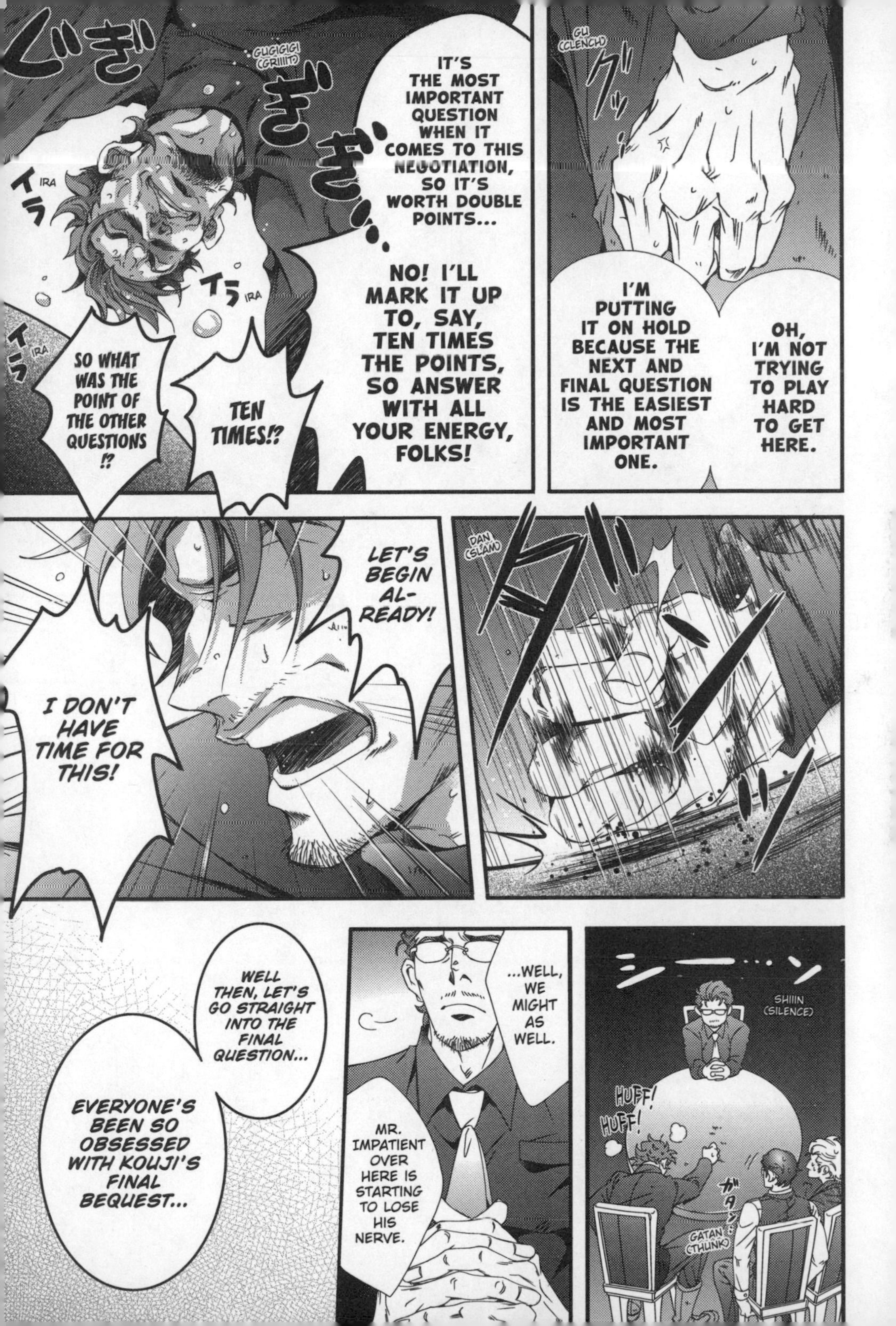
GU (CLENCH)
OH, I'M NOT TRYING TO PLAY HARD TO GET HERE.
I'M PUTTING IT ON HOLD BECAUSE THE NEXT AND FINAL QUESTION IS THE EASIEST AND MOST IMPORTANT ONE.
IT'S THE MOST IMPORTANT QUESTION WHEN IT COMES TO THIS NEGOTIATION, SO IT'S WORTH DOUBLE POINTS...
NO! I'LL MARK IT UP TO, SAY, TEN TIMES THE POINTS, SO ANSWER WITH ALL YOUR ENERGY, FOLKS!
GUGIGIGI (GRIIIIT)
IRA
IRA
IRA
TEN TIMES!?
SO WHAT WAS THE POINT OF THE OTHER QUESTIONS!?
DAN (SLAM)
LET'S BEGIN AL-READY!
I DON'T HAVE TIME FOR THIS!
SHIIIN (SILENCE)
HUFF! HUFF!
GATAN (THUNK)
...WELL, WE MIGHT AS WELL.
MR. IMPATIENT OVER HERE IS STARTING TO LOSE HIS NERVE.
WELL THEN, LET'S GO STRAIGHT INTO THE FINAL QUESTION...
EVERYONE'S BEEN SO OBSESSED WITH KOUJI'S FINAL BEQUEST...

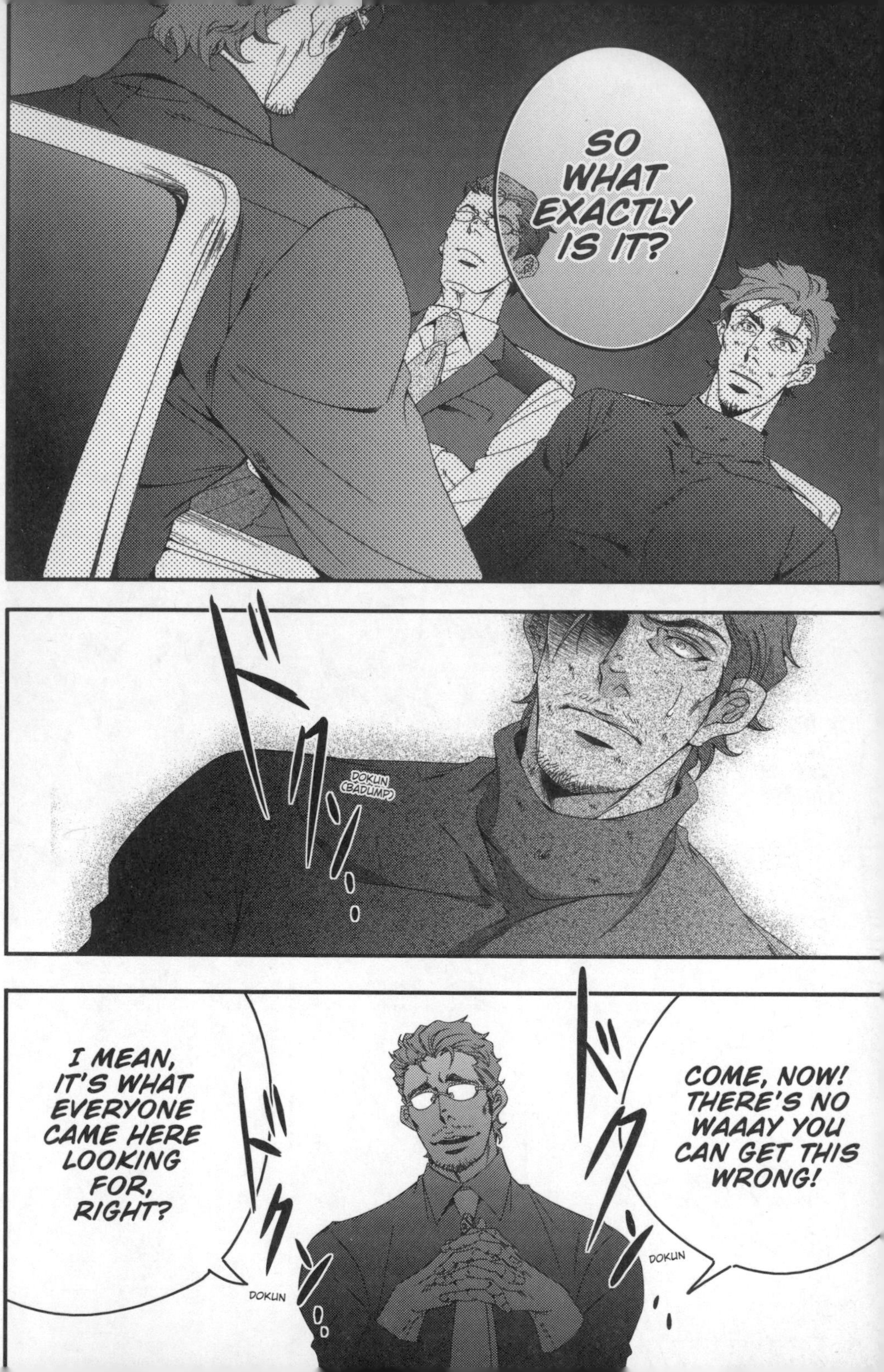
SO WHAT EXACTLY IS IT?
DOKUN (BADUMP)
COME, NOW! THERE'S NO WAAAY YOU CAN GET THIS WRONG!
DOKUN
I MEAN, IT'S WHAT EVERYONE CAME HERE LOOKING FOR, RIGHT?
DOKUN

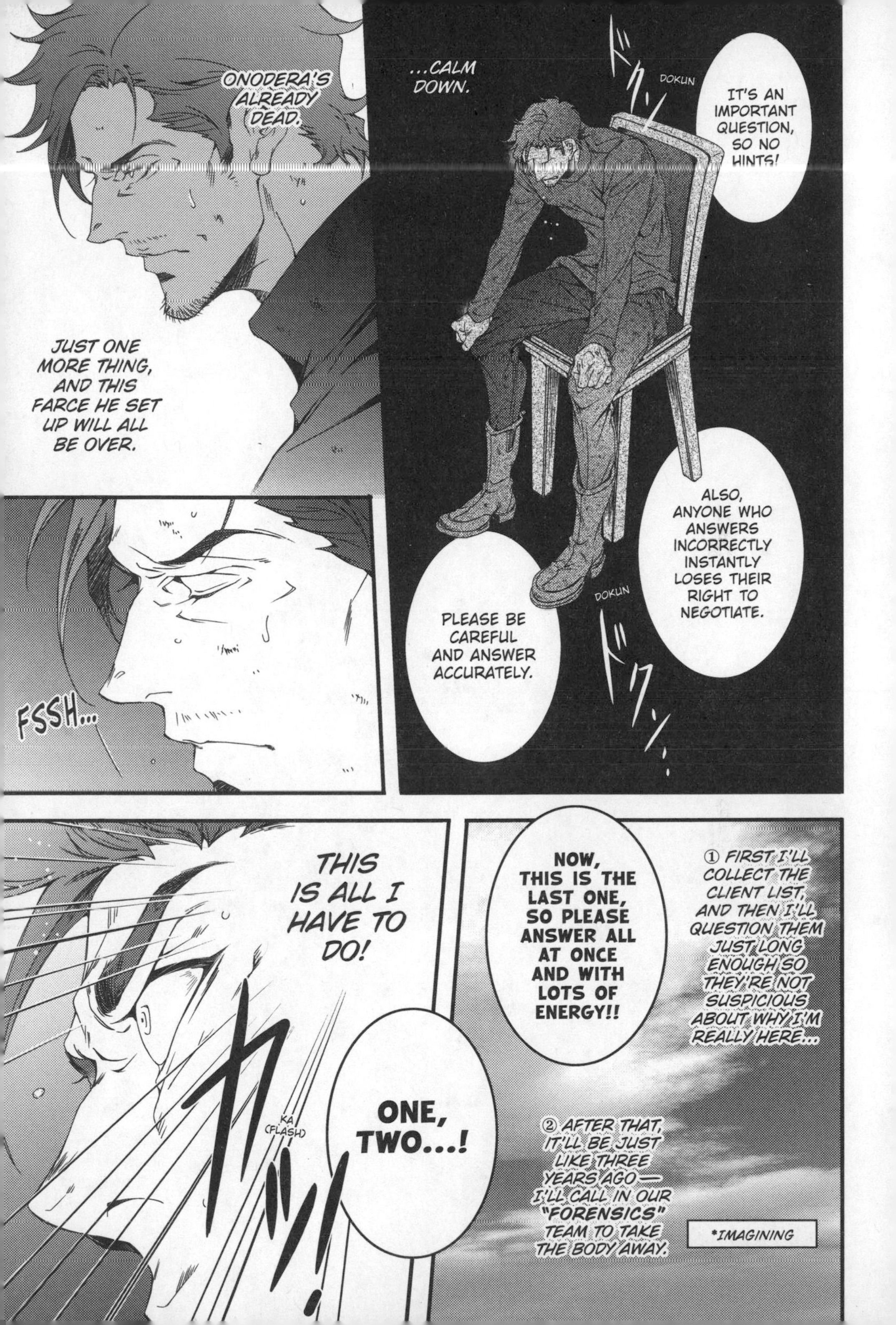
DOKUN
IT'S AN IMPORTANT QUESTION, SO NO HINTS!
...CALM DOWN.
ALSO, ANYONE WHO ANSWERS INCORRECTLY INSTANTLY LOSES THEIR RIGHT TO NEGOTIATE.
PLEASE BE CAREFUL AND ANSWER ACCURATELY.
DOKUN
ONODERA'S ALREADY DEAD.
JUST ONE MORE THING, AND THIS FARCE HE SET UP WILL ALL BE OVER.
FSSH...
① FIRST I'LL COLLECT THE CLIENT LIST, AND THEN I'LL QUESTION THEM JUST LONG ENOUGH SO THEY'RE NOT SUSPICIOUS ABOUT WHY I'M REALLY HERE...
NOW, THIS IS THE LAST ONE, SO PLEASE ANSWER ALL AT ONCE AND WITH LOTS OF ENERGY!!
② AFTER THAT, IT'LL BE JUST LIKE THREE YEARS AGO— I'LL CALL IN OUR "FORENSICS" TEAM TO TAKE THE BODY AWAY.
*IMAGINING
THIS IS ALL I HAVE TO DO!
ONE, TWO...!
KA (FLASH)

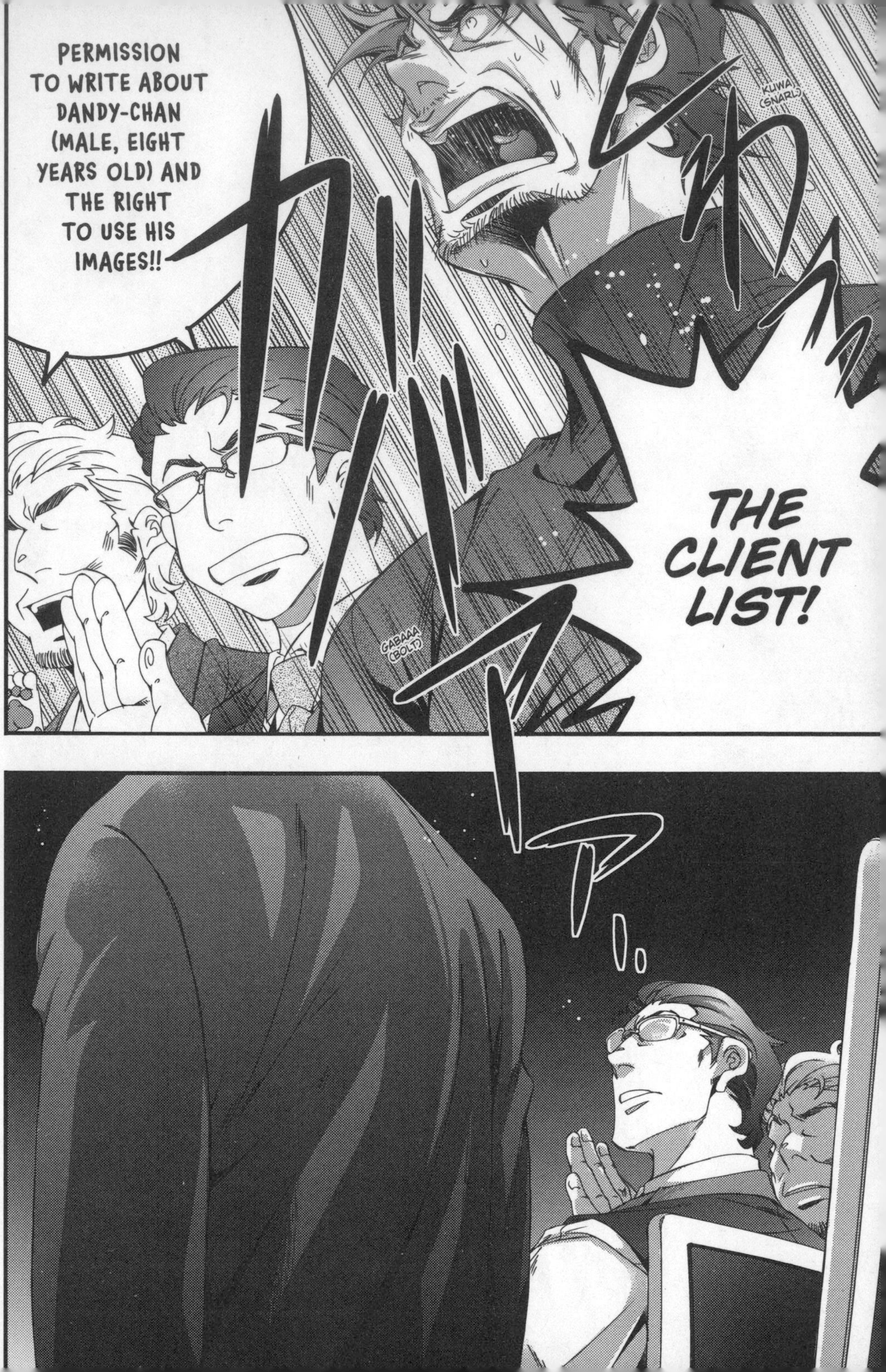
KUWA (SNARL)
THE CLIENT LIST!
PERMISSION TO WRITE ABOUT DANDY-CHAN (MALE, EIGHT YEARS OLD) AND THE RIGHT TO USE HIS IMAGES!!
GABAAA (BOLT)

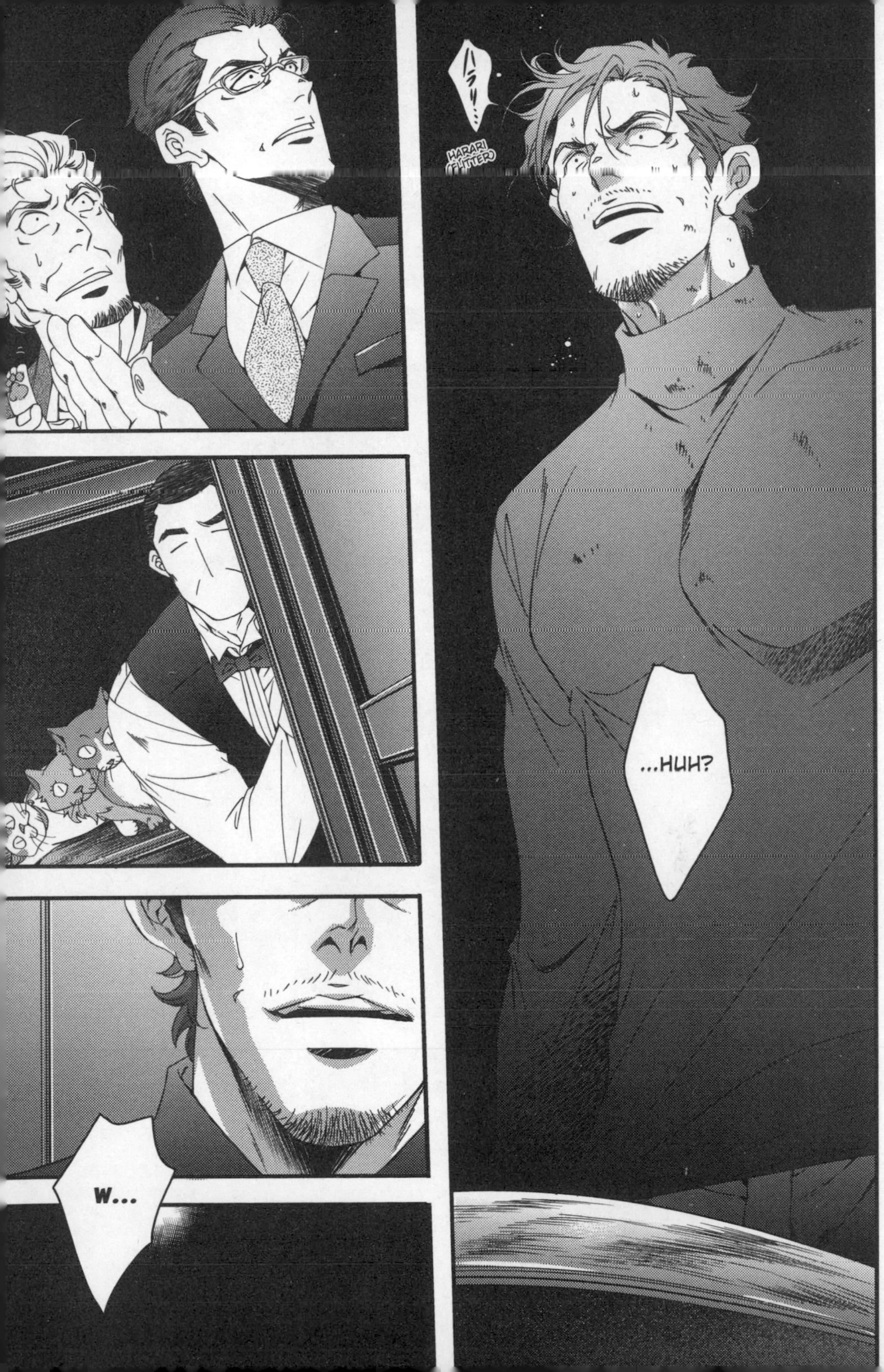
ハラリ…
HARARI (FLITTER)
...HUH?
W...

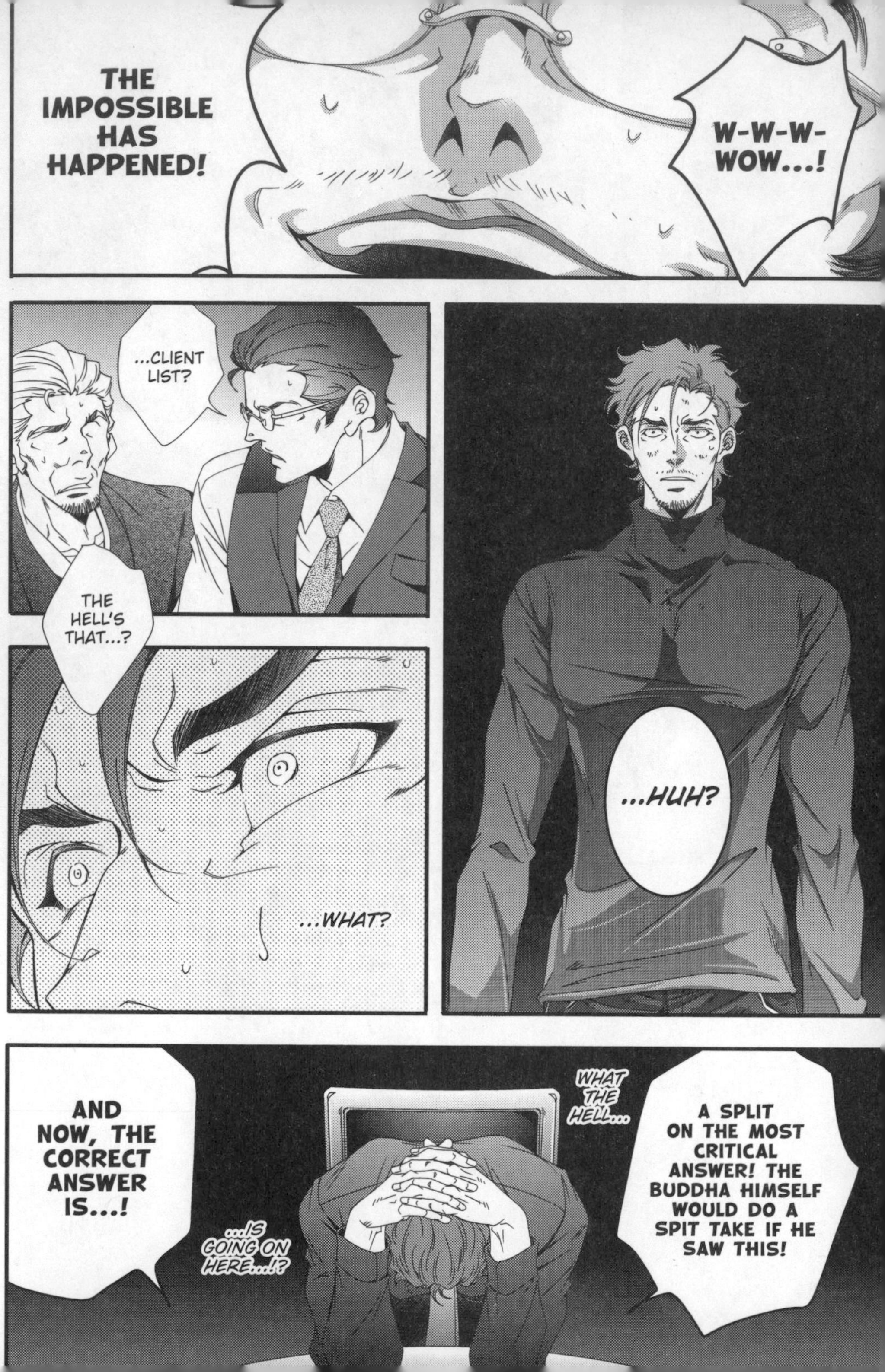
W-W-W-WOW...!
THE IMPOSSIBLE HAS HAPPENED!
...HUH?
...CLIENT LIST?
THE HELL'S THAT...?
...WHAT?
A SPLIT ON THE MOST CRITICAL ANSWER! THE BUDDHA HIMSELF WOULD DO A SPIT TAKE IF HE SAW THIS!
WHAT THE HELL...
...IS GOING ON HERE...!?
AND NOW, THE CORRECT ANSWER IS...!

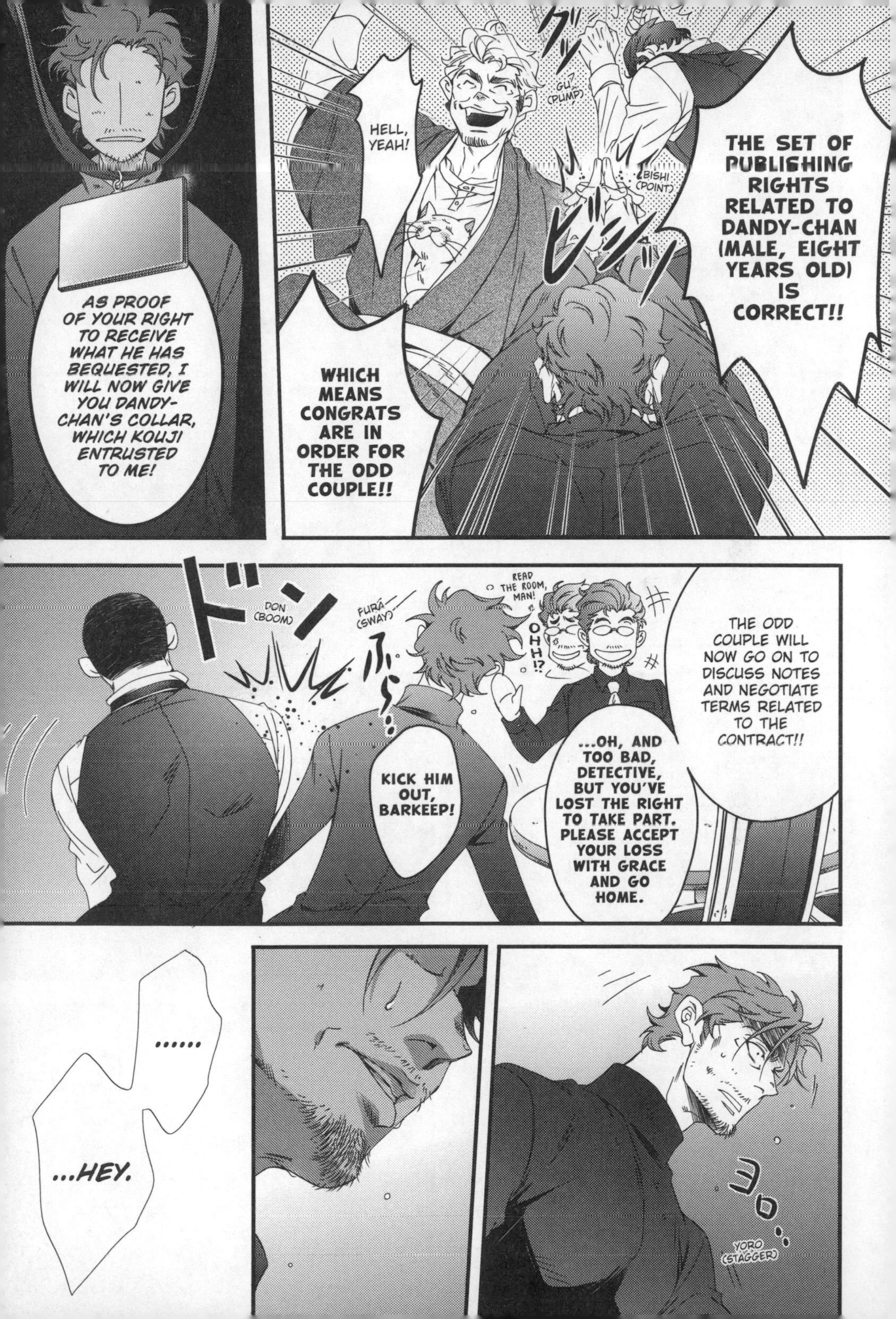
THE SET OF PUBLISHING RIGHTS RELATED TO DANDY-CHAN (MALE, EIGHT YEARS OLD) IS CORRECT!!
GU (PUMP)
HELL, YEAH!
BISHI (POINT)
WHICH MEANS CONGRATS ARE IN ORDER FOR THE ODD COUPLE!!
AS PROOF OF YOUR RIGHT TO RECEIVE WHAT HE HAS BEQUESTED, I WILL NOW GIVE YOU DANDY-CHAN'S COLLAR, WHICH KOUJI ENTRUSTED TO ME!
THE ODD COUPLE WILL NOW GO ON TO DISCUSS NOTES AND NEGOTIATE TERMS RELATED TO THE CONTRACT!!
READ THE ROOM, MAN!
OHH!?
...OH, AND TOO BAD, DETECTIVE, BUT YOU'VE LOST THE RIGHT TO TAKE PART. PLEASE ACCEPT YOUR LOSS WITH GRACE AND GO HOME.
FURA (SWAY)
DON (BOOM)
KICK HIM OUT, BARKEEP!
YORO (STAGGER)
......
...HEY.

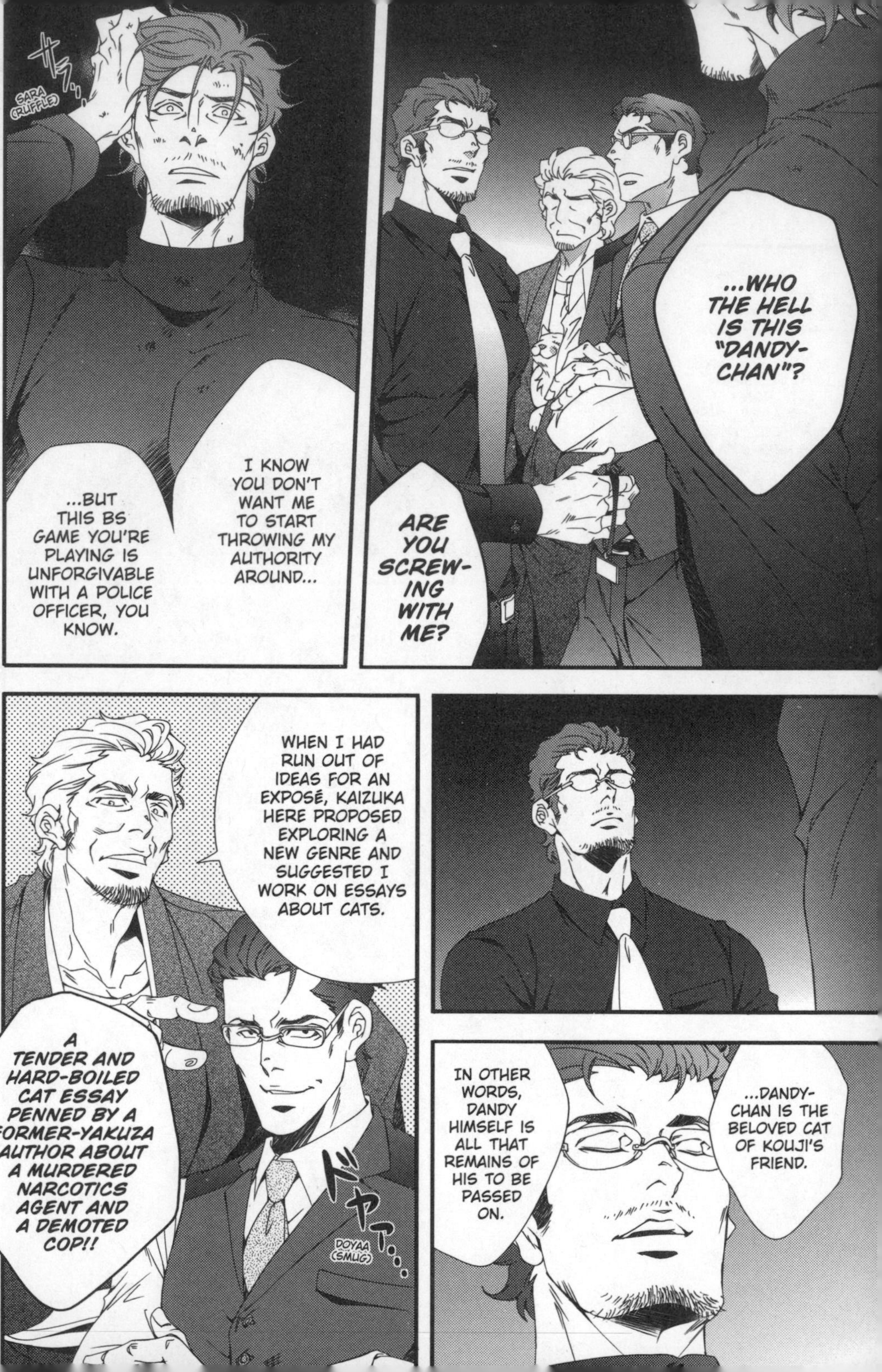
...WHO THE HELL IS THIS "DANDY-CHAN"?
ARE YOU SCREWING WITH ME?
SARA (RUFFLE)
I KNOW YOU DON'T WANT ME TO START THROWING MY AUTHORITY AROUND...
...BUT THIS BS GAME YOU'RE PLAYING IS UNFORGIVABLE WITH A POLICE OFFICER, YOU KNOW.
...DANDY-CHAN IS THE BELOVED CAT OF KOUJI'S FRIEND.
IN OTHER WORDS, DANDY HIMSELF IS ALL THAT REMAINS OF HIS TO BE PASSED ON.
WHEN I HAD RUN OUT OF IDEAS FOR AN EXPOSÉ, KAIZUKA HERE PROPOSED EXPLORING A NEW GENRE AND SUGGESTED I WORK ON ESSAYS ABOUT CATS.
A TENDER AND HARD-BOILED CAT ESSAY PENNED BY A FORMER-YAKUZA AUTHOR ABOUT A MURDERED NARCOTICS AGENT AND A DEMOTED COP!!
DOYAA (SMUG)

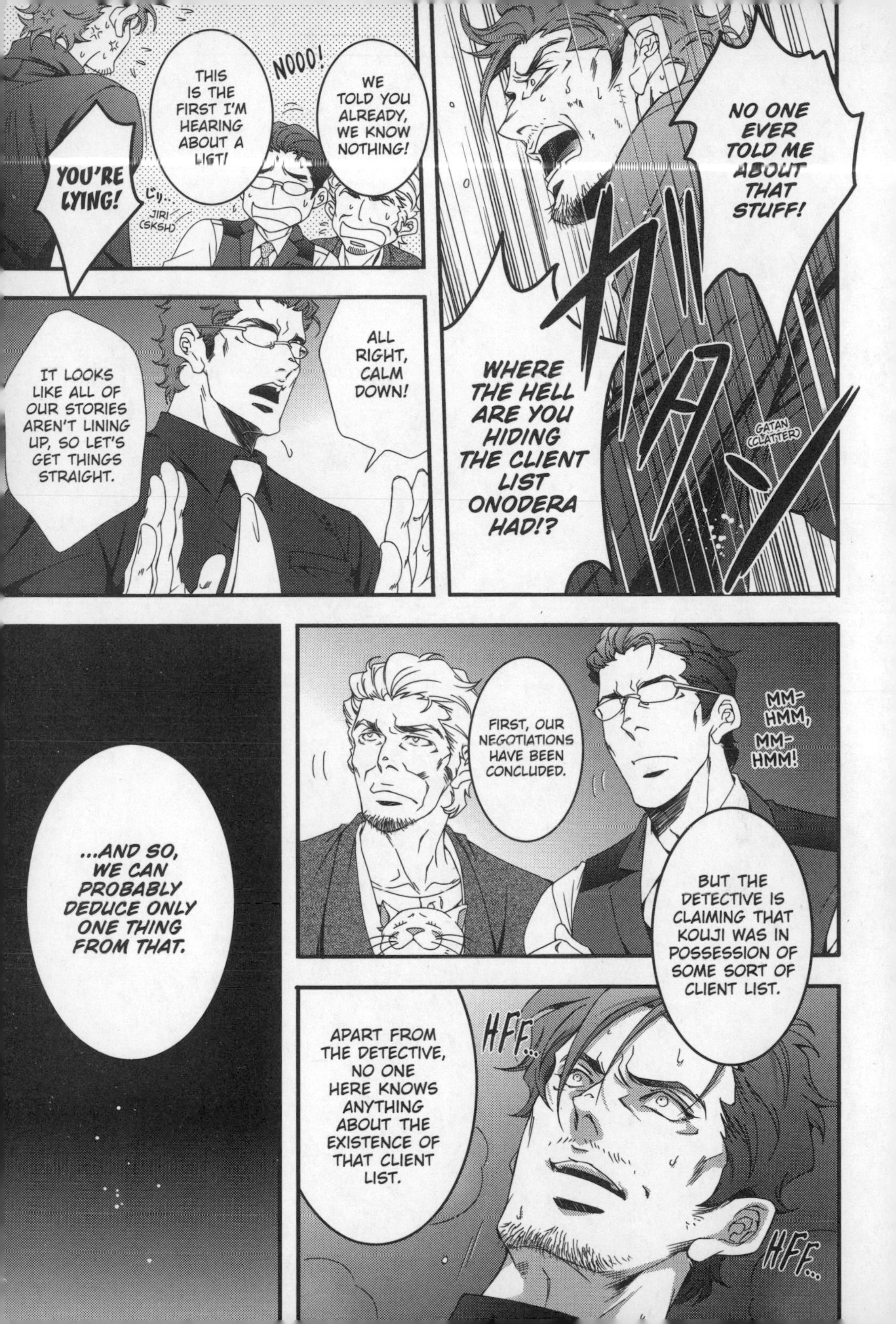
NO ONE EVER TOLD ME ABOUT THAT STUFF!
WHERE THE HELL ARE YOU HIDING THE CLIENT LIST ONODERA HAD!?
GATAN (CLATTER)
WE TOLD YOU ALREADY, WE KNOW NOTHING!
NOOO!
THIS IS THE FIRST I'M HEARING ABOUT A LIST!
じり…
JIRI (SKSH)
YOU'RE LYING!
ALL RIGHT, CALM DOWN!
IT LOOKS LIKE ALL OF OUR STORIES AREN'T LINING UP, SO LET'S GET THINGS STRAIGHT.
MM-HMM, MM-HMM!
FIRST, OUR NEGOTIATIONS HAVE BEEN CONCLUDED.
BUT THE DETECTIVE IS CLAIMING THAT KOUJI WAS IN POSSESSION OF SOME SORT OF CLIENT LIST.
HFF...
APART FROM THE DETECTIVE, NO ONE HERE KNOWS ANYTHING ABOUT THE EXISTENCE OF THAT CLIENT LIST.
HFF...
...AND SO, WE CAN PROBABLY DEDUCE ONLY ONE THING FROM THAT.

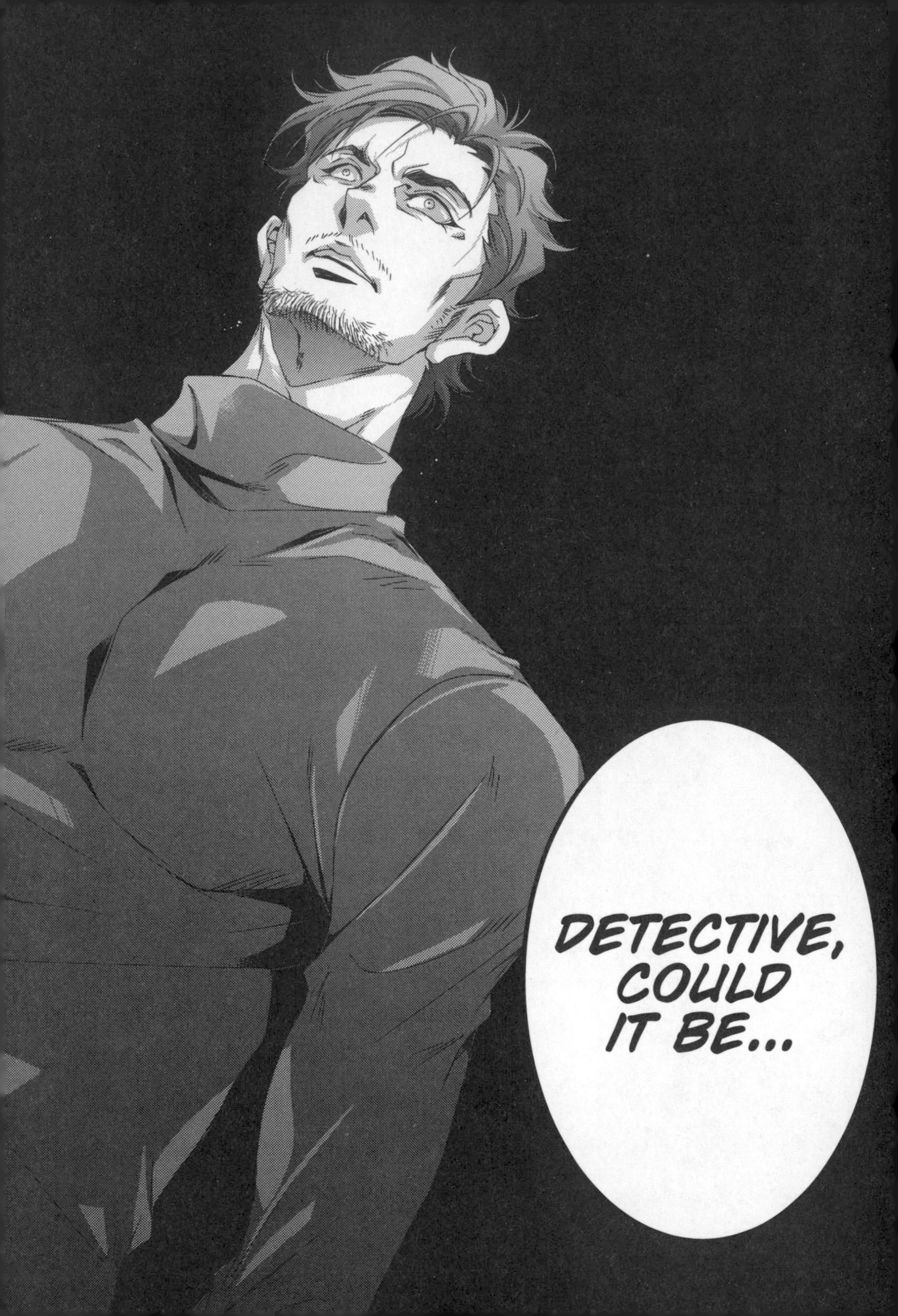
DETECTIVE, COULD IT BE...

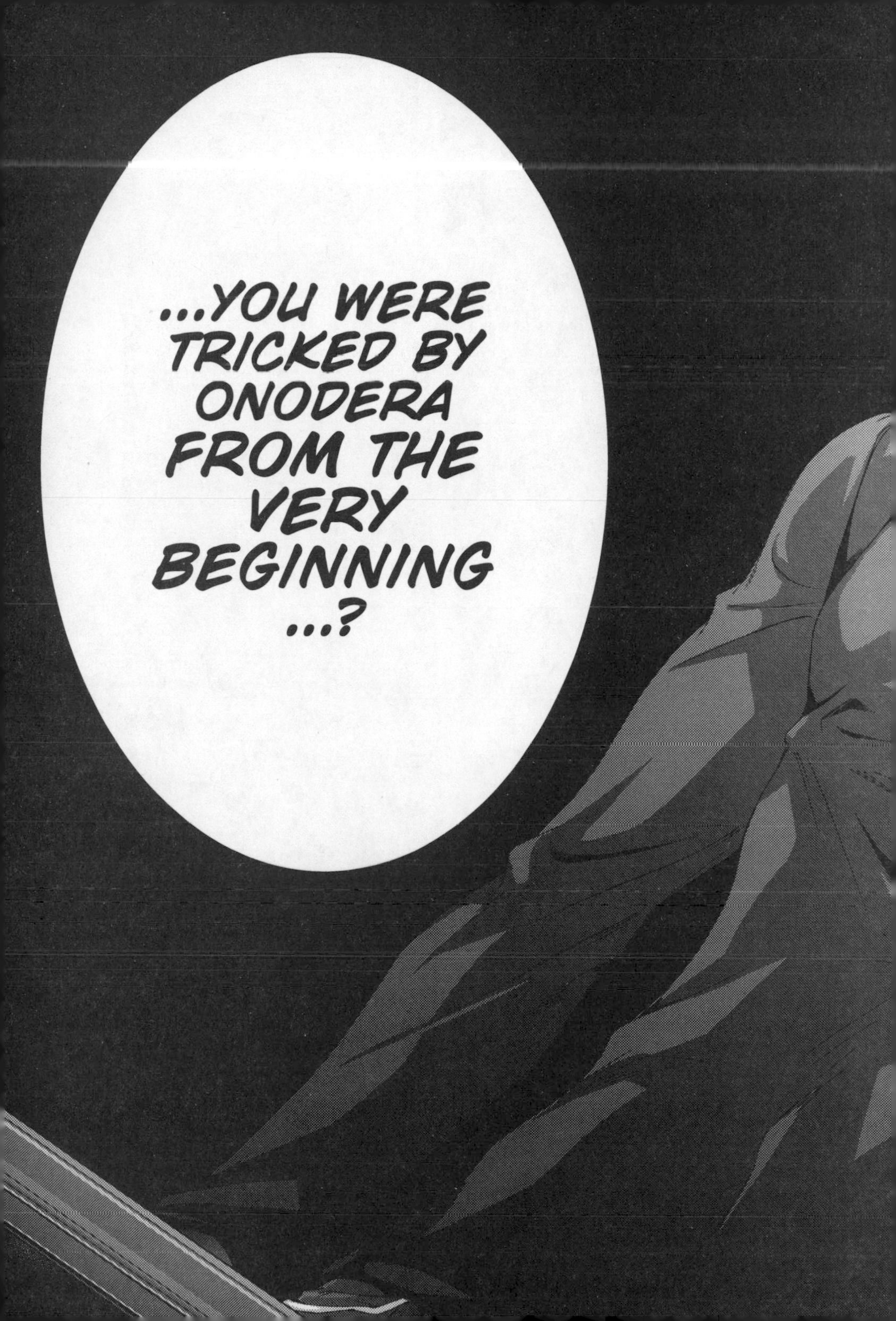
...YOU WERE TRICKED BY ONODERA FROM THE VERY BEGINNING ...?

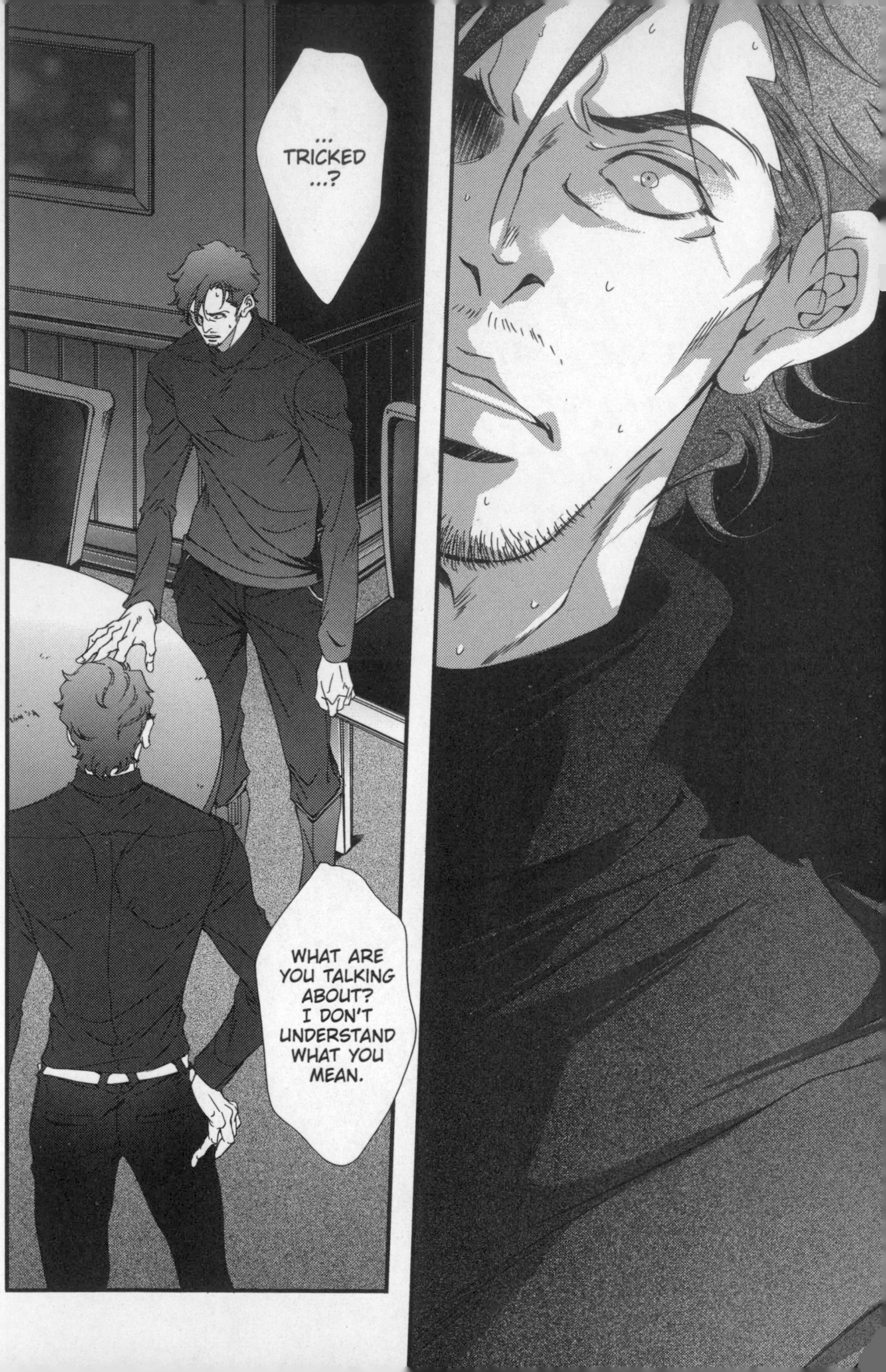
... TRICKED ...?
WHAT ARE YOU TALKING ABOUT? I DON'T UNDERSTAND WHAT YOU MEAN.

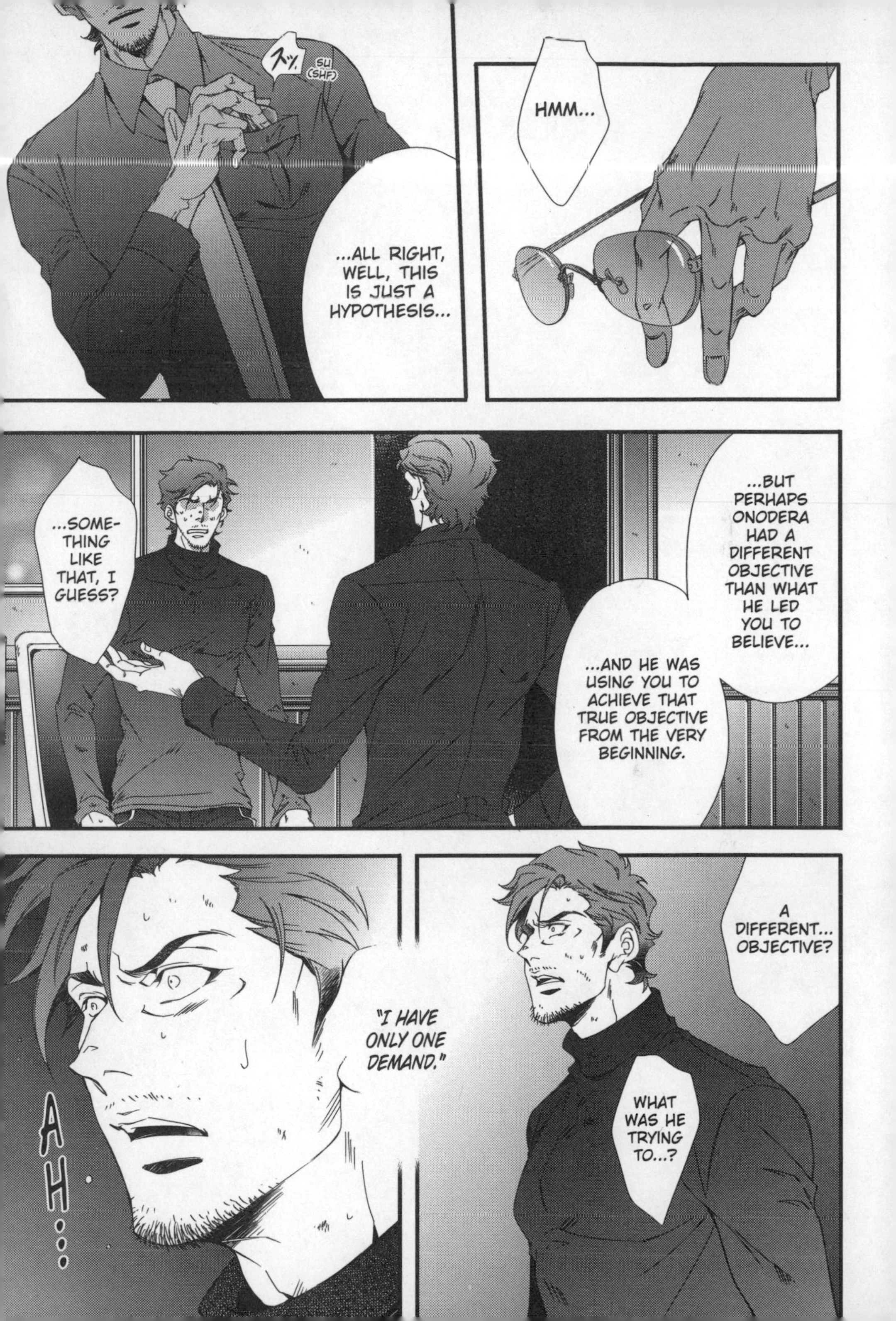
HMM...
スッ
SU (SHF)
...ALL RIGHT, WELL, THIS IS JUST A HYPOTHESIS...
...BUT PERHAPS ONODERA HAD A DIFFERENT OBJECTIVE THAN WHAT HE LED YOU TO BELIEVE...
...AND HE WAS USING YOU TO ACHIEVE THAT TRUE OBJECTIVE FROM THE VERY BEGINNING.
...SOME-THING LIKE THAT, I GUESS?
A DIFFERENT... OBJECTIVE?
WHAT WAS HE TRYING TO...?
"I HAVE ONLY ONE DEMAND."
AH...

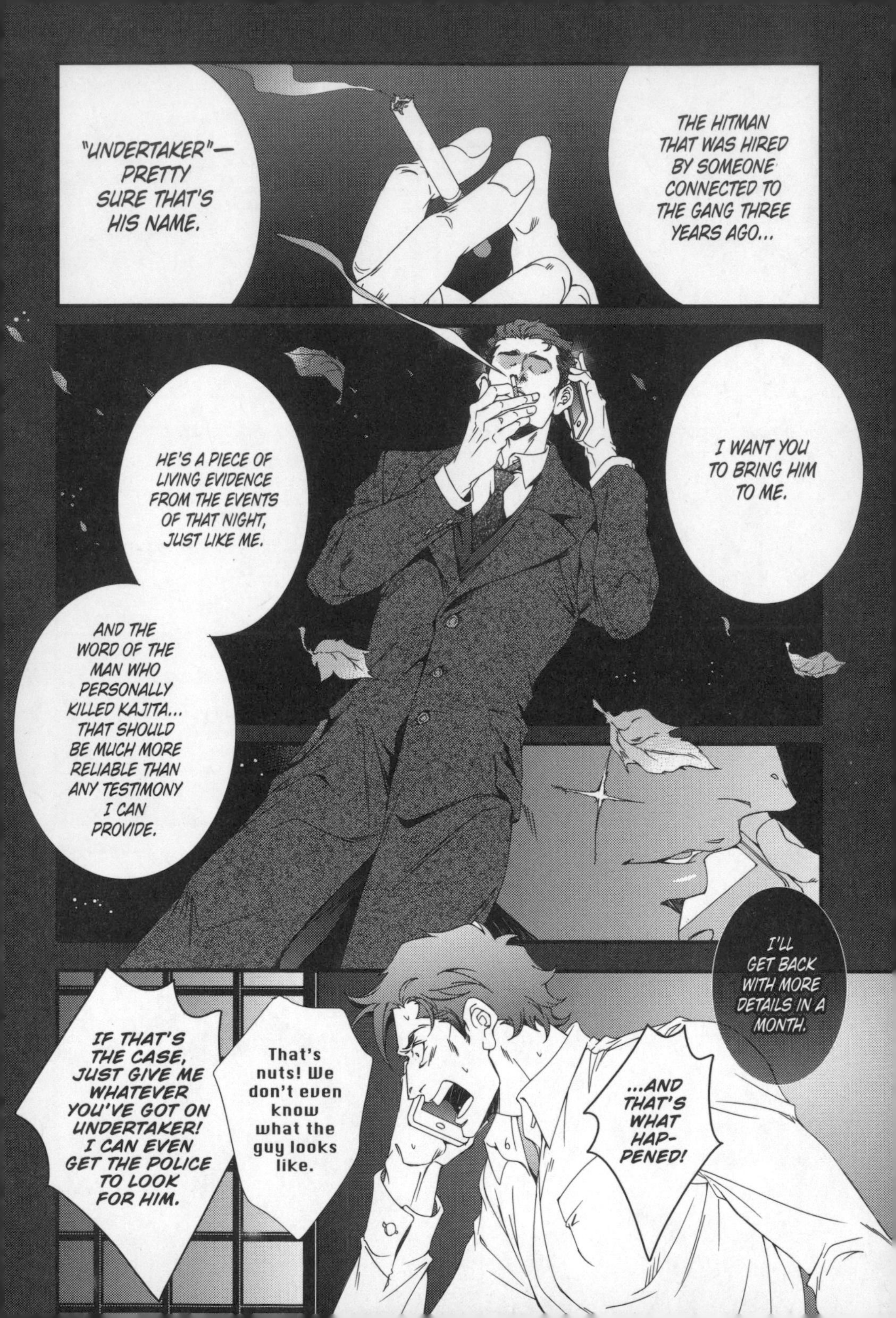

THE HITMAN THAT WAS HIRED BY SOMEONE CONNECTED TO THE GANG THREE YEARS AGO...
"UNDERTAKER"—PRETTY SURE THAT'S HIS NAME.
I WANT YOU TO BRING HIM TO ME.
HE'S A PIECE OF LIVING EVIDENCE FROM THE EVENTS OF THAT NIGHT, JUST LIKE ME.
AND THE WORD OF THE MAN WHO PERSONALLY KILLED KAJITA... THAT SHOULD BE MUCH MORE RELIABLE THAN ANY TESTIMONY I CAN PROVIDE.
I'LL GET BACK WITH MORE DETAILS IN A MONTH.
...AND THAT'S WHAT HAP-PENED!
That's nuts! We don't even know what the guy looks like.
IF THAT'S THE CASE, JUST GIVE ME WHATEVER YOU'VE GOT ON UNDERTAKER! I CAN EVEN GET THE POLICE TO LOOK FOR HIM.

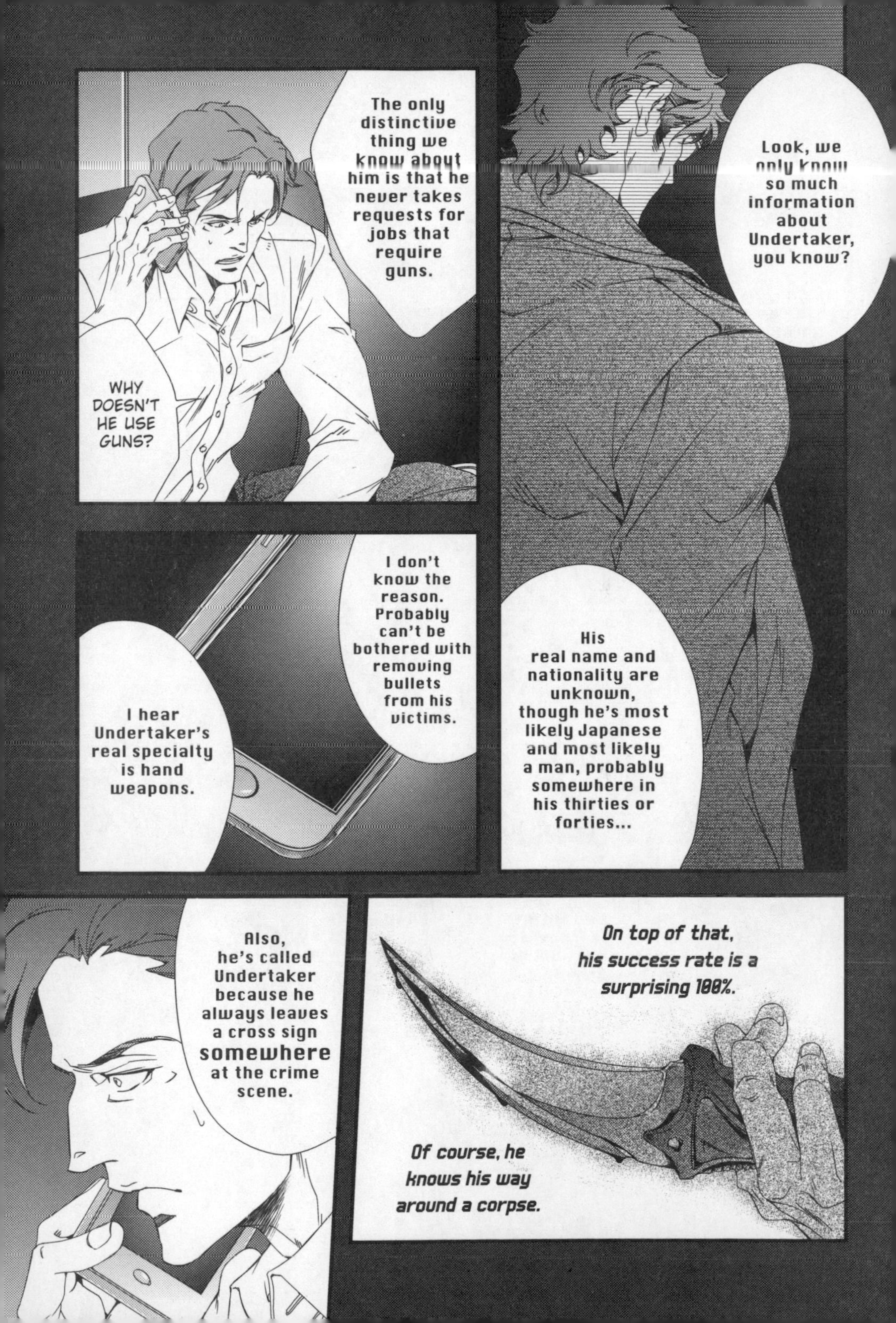
Look, we only know so much information about Undertaker, you know?
His real name and nationality are unknown, though he's most likely Japanese and most likely a man, probably somewhere in his thirties or forties...
The only distinctive thing we know about him is that he never takes requests for jobs that require guns.
WHY DOESN'T HE USE GUNS?
I don't know the reason. Probably can't be bothered with removing bullets from his victims.
I hear Undertaker's real specialty is hand weapons.
On top of that, his success rate is a surprising 100%.
Of course, he knows his way around a corpse.
Also, he's called Undertaker because he always leaves a cross sign somewhere at the crime scene.

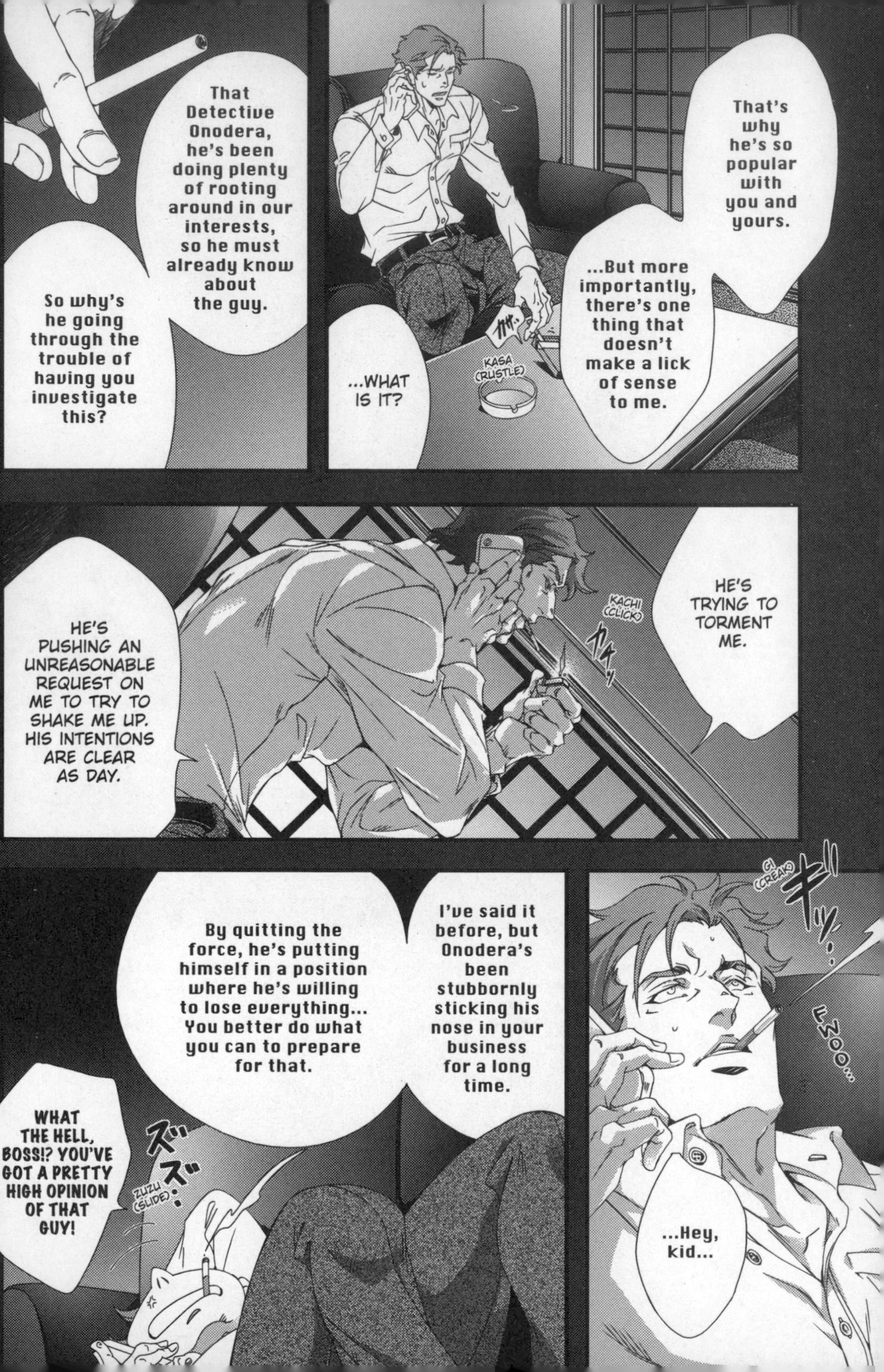
That's why he's so popular with you and yours.
...But more importantly, there's one thing that doesn't make a lick of sense to me.
KASA (RUSTLE)
...WHAT IS IT?
That Detective Onodera, he's been doing plenty of rooting around in our interests, so he must already know about the guy.
So why's he going through the trouble of having you investigate this?
HE'S TRYING TO TORMENT ME.
KACHI (CLICK)
HE'S PUSHING AN UNREASONABLE REQUEST ON ME TO TRY TO SHAKE ME UP. HIS INTENTIONS ARE CLEAR AS DAY.
GI (CREAK)
FWOO...
...Hey, kid...
I've said it before, but Onodera's been stubbornly sticking his nose in your business for a long time.
By quitting the force, he's putting himself in a position where he's willing to lose everything... You better do what you can to prepare for that.
WHAT THE HELL, BOSS!? YOU'VE GOT A PRETTY HIGH OPINION OF THAT GUY!
ZUZU (SLIDE)

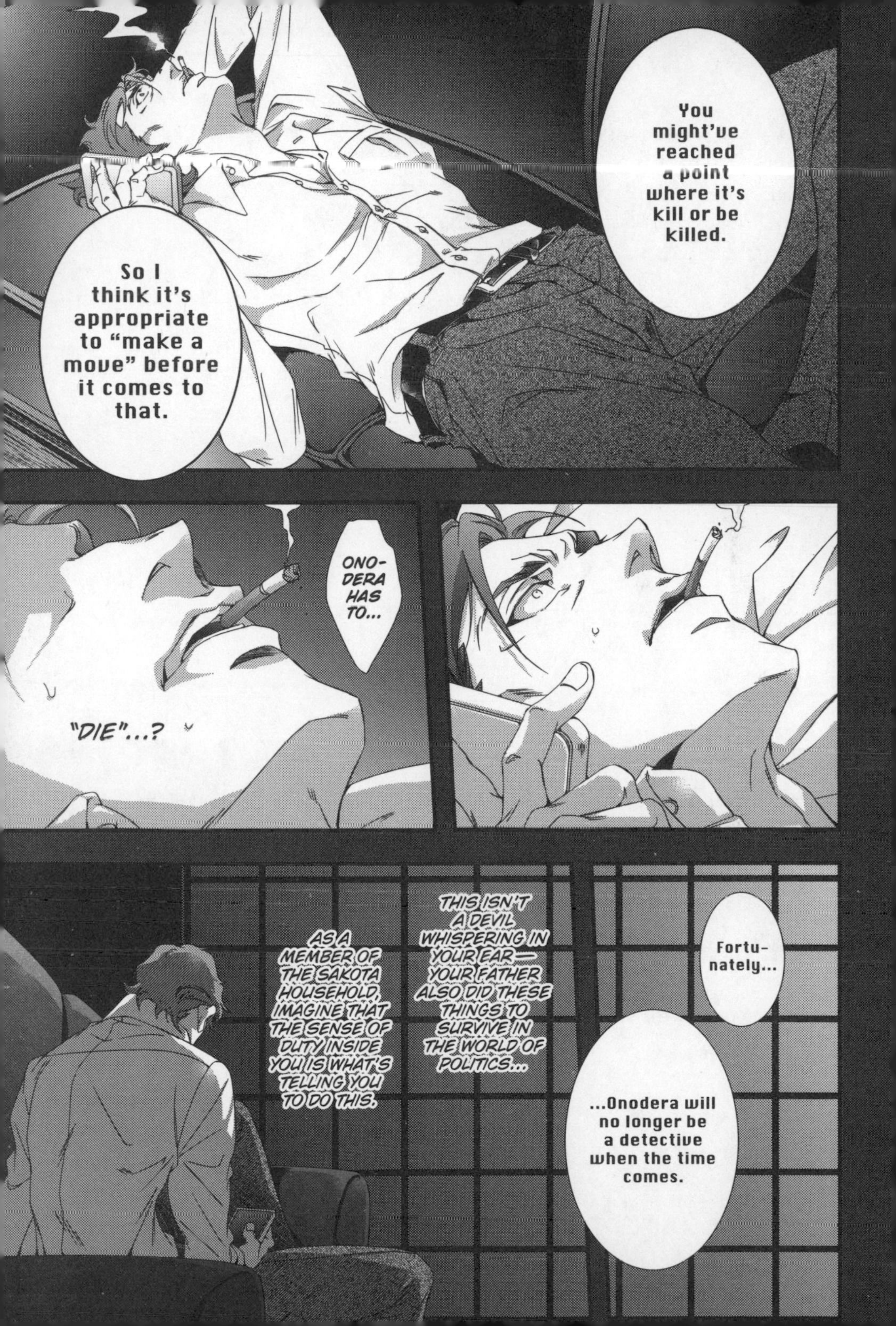
You might've reached a point where it's kill or be killed.
So I think it's appropriate to "make a move" before it comes to that.
ONODERA HAS TO...
"DIE"...?
Fortunately...
...Onodera will no longer be a detective when the time comes.
THIS ISN'T A DEVIL WHISPERING IN YOUR EAR—YOUR FATHER ALSO DID THESE THINGS TO SURVIVE IN THE WORLD OF POLITICS...
AS A MEMBER OF THE SAKOTA HOUSEHOLD, IMAGINE THAT THE SENSE OF DUTY INSIDE YOU IS WHAT'S TELLING YOU TO DO THIS.

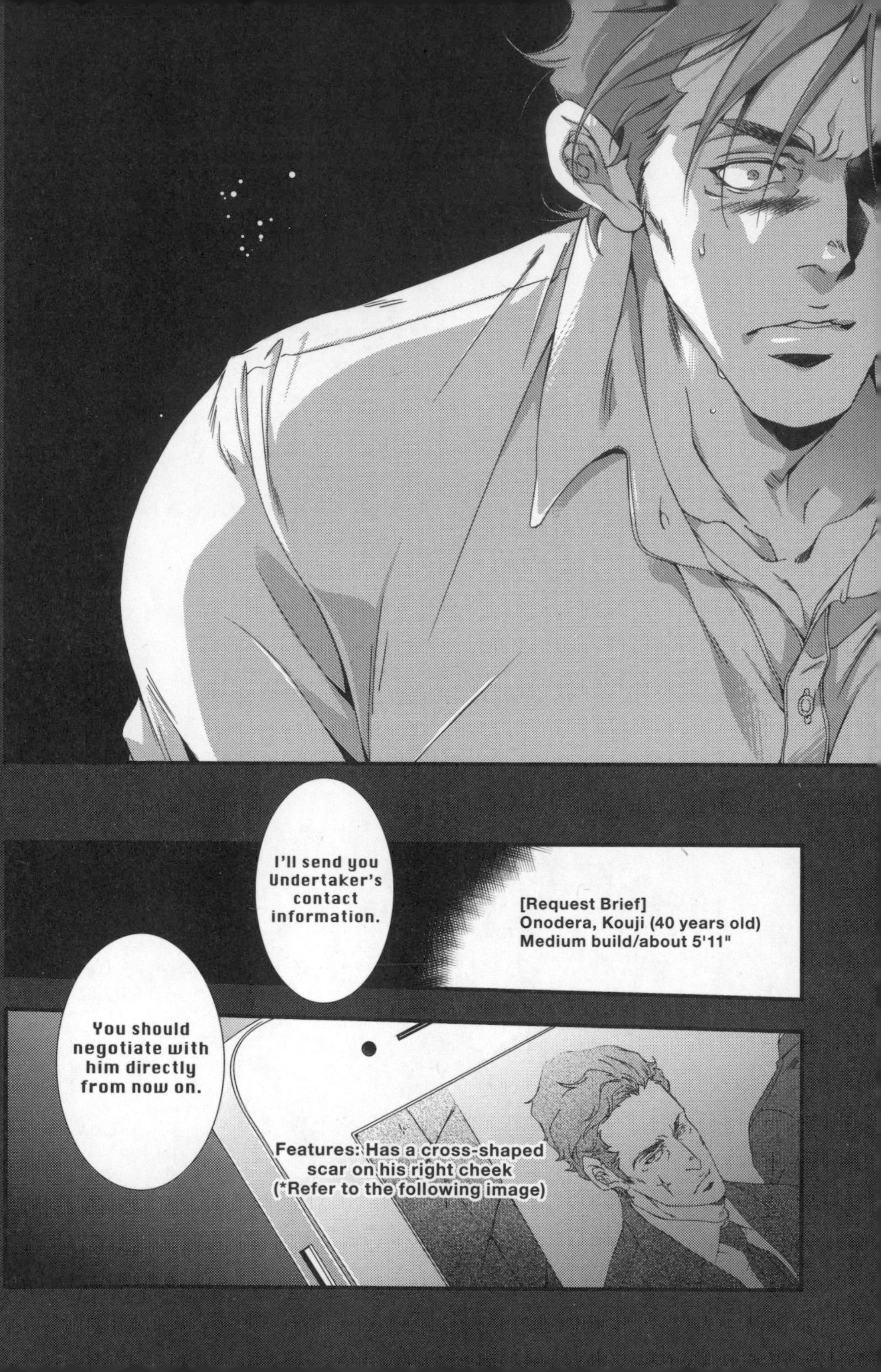
I'll send you Undertaker's contact information.
[Request Brief]
Onodera, Kouji (40 years old)
Medium build/about 5'11"
You should negotiate with him directly from now on.
Features: Has a cross-shaped scar on his right cheek
(*Refer to the following image)

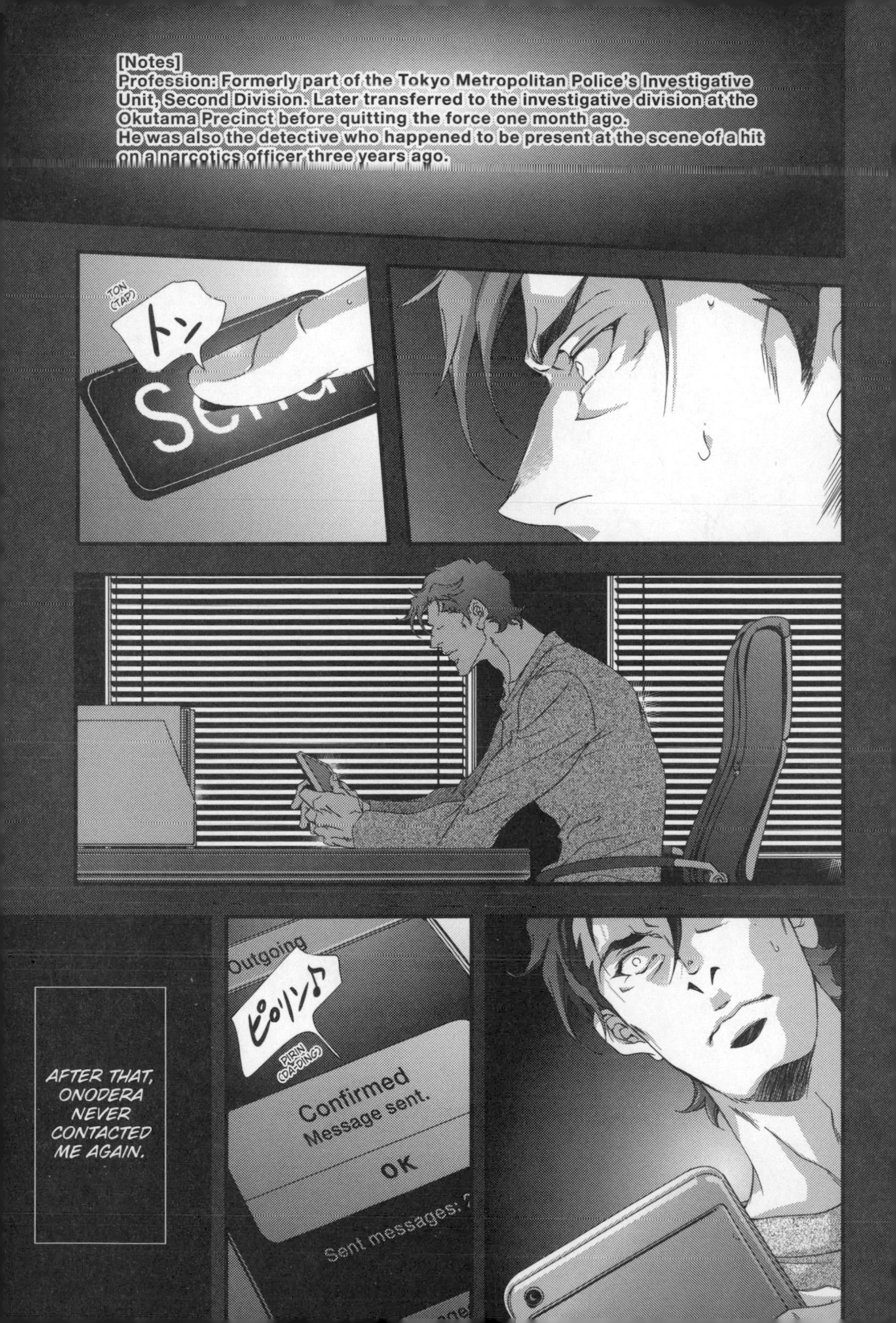
[Notes]
Profession: Formerly part of the Tokyo Metropolitan Police's Investigative Unit, Second Division. Later transferred to the investigative division at the Okutama Precinct before quitting the force one month ago.
He was also the detective who happened to be present at the scene of a hit on a narcotics officer three years ago.
トン
TON (TAP)
Outgoing
ピロリン♪
PIRIN (DA-DING)
Confirmed
Message sent.
OK
Sent messages:
AFTER THAT, ONODERA NEVER CONTACTED ME AGAIN.

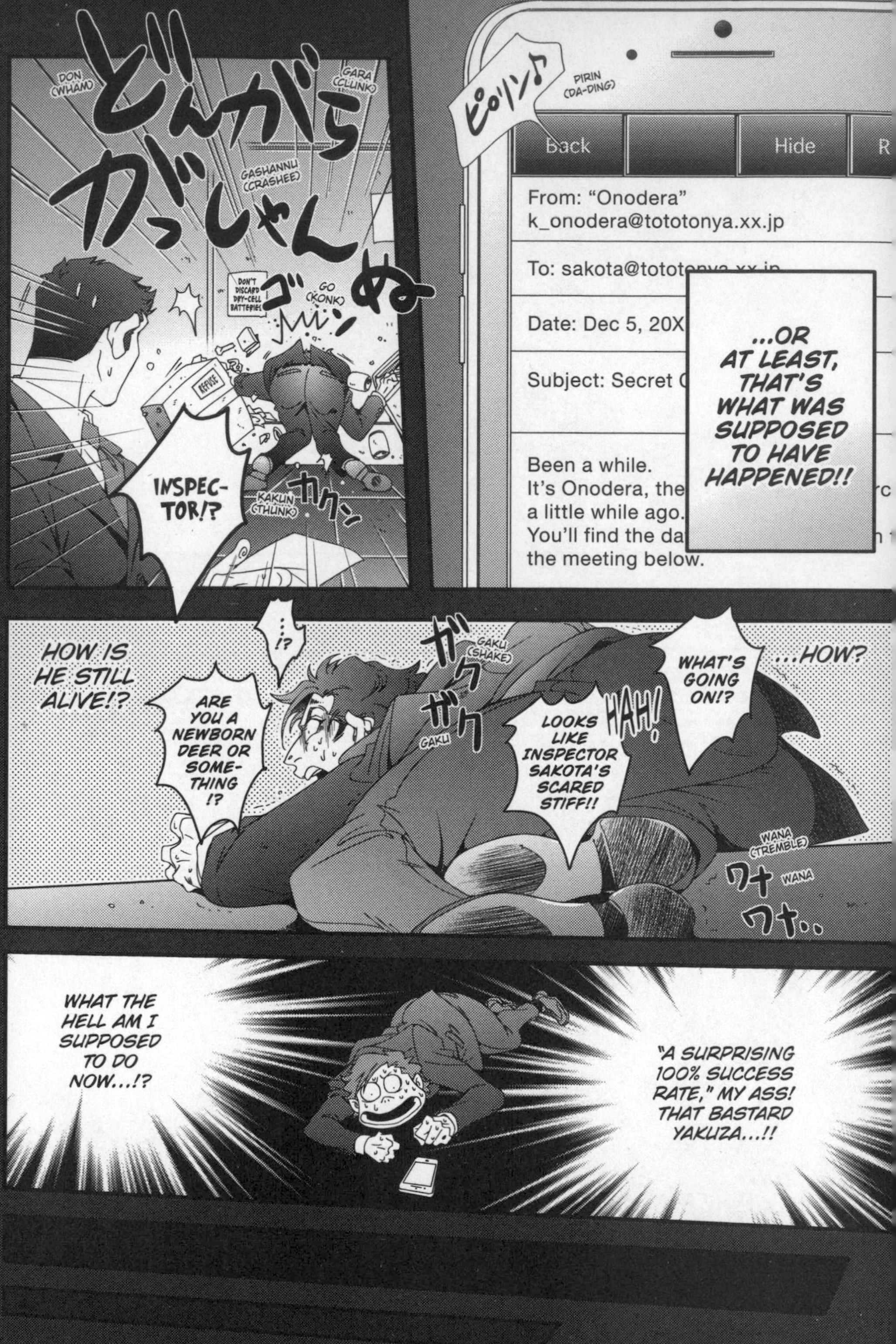
ピロリン♪
PIRIN (DA-DING)
Back
Hide
From: "Onodera"
k_onodera@tototonya.xx.jp
To: sakota@tototo
Date: Dec 5, 20X
Subject: Secret
Been a while.
It's Onodera, the
a little while ago.
You'll find the da
the meeting below.
...OR AT LEAST, THAT'S WHAT WAS SUPPOSED TO HAVE HAPPENED!!
DON (WHAM)
GARA (CLUNK)
GASHANNU (CRASHEE)
DON'T DISCARD DRY-CELL BATTERIES
GO (KONK)
REFUSE
INSPECTOR!?
KAKUN (THUNK)
...HOW?
WHAT'S GOING ON!?
LOOKS LIKE INSPECTOR SAKOTA'S SCARED STIFF!!
HAH!
WANA (TREMBLE)
WANA
GAKU (SHAKE)
GAKU
ARE YOU A NEWBORN DEER OR SOMETHING!?
...!?
HOW IS HE STILL ALIVE!?
"A SURPRISING 100% SUCCESS RATE," MY ASS! THAT BASTARD YAKUZA...!!
WHAT THE HELL AM I SUPPOSED TO DO NOW...!?

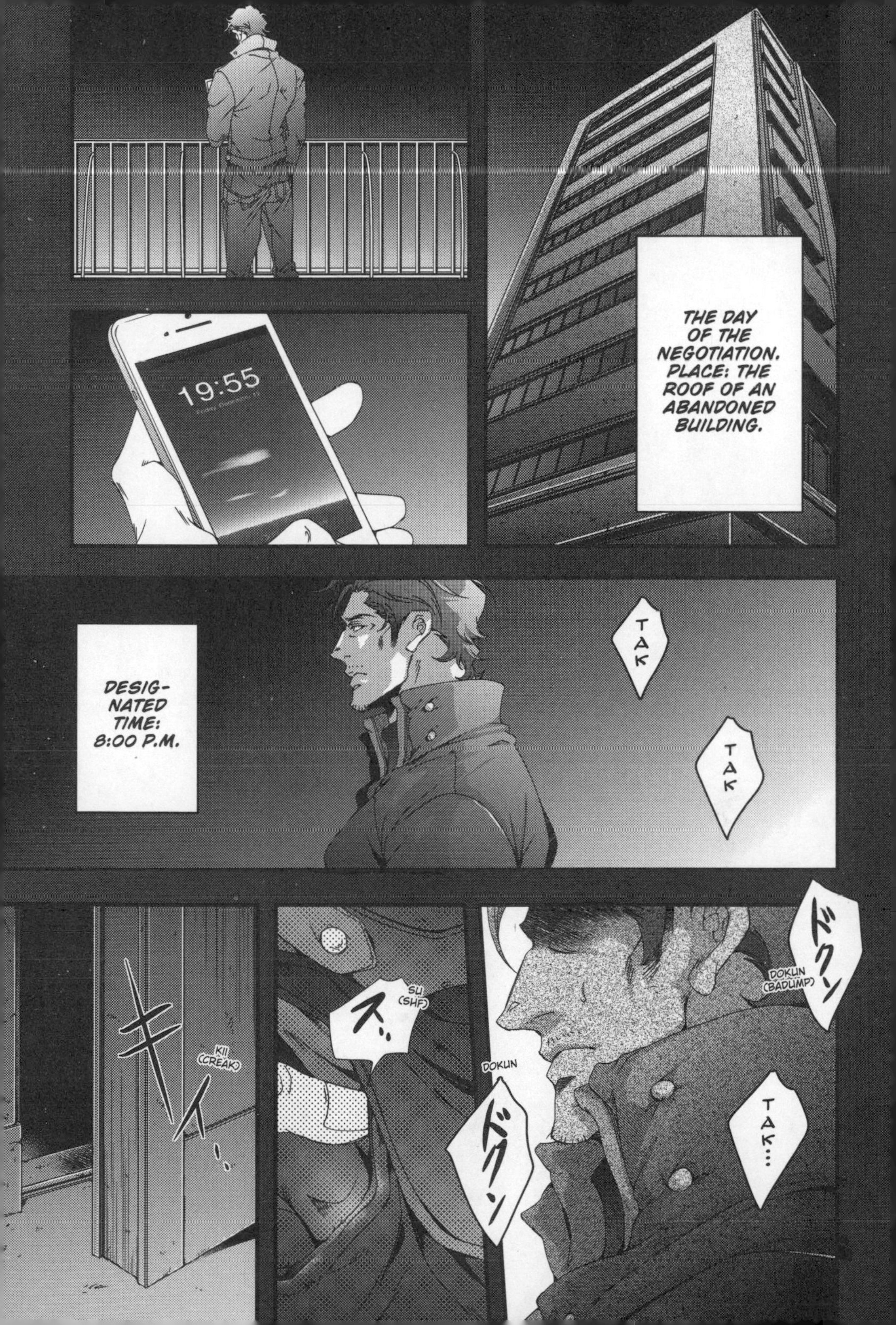

THE DAY OF THE NEGOTIATION. PLACE: THE ROOF OF AN ABANDONED BUILDING.
19:55
TAK
TAK
DESIGNATED TIME: 8:00 P.M.
ドクン
DOKUN (BADUMP)
TAK...
DOKUN
ドクン
ス
SU (SHF)
キイ
KII (CREAK)

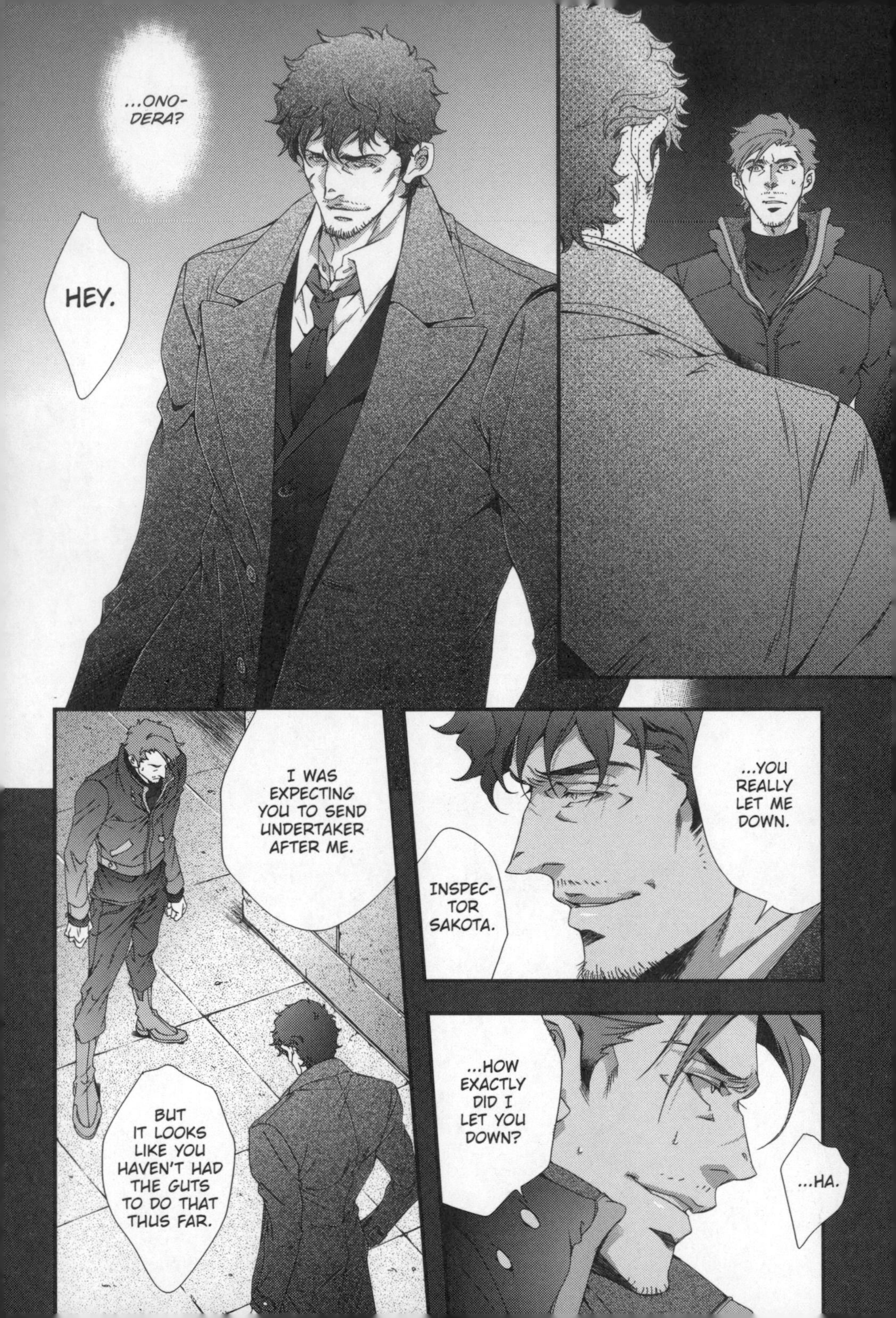
...ONO-
DERA?
HEY.
...YOU REALLY LET ME DOWN.
INSPECTOR SAKOTA.
...HA.
...HOW EXACTLY DID I LET YOU DOWN?
I WAS EXPECTING YOU TO SEND UNDERTAKER AFTER ME.
BUT IT LOOKS LIKE YOU HAVEN'T HAD THE GUTS TO DO THAT THUS FAR.

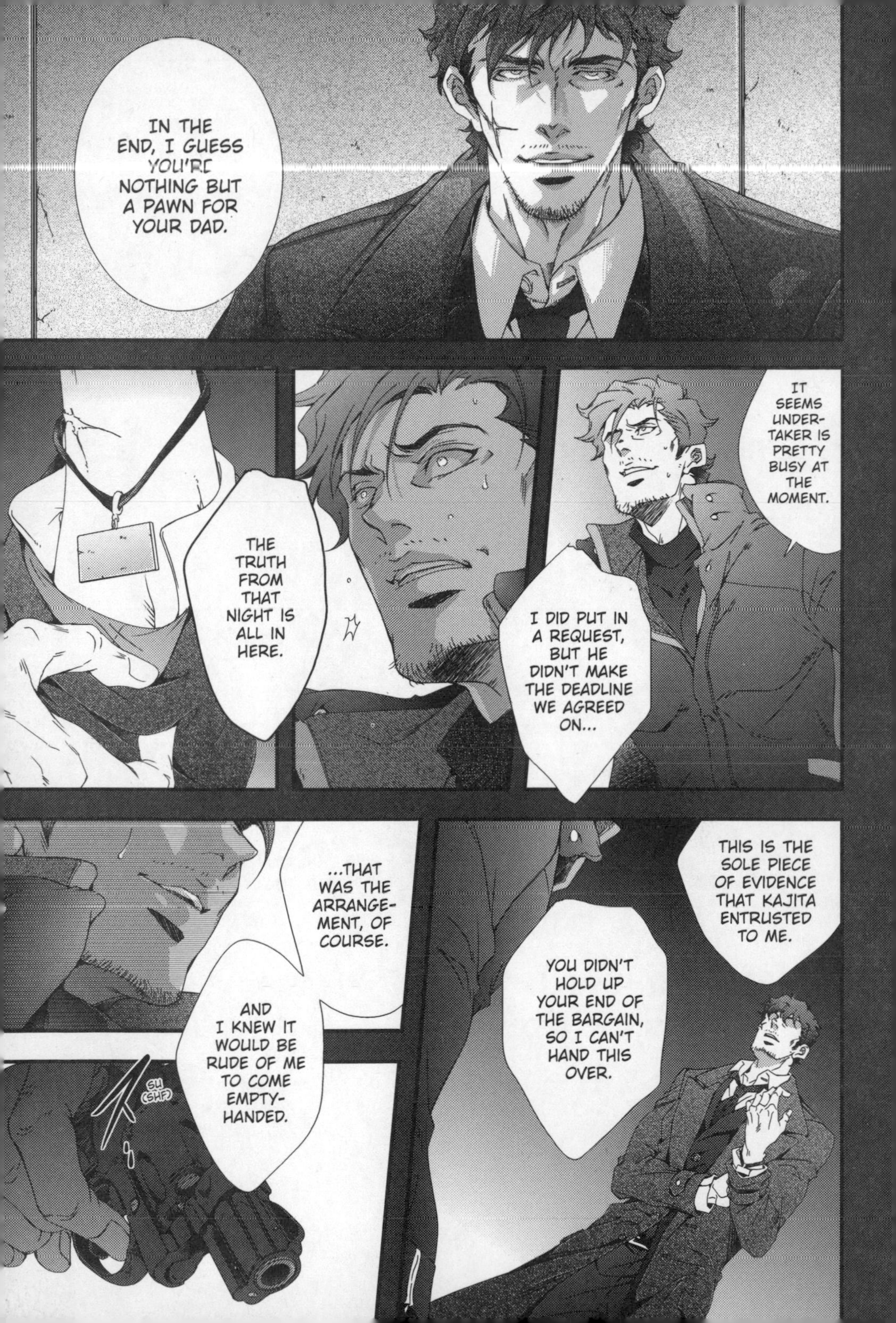
IN THE END, I GUESS YOU'RE NOTHING BUT A PAWN FOR YOUR DAD.
IT SEEMS UNDER-TAKER IS PRETTY BUSY AT THE MOMENT.
I DID PUT IN A REQUEST, BUT HE DIDN'T MAKE THE DEADLINE WE AGREED ON...
THE TRUTH FROM THAT NIGHT IS ALL IN HERE.
THIS IS THE SOLE PIECE OF EVIDENCE THAT KAJITA ENTRUSTED TO ME.
YOU DIDN'T HOLD UP YOUR END OF THE BARGAIN, SO I CAN'T HAND THIS OVER.
...THAT WAS THE ARRANGE-MENT, OF COURSE.
AND I KNEW IT WOULD BE RUDE OF ME TO COME EMPTY-HANDED.
SU (SHF)

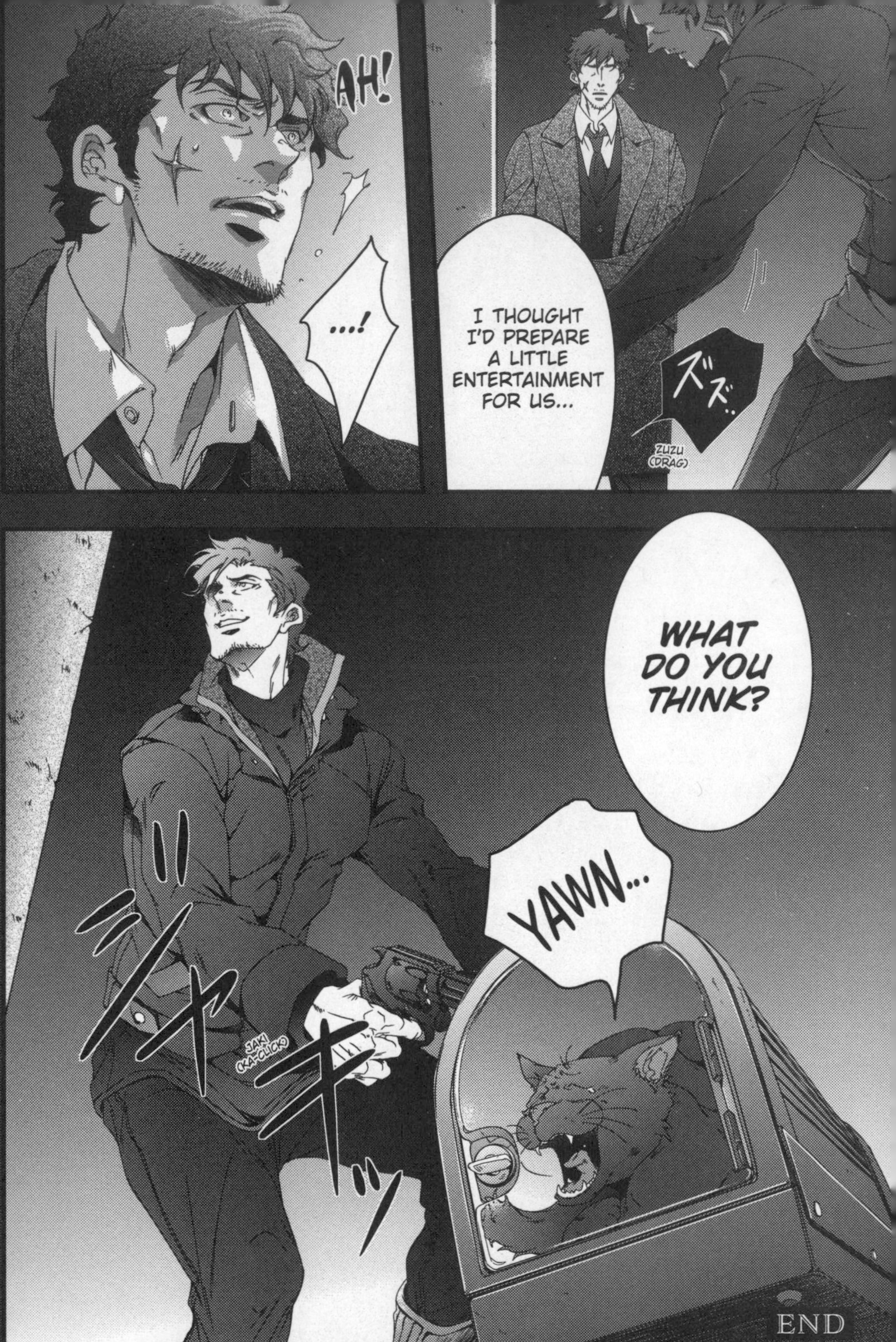
I THOUGHT I'D PREPARE A LITTLE ENTERTAINMENT FOR US...
ズズ..
ZUZU (DRAG)
AH!
...!
WHAT DO YOU THINK?
YAWN...
ジャキ
JAKI (KA-CLICK)

END

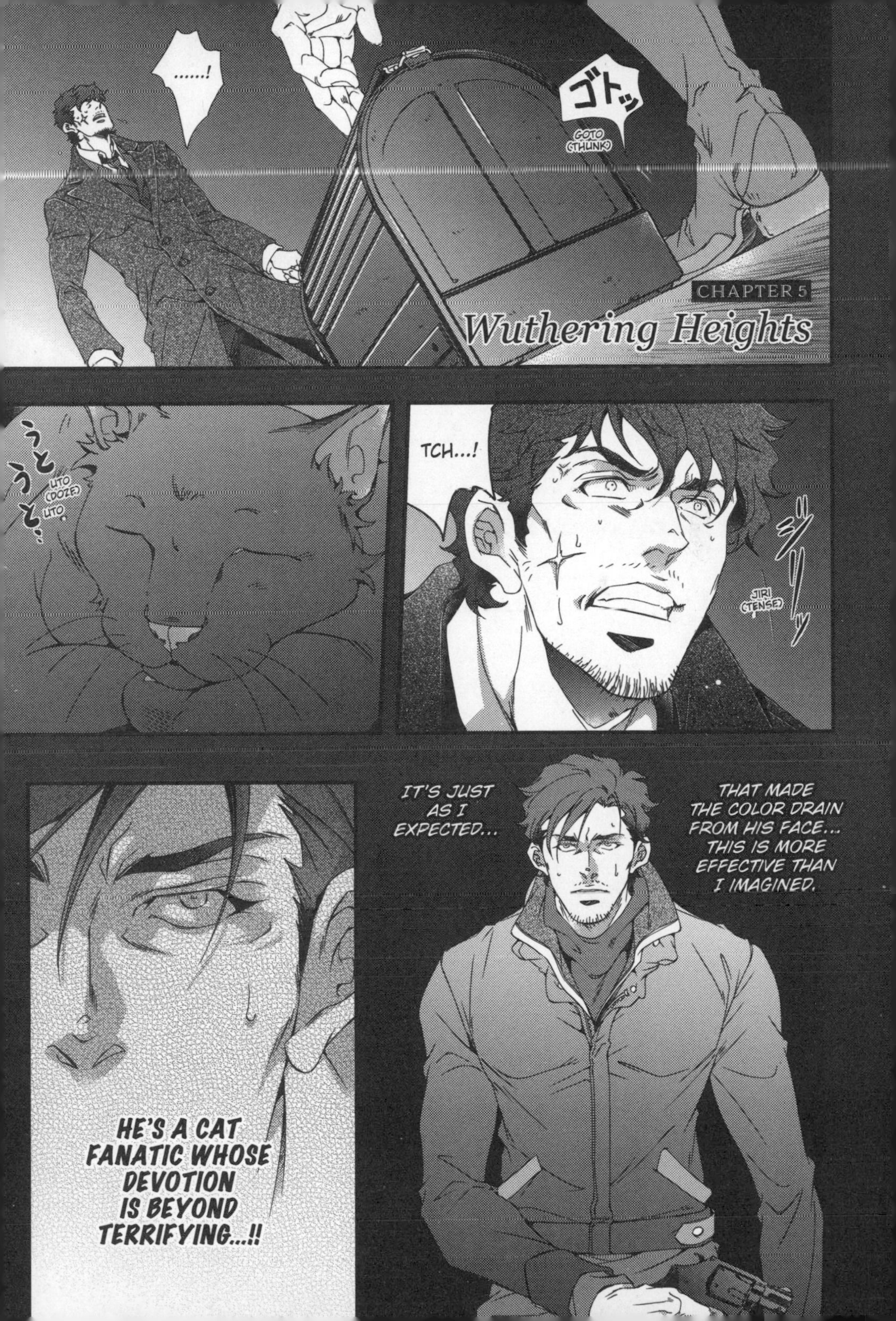
ゴトッ
GOTO (THUNK)
......!
CHAPTER 5
Wuthering Heights
TCH...!
ジリッ
JIRI (TENSE)
うとうと
UTO (DOZE) UTO
IT'S JUST AS I EXPECTED...
THAT MADE THE COLOR DRAIN FROM HIS FACE... THIS IS MORE EFFECTIVE THAN I IMAGINED.
HE'S A CAT FANATIC WHOSE DEVOTION IS BEYOND TERRIFYING...!!

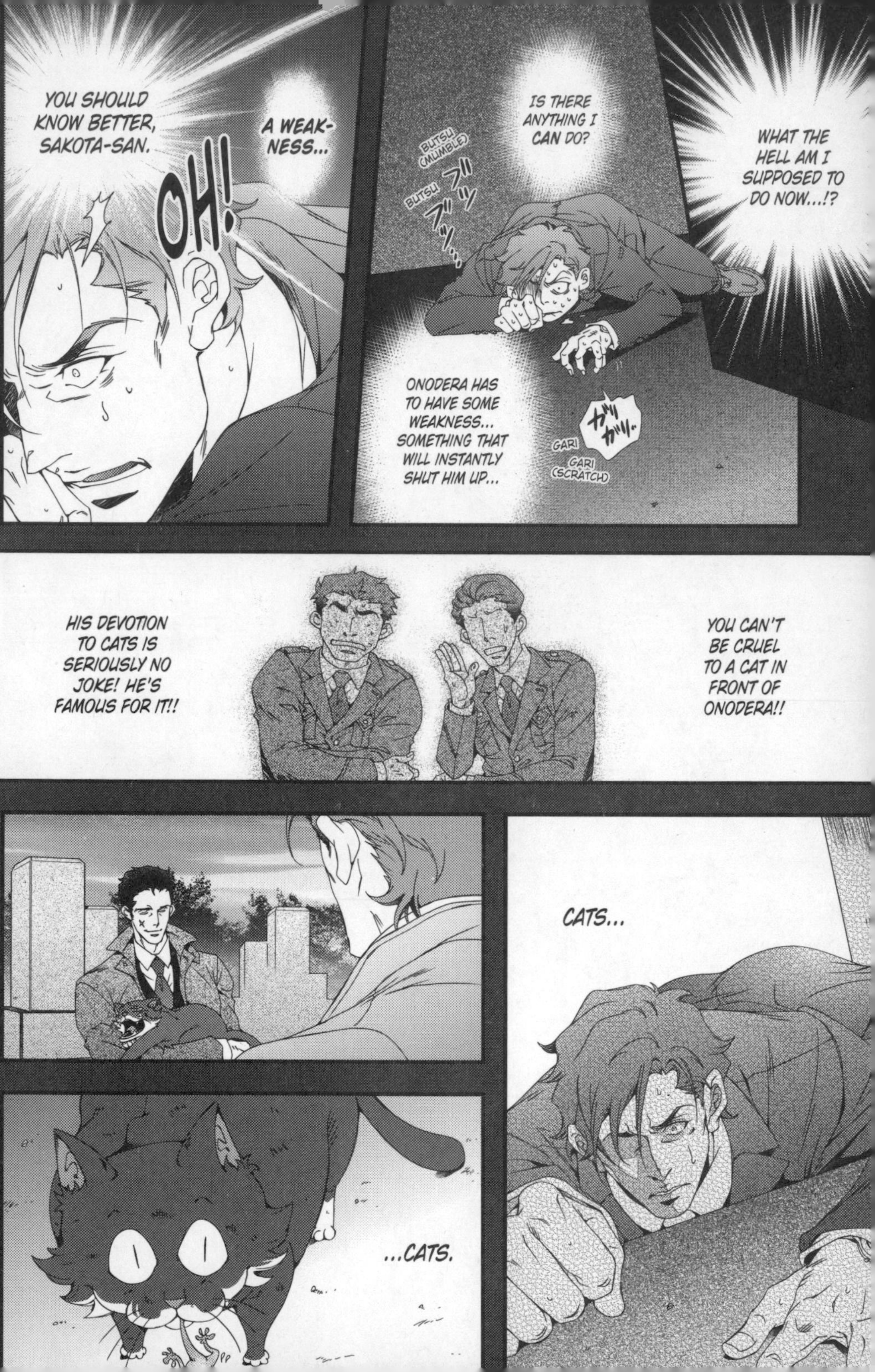
WHAT THE HELL AM I SUPPOSED TO DO NOW...!?
IS THERE ANYTHING I CAN DO?
BUTSU (MUMBLE) BUTSU
ONODERA HAS TO HAVE SOME WEAKNESS... SOMETHING THAT WILL INSTANTLY SHUT HIM UP...
GARI GARI (SCRATCH)
A WEAK-NESS...
OH!
YOU SHOULD KNOW BETTER, SAKOTA-SAN.
YOU CAN'T BE CRUEL TO A CAT IN FRONT OF ONODERA!!
HIS DEVOTION TO CATS IS SERIOUSLY NO JOKE! HE'S FAMOUS FOR IT!!
CATS...
...CATS.

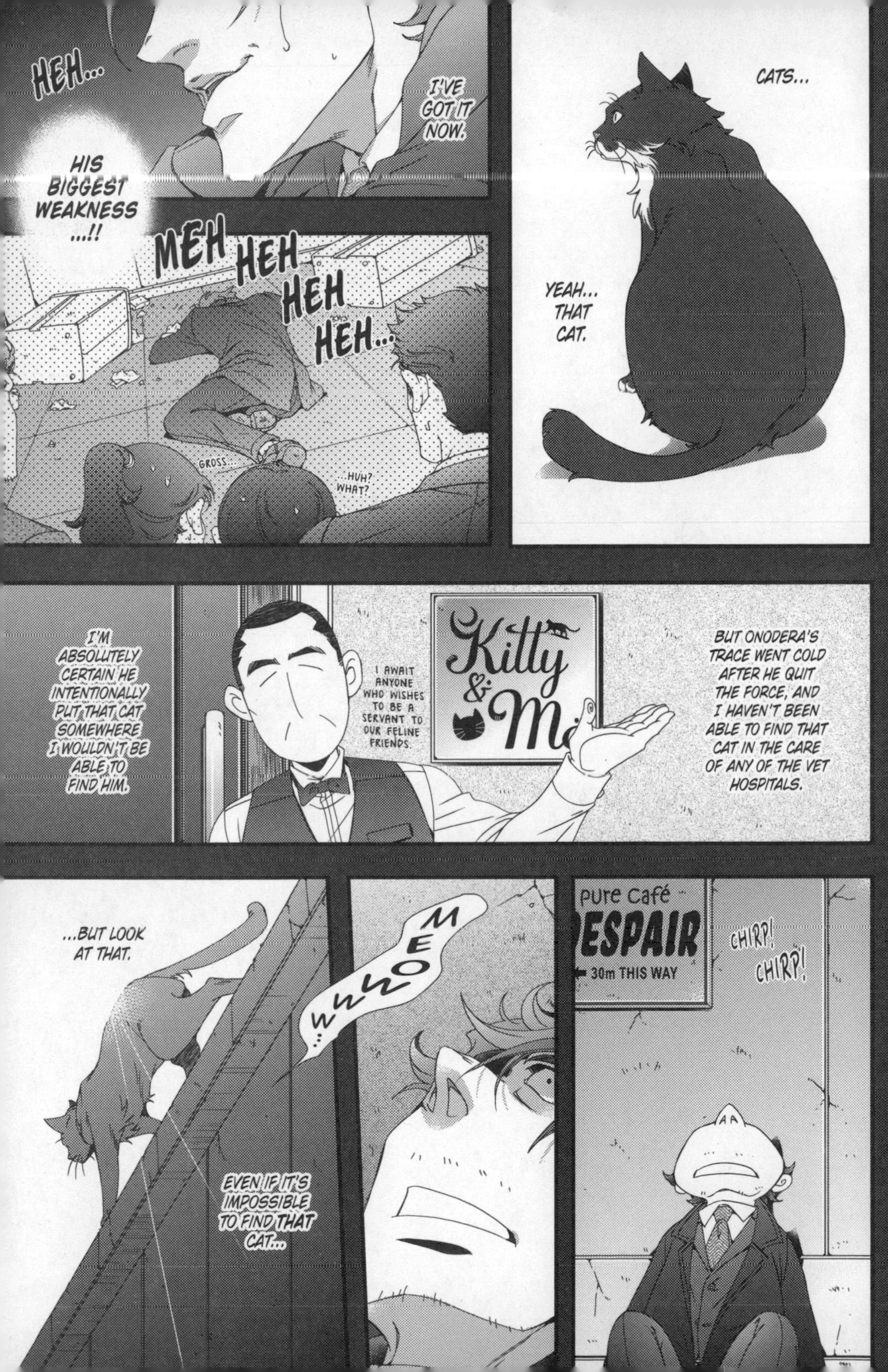
CATS...
YEAH... THAT CAT.
I'VE GOT IT NOW.
HEH...
HIS BIGGEST WEAKNESS ...!!
MEH HEH HEH HEH...
...HUH? WHAT?
GROSS...
BUT ONODERA'S TRACE WENT COLD AFTER HE QUIT THE FORCE, AND I HAVEN'T BEEN ABLE TO FIND THAT CAT IN THE CARE OF ANY OF THE VET HOSPITALS.
Kitty & M
I AWAIT ANYONE WHO WISHES TO BE A SERVANT TO OUR FELINE FRIENDS.
I'M ABSOLUTELY CERTAIN HE INTENTIONALLY PUT THAT CAT SOMEWHERE I WOULDN'T BE ABLE TO FIND HIM.
pure Café
ESPAIR
← 30m THIS WAY
CHIRP! CHIRP!
MEOWWW...
EVEN IF IT'S IMPOSSIBLE TO FIND THAT CAT...
...BUT LOOK AT THAT.

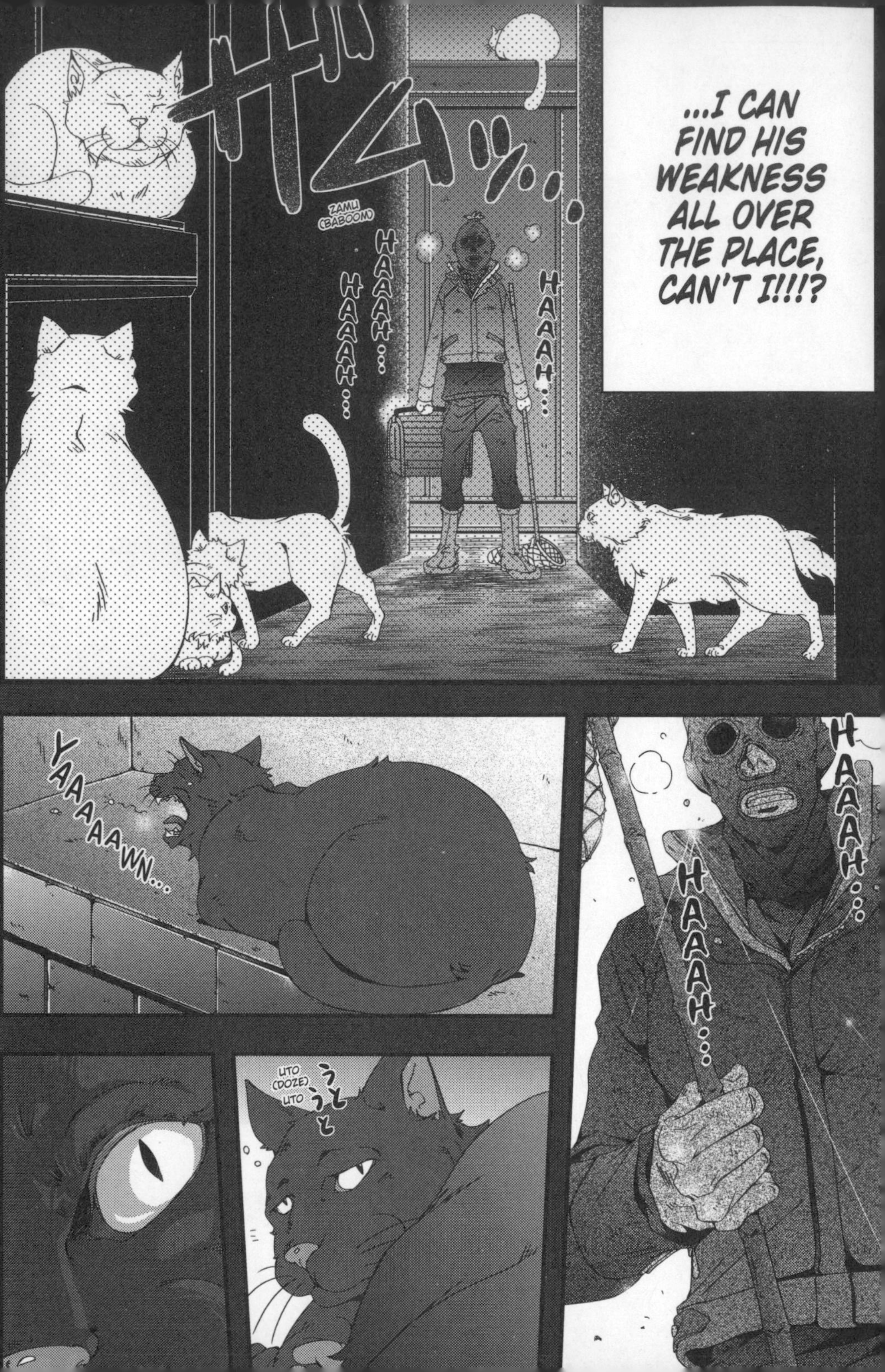

...I CAN FIND HIS WEAKNESS ALL OVER THE PLACE, CAN'T I!!!?
HAAAAH...
HAAAAH... HAAAAH...
ザムッ...
ZAMU (BABOOM)
HAAAAH...
HAAAAH...
YAAAAAAWN...
うと うと
UTO (DOZE) UTO

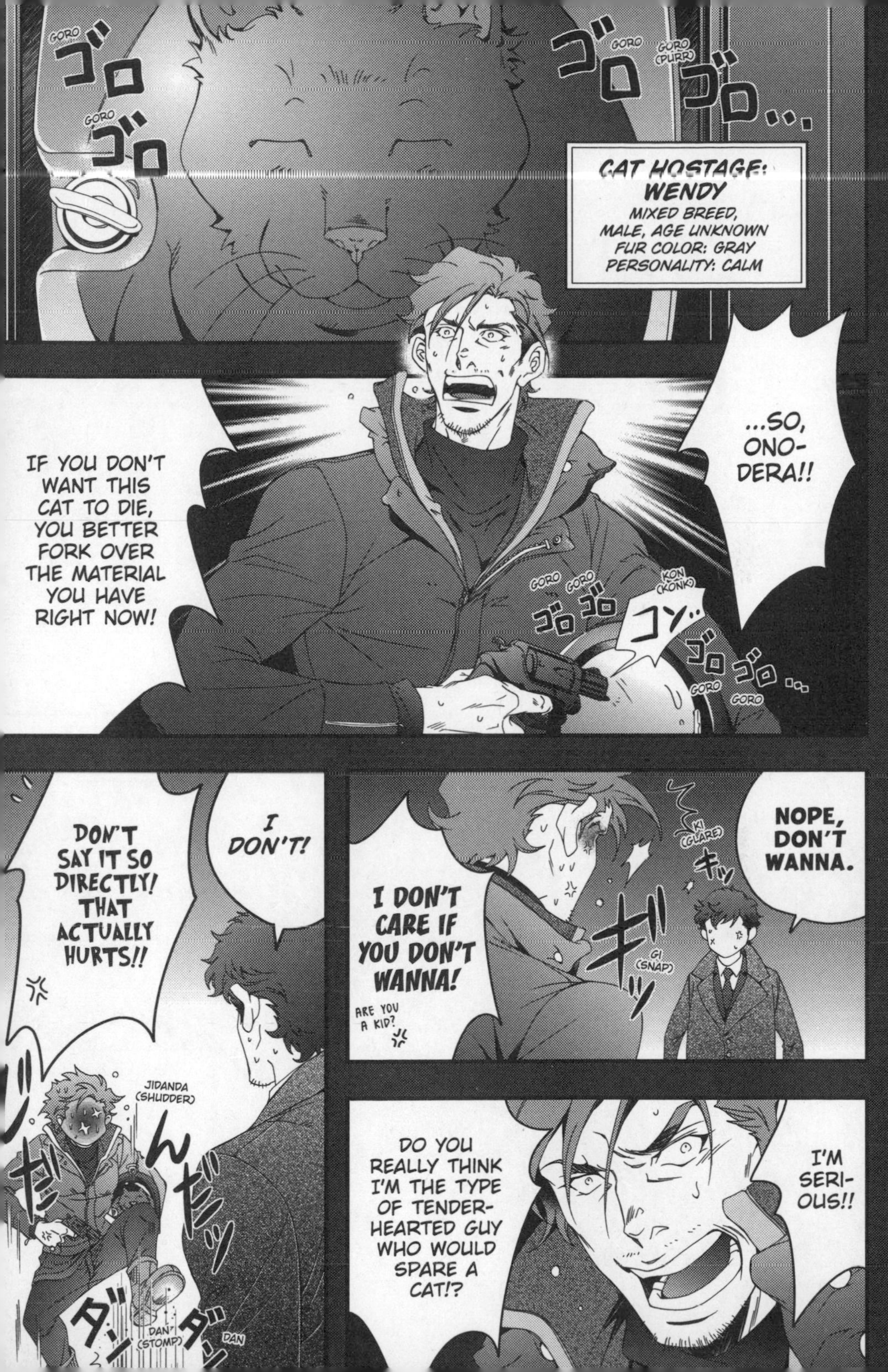
GORO (PURR) ゴロ...
GORO ゴロ
GORO ゴロ
GORO ゴロ
CAT HOSTAGE: WENDY
MIXED BREED, MALE, AGE UNKNOWN
FUR COLOR: GRAY
PERSONALITY: CALM
...SO, ONO-DERA!!
IF YOU DON'T WANT THIS CAT TO DIE, YOU BETTER FORK OVER THE MATERIAL YOU HAVE RIGHT NOW!
KON (KONK) コン
GORO ゴロ GORO ゴロ
GORO ゴロ GORO ゴロ...
NOPE, DON'T WANNA.
KI (GLARE) キッ
GI (SNAP) ギッ
I DON'T CARE IF YOU DON'T WANNA!
ARE YOU A KID?
I'M SERI-OUS!!
DO YOU REALLY THINK I'M THE TYPE OF TENDER-HEARTED GUY WHO WOULD SPARE A CAT!?
I DON'T!
DON'T SAY IT SO DIRECTLY! THAT ACTUALLY HURTS!!
JIDANDA (SHUDDER)
DAN (STOMP) ダン
DAN ダン

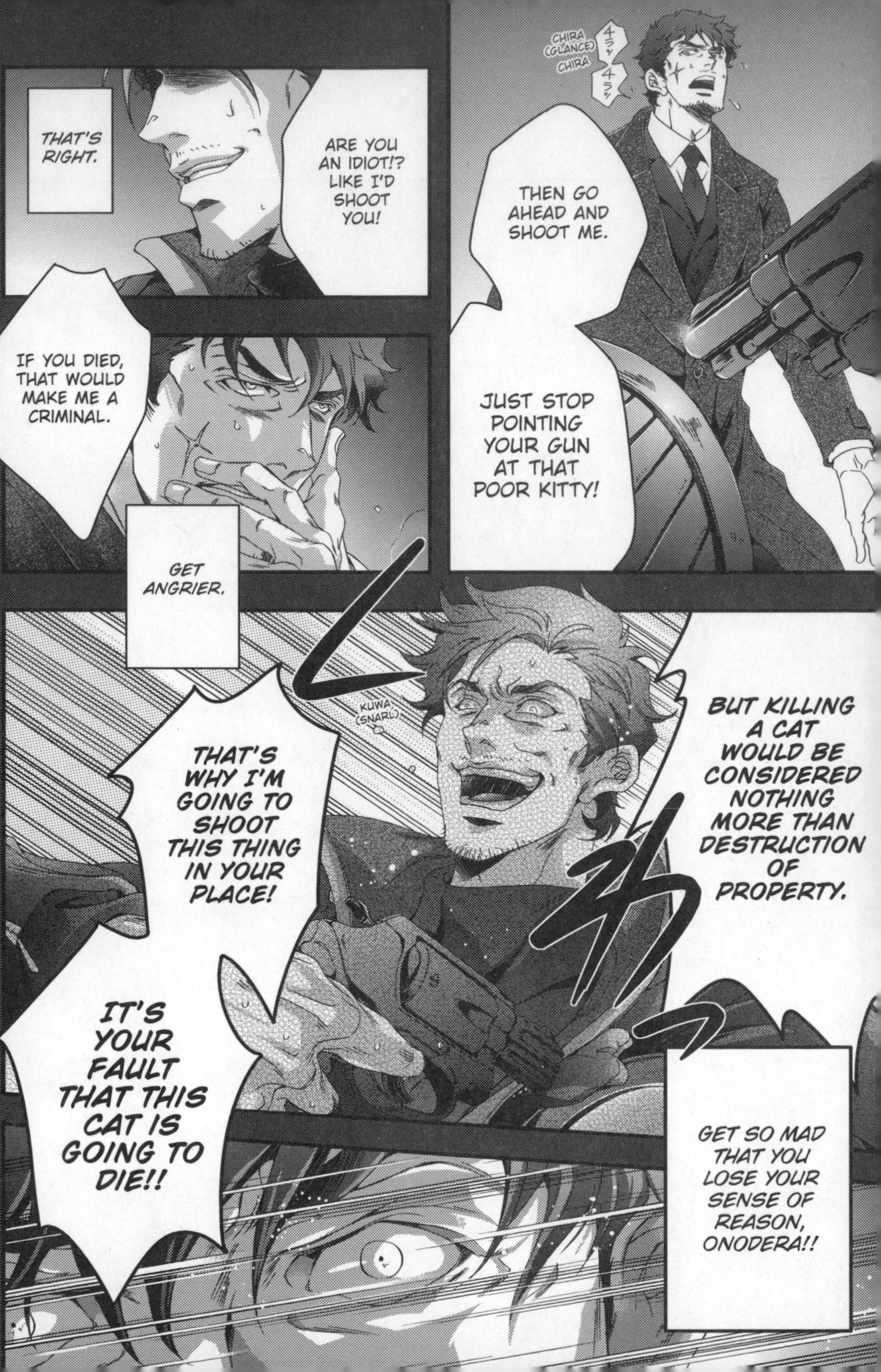
CHIRA (GLANCE) CHIRA
THEN GO AHEAD AND SHOOT ME.
JUST STOP POINTING YOUR GUN AT THAT POOR KITTY!
ARE YOU AN IDIOT!? LIKE I'D SHOOT YOU!
THAT'S RIGHT.
IF YOU DIED, THAT WOULD MAKE ME A CRIMINAL.
GET ANGRIER.
BUT KILLING A CAT WOULD BE CONSIDERED NOTHING MORE THAN DESTRUCTION OF PROPERTY.
KUWA (SNARL)
THAT'S WHY I'M GOING TO SHOOT THIS THING IN YOUR PLACE!
IT'S YOUR FAULT THAT THIS CAT IS GOING TO DIE!!
GET SO MAD THAT YOU LOSE YOUR SENSE OF REASON, ONODERA!!

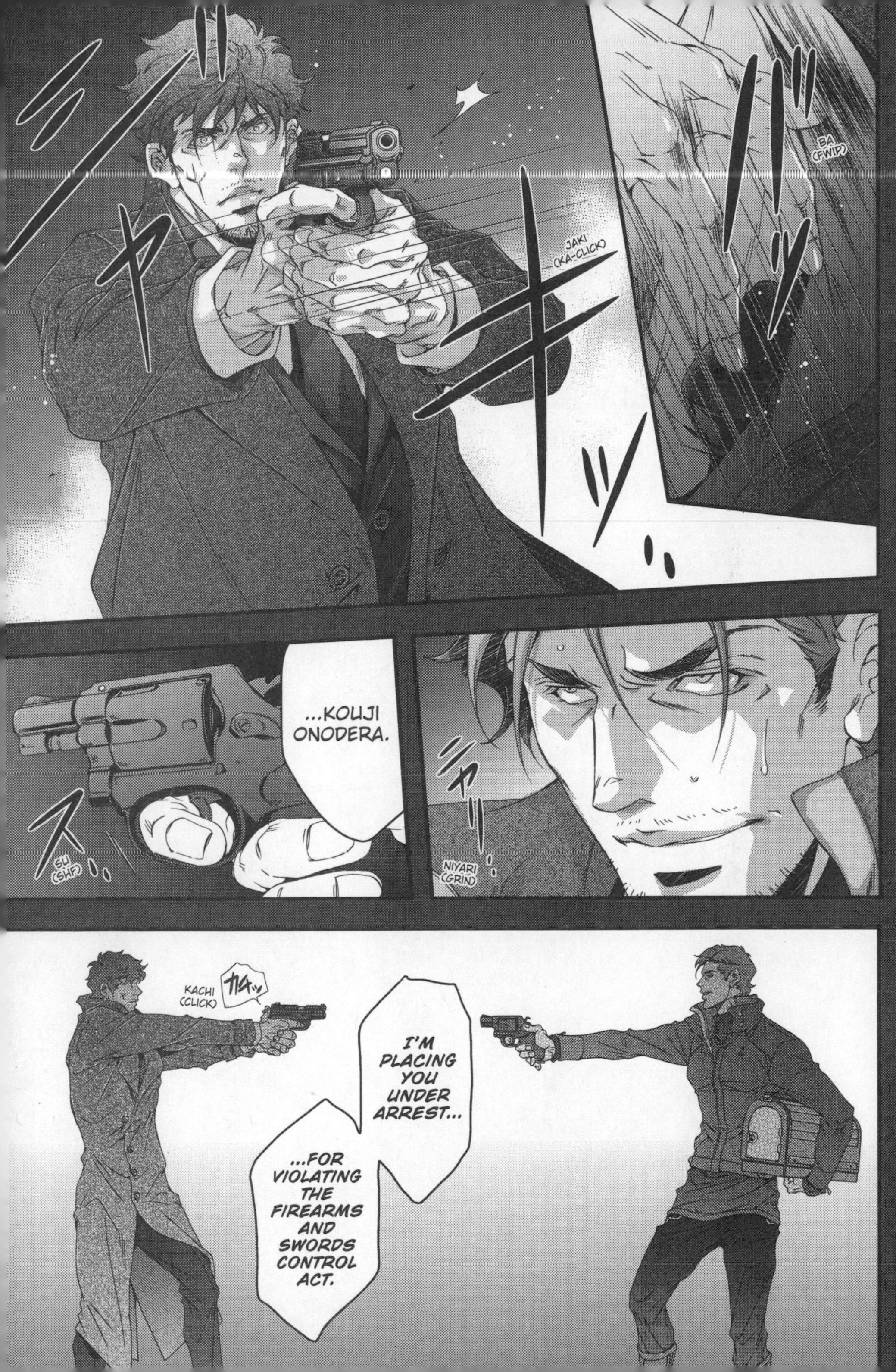
BA (FWIP)
JAKI (KA-CLICK)
NIYARI (GRIN)
...KOUJI ONODERA.
SU (SHF)
I'M PLACING YOU UNDER ARREST...
...FOR VIOLATING THE FIREARMS AND SWORDS CONTROL ACT.
KACHI (CLICK)

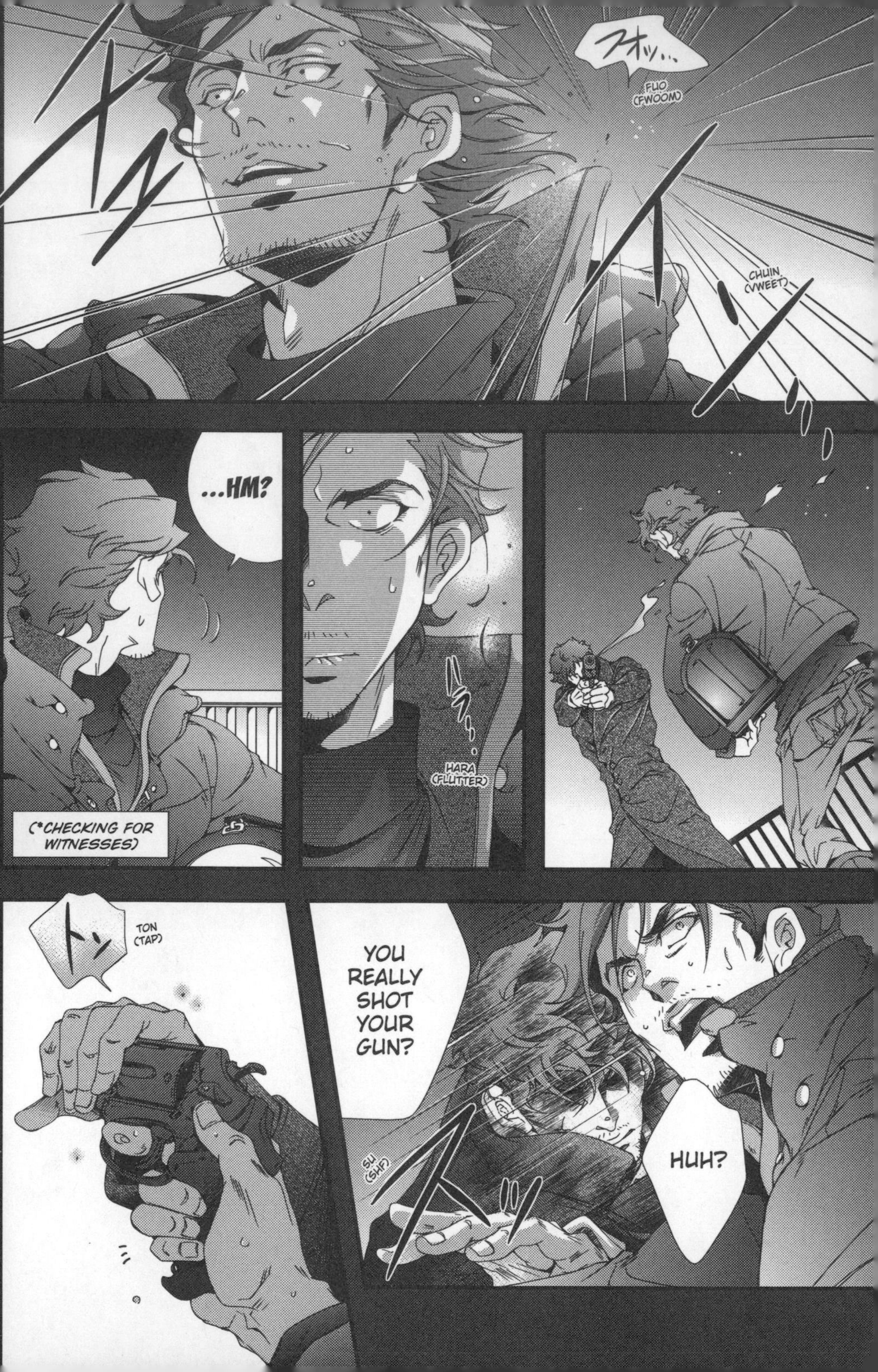
フオッ…
FUO (FWOOM)
CHUIN (VWEET)
HARA (FLUTTER)
...HM?
(*CHECKING FOR WITNESSES)
YOU REALLY SHOT YOUR GUN?
HUH?
SU (SHF)
TON (TAP)

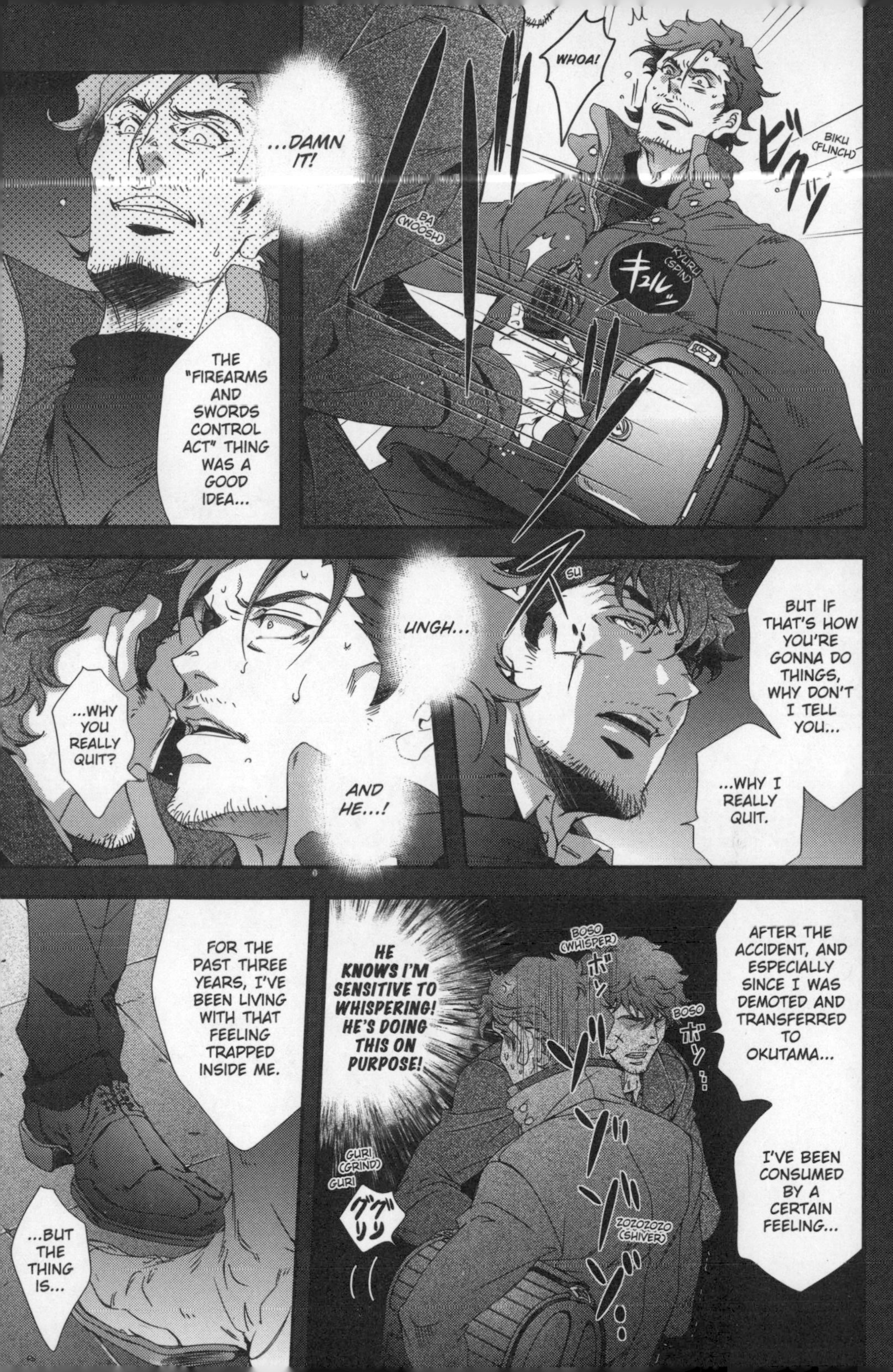
WHOA!
BIKU (FLINCH)
BA (WOOSH)
KYURU (SPIN)
...DAMN IT!
THE "FIREARMS AND SWORDS CONTROL ACT" THING WAS A GOOD IDEA...
SU
BUT IF THAT'S HOW YOU'RE GONNA DO THINGS, WHY DON'T I TELL YOU...
...WHY I REALLY QUIT.
UNGH...
...WHY YOU REALLY QUIT?
AND HE...!
AFTER THE ACCIDENT, AND ESPECIALLY SINCE I WAS DEMOTED AND TRANSFERRED TO OKUTAMA...
BOSO (WHISPER)
BOSO
HE KNOWS I'M SENSITIVE TO WHISPERING! HE'S DOING THIS ON PURPOSE!
I'VE BEEN CONSUMED BY A CERTAIN FEELING...
ZOZOZOZO (SHIVER)
GURI (GRIND) GURI
FOR THE PAST THREE YEARS, I'VE BEEN LIVING WITH THAT FEELING TRAPPED INSIDE ME.
...BUT THE THING IS...

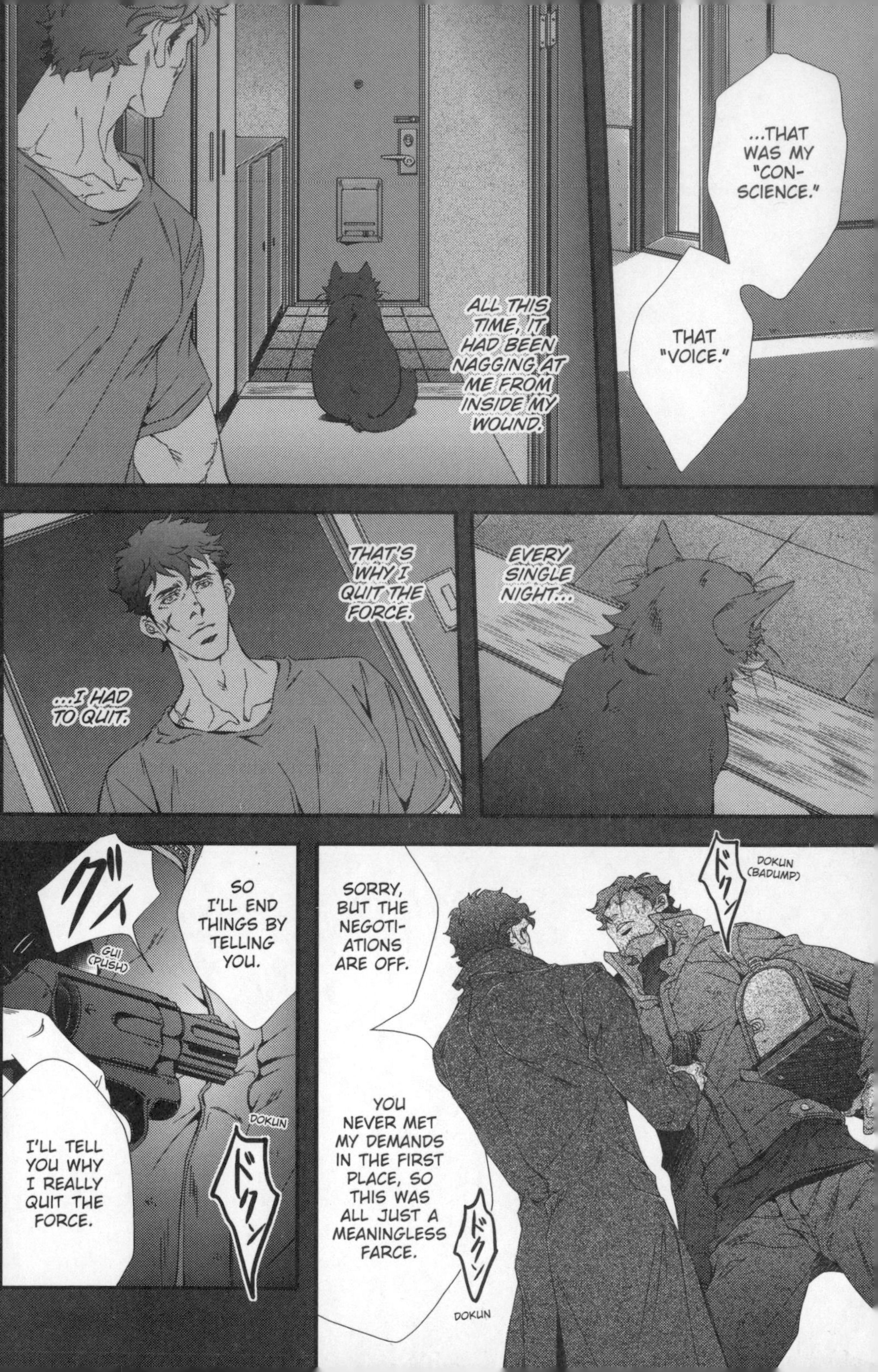
...THAT WAS MY "CON-SCIENCE."
THAT "VOICE."
ALL THIS TIME, IT HAD BEEN NAGGING AT ME FROM INSIDE MY WOUND.
EVERY SINGLE NIGHT...
THAT'S WHY I QUIT THE FORCE.
...I HAD TO QUIT.
ドクン
DOKUN (BADUMP)
SORRY, BUT THE NEGOTI-ATIONS ARE OFF.
YOU NEVER MET MY DEMANDS IN THE FIRST PLACE, SO THIS WAS ALL JUST A MEANINGLESS FARCE.
ドクン
DOKUN
グイ
GUI (PUSH)
SO I'LL END THINGS BY TELLING YOU.
I'LL TELL YOU WHY I REALLY QUIT THE FORCE.
ドクン
DOKUN

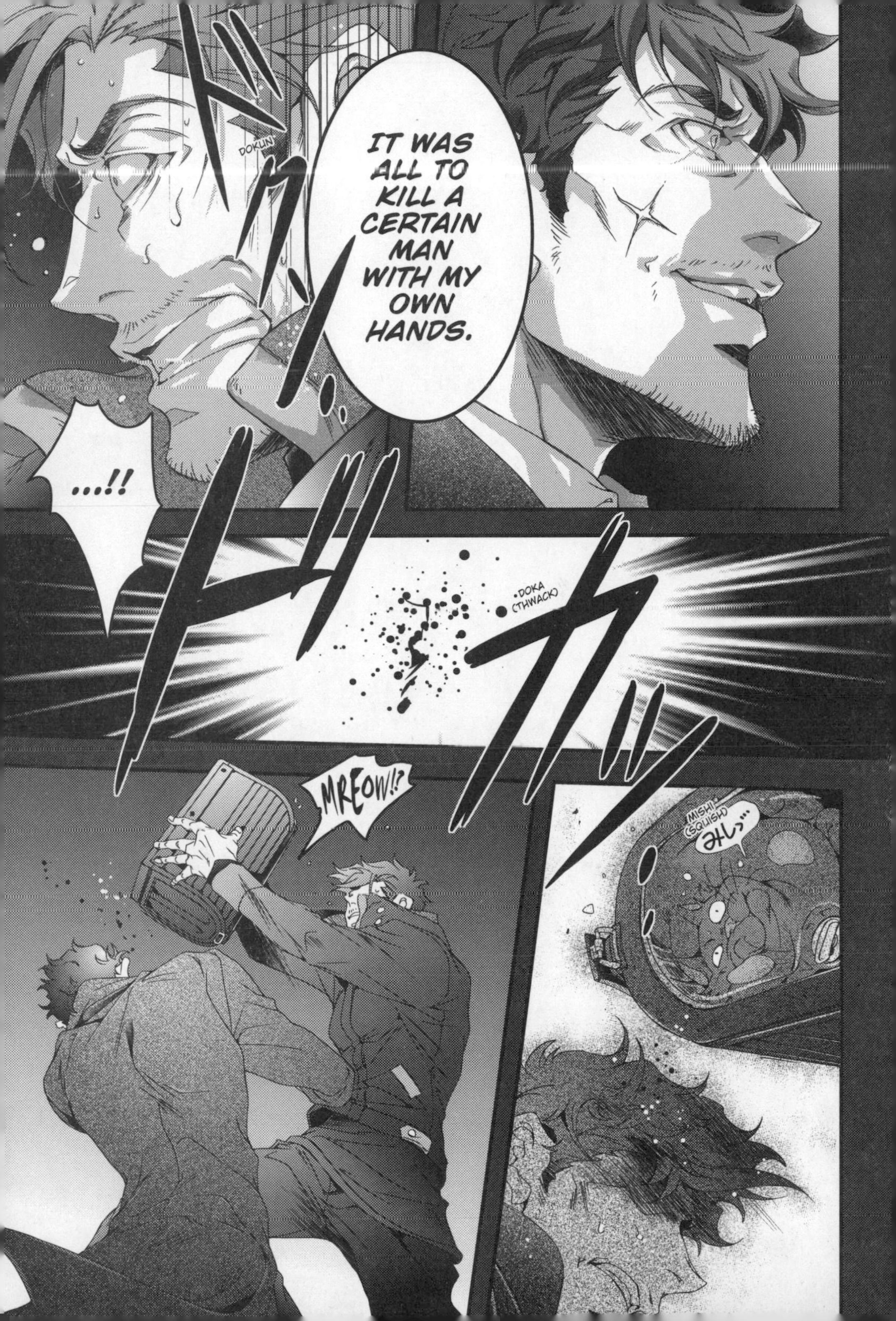
IT WAS ALL TO KILL A CERTAIN MAN WITH MY OWN HANDS.
DOKUN
...!!
DOKA (THWACK)
MISHI (SQUISH)
みしっ…
MREOW!?

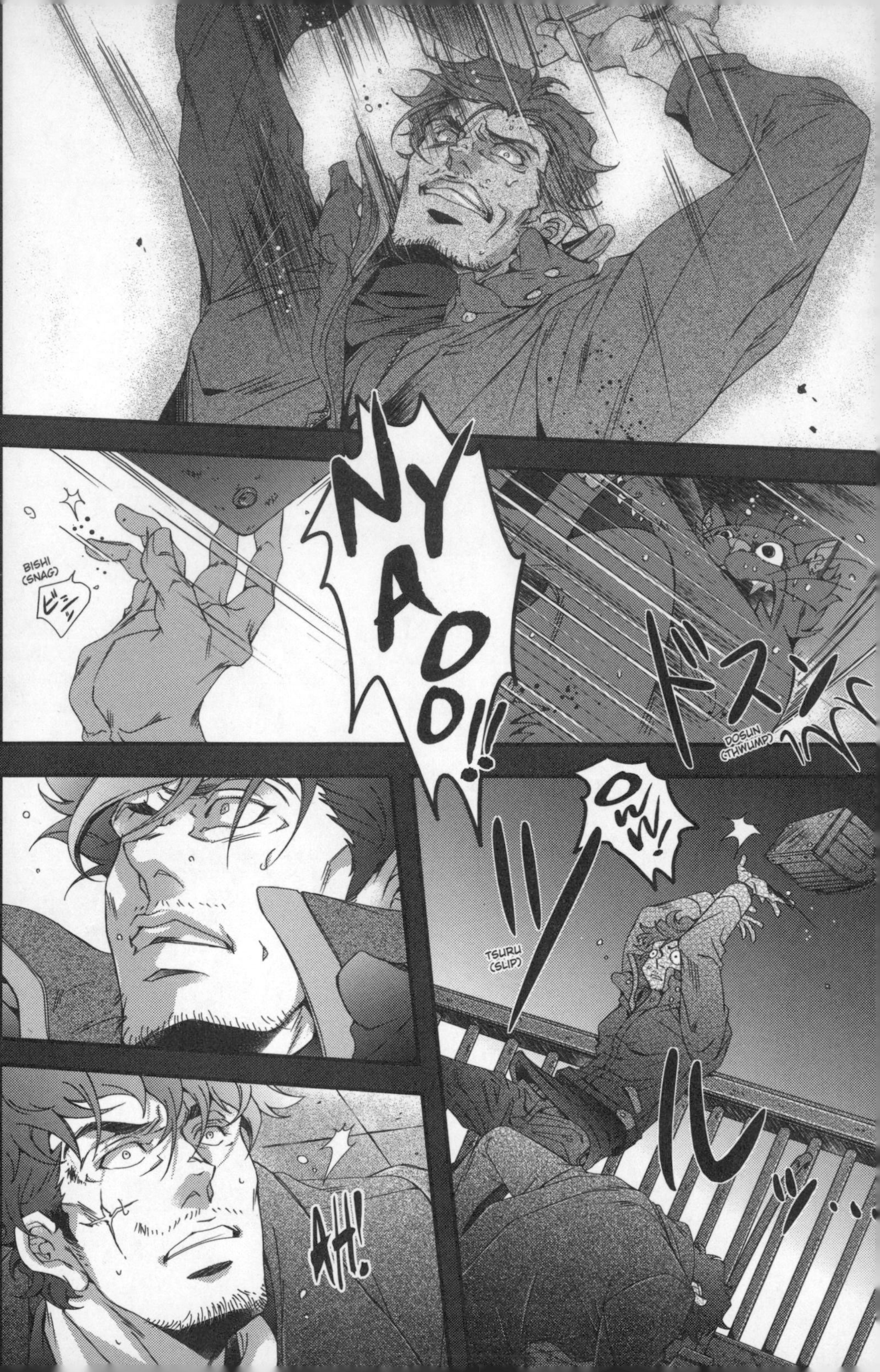
ドスン
DOSUN (THWUMP)
NYAOO!!
BISHI (SNAG)
ビシッ
OWW!
ツルッ
TSURU (SLIP)
AH!

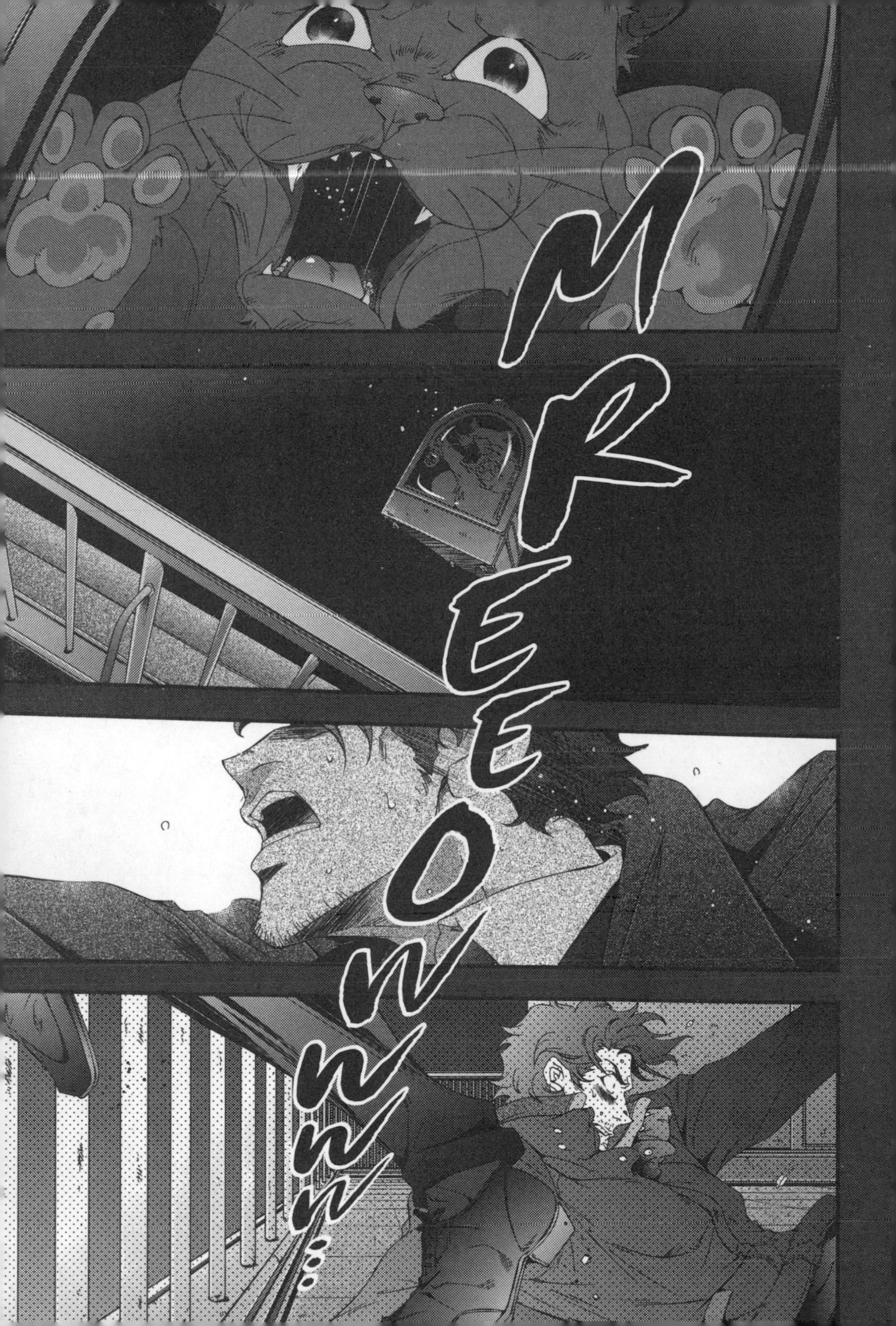
MRREOWWnnn...

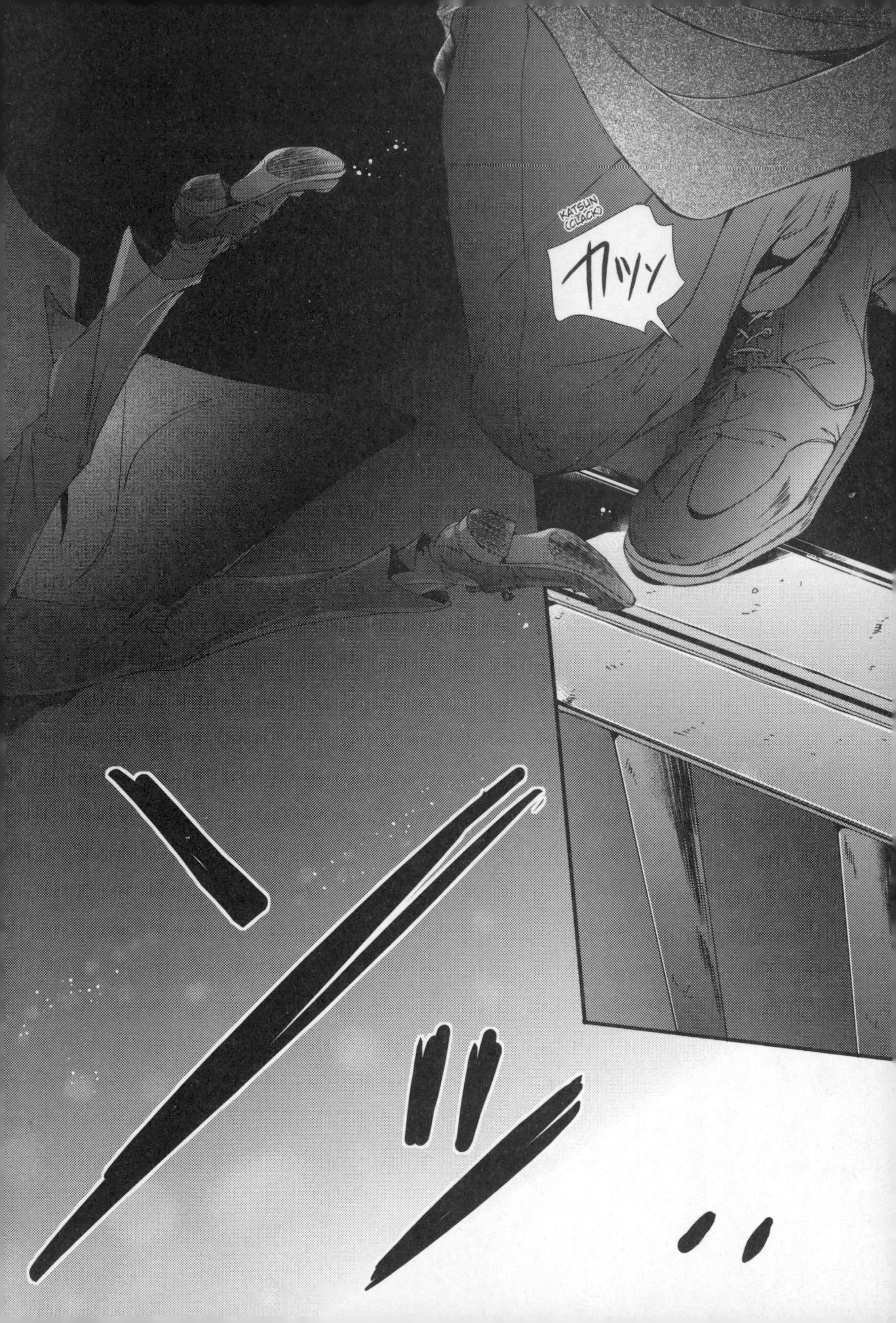
KATSUN (CLACK)
カツン

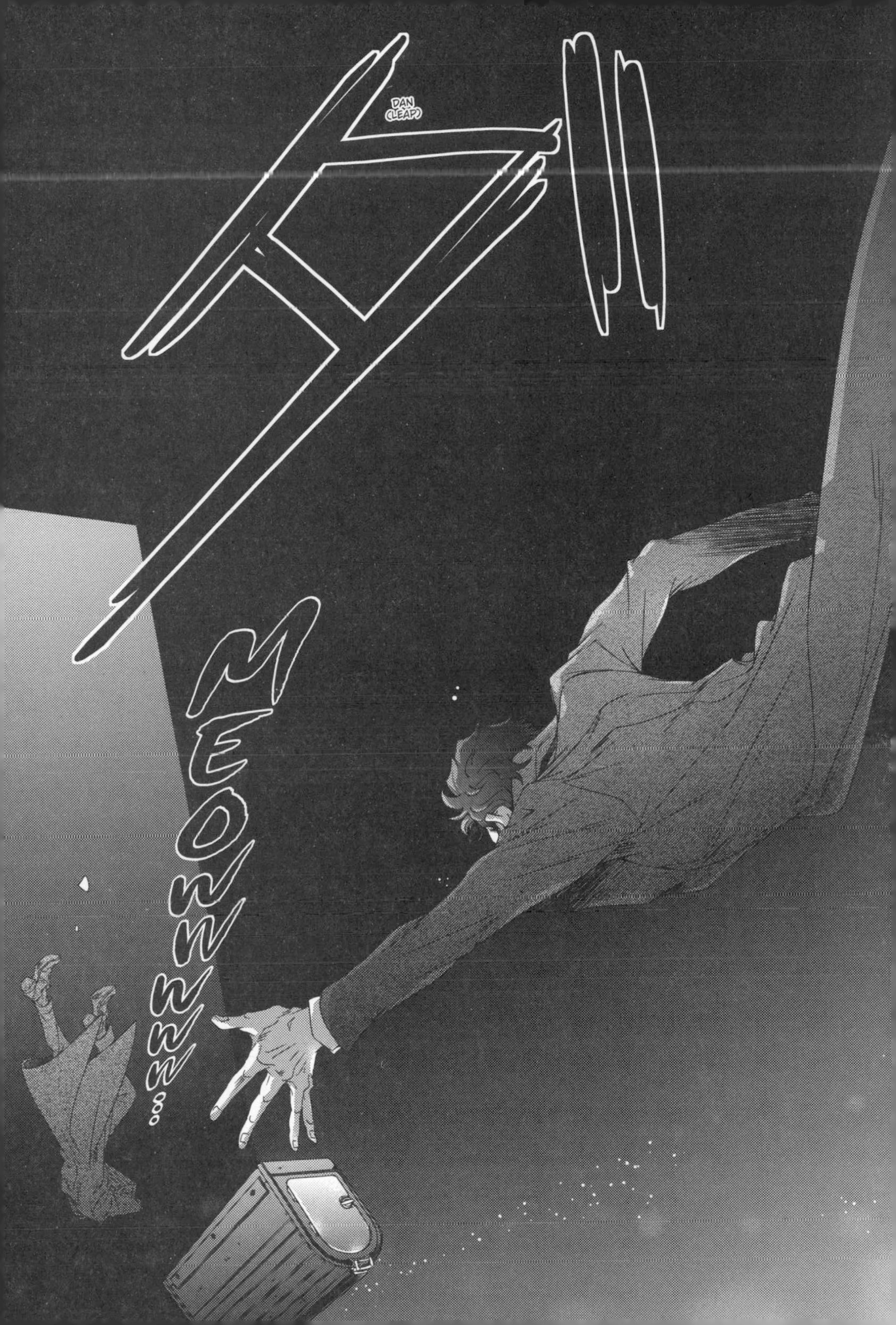
DAN (LEAP)
MEOWWWWWW..

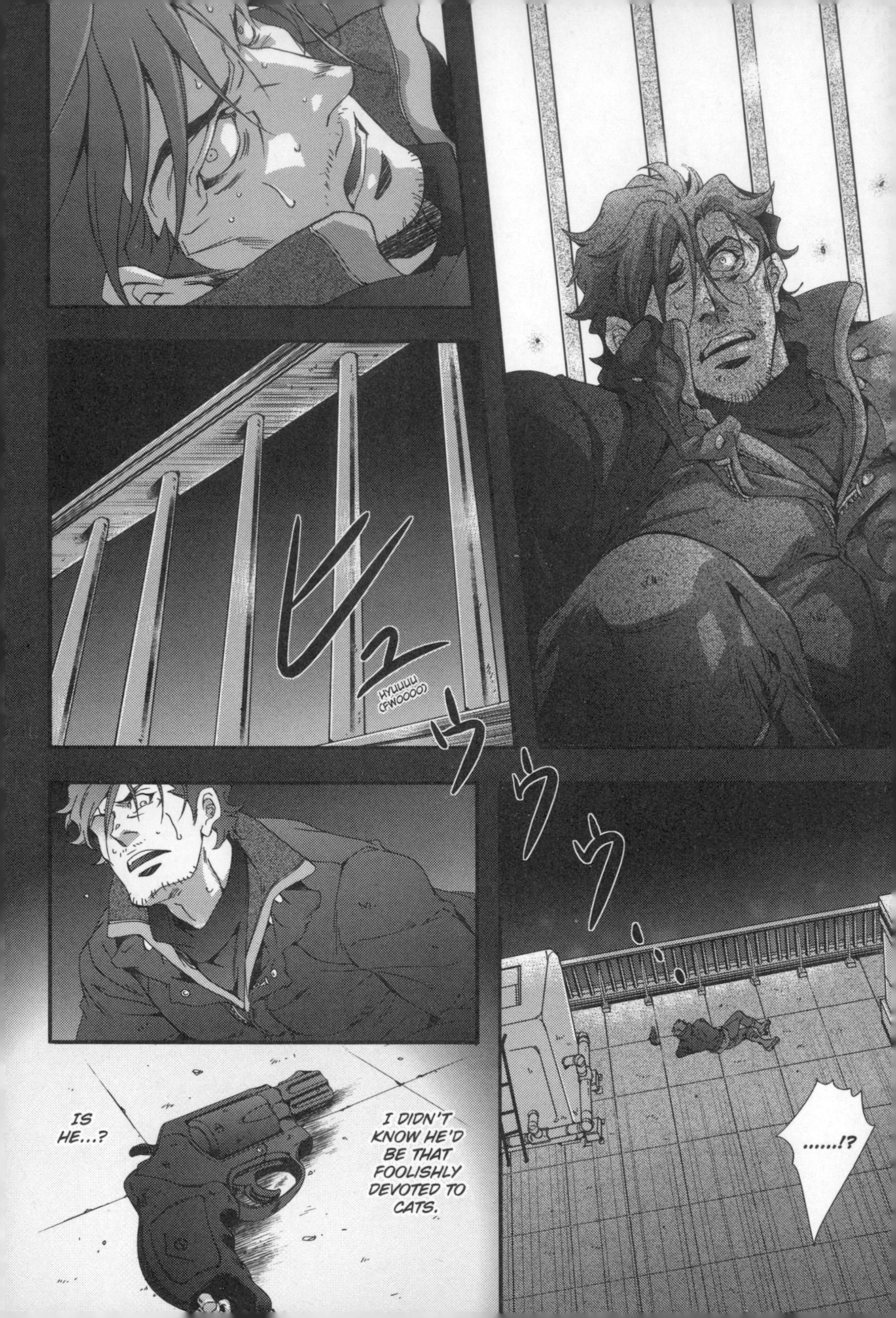
HYUUUU
(FWOOOO)
......!?
I DIDN'T KNOW HE'D BE THAT FOOLISHLY DEVOTED TO CATS.
IS HE...?

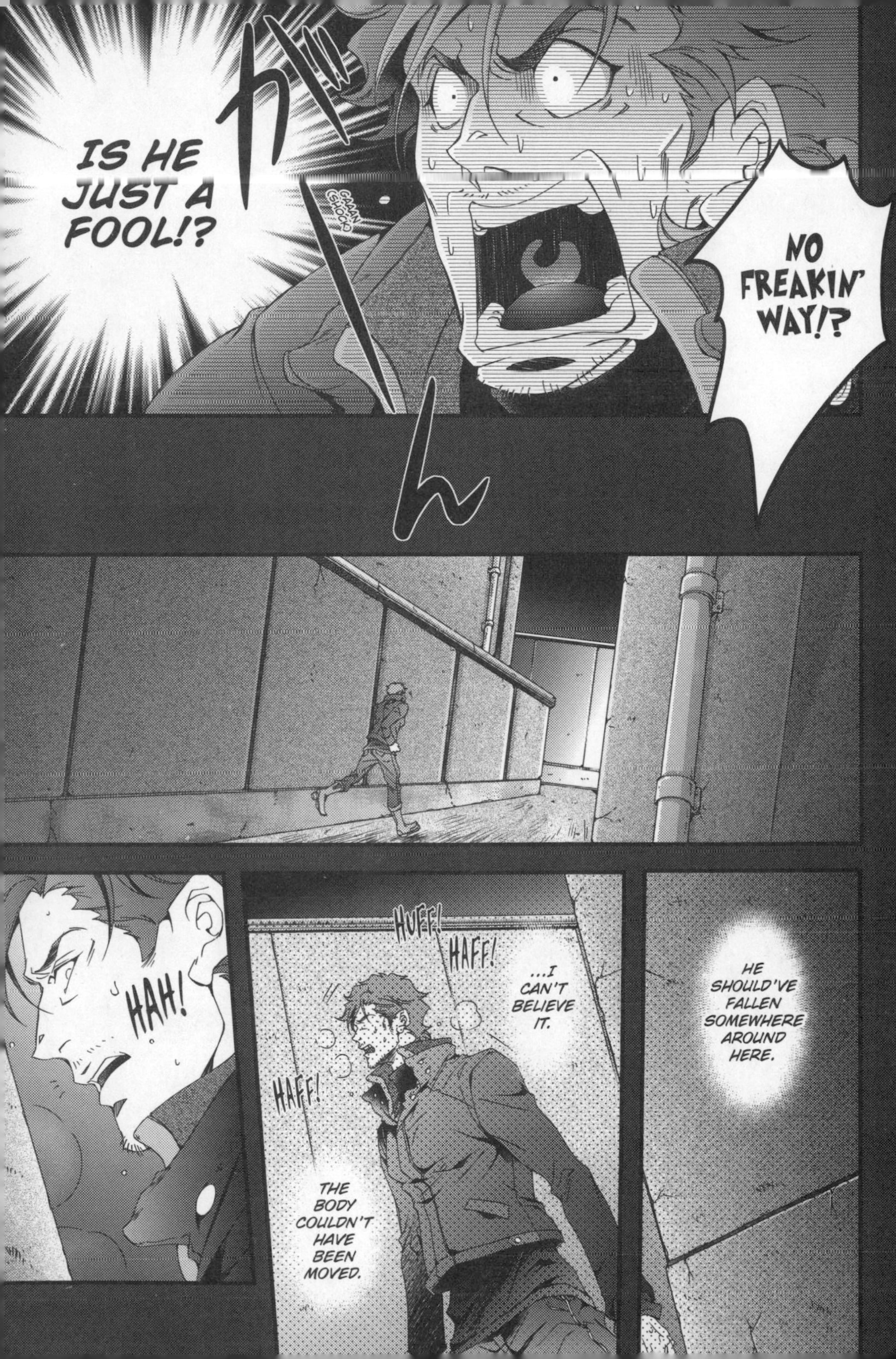
NO FREAKIN' WAY!?
GAAAN (SHOCK)
IS HE JUST A FOOL!?
HE SHOULD'VE FALLEN SOMEWHERE AROUND HERE.
HUFF!
HAFF!
...I CAN'T BELIEVE IT.
HAFF!
THE BODY COULDN'T HAVE BEEN MOVED.
HAH!

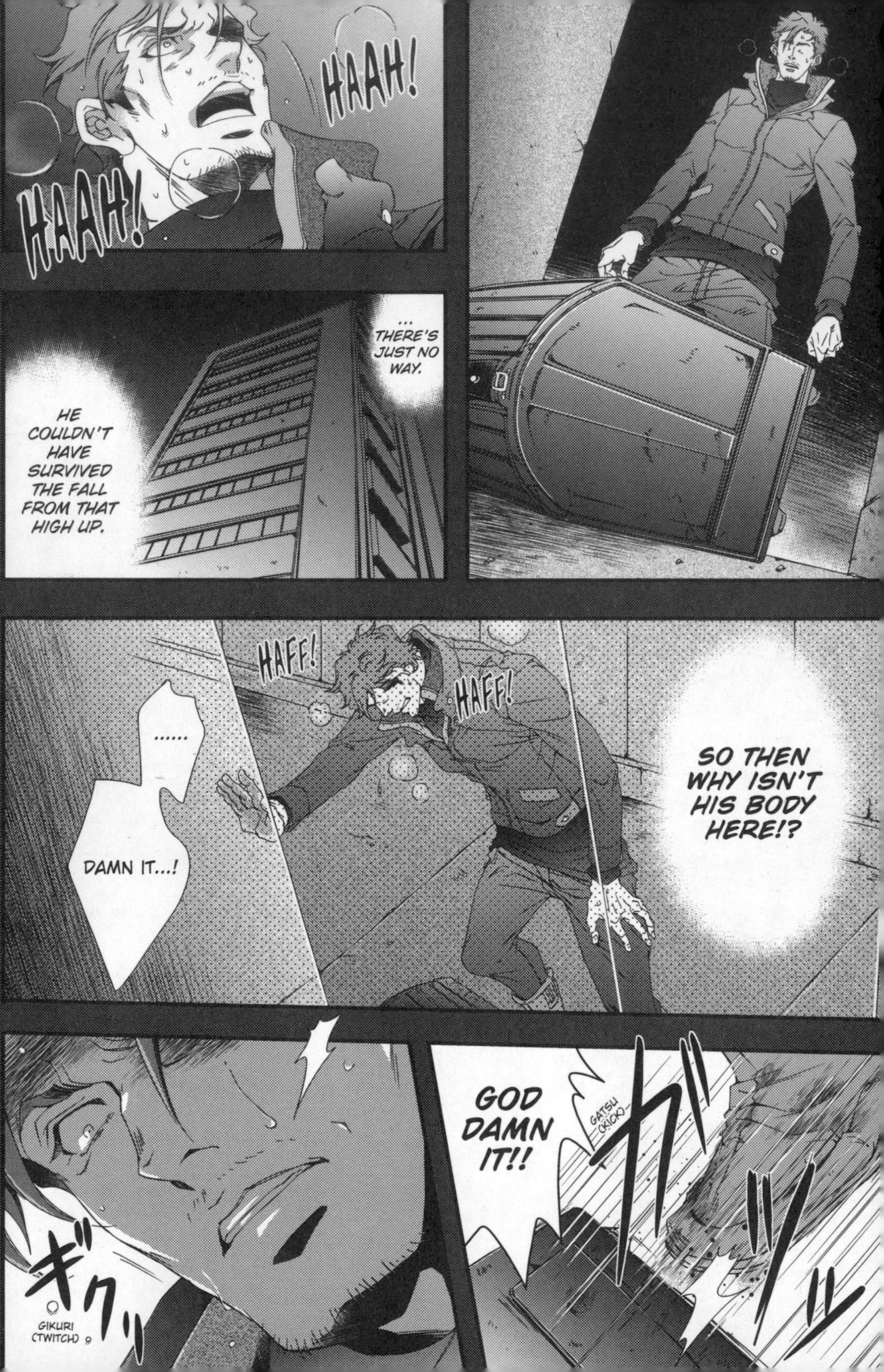
HAAH!
HAAH!
HE COULDN'T HAVE SURVIVED THE FALL FROM THAT HIGH UP.
... THERE'S JUST NO WAY.
HAFF!
HAFF!
SO THEN WHY ISN'T HIS BODY HERE!?
......
DAMN IT...!
GOD DAMN IT!!
ガッ
GATSU (KICK)
ギクッ
GIKURI (TWITCH)

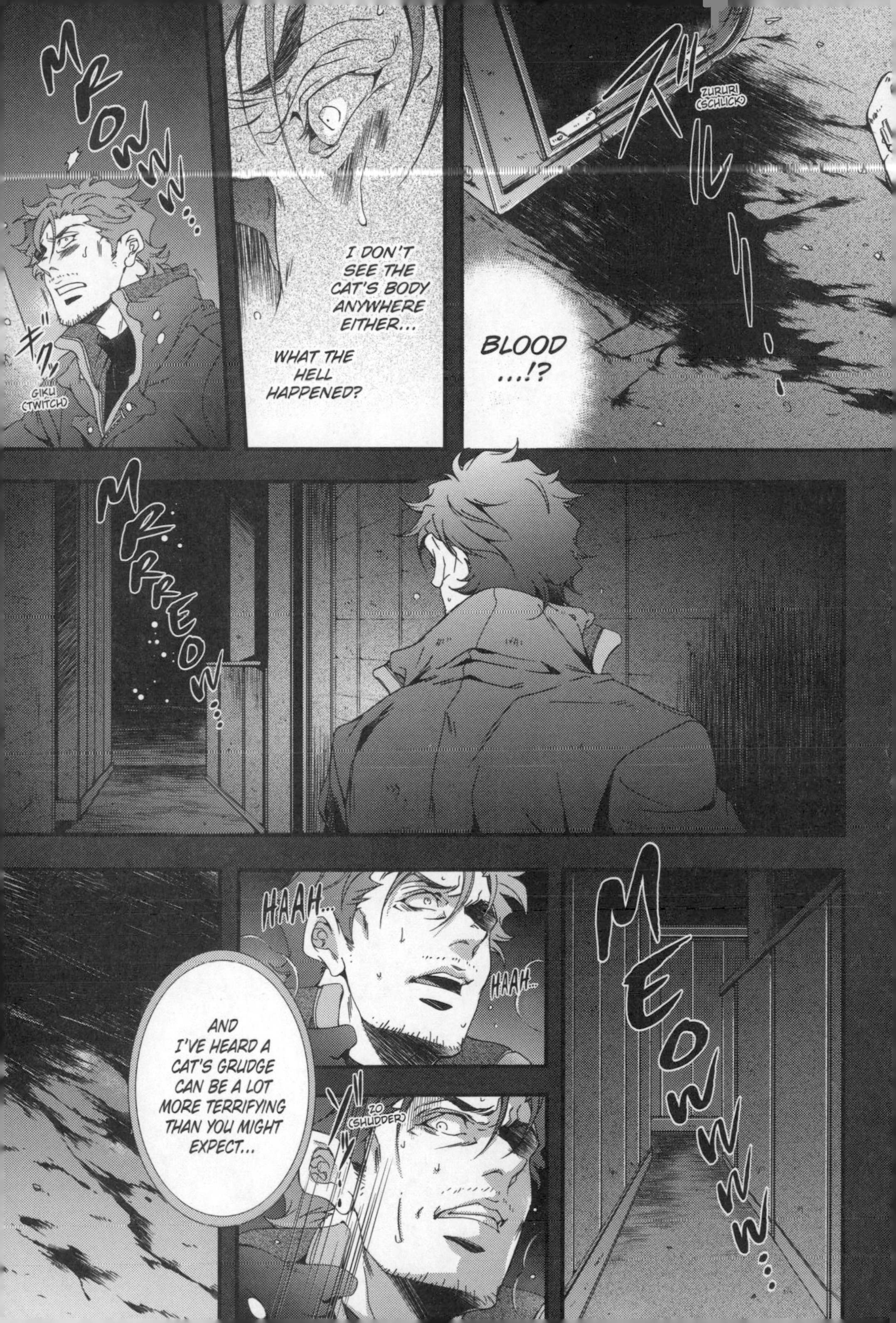
ZURURI (SCHLICK)
BLOOD ...!?
I DON'T SEE THE CAT'S BODY ANYWHERE EITHER...
WHAT THE HELL HAPPENED?
MROWWW...
GIKU (TWITCH)
MRRREOWW...
MEOWWWW...
HAAH...
HAAH...
AND I'VE HEARD A CAT'S GRUDGE CAN BE A LOT MORE TERRIFYING THAN YOU MIGHT EXPECT...
ZO (SHUDDER)

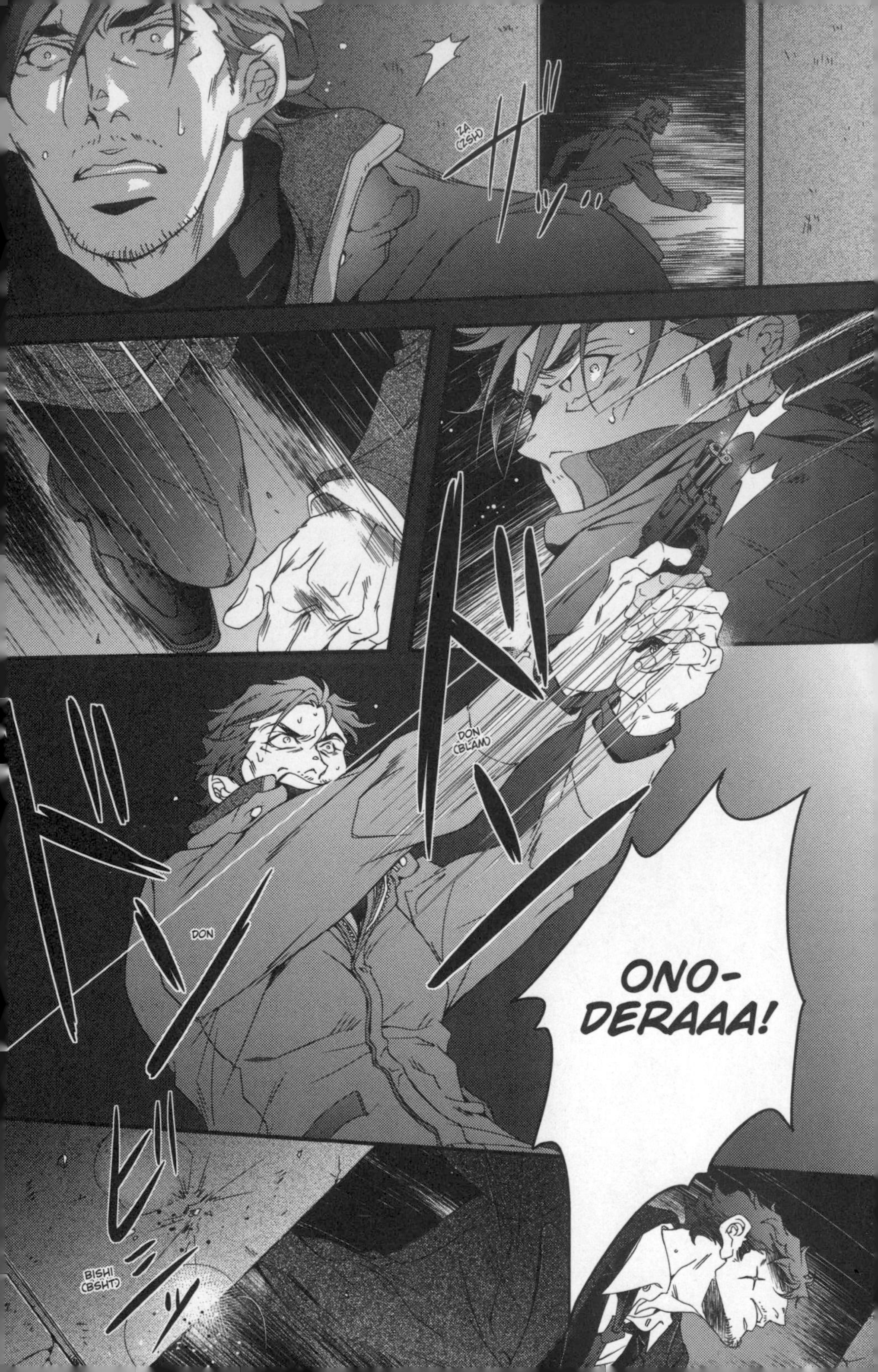
ZA (ZSH)
DON (BLAM)
ONO-DERAAA!
DON
BISHI (BSHT)

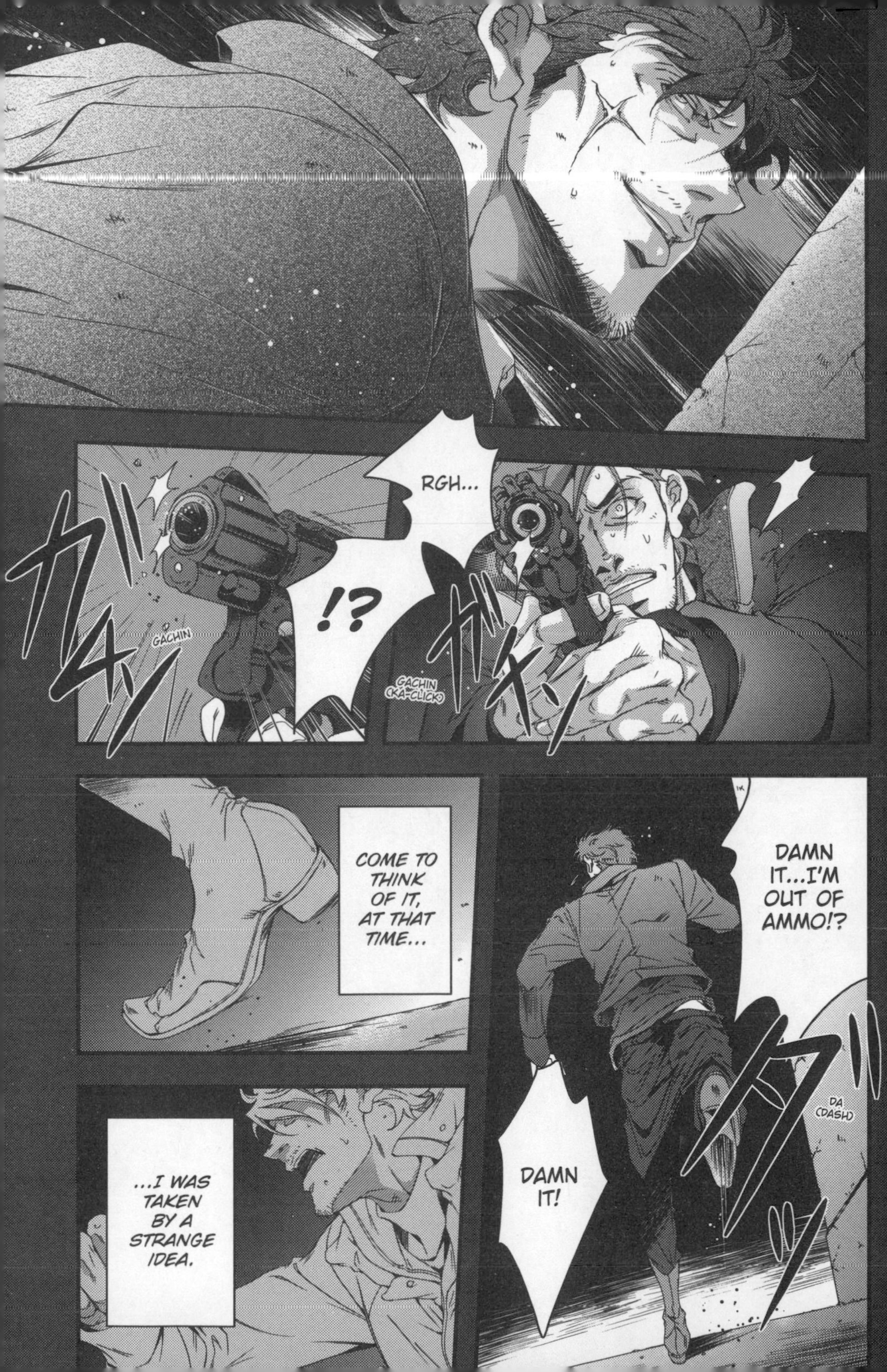
RGH...
GACHIN (KA-CLICK)
!?
GACHIN
DAMN IT...I'M OUT OF AMMO!?
DA (DASH)
DAMN IT!
COME TO THINK OF IT, AT THAT TIME...
...I WAS TAKEN BY A STRANGE IDEA.

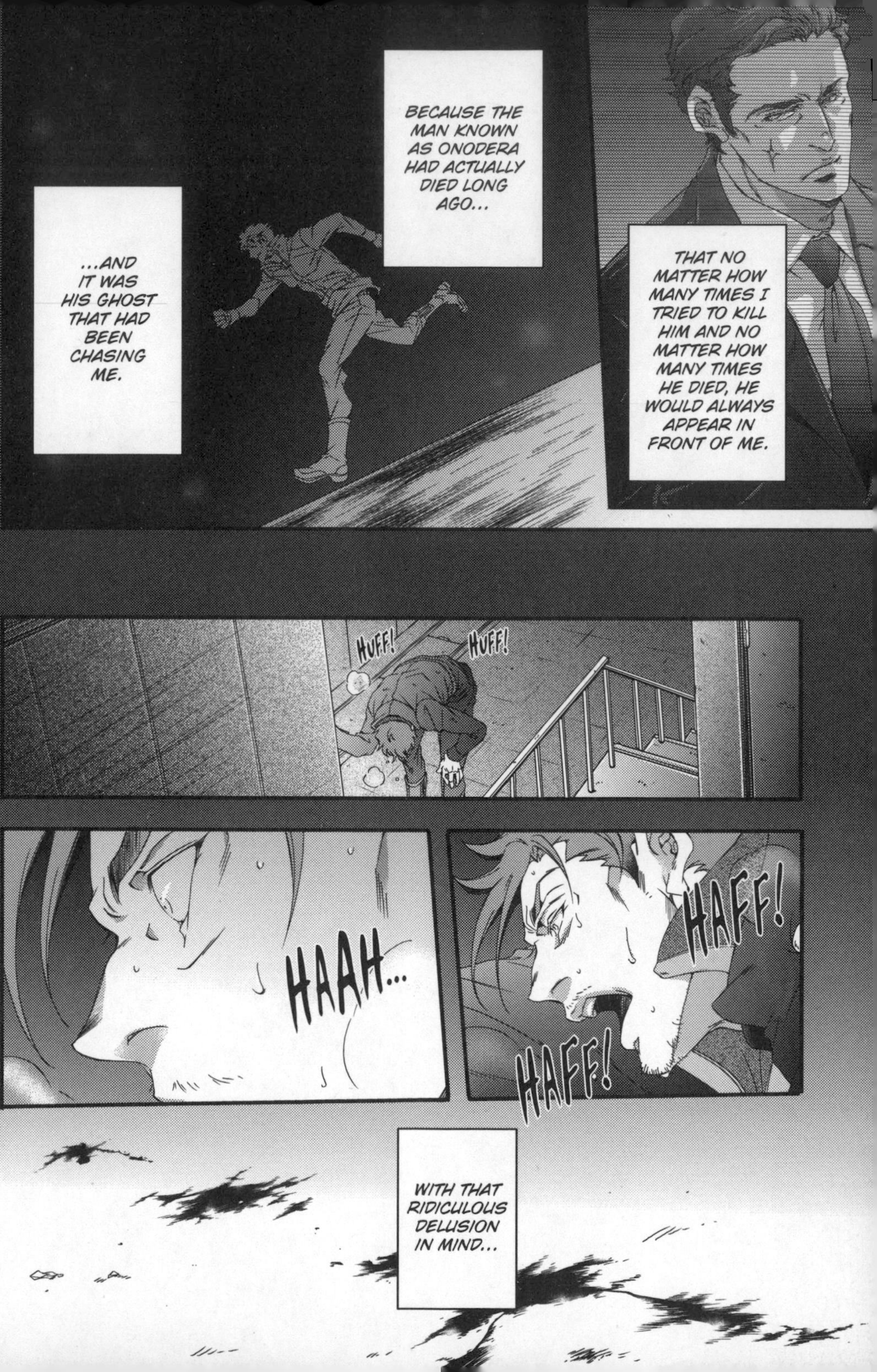
THAT NO MATTER HOW MANY TIMES I TRIED TO KILL HIM AND NO MATTER HOW MANY TIMES HE DIED, HE WOULD ALWAYS APPEAR IN FRONT OF ME.
BECAUSE THE MAN KNOWN AS ONODERA HAD ACTUALLY DIED LONG AGO...
...AND IT WAS HIS GHOST THAT HAD BEEN CHASING ME.
HUFF!
HUFF!
HAFF!
HAFF!
HAAH...
WITH THAT RIDICULOUS DELUSION IN MIND...

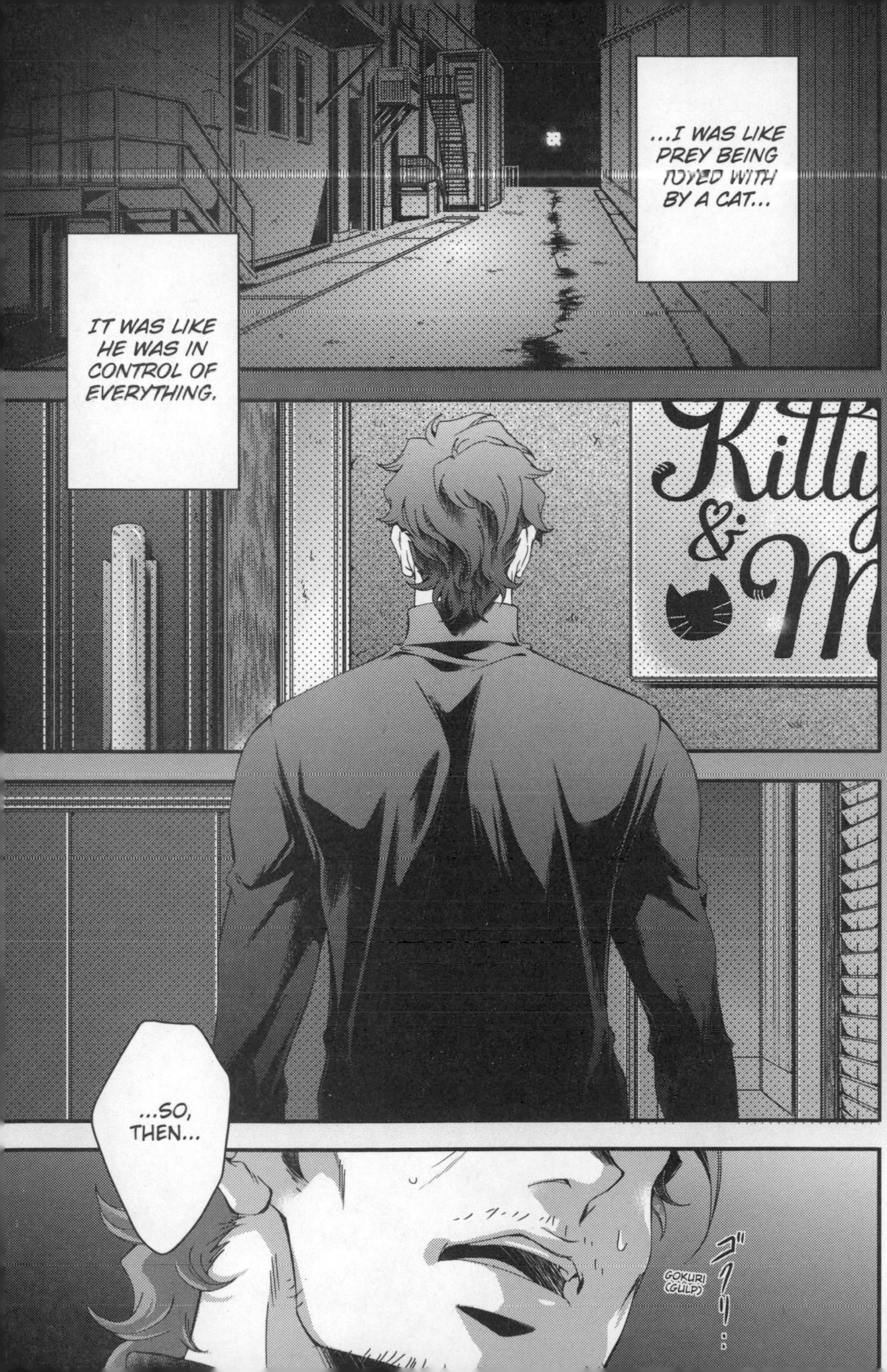
...I WAS LIKE PREY BEING TOYED WITH BY A CAT...
IT WAS LIKE HE WAS IN CONTROL OF EVERYTHING.
...SO, THEN...
ゴクリ…
GOKURI (GULP)

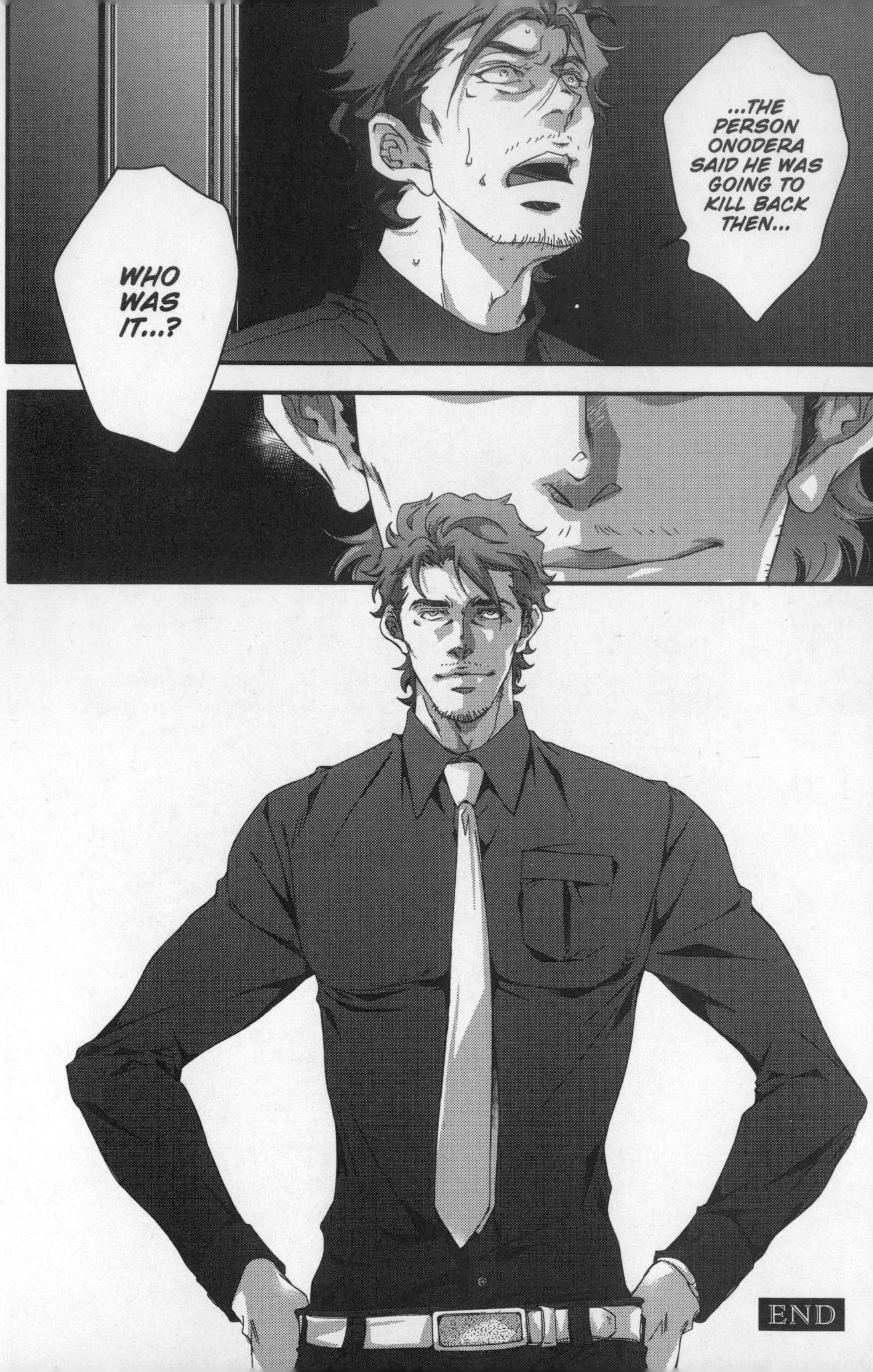
...THE PERSON ONODERA SAID HE WAS GOING TO KILL BACK THEN...
WHO WAS IT...?
END

CHAPTER 6

Still, the Morning Comes

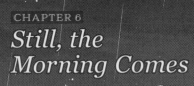

ZAAA (FSHHH)

HEY,
DETECTIVE...

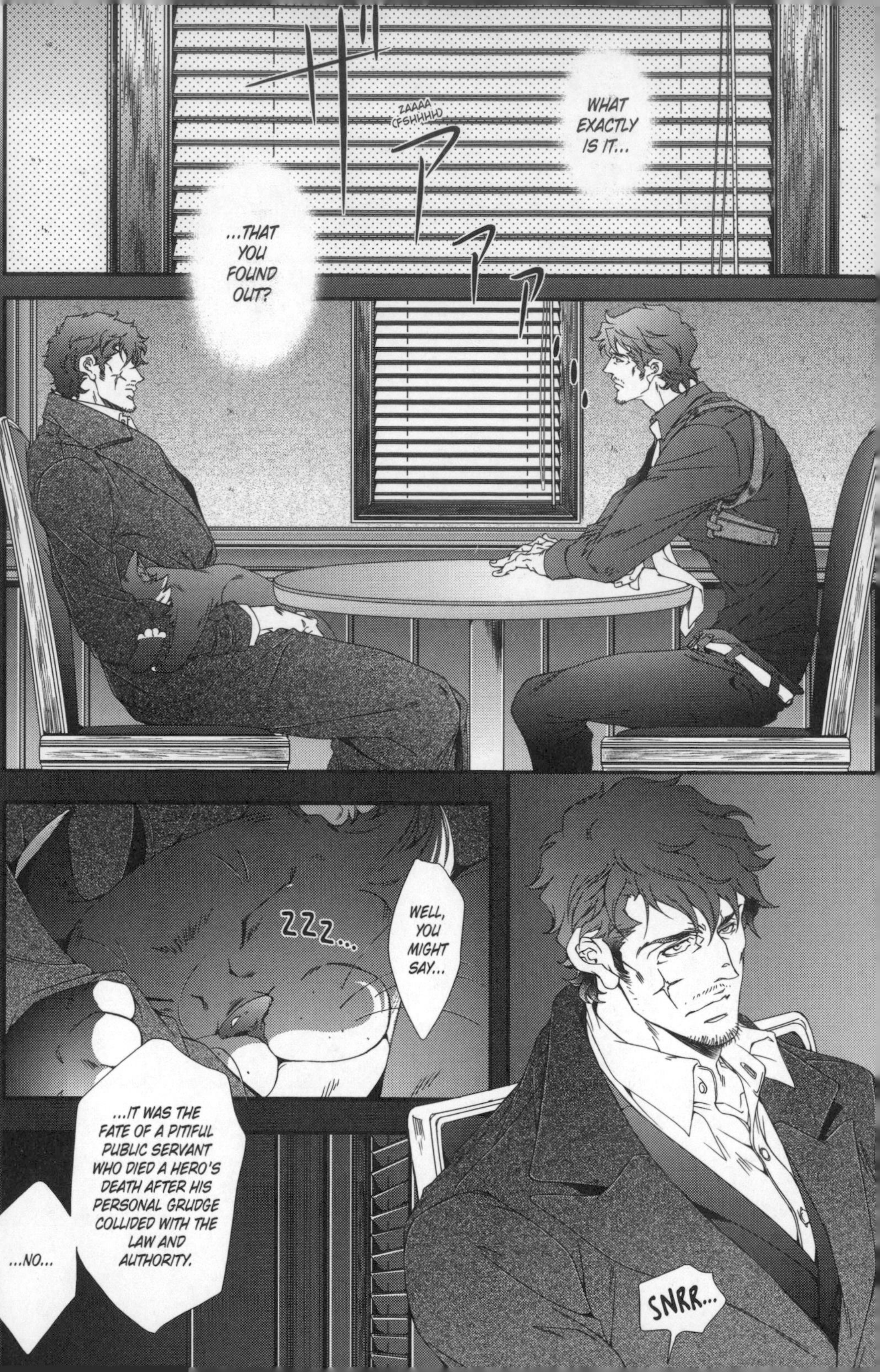
WHAT EXACTLY IS IT...
ZAAAA (FSHHHH)
...THAT YOU FOUND OUT?
SNRR...
ZZZ...
WELL, YOU MIGHT SAY...
...IT WAS THE FATE OF A PITIFUL PUBLIC SERVANT WHO DIED A HERO'S DEATH AFTER HIS PERSONAL GRUDGE COLLIDED WITH THE LAW AND AUTHORITY.
...NO...

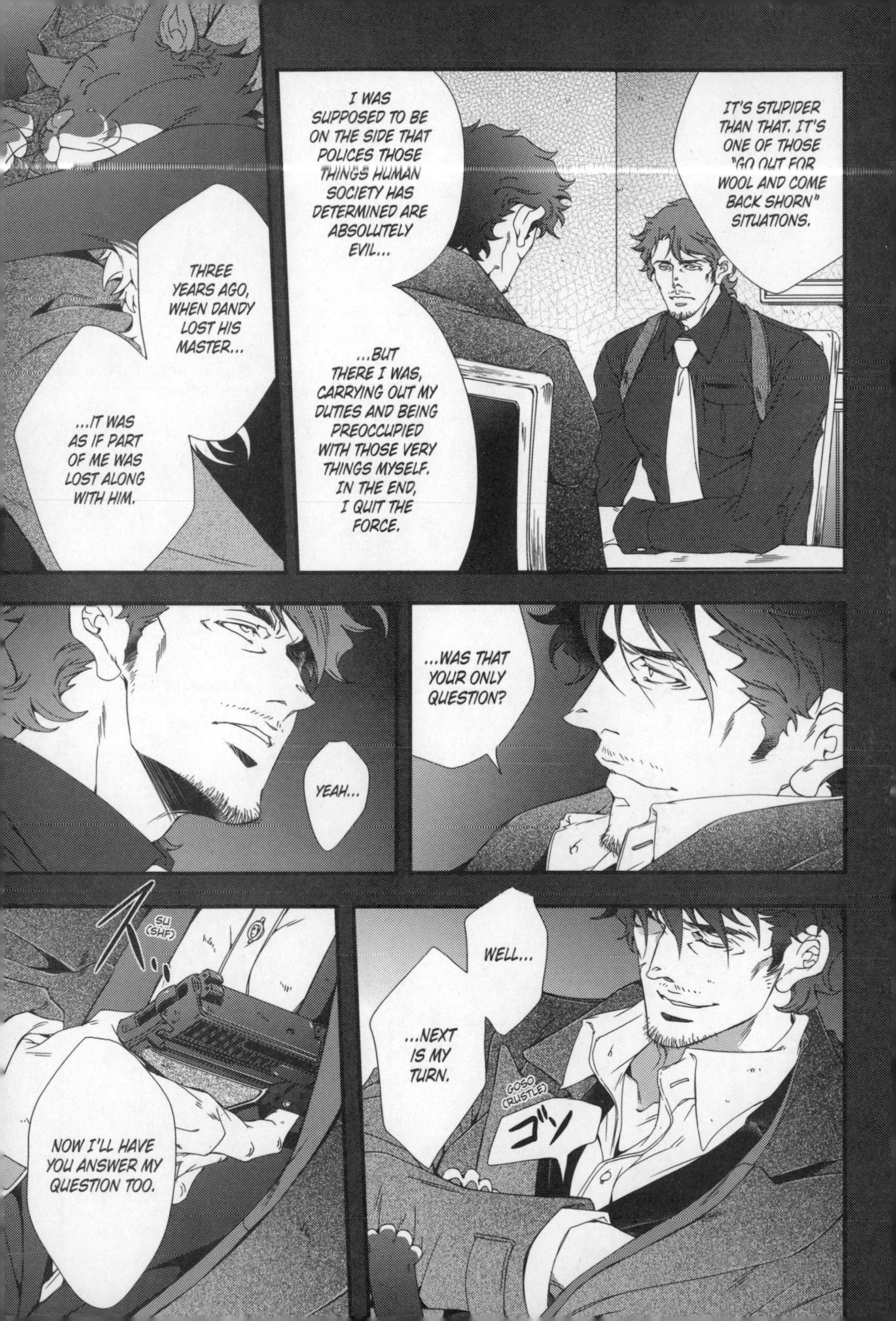
IT'S STUPIDER THAN THAT. IT'S ONE OF THOSE "GO OUT FOR WOOL AND COME BACK SHORN" SITUATIONS.
I WAS SUPPOSED TO BE ON THE SIDE THAT POLICES THOSE THINGS HUMAN SOCIETY HAS DETERMINED ARE ABSOLUTELY EVIL...
...BUT THERE I WAS, CARRYING OUT MY DUTIES AND BEING PREOCCUPIED WITH THOSE VERY THINGS MYSELF. IN THE END, I QUIT THE FORCE.
THREE YEARS AGO, WHEN DANDY LOST HIS MASTER...
...IT WAS AS IF PART OF ME WAS LOST ALONG WITH HIM.
...WAS THAT YOUR ONLY QUESTION?
YEAH...
WELL...
...NEXT IS MY TURN.
GOSO (RUSTLE)
ゴソ
SU (SHF)
ス
NOW I'LL HAVE YOU ANSWER MY QUESTION TOO.

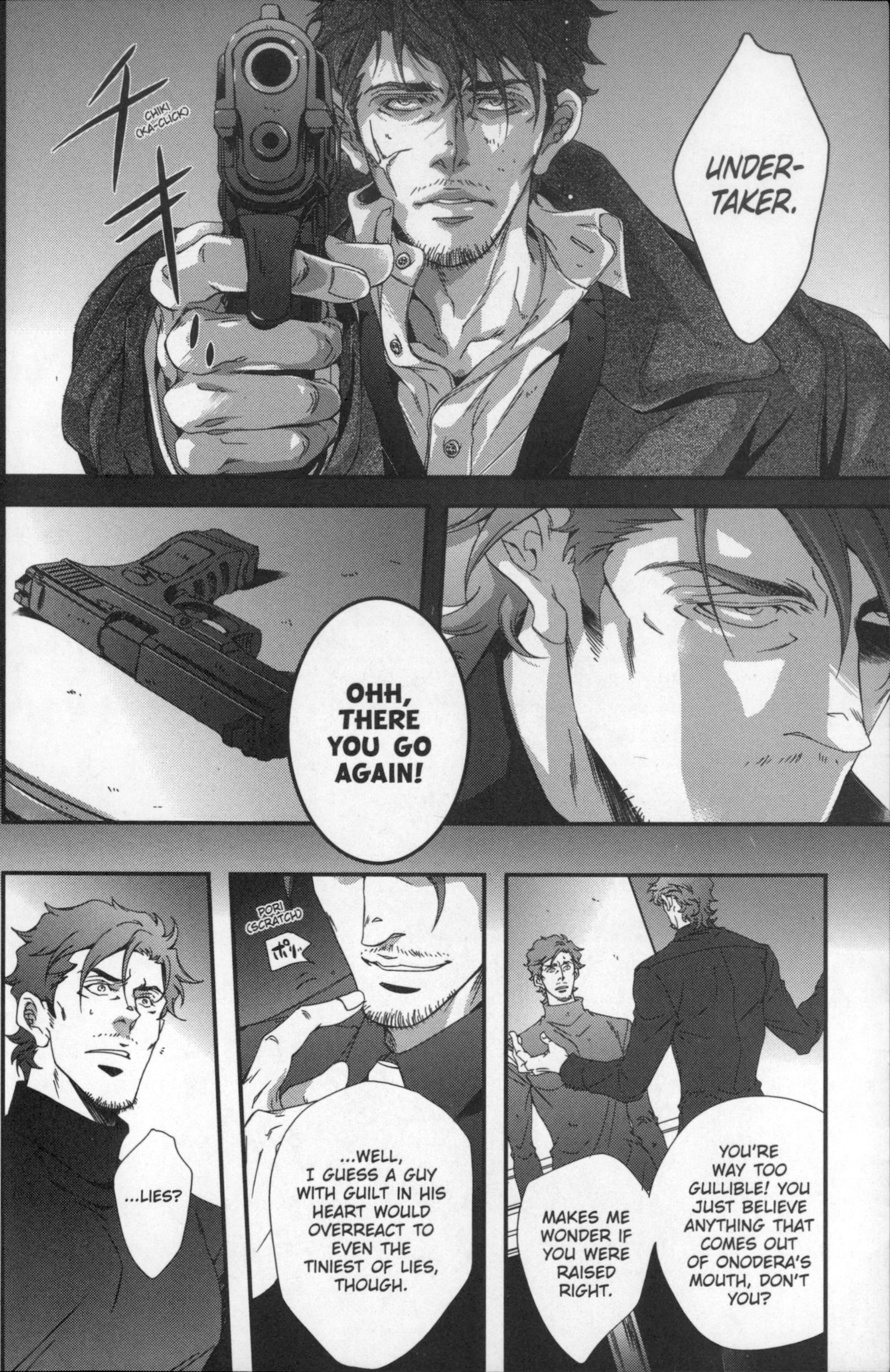
UNDER-TAKER.
CHIKI (KA-CLICK)
OHH, THERE YOU GO AGAIN!
YOU'RE WAY TOO GULLIBLE! YOU JUST BELIEVE ANYTHING THAT COMES OUT OF ONODERA'S MOUTH, DON'T YOU?
MAKES ME WONDER IF YOU WERE RAISED RIGHT.
PORI (SCRATCH)
...WELL, I GUESS A GUY WITH GUILT IN HIS HEART WOULD OVERREACT TO EVEN THE TINIEST OF LIES, THOUGH.
...LIES?

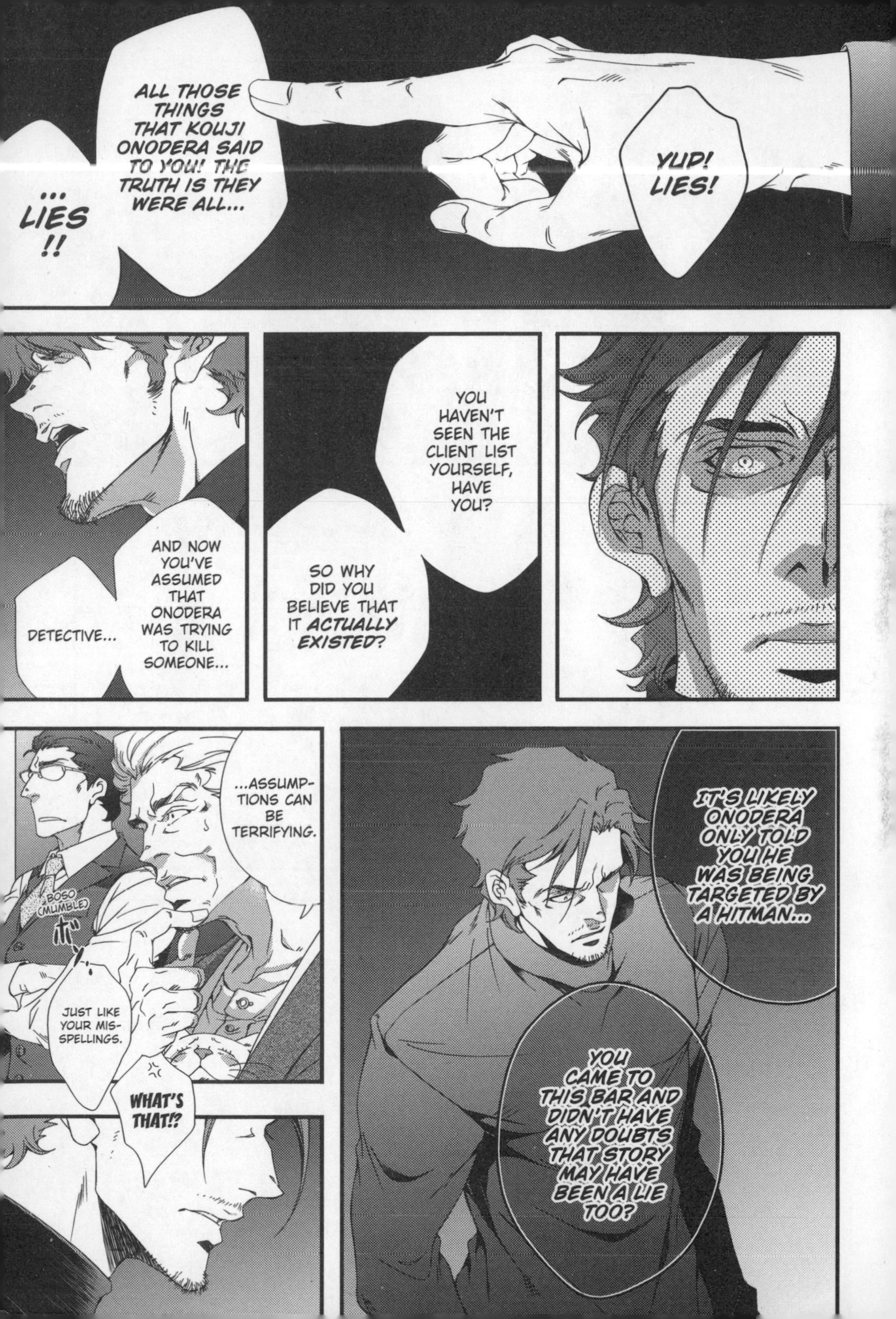
ALL THOSE THINGS THAT KOUJI ONODERA SAID TO YOU! THE TRUTH IS THEY WERE ALL...
...LIES!!
YUP! LIES!
YOU HAVEN'T SEEN THE CLIENT LIST YOURSELF, HAVE YOU?
SO WHY DID YOU BELIEVE THAT IT ACTUALLY EXISTED?
AND NOW YOU'VE ASSUMED THAT ONODERA WAS TRYING TO KILL SOMEONE...
DETECTIVE...
IT'S LIKELY ONODERA ONLY TOLD YOU HE WAS BEING TARGETED BY A HITMAN...
YOU CAME TO THIS BAR AND DIDN'T HAVE ANY DOUBTS THAT STORY MAY HAVE BEEN A LIE TOO?
...ASSUMPTIONS CAN BE TERRIFYING.
BOSO (MUMBLE)
JUST LIKE YOUR MIS-SPELLINGS.
WHAT'S THAT!?

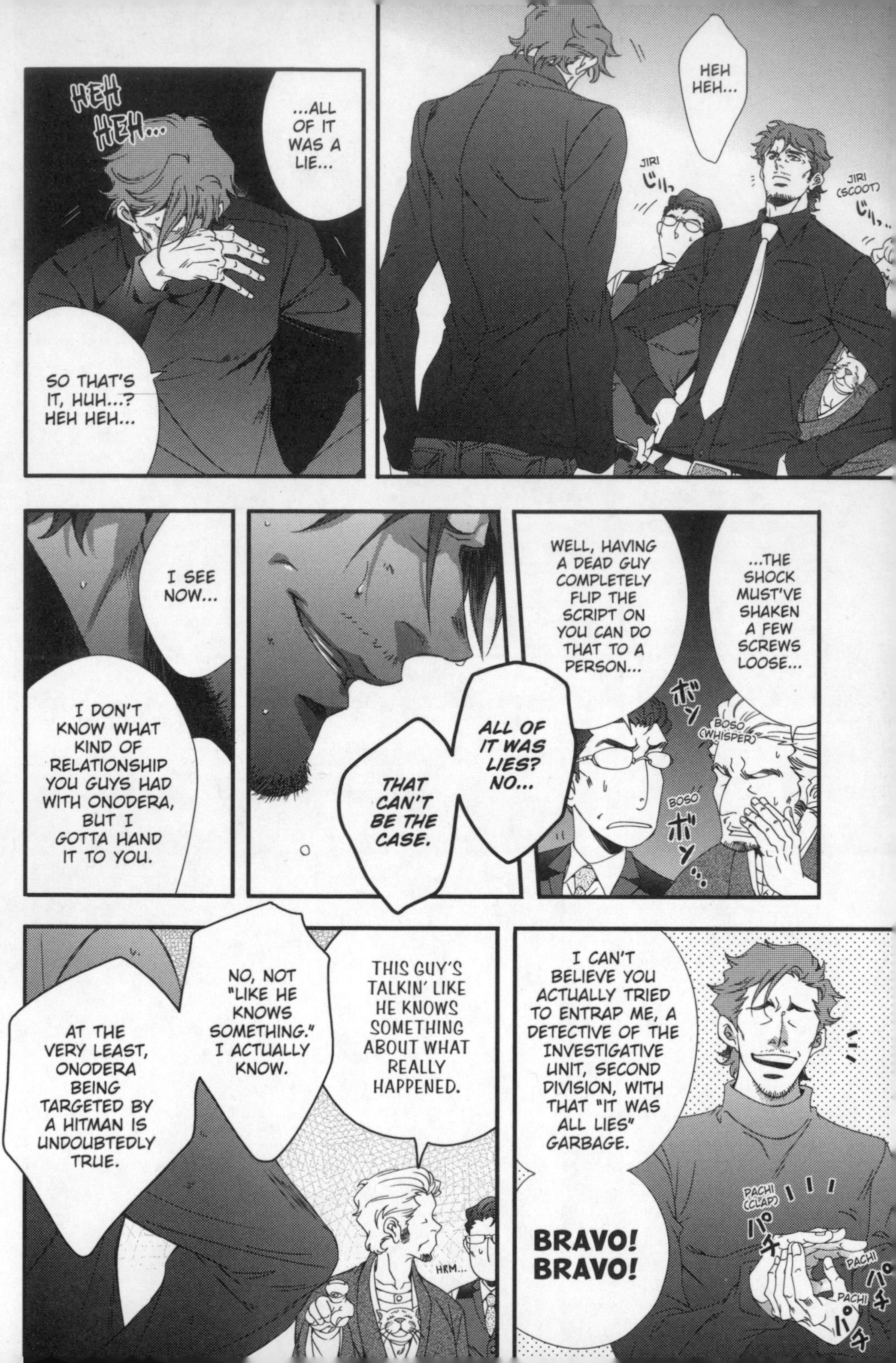
HEH HEH...
JIRI
じりっ
JIRI (SCOOT)
じりっ
HEH HEH...
...ALL OF IT WAS A LIE...
SO THAT'S IT, HUH...? HEH HEH...
...THE SHOCK MUST'VE SHAKEN A FEW SCREWS LOOSE...
WELL, HAVING A DEAD GUY COMPLETELY FLIP THE SCRIPT ON YOU CAN DO THAT TO A PERSON...
BOSO (WHISPER)
ボソ
BOSO
ボソ…
ALL OF IT WAS LIES? NO...
THAT CAN'T BE THE CASE.
I SEE NOW...
I DON'T KNOW WHAT KIND OF RELATIONSHIP YOU GUYS HAD WITH ONODERA, BUT I GOTTA HAND IT TO YOU.
I CAN'T BELIEVE YOU ACTUALLY TRIED TO ENTRAP ME, A DETECTIVE OF THE INVESTIGATIVE UNIT, SECOND DIVISION, WITH THAT "IT WAS ALL LIES" GARBAGE.
BRAVO! BRAVO!
PACHI (CLAP)
パチ
PACHI
パチ
PACHI
パチ
THIS GUY'S TALKIN' LIKE HE KNOWS SOMETHING ABOUT WHAT REALLY HAPPENED.
NO, NOT "LIKE HE KNOWS SOMETHING." I ACTUALLY KNOW.
AT THE VERY LEAST, ONODERA BEING TARGETED BY A HITMAN IS UNDOUBTEDLY TRUE.
HRM...

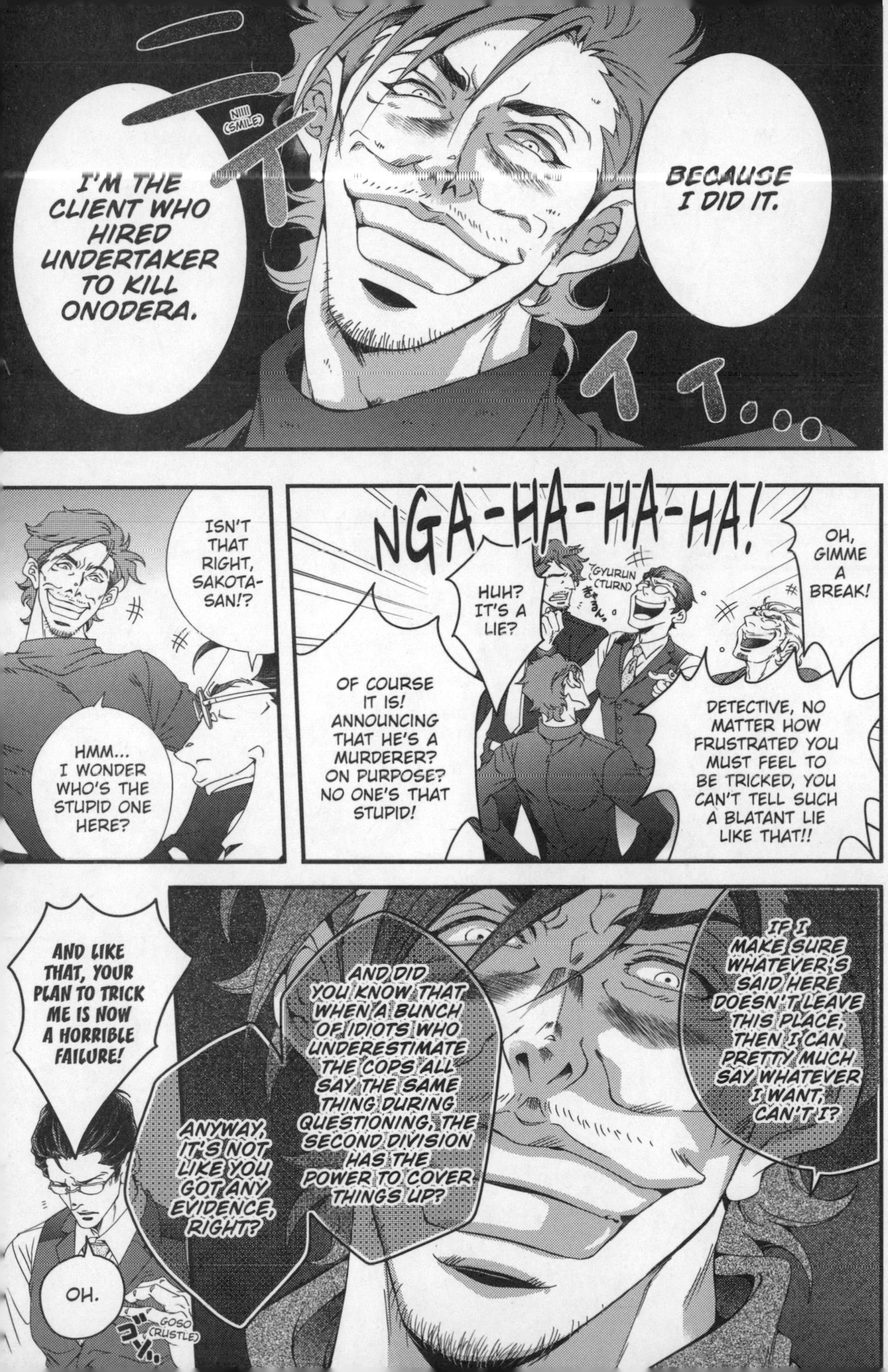
BECAUSE I DID IT.
NIIII (SMILE)
I'M THE CLIENT WHO HIRED UNDERTAKER TO KILL ONODERA.
NGA-HA-HA-HA!
OH, GIMME A BREAK!
(GYURUN (TURN)
HUH? IT'S A LIE?
DETECTIVE, NO MATTER HOW FRUSTRATED YOU MUST FEEL TO BE TRICKED, YOU CAN'T TELL SUCH A BLATANT LIE LIKE THAT!!
OF COURSE IT IS! ANNOUNCING THAT HE'S A MURDERER? ON PURPOSE? NO ONE'S THAT STUPID!
ISN'T THAT RIGHT, SAKOTA-SAN!?
HMM... I WONDER WHO'S THE STUPID ONE HERE?
IF I MAKE SURE WHATEVER'S SAID HERE DOESN'T LEAVE THIS PLACE, THEN I CAN PRETTY MUCH SAY WHATEVER I WANT, CAN'T I?
AND DID YOU KNOW THAT WHEN A BUNCH OF IDIOTS WHO UNDERESTIMATE THE COPS ALL SAY THE SAME THING DURING QUESTIONING, THE SECOND DIVISION HAS THE POWER TO COVER THINGS UP?
ANYWAY, IT'S NOT LIKE YOU GOT ANY EVIDENCE, RIGHT?
AND LIKE THAT, YOUR PLAN TO TRICK ME IS NOW A HORRIBLE FAILURE!
OH.
GOSO (RUSTLE)

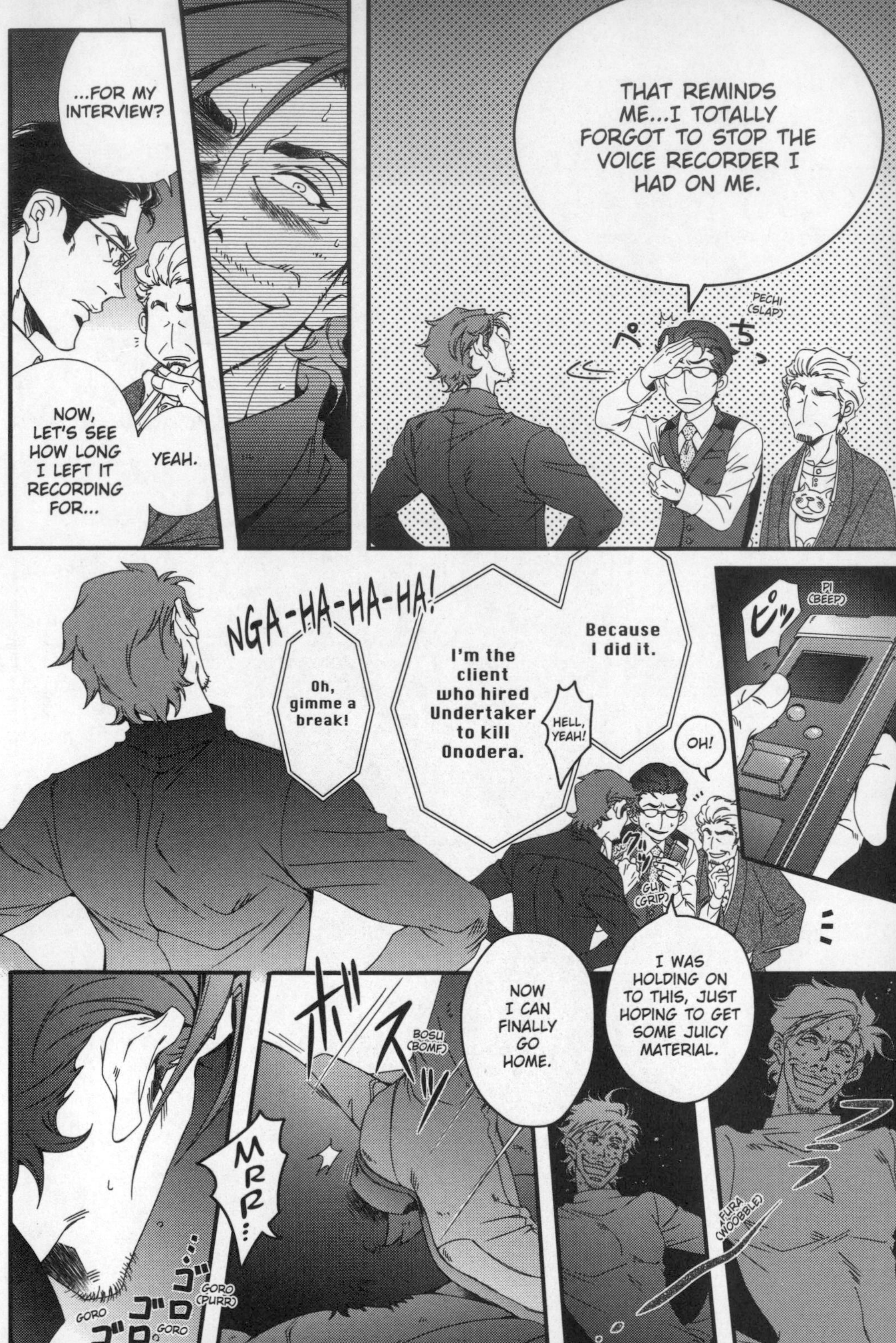
THAT REMINDS ME...I TOTALLY FORGOT TO STOP THE VOICE RECORDER I HAD ON ME.
PECHI (SLAP)
...FOR MY INTERVIEW?
YEAH.
NOW, LET'S SEE HOW LONG I LEFT IT RECORDING FOR...
PI (BEEP)
OH!
Because I did it.
I'm the client who hired Undertaker to kill Onodera.
HELL, YEAH!
Oh, gimme a break!
NGA-HA-HA-HA!
GU (GRIP)
I WAS HOLDING ON TO THIS, JUST HOPING TO GET SOME JUICY MATERIAL.
FURA (WOOBBLE)
NOW I CAN FINALLY GO HOME.
BOSU (BOMF)
MRR...
GORO (PURR)
GORO
GORO

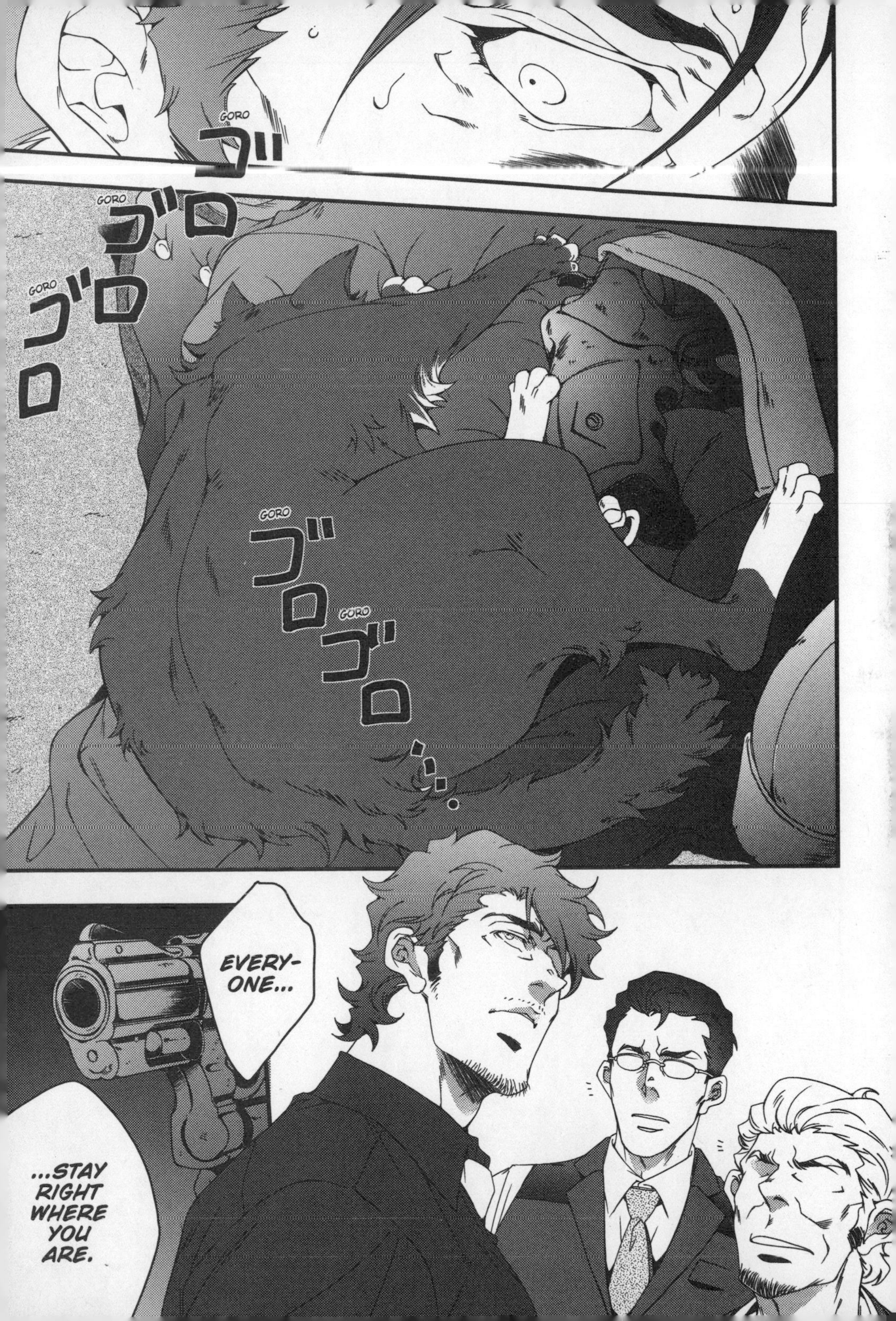
GORO
GORO
GORO
GORO
GORO
EVERY-ONE...
...STAY RIGHT WHERE YOU ARE.

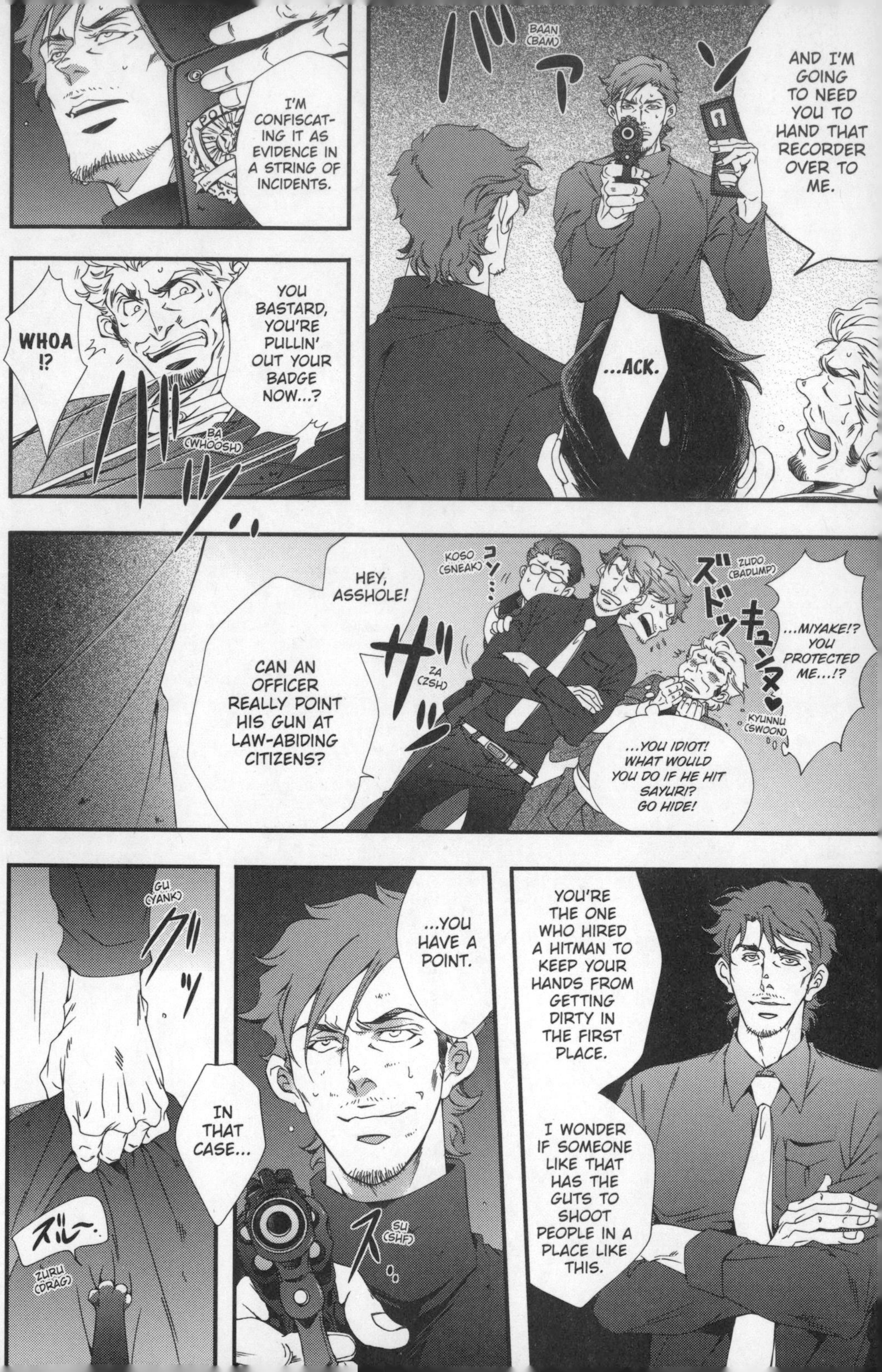
BAAN (BAM)
AND I'M GOING TO NEED YOU TO HAND THAT RECORDER OVER TO ME.
...ACK.
I'M CONFISCAT-ING IT AS EVIDENCE IN A STRING OF INCIDENTS.
YOU BASTARD, YOU'RE PULLIN' OUT YOUR BADGE NOW...?
WHOA!?
BA (WHOOSH)
...MIYAKE!? YOU PROTECTED ME...!?
ZUDO (BADUMP)
KYUNNU (SWOON)
...YOU IDIOT! WHAT WOULD YOU DO IF HE HIT SAYURI? GO HIDE!
KOSO (SNEAK)
HEY, ASSHOLE!
ZA (ZSH)
CAN AN OFFICER REALLY POINT HIS GUN AT LAW-ABIDING CITIZENS?
YOU'RE THE ONE WHO HIRED A HITMAN TO KEEP YOUR HANDS FROM GETTING DIRTY IN THE FIRST PLACE.
I WONDER IF SOMEONE LIKE THAT HAS THE GUTS TO SHOOT PEOPLE IN A PLACE LIKE THIS.
...YOU HAVE A POINT.
IN THAT CASE...
SU (SHF)
GU (YANK)
ZURU (DRAG)

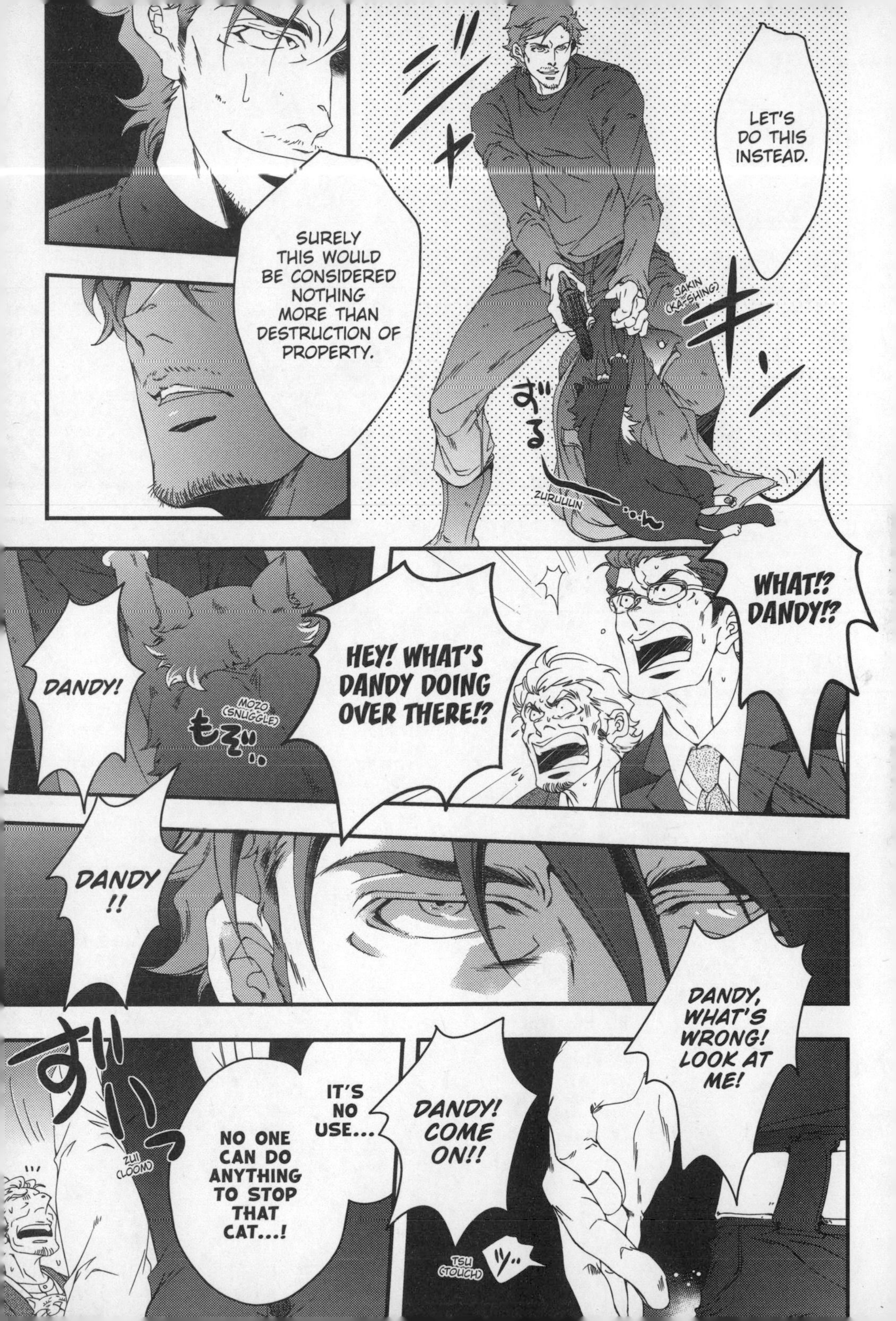
LET'S DO THIS INSTEAD.
JAKIN (KA-SHING)
ZURUUUN
SURELY THIS WOULD BE CONSIDERED NOTHING MORE THAN DESTRUCTION OF PROPERTY.
WHAT!? DANDY!?
HEY! WHAT'S DANDY DOING OVER THERE!?
MOZO (SNUGGLE)
DANDY!
DANDY !!
DANDY, WHAT'S WRONG! LOOK AT ME!
DANDY! COME ON!!
TSU (TOUCH)
IT'S NO USE...
NO ONE CAN DO ANYTHING TO STOP THAT CAT...!
ZUI (LOOM)

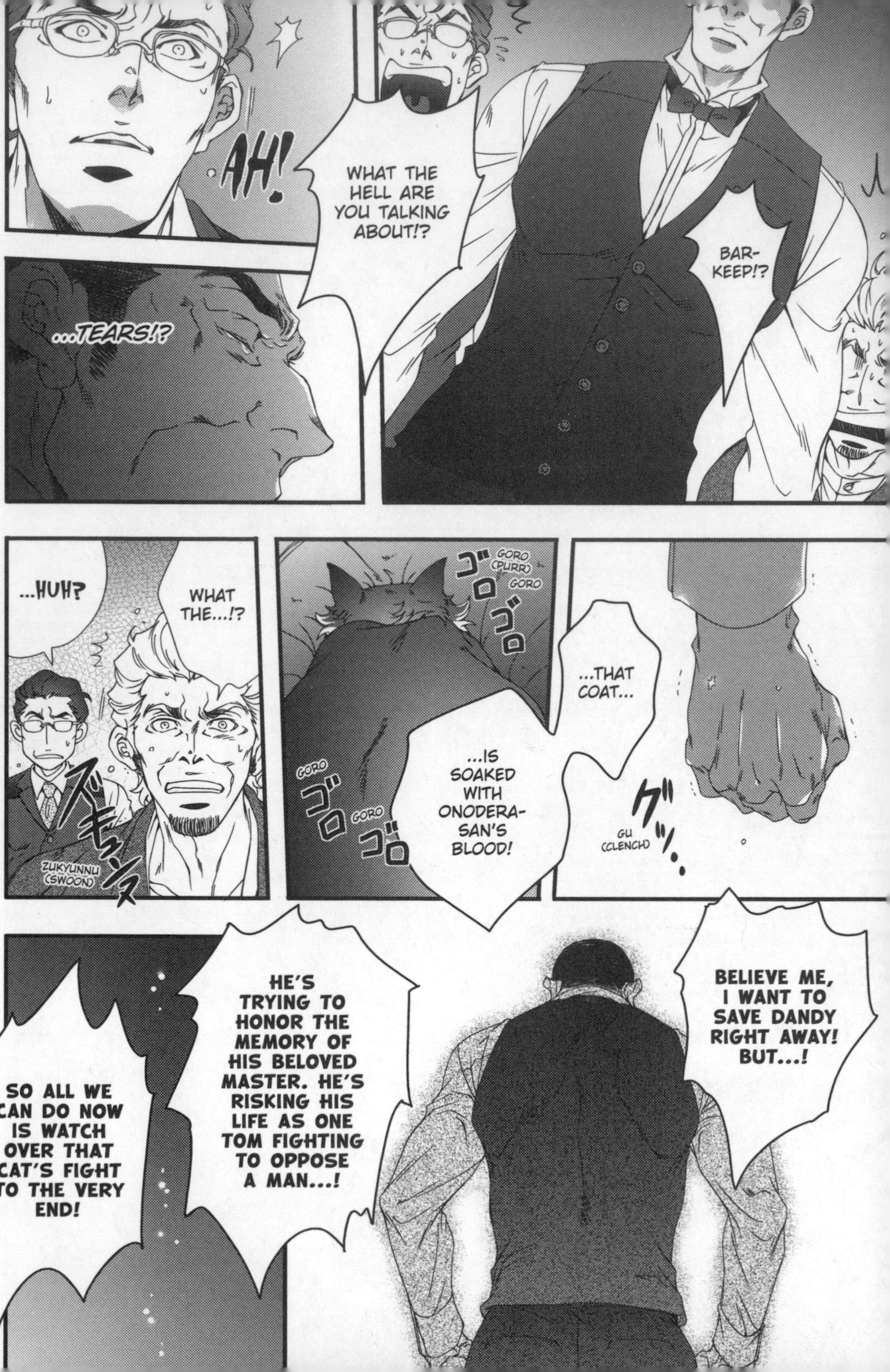
BAR-KEEP!?
WHAT THE HELL ARE YOU TALKING ABOUT!?
AH!
...TEARS!?
...THAT COAT...
GU (CLENCH)
GORO (PURR) GORO
GORO
GORO
...IS SOAKED WITH ONODERA-SAN'S BLOOD!
WHAT THE...!?
...HUH?
ZUKYUNNU (SWOON)
BELIEVE ME, I WANT TO SAVE DANDY RIGHT AWAY! BUT...!
HE'S TRYING TO HONOR THE MEMORY OF HIS BELOVED MASTER. HE'S RISKING HIS LIFE AS ONE TOM FIGHTING TO OPPOSE A MAN...!
SO ALL WE CAN DO NOW IS WATCH OVER THAT CAT'S FIGHT TO THE VERY END!

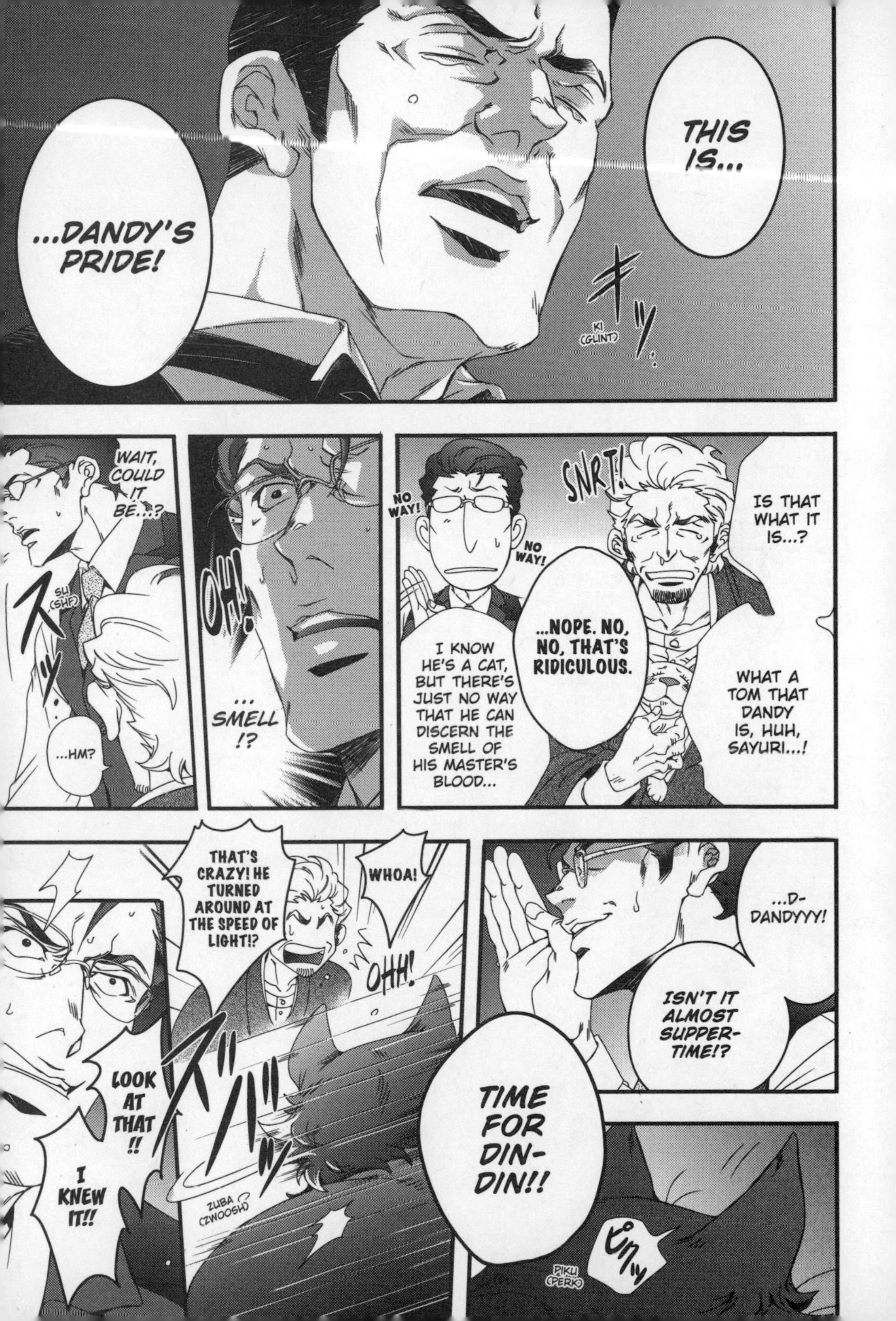
THIS IS...
...DANDY'S PRIDE!
KI (GLINT)
IS THAT WHAT IT IS...?
SNRT!
WHAT A TOM THAT DANDY IS, HUH, SAYURI...!
NO WAY!
NO WAY!
...NOPE. NO, NO, THAT'S RIDICULOUS.
I KNOW HE'S A CAT, BUT THERE'S JUST NO WAY THAT HE CAN DISCERN THE SMELL OF HIS MASTER'S BLOOD...
OHH!
...SMELL!?
WAIT, COULD IT BE...?
SU (SHF)
...HM?
...D-DANDYYY!
ISN'T IT ALMOST SUPPER-TIME!?
TIME FOR DIN-DIN!!
PIKU (PERK)
WHOA!
THAT'S CRAZY! HE TURNED AROUND AT THE SPEED OF LIGHT!?
OHH!
ZUBA (ZWOOSH)
LOOK AT THAT!!
I KNEW IT!!

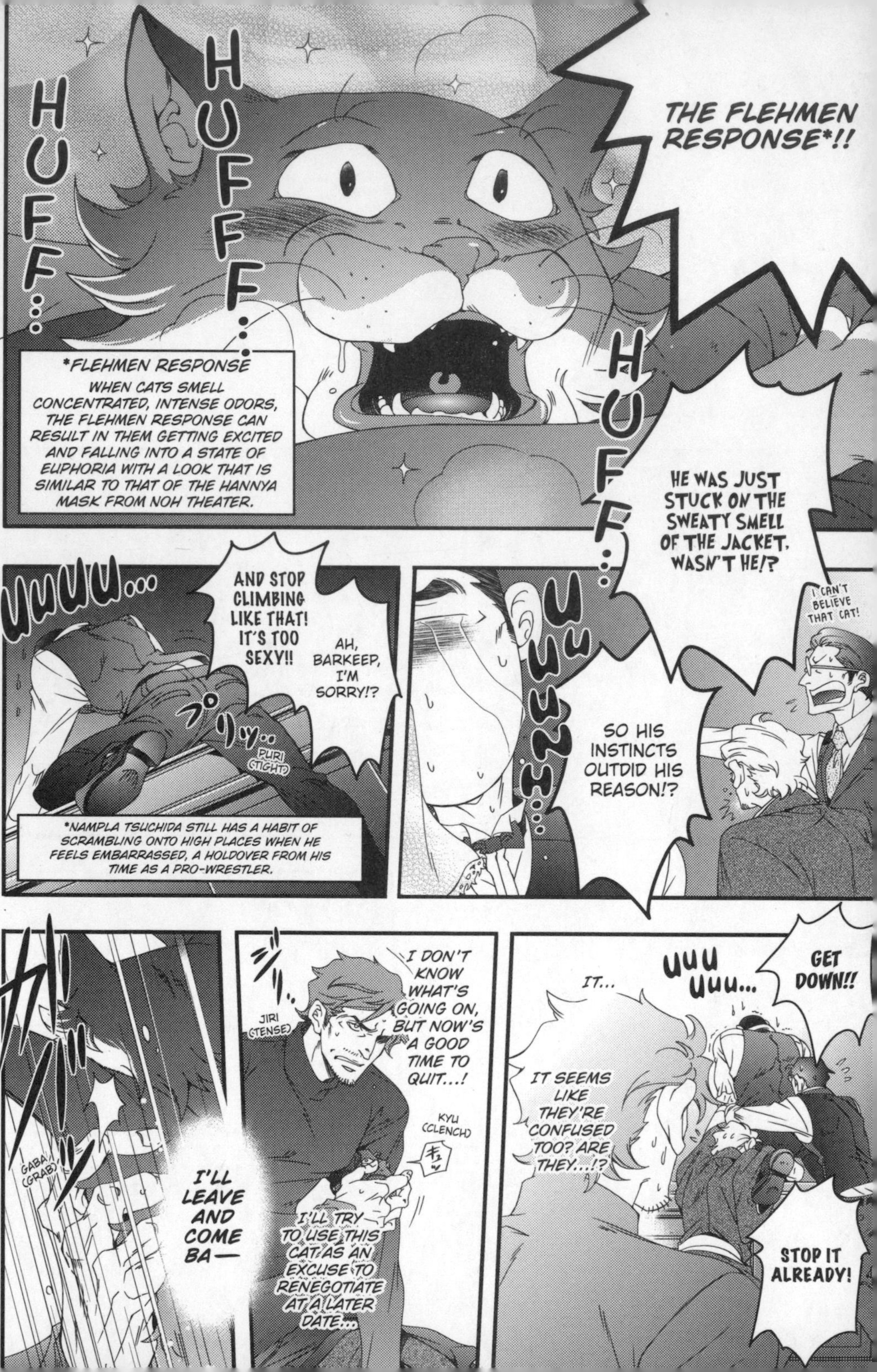
THE FLEHMEN RESPONSE*!!
HUFF HUFF...
HUFF...
HUFF...
*FLEHMEN RESPONSE
WHEN CATS SMELL CONCENTRATED, INTENSE ODORS, THE FLEHMEN RESPONSE CAN RESULT IN THEM GETTING EXCITED AND FALLING INTO A STATE OF EUPHORIA WITH A LOOK THAT IS SIMILAR TO THAT OF THE HANNYA MASK FROM NOH THEATER.
HE WAS JUST STUCK ON THE SWEATY SMELL OF THE JACKET, WASN'T HE!?
I CAN'T BELIEVE THAT CAT!
SO HIS INSTINCTS OUTDID HIS REASON!?
UU UUUNH...
AND STOP CLIMBING LIKE THAT! IT'S TOO SEXY!!
AH, BARKEEP, I'M SORRY!?
UUUU...
プリッ
PURI (TIGHT)
*NAMPLA TSUCHIDA STILL HAS A HABIT OF SCRAMBLING ONTO HIGH PLACES WHEN HE FEELS EMBARRASSED, A HOLDOVER FROM HIS TIME AS A PRO-WRESTLER.
GET DOWN!!
UUU UUU...
IT...
IT SEEMS LIKE THEY'RE CONFUSED TOO? ARE THEY...!?
STOP IT ALREADY!
I DON'T KNOW WHAT'S GOING ON, BUT NOW'S A GOOD TIME TO QUIT...!
JIRI (TENSE)
KYU (CLENCH)
I'LL TRY TO USE THIS CAT AS AN EXCUSE TO RENEGOTIATE AT A LATER DATE...
GABA (GRAB)
I'LL LEAVE AND COME BA—

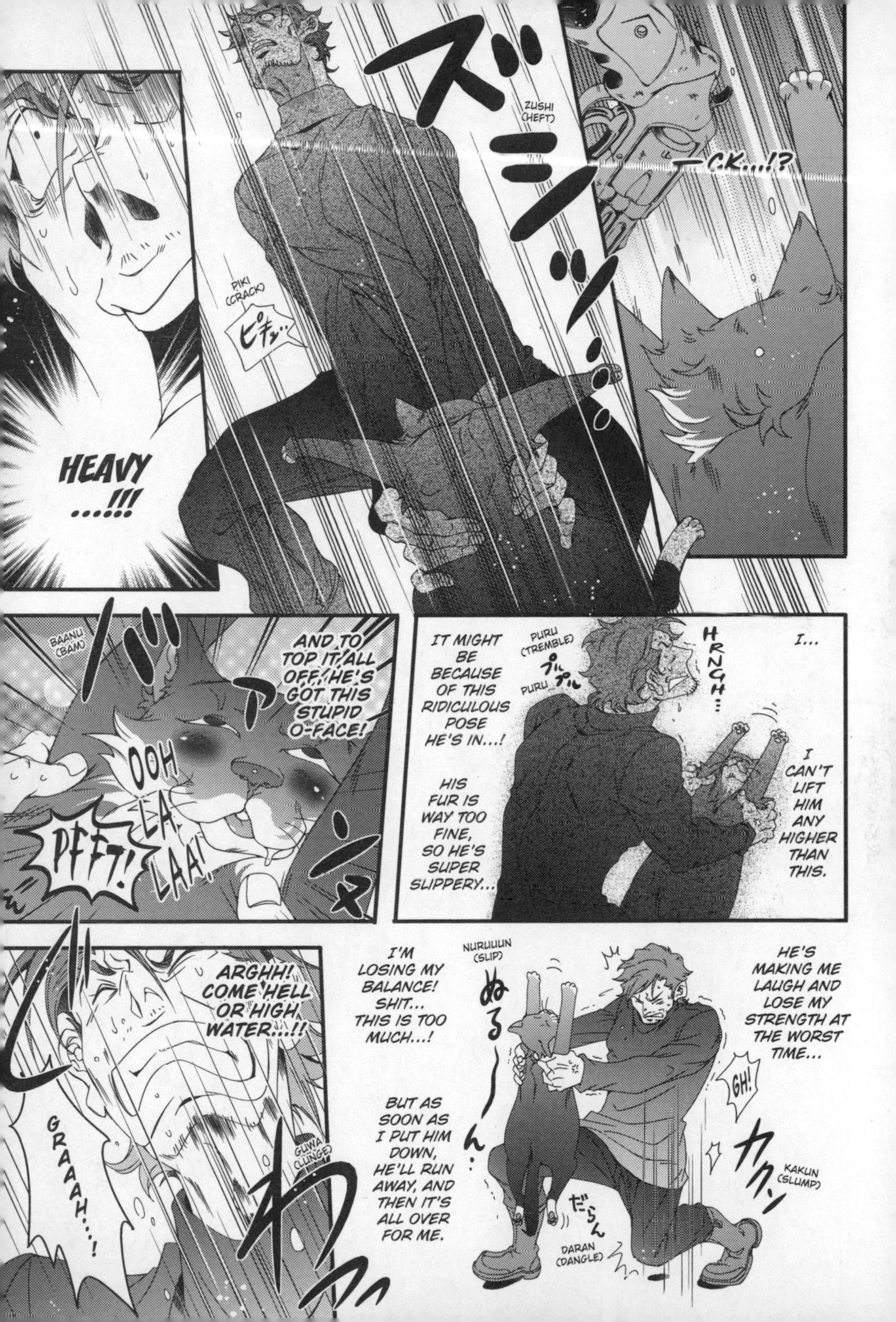
—CK...!?
ZUSHI (HEFT)
PIKI (CRACK)
ピキッ
HEAVY ......!!!
I...
HRNGH...
I CAN'T LIFT HIM ANY HIGHER THAN THIS.
PURU (TREMBLE) PURU
IT MIGHT BE BECAUSE OF THIS RIDICULOUS POSE HE'S IN...!
HIS FUR IS WAY TOO FINE, SO HE'S SUPER SLIPPERY...
BAANU (BAM)
AND TO TOP IT ALL OFF, HE'S GOT THIS STUPID O-FACE!
OOH LA LA LAA!
PFFFT!
HE'S MAKING ME LAUGH AND LOSE MY STRENGTH AT THE WORST TIME...
GH!
KAKUN (SLUMP)
NURUUUN (SLIP)
ぬるーん
I'M LOSING MY BALANCE! SHIT... THIS IS TOO MUCH...!
BUT AS SOON AS I PUT HIM DOWN, HE'LL RUN AWAY, AND THEN IT'S ALL OVER FOR ME.
だらん
DARAN (DANGLE)
ARGHH! COME HELL OR HIGH WATER...!!
GUWA (LUNGE)
GRAAAH...!

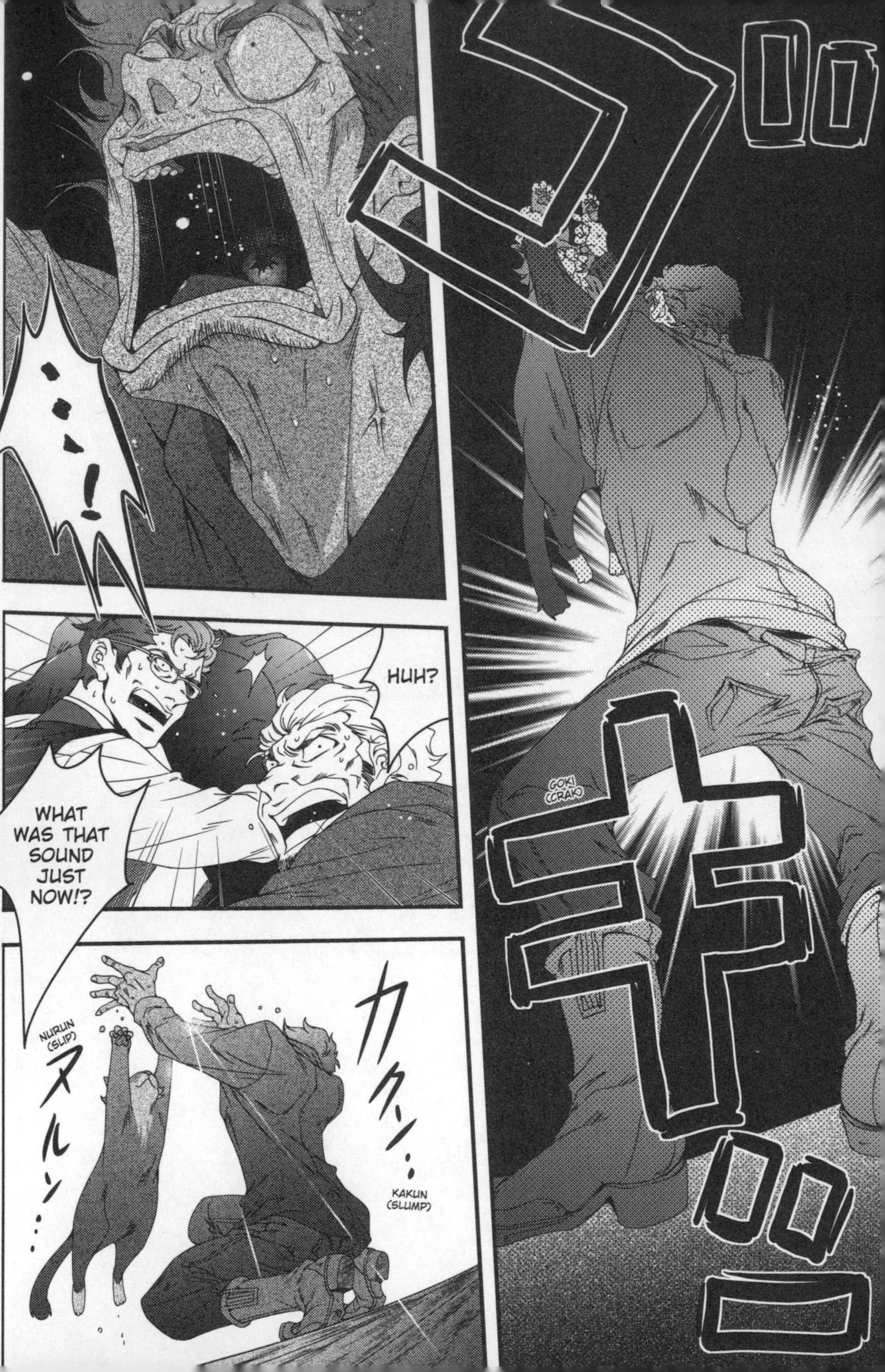
GOKI
(CRAK)
...!
HUH?
WHAT WAS THAT SOUND JUST NOW!?
カクン...
KAKUN
(SLUMP)
ヌルン...
NURUN
(SLIP)

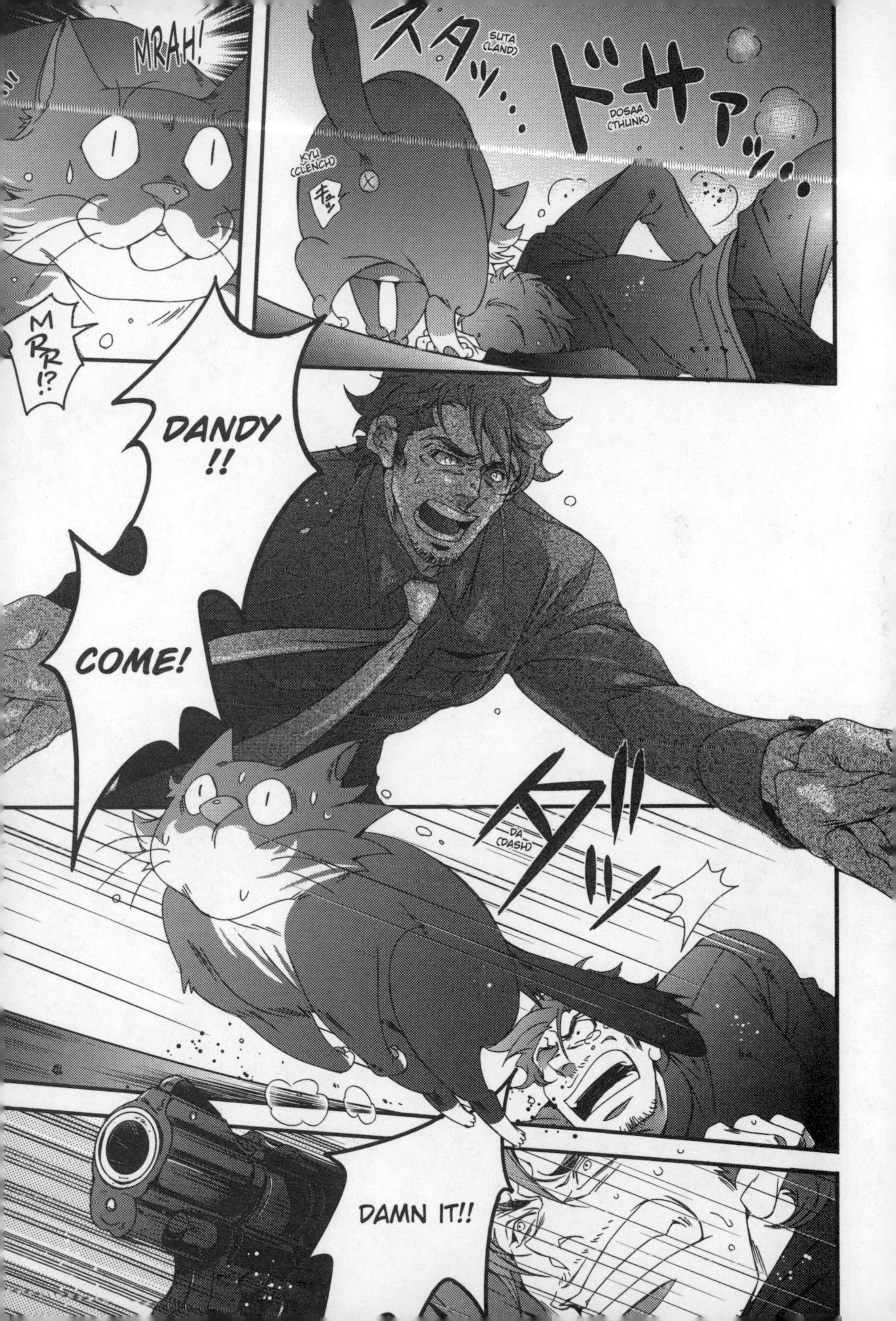

スタッ…
SUTA (LAND)
ドサァッ…
DOSAA (THUNK)
KYU (CLENCH)
MRAH!
MRR!?
DANDY!!
COME!
タッ
DA (DASH)
DAMN IT!!

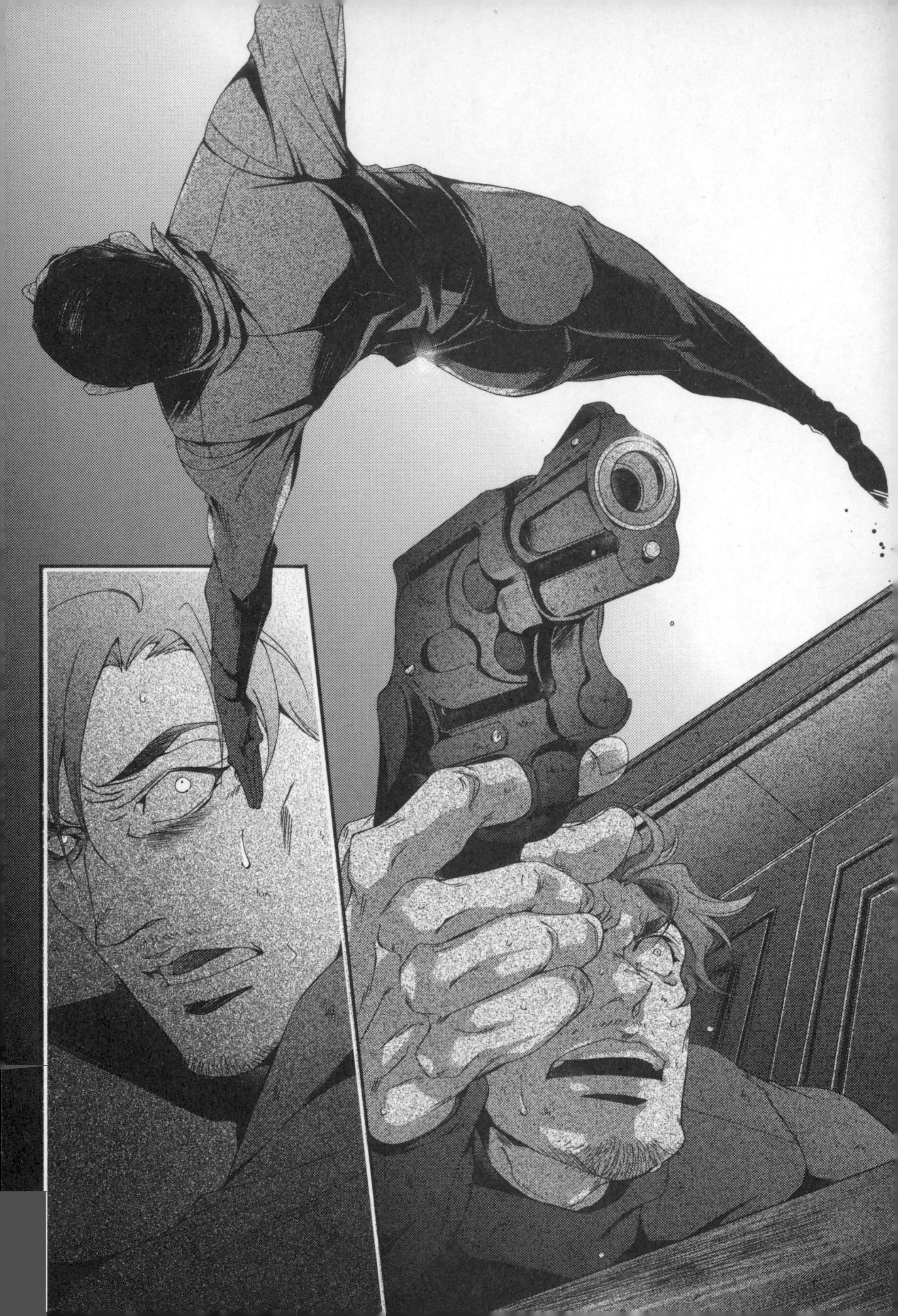

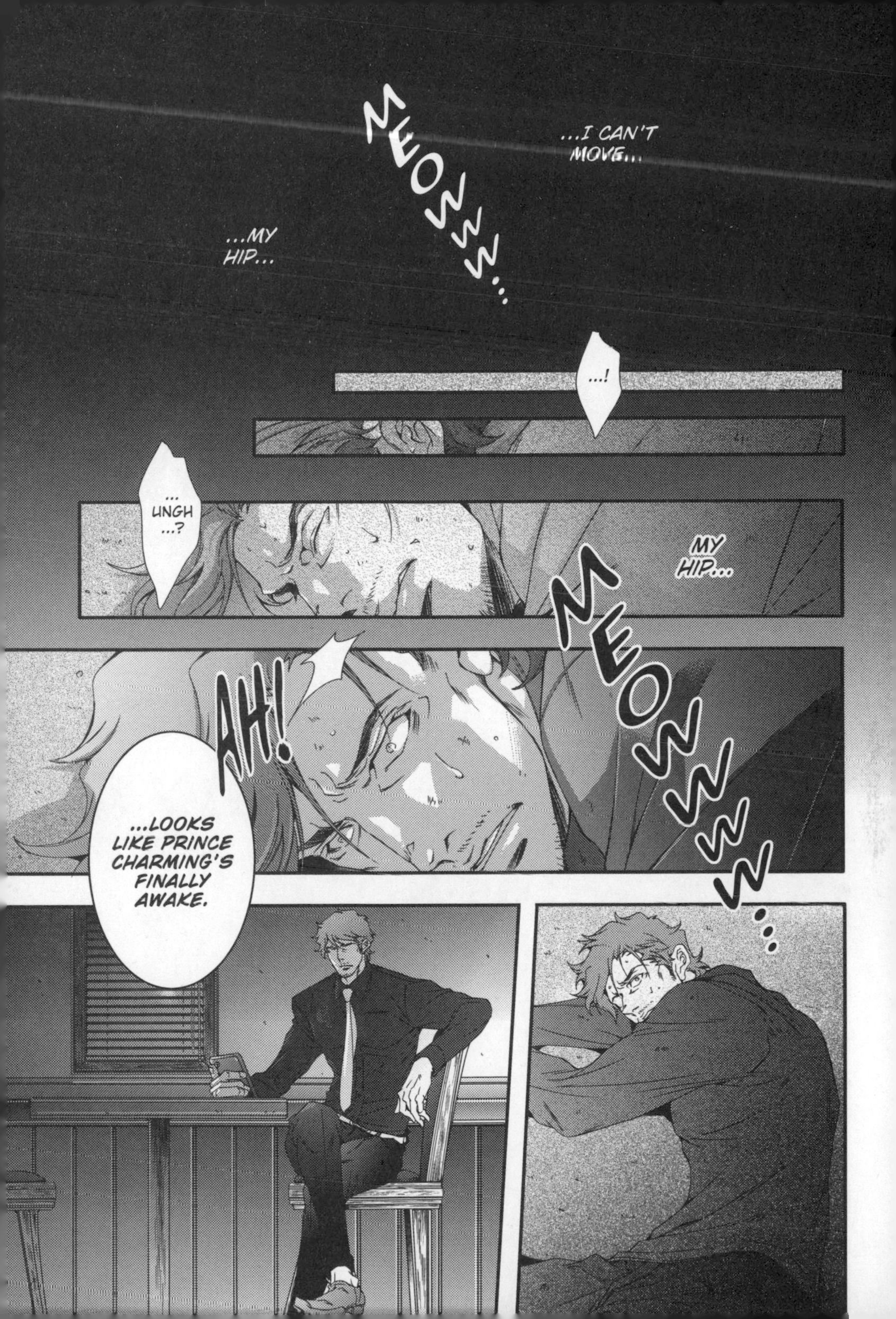
...I CAN'T MOVE...
MEOWWW...
...MY HIP...
...!
... UNGH ...?
MY HIP...
MEOWWWWW...
AH!
...LOOKS LIKE PRINCE CHARMING'S FINALLY AWAKE.

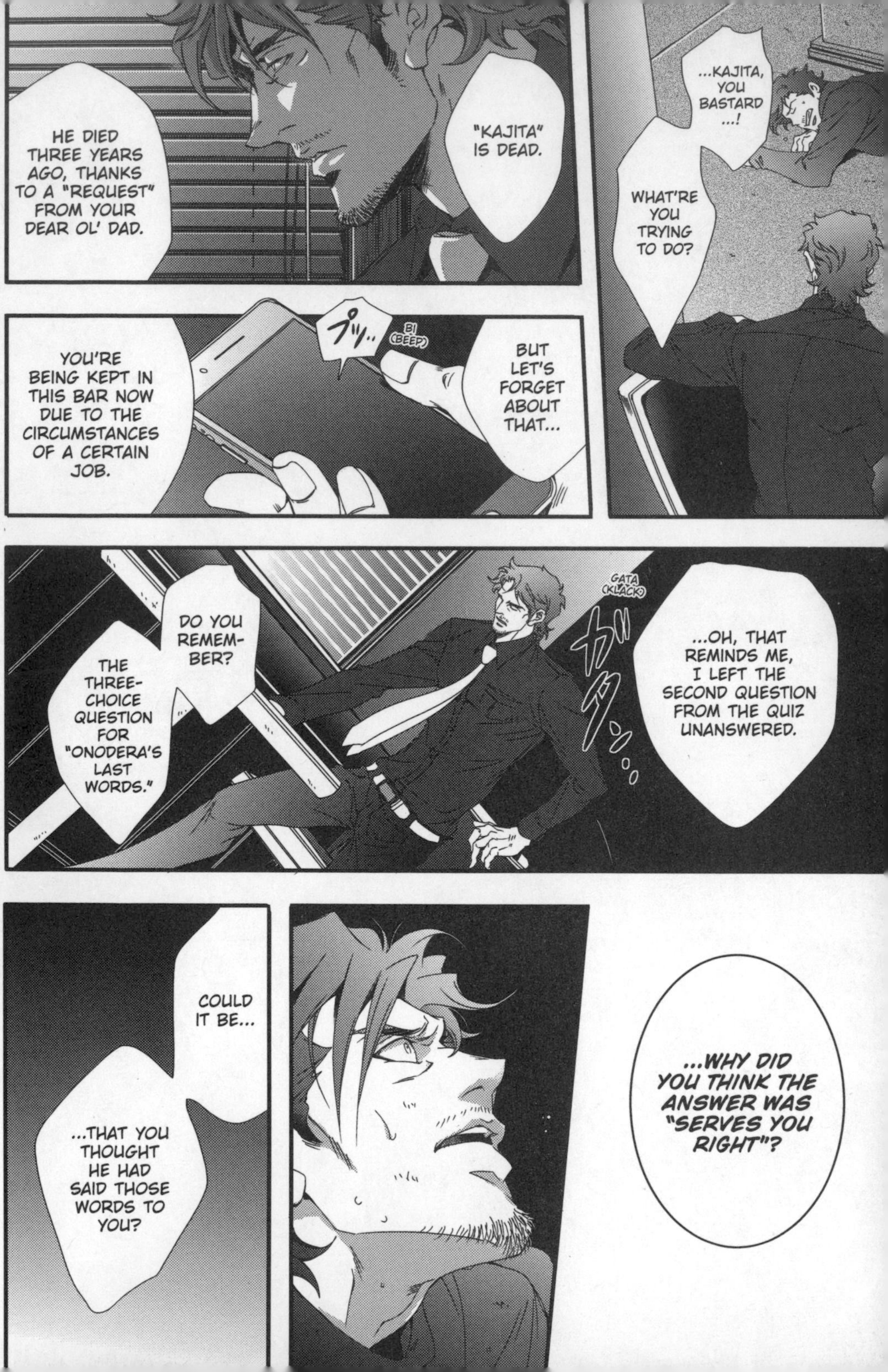
...KAJITA, YOU BASTARD ...!
WHAT'RE YOU TRYING TO DO?
"KAJITA" IS DEAD.
HE DIED THREE YEARS AGO, THANKS TO A "REQUEST" FROM YOUR DEAR OL' DAD.
BI (BEEP)
BUT LET'S FORGET ABOUT THAT...
YOU'RE BEING KEPT IN THIS BAR NOW DUE TO THE CIRCUMSTANCES OF A CERTAIN JOB.
GATA (KLACK)
...OH, THAT REMINDS ME, I LEFT THE SECOND QUESTION FROM THE QUIZ UNANSWERED.
DO YOU REMEMBER?
THE THREE-CHOICE QUESTION FOR "ONODERA'S LAST WORDS."
...WHY DID YOU THINK THE ANSWER WAS "SERVES YOU RIGHT"?
COULD IT BE...
...THAT YOU THOUGHT HE HAD SAID THOSE WORDS TO YOU?

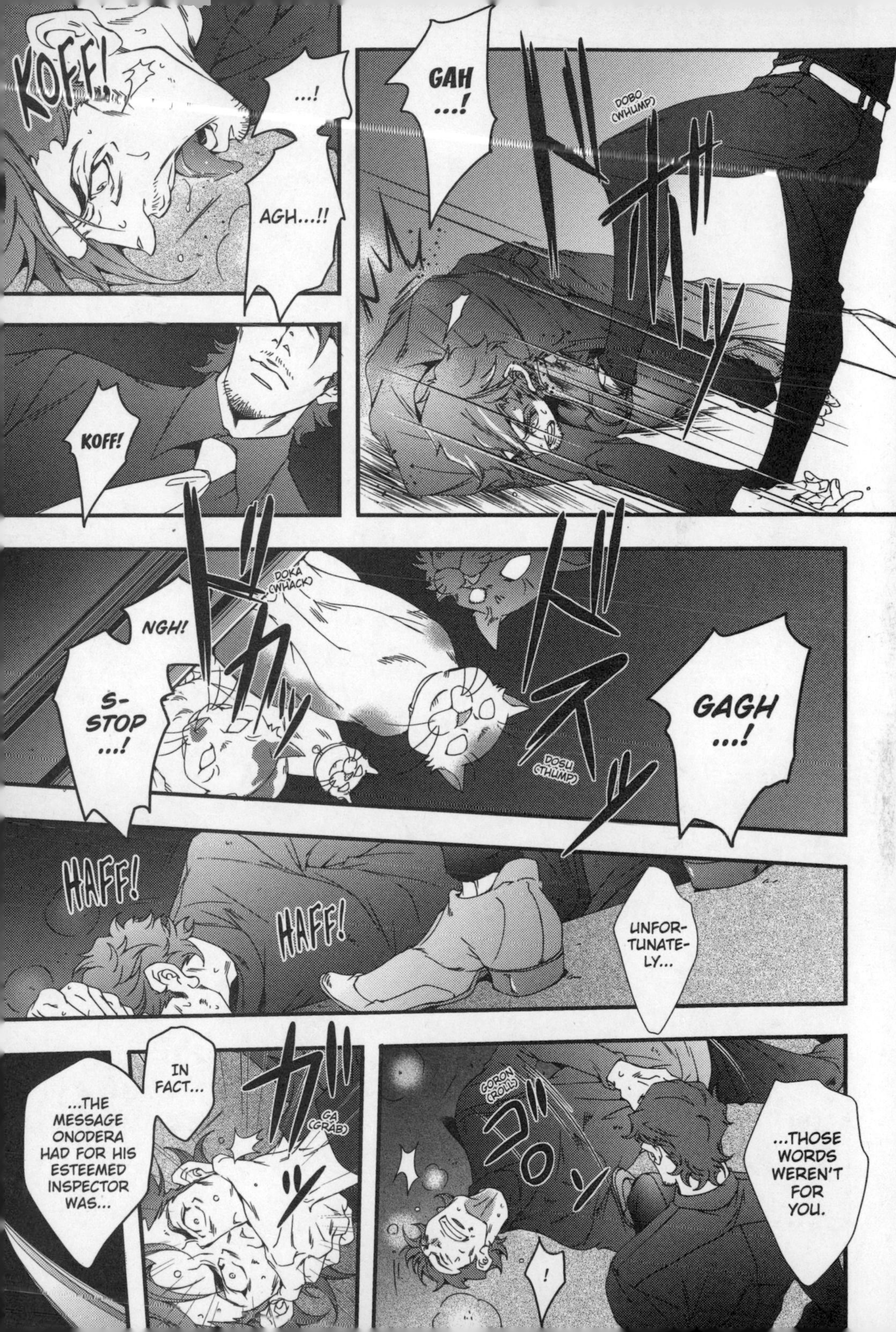
GAH ...!
DOBO (WHUMP)
KOFF!
...!
AGH...!!
KOFF!
GAGH ...!
DOSU (THUMP)
DOKA (WHACK)
NGH!
S-STOP ...!
UNFORTUNATELY...
HAFF!
HAFF!
GORON (ROLL)
...THOSE WORDS WEREN'T FOR YOU.
!
IN FACT...
GA (GRAB)
...THE MESSAGE ONODERA HAD FOR HIS ESTEEMED INSPECTOR WAS...

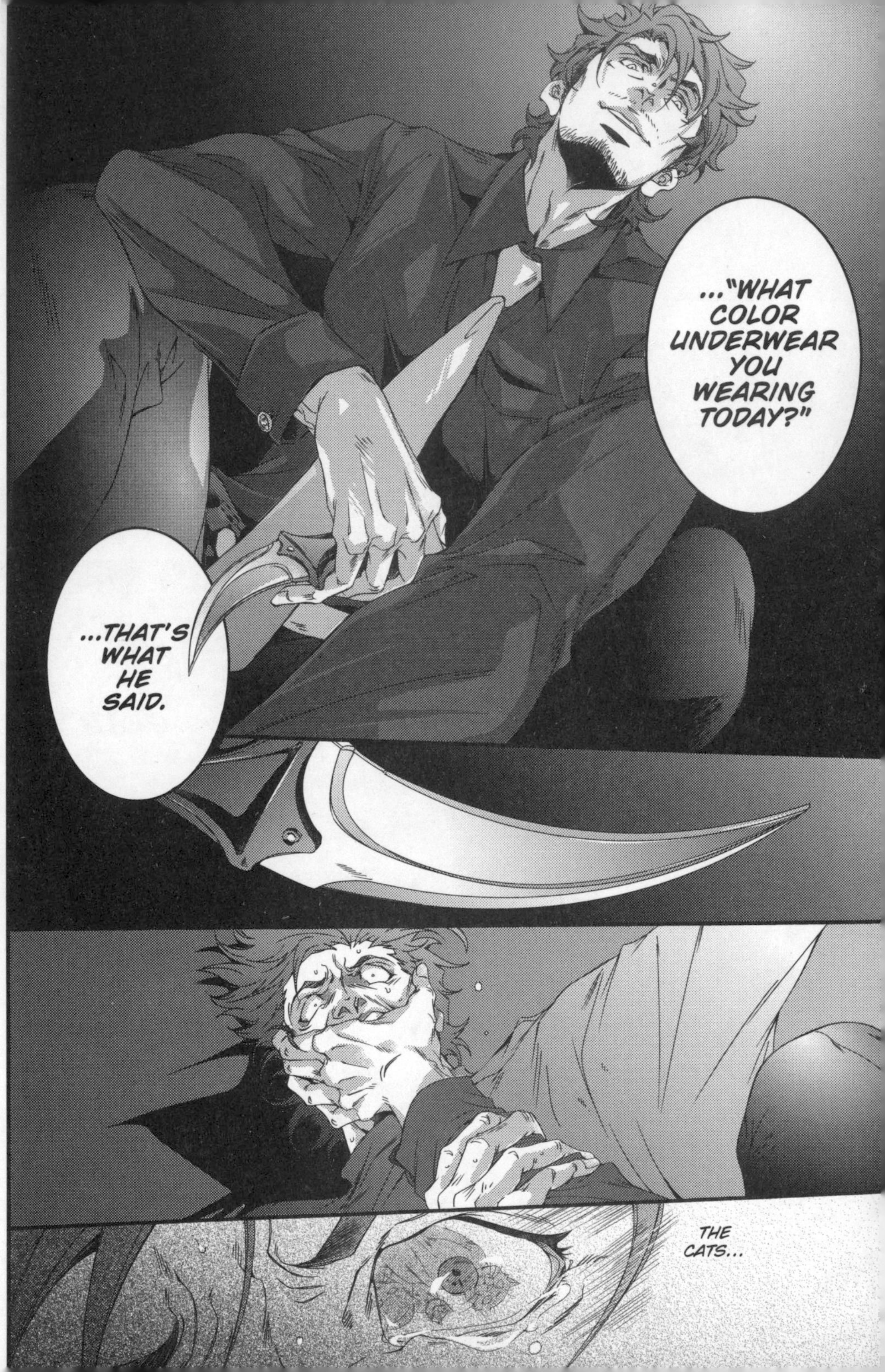
..."WHAT COLOR UNDERWEAR YOU WEARING TODAY?"
...THAT'S WHAT HE SAID.
THE CATS...

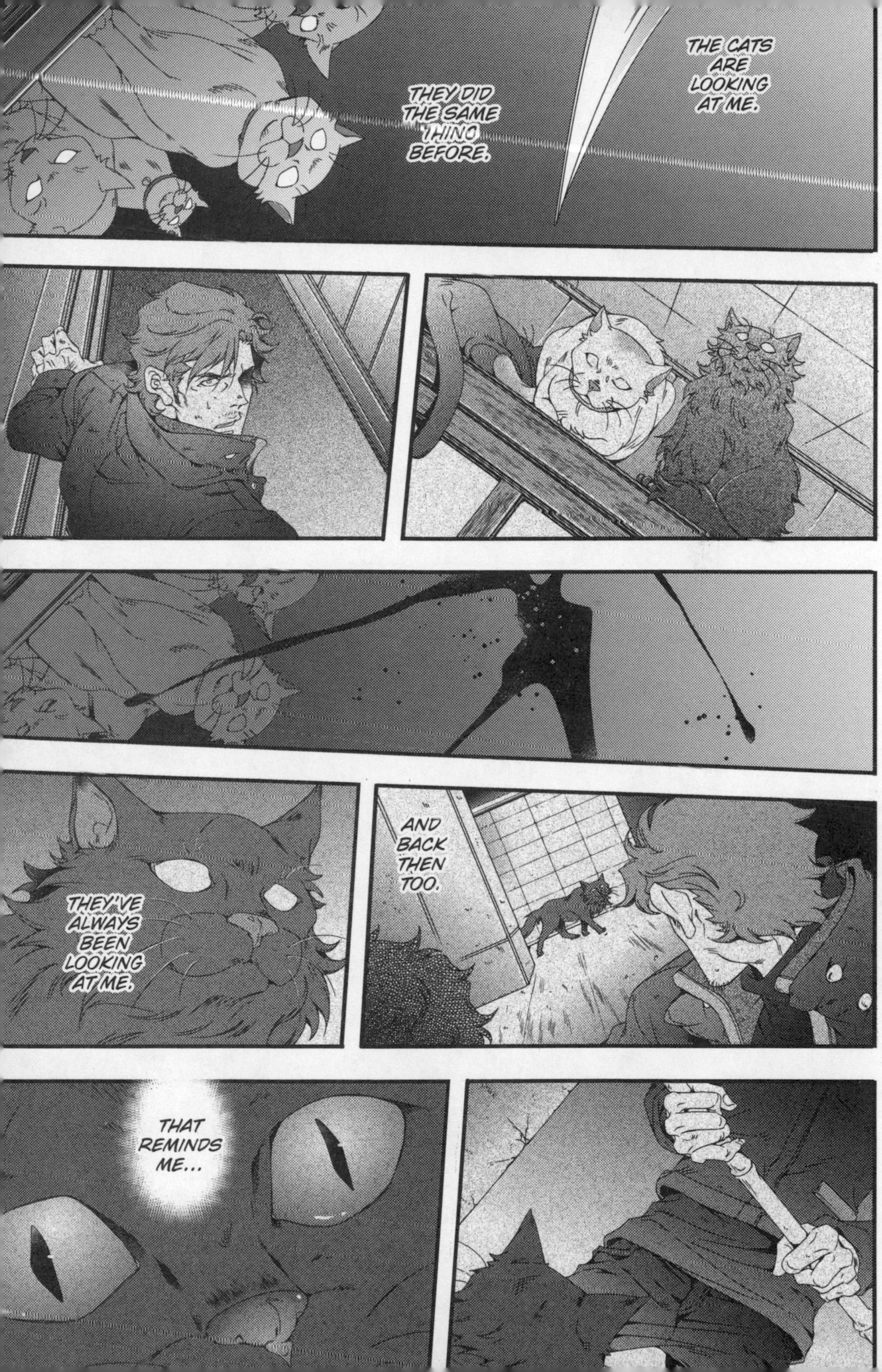
THE CATS ARE LOOKING AT ME.
THEY DID THE SAME THING BEFORE.
AND BACK THEN TOO.
THEY'VE ALWAYS BEEN LOOKING AT ME.
THAT REMINDS ME...

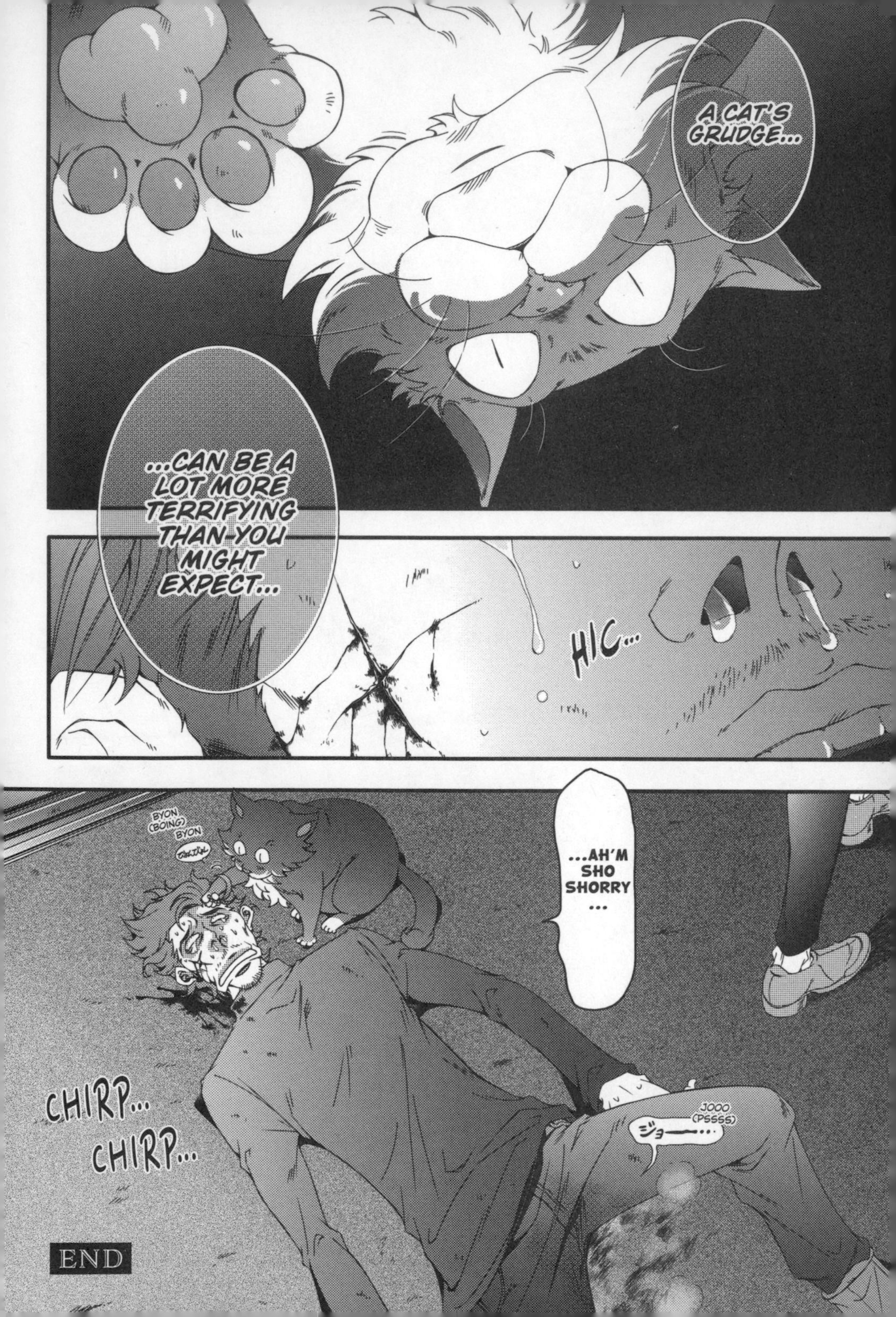
A CAT'S GRUDGE...
...CAN BE A LOT MORE TERRIFYING THAN YOU MIGHT EXPECT...
HIC...
...AH'M SHO SHORRY ...
BYON (BOING) BYON
ぴょんぴょん
CHIRP... CHIRP...
JOOO (PSSSS)
ジョ——...
END

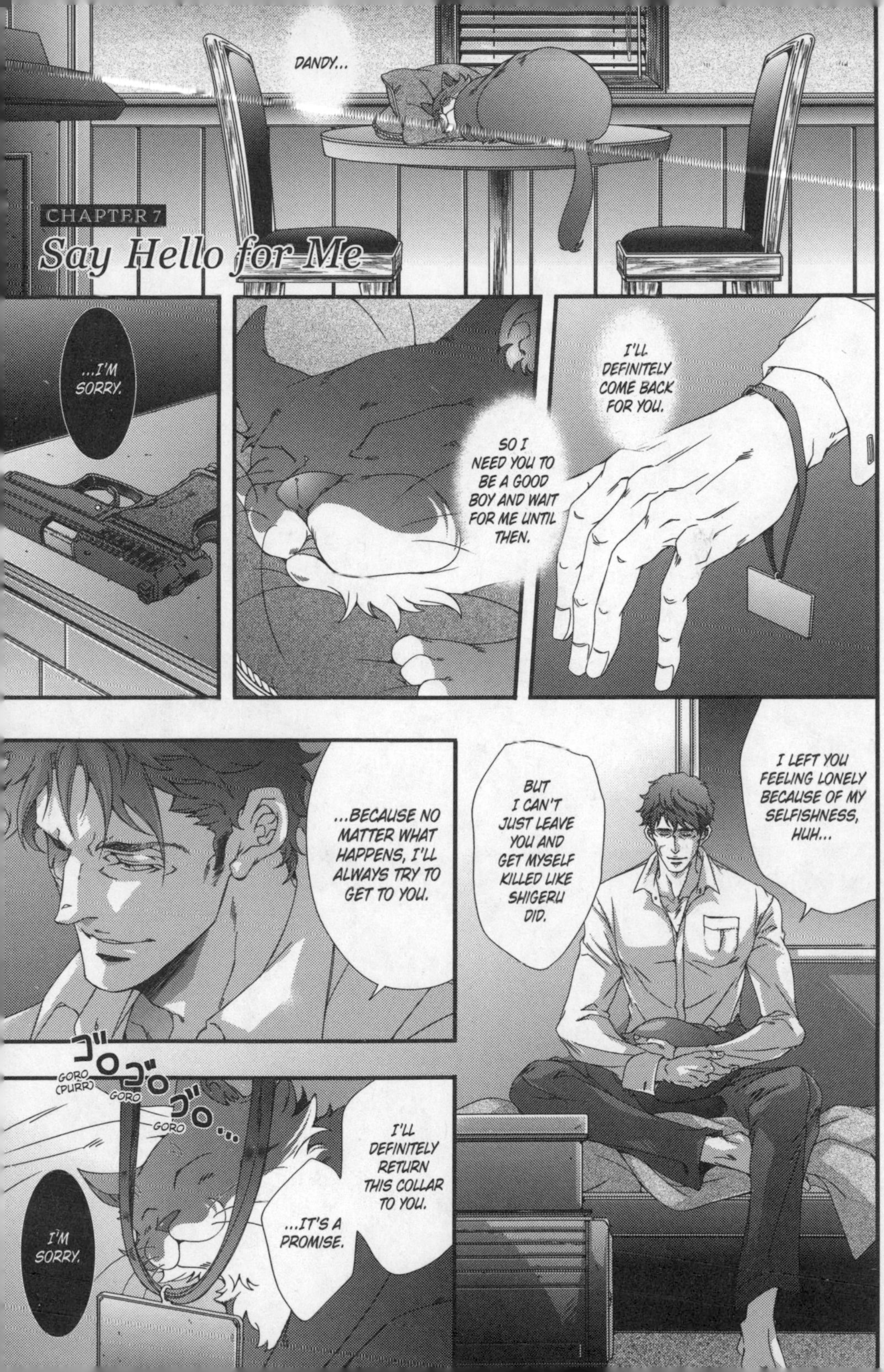
DANDY...
CHAPTER 7
Say Hello for Me
I'LL DEFINITELY COME BACK FOR YOU.
SO I NEED YOU TO BE A GOOD BOY AND WAIT FOR ME UNTIL THEN.
...I'M SORRY.
I LEFT YOU FEELING LONELY BECAUSE OF MY SELFISHNESS, HUH...
BUT I CAN'T JUST LEAVE YOU AND GET MYSELF KILLED LIKE SHIGERU DID.
...BECAUSE NO MATTER WHAT HAPPENS, I'LL ALWAYS TRY TO GET TO YOU.
ゴロゴロゴロ...
GORO (PURR)
GORO
GORO
I'LL DEFINITELY RETURN THIS COLLAR TO YOU.
...IT'S A PROMISE.
I'M SORRY.

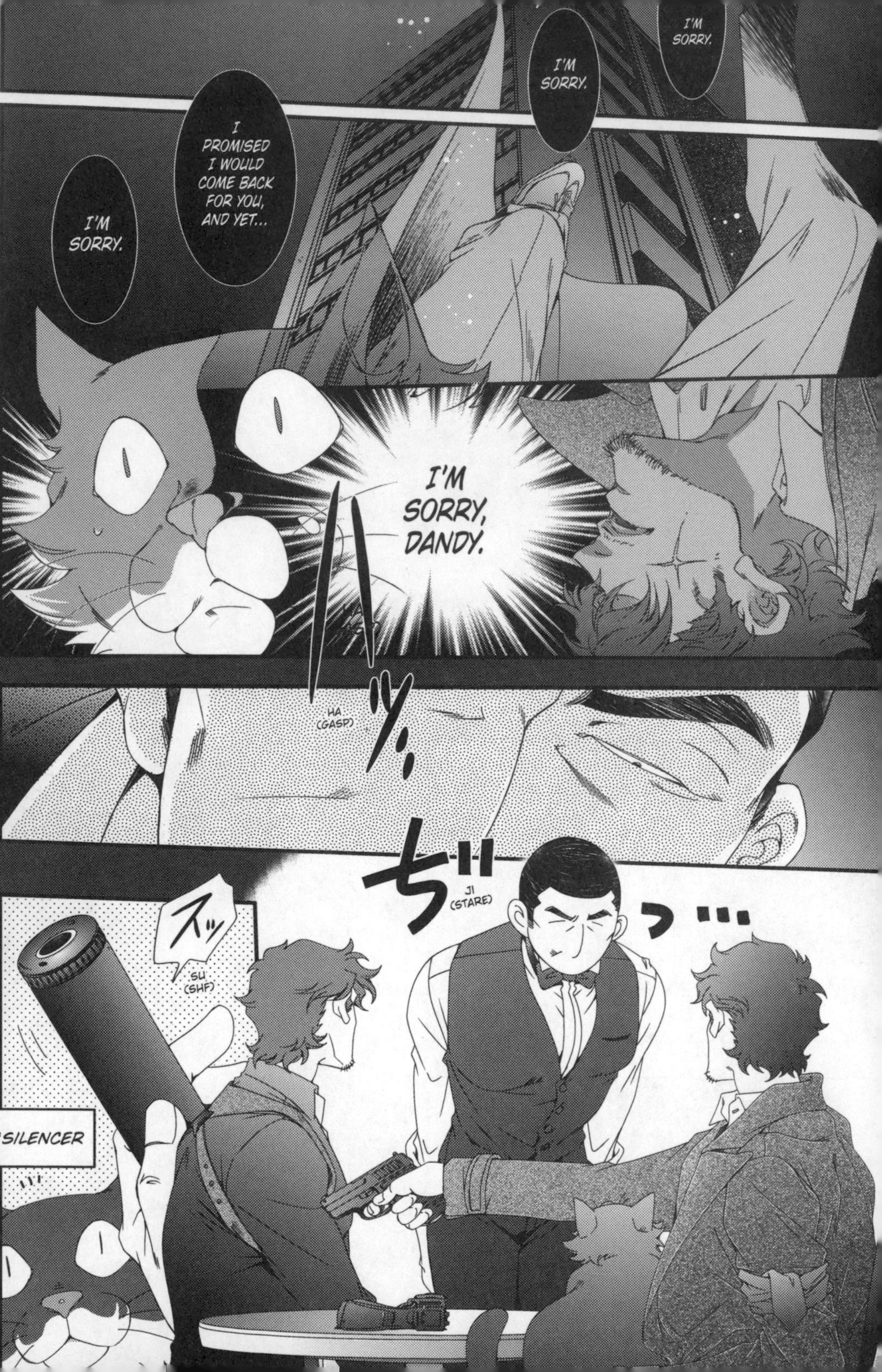
I'M SORRY.
I'M SORRY.
I PROMISED I WOULD COME BACK FOR YOU, AND YET...
I'M SORRY.
I'M SORRY, DANDY.
ッ
HA (GASP)
ぢー
JI (STARE)
っ...
スッ
SU (SHF)
*SILENCER

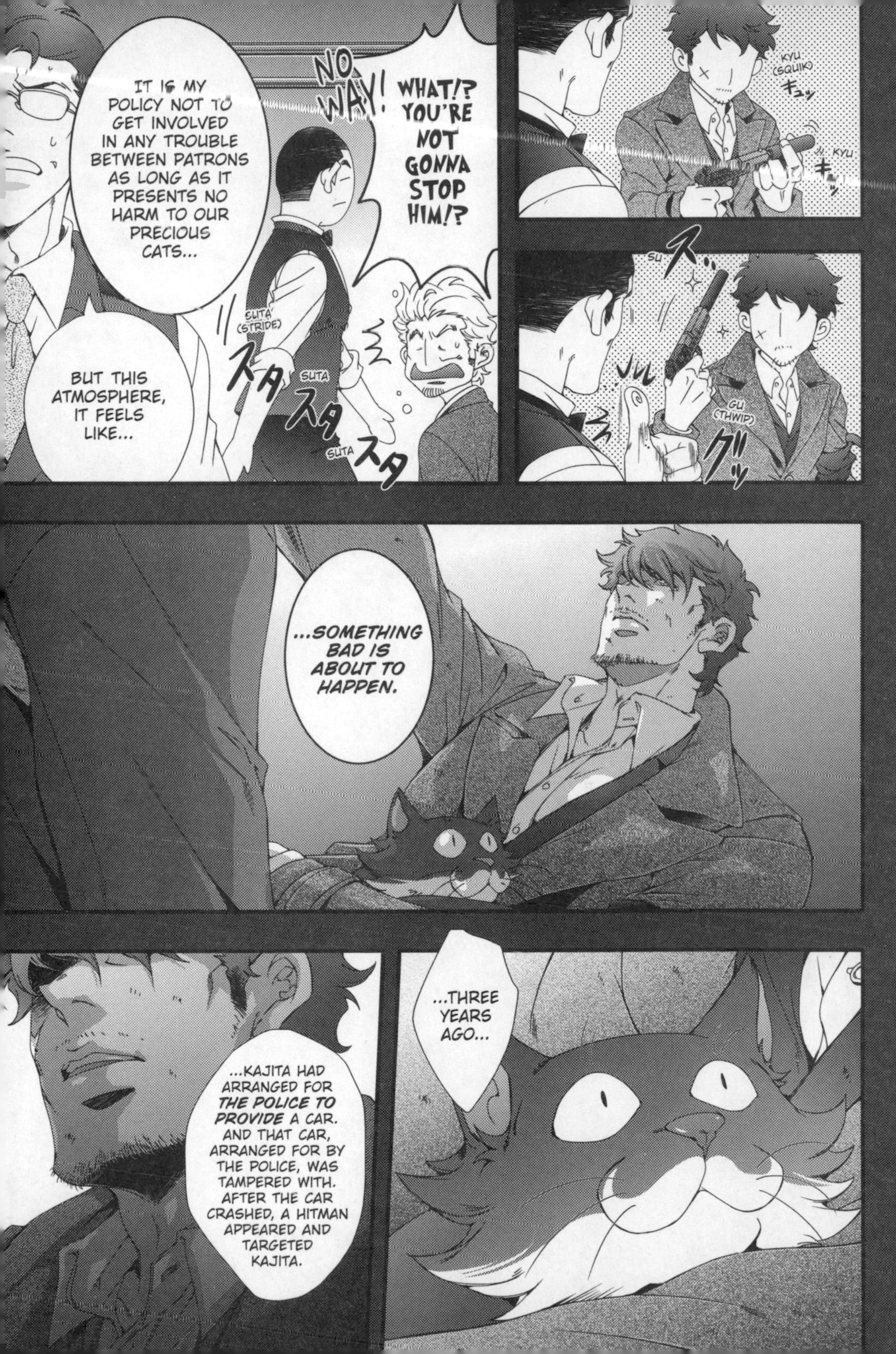
KYU (SQUIK)
キュッ
KYU
キュッ
SU
ス…
GU (THWIP)
グッ
NO WAY!
WHAT!? YOU'RE NOT GONNA STOP HIM!?
IT IS MY POLICY NOT TO GET INVOLVED IN ANY TROUBLE BETWEEN PATRONS AS LONG AS IT PRESENTS NO HARM TO OUR PRECIOUS CATS...
SUTA (STRIDE)
スタ
SUTA
スタ
SUTA
スタ
BUT THIS ATMOSPHERE, IT FEELS LIKE...
...SOMETHING BAD IS ABOUT TO HAPPEN.
...THREE YEARS AGO...
...KAJITA HAD ARRANGED FOR THE POLICE TO PROVIDE A CAR. AND THAT CAR, ARRANGED FOR BY THE POLICE, WAS TAMPERED WITH. AFTER THE CAR CRASHED, A HITMAN APPEARED AND TARGETED KAJITA.

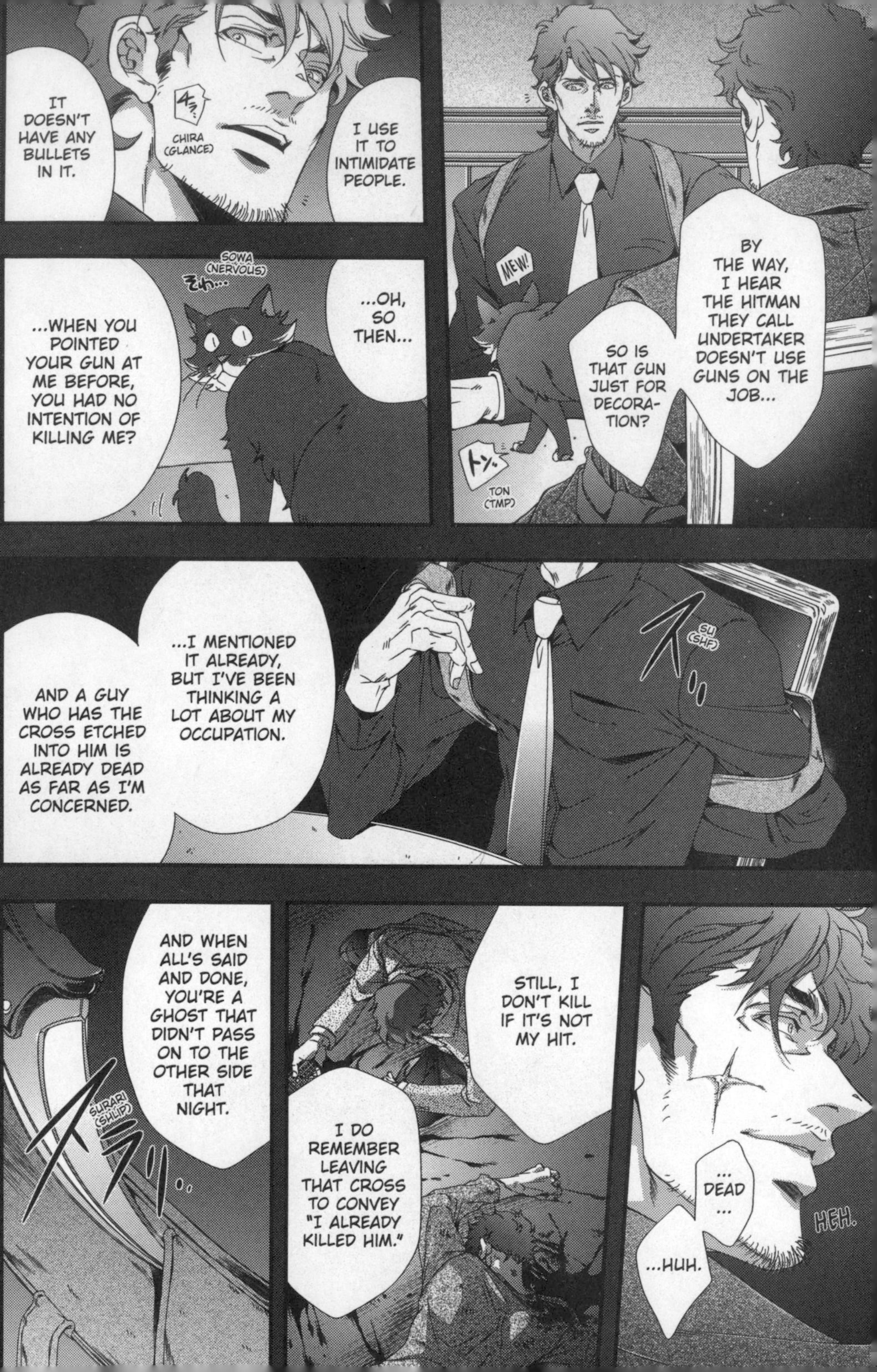
BY THE WAY, I HEAR THE HITMAN THEY CALL UNDERTAKER DOESN'T USE GUNS ON THE JOB...
SO IS THAT GUN JUST FOR DECORATION?
MEW!
TON (TMP)
I USE IT TO INTIMIDATE PEOPLE.
CHIRA (GLANCE)
IT DOESN'T HAVE ANY BULLETS IN IT.
...OH, SO THEN...
SOWA (NERVOUS)
...WHEN YOU POINTED YOUR GUN AT ME BEFORE, YOU HAD NO INTENTION OF KILLING ME?
SU (SHF)
...I MENTIONED IT ALREADY, BUT I'VE BEEN THINKING A LOT ABOUT MY OCCUPATION.
AND A GUY WHO HAS THE CROSS ETCHED INTO HIM IS ALREADY DEAD AS FAR AS I'M CONCERNED.
HEH.
...DEAD...
...HUH.
STILL, I DON'T KILL IF IT'S NOT MY HIT.
I DO REMEMBER LEAVING THAT CROSS TO CONVEY "I ALREADY KILLED HIM."
AND WHEN ALL'S SAID AND DONE, YOU'RE A GHOST THAT DIDN'T PASS ON TO THE OTHER SIDE THAT NIGHT.
SURARI (SHLIP)

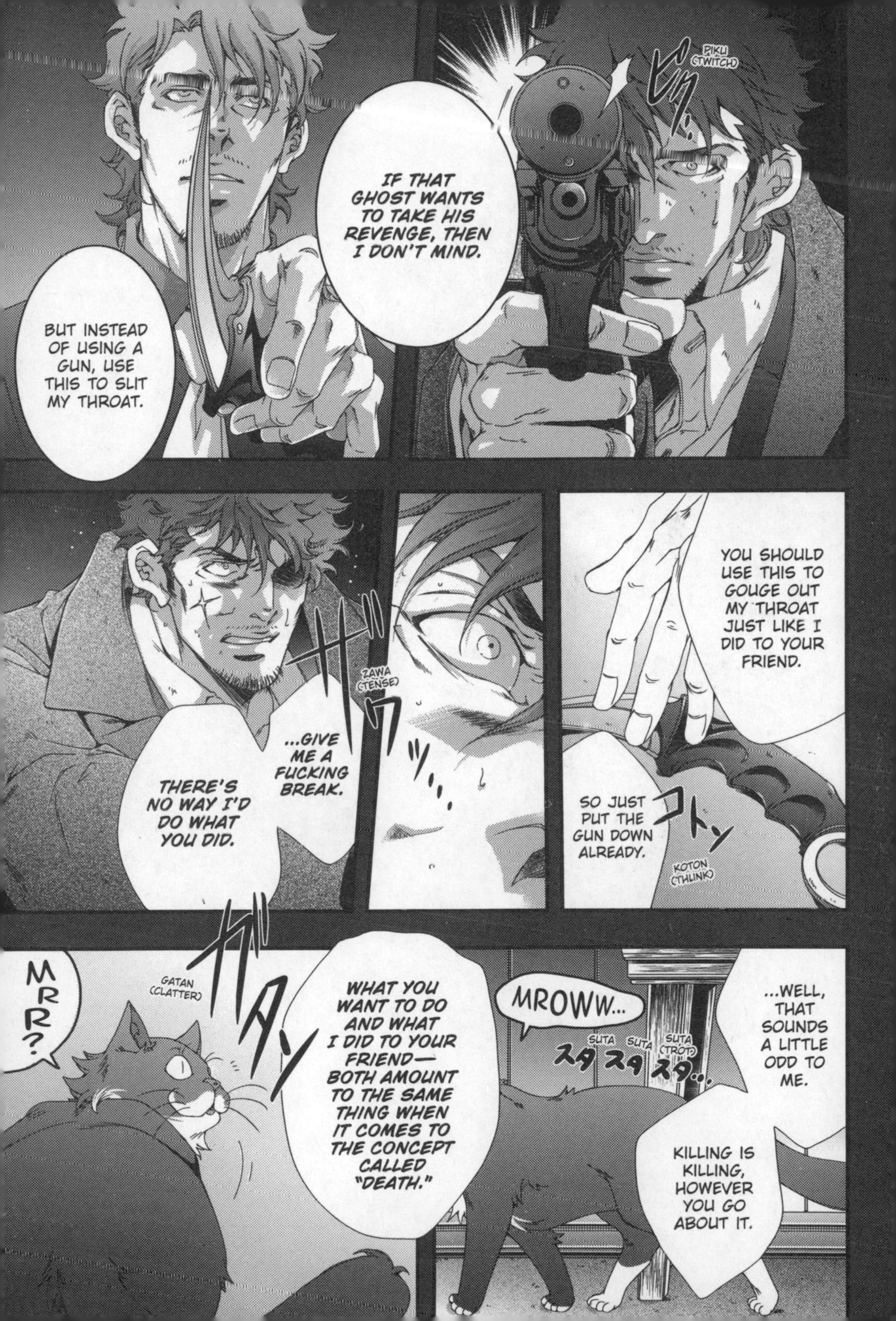
PIKU (TWITCH)
IF THAT GHOST WANTS TO TAKE HIS REVENGE, THEN I DON'T MIND.
BUT INSTEAD OF USING A GUN, USE THIS TO SLIT MY THROAT.
YOU SHOULD USE THIS TO GOUGE OUT MY THROAT JUST LIKE I DID TO YOUR FRIEND.
SO JUST PUT THE GUN DOWN ALREADY.
KOTON (THLINK)
ZAWA (TENSE)
...GIVE ME A FUCKING BREAK.
THERE'S NO WAY I'D DO WHAT YOU DID.
...WELL, THAT SOUNDS A LITTLE ODD TO ME.
MROWW...
SUTA SUTA SUTA (TROT)
KILLING IS KILLING, HOWEVER YOU GO ABOUT IT.
WHAT YOU WANT TO DO AND WHAT I DID TO YOUR FRIEND—BOTH AMOUNT TO THE SAME THING WHEN IT COMES TO THE CONCEPT CALLED "DEATH."
GATAN (CLATTER)
MRR?

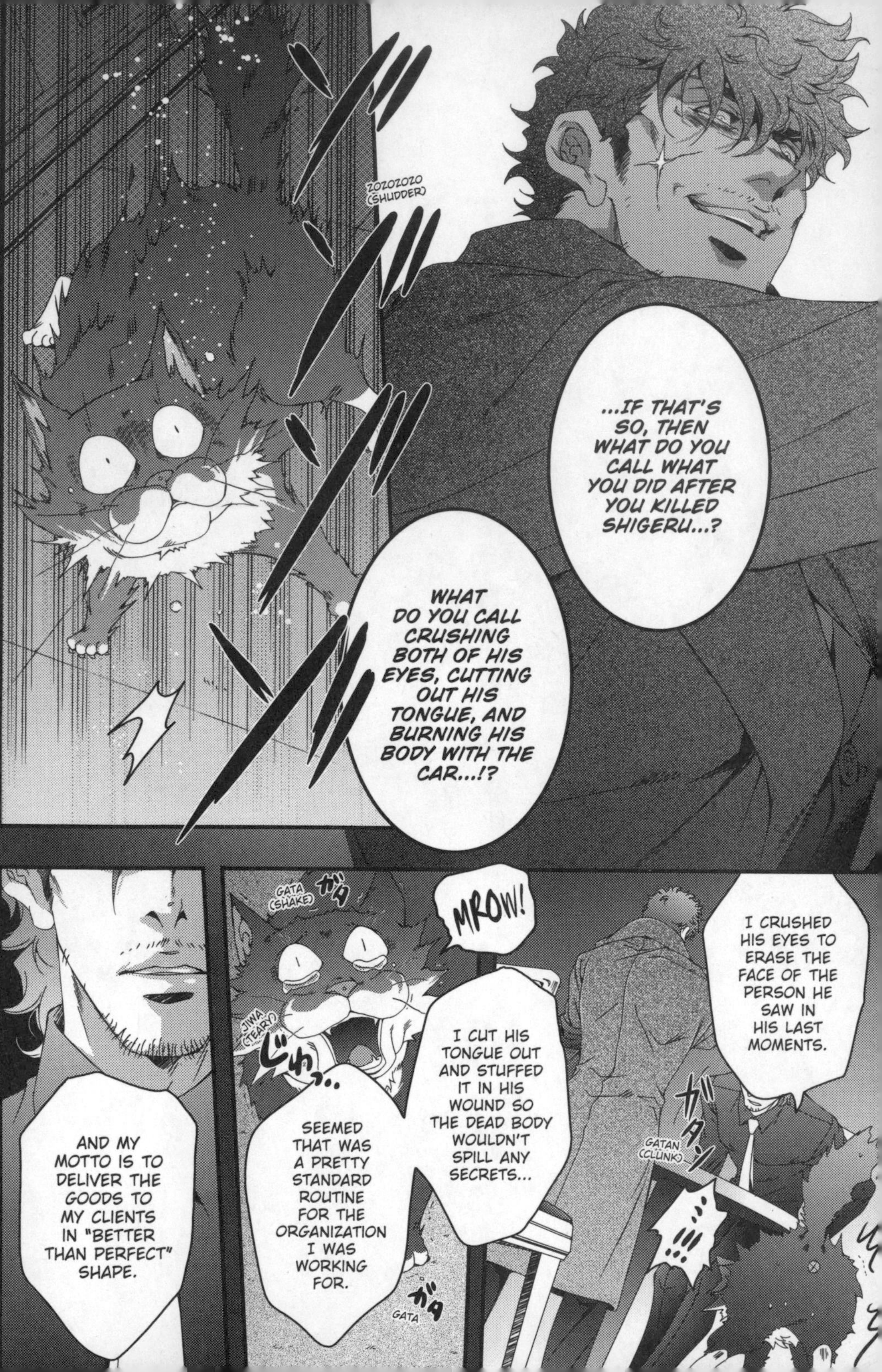
ZOZOZOZO (SHUDDER)
...IF THAT'S SO, THEN WHAT DO YOU CALL WHAT YOU DID AFTER YOU KILLED SHIGERU...?
WHAT DO YOU CALL CRUSHING BOTH OF HIS EYES, CUTTING OUT HIS TONGUE, AND BURNING HIS BODY WITH THE CAR...!?
I CRUSHED HIS EYES TO ERASE THE FACE OF THE PERSON HE SAW IN HIS LAST MOMENTS.
GATAN (CLUNK)
MROW!
GATA (SHAKE)
I CUT HIS TONGUE OUT AND STUFFED IT IN HIS WOUND SO THE DEAD BODY WOULDN'T SPILL ANY SECRETS...
JIWA (TEARY)
SEEMED THAT WAS A PRETTY STANDARD ROUTINE FOR THE ORGANIZATION I WAS WORKING FOR.
GATA
AND MY MOTTO IS TO DELIVER THE GOODS TO MY CLIENTS IN "BETTER THAN PERFECT" SHAPE.

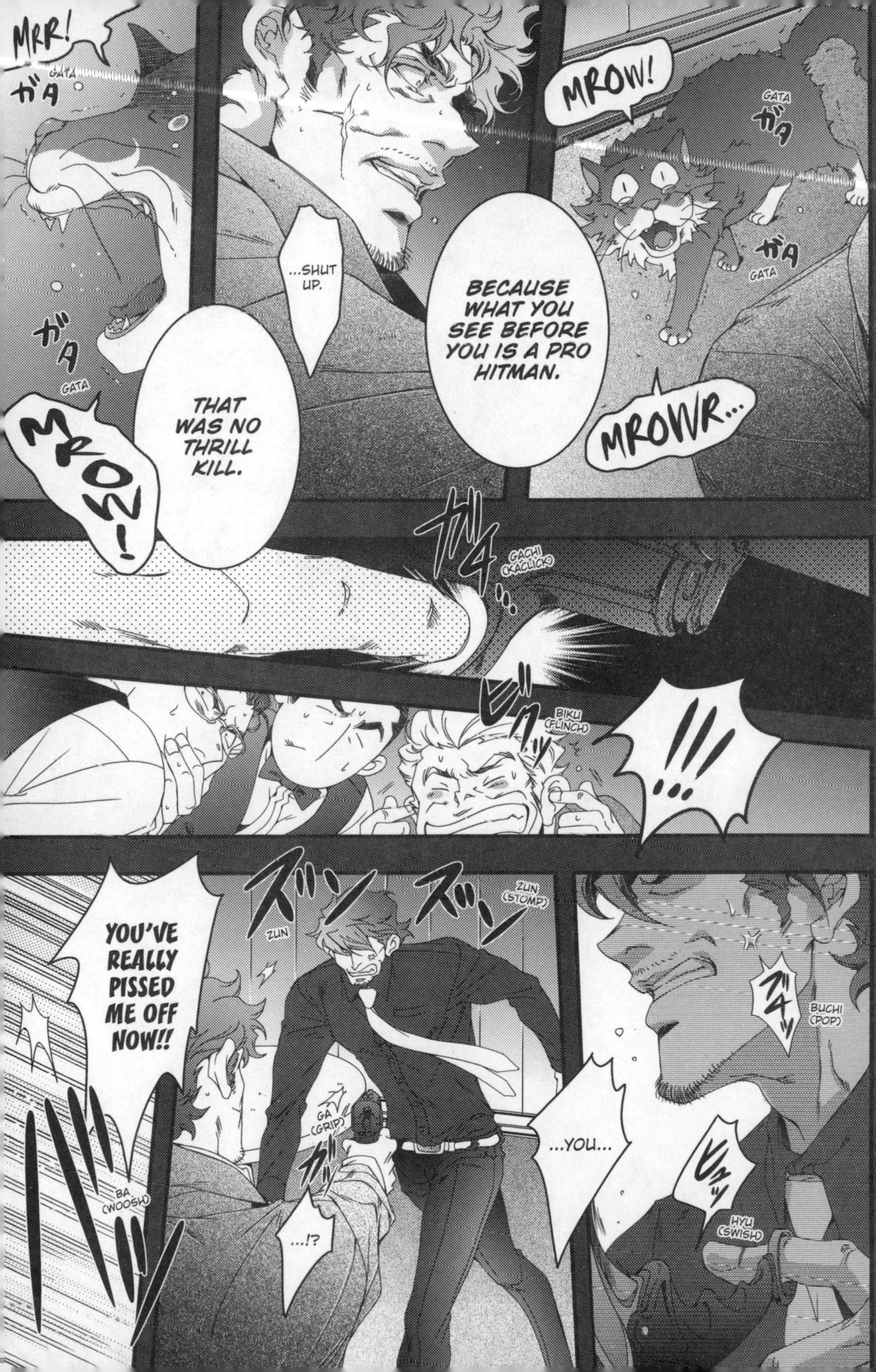
MROW!
GATA
GATA
MROWR...
BECAUSE WHAT YOU SEE BEFORE YOU IS A PRO HITMAN.
...SHUT UP.
THAT WAS NO THRILL KILL.
MRR!
GATA
GATA
MROW!
GACHI (KACLICK)
!!!...
BIKU (FLINCH)
BUCHI (POP)
...YOU...
HYU (SWISH)
ZUN (STOMP)
ZUN
YOU'VE REALLY PISSED ME OFF NOW!!
GA (GRIP)
...!?
BA (WOOSH)

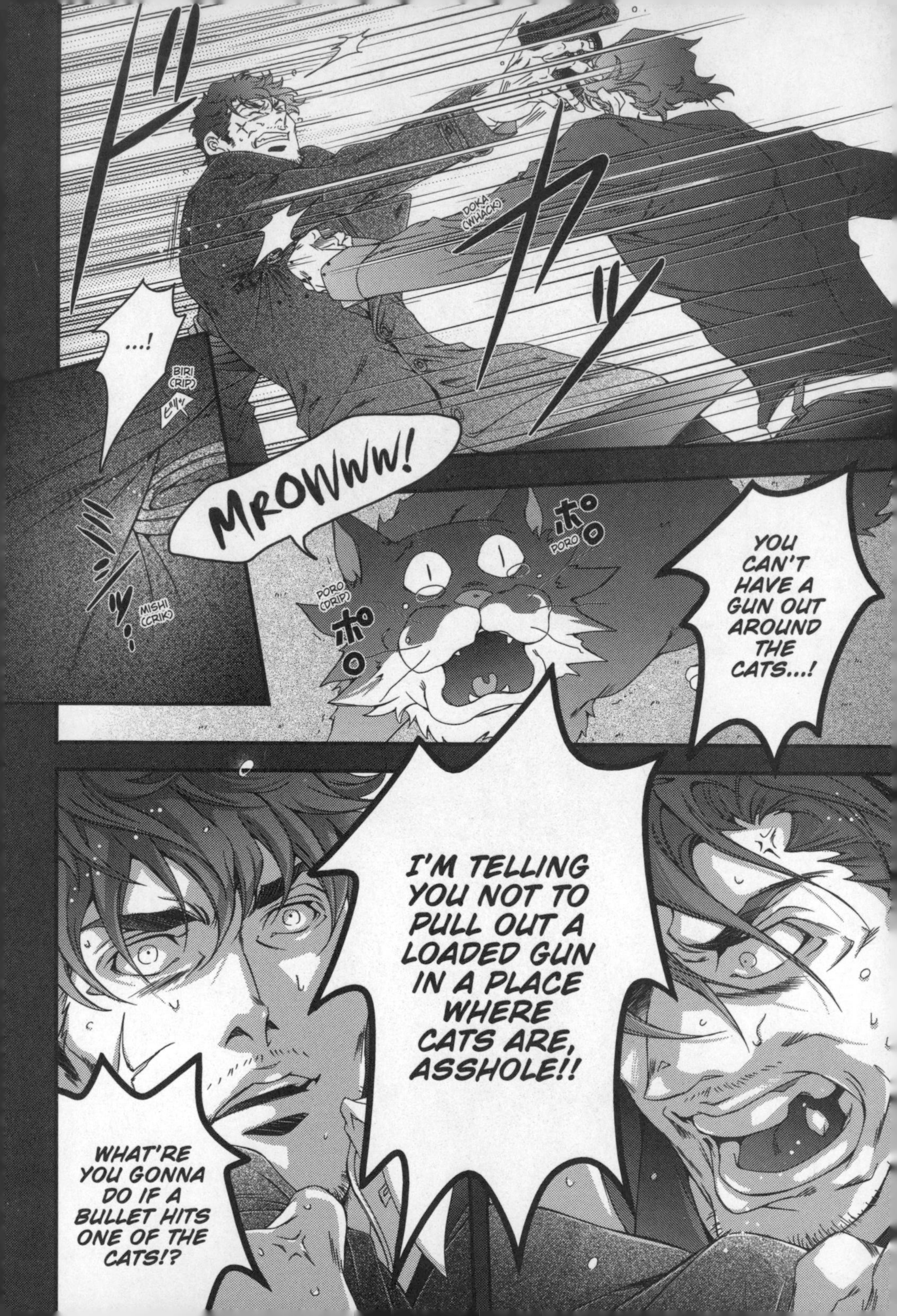

DOKA (WHACK)
...!
BIRI (RIP)
YOU CAN'T HAVE A GUN OUT AROUND THE CATS...!
PORO
MROWWW!
PORO (DRIP)
MISHI (CRIK)
I'M TELLING YOU NOT TO PULL OUT A LOADED GUN IN A PLACE WHERE CATS ARE, ASSHOLE!!
WHAT'RE YOU GONNA DO IF A BULLET HITS ONE OF THE CATS!?

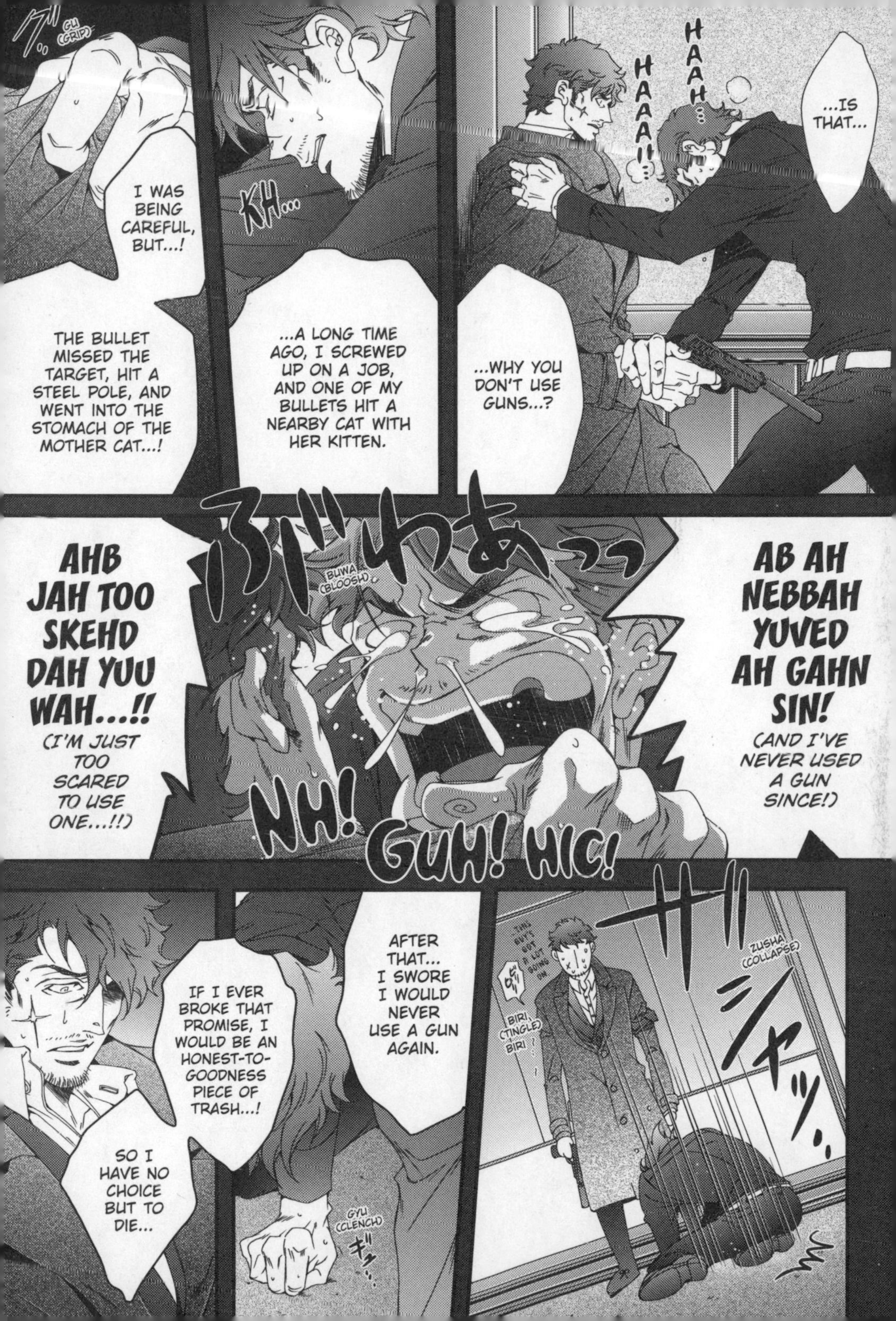
HAAAA!!...
HAAAH...
...IS THAT...
...WHY YOU DON'T USE GUNS...?
KH...
...A LONG TIME AGO, I SCREWED UP ON A JOB, AND ONE OF MY BULLETS HIT A NEARBY CAT WITH HER KITTEN.
GU (GRIP)
I WAS BEING CAREFUL, BUT...!
THE BULLET MISSED THE TARGET, HIT A STEEL POLE, AND WENT INTO THE STOMACH OF THE MOTHER CAT...!
AB AH NEBBAH YUVED AH GAHN SIN!
(AND I'VE NEVER USED A GUN SINCE!)
BUWA (BLOOSH)
AHB JAH TOO SKEHD DAH YUU WAH...!!
(I'M JUST TOO SCARED TO USE ONE...!!)
NH!
GUH! HIC!
ZUSHA (COLLAPSE)
THIS GUY'S GOT A LOT GOING ON
BIRI (TINGLE) BIRI
AFTER THAT... I SWORE I WOULD NEVER USE A GUN AGAIN.
GYU (CLENCH)
IF I EVER BROKE THAT PROMISE, I WOULD BE AN HONEST-TO-GOODNESS PIECE OF TRASH...!
SO I HAVE NO CHOICE BUT TO DIE...

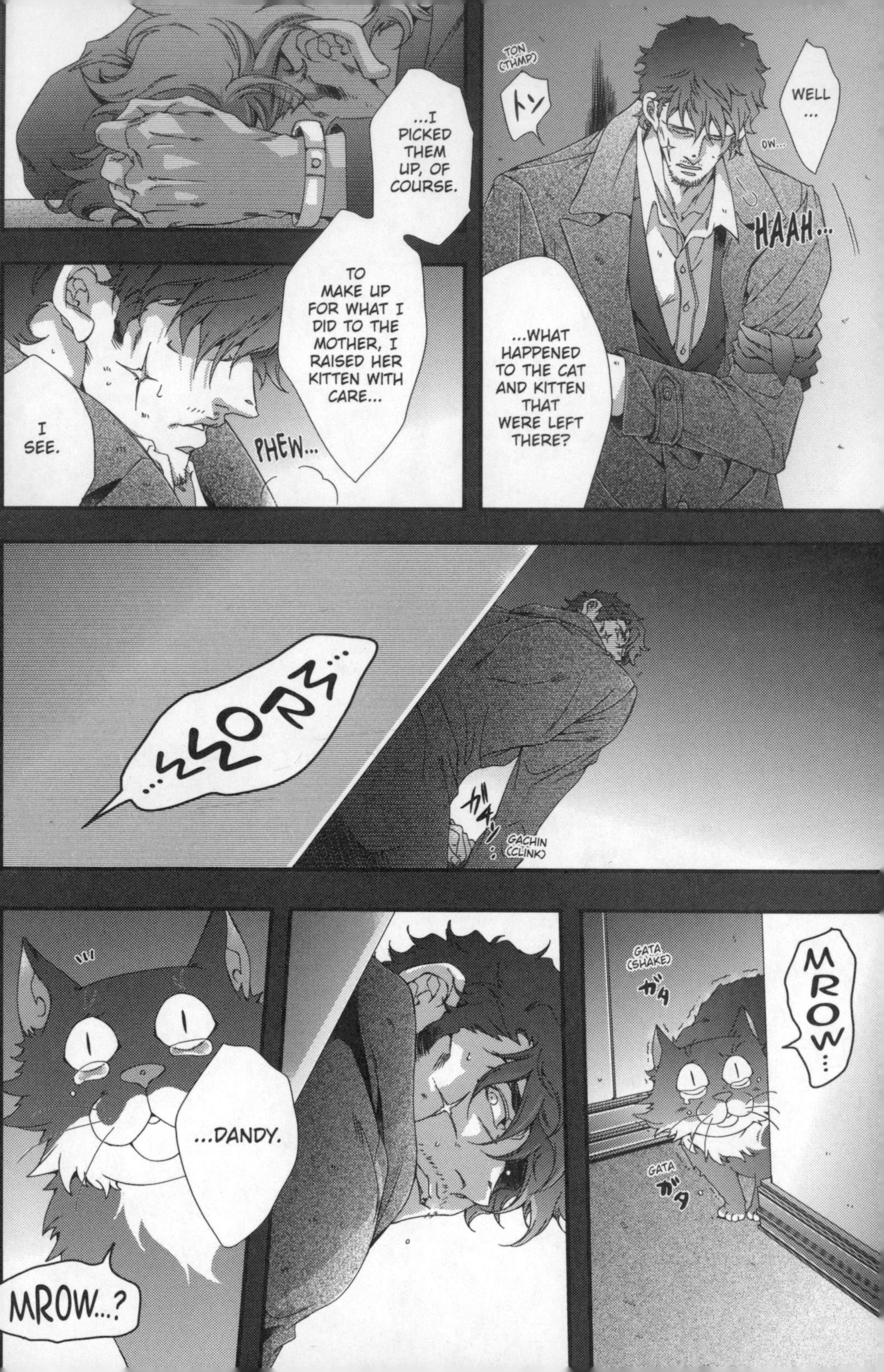
TON (THMP)
トン
WELL...
OW...
HAAH...
...WHAT HAPPENED TO THE CAT AND KITTEN THAT WERE LEFT THERE?
...I PICKED THEM UP, OF COURSE.
TO MAKE UP FOR WHAT I DID TO THE MOTHER, I RAISED HER KITTEN WITH CARE...
PHEW...
I SEE.
...MROWW...
ガチン
GACHIN (CLINK)
MROW...
GATA (SHAKE)
ガタ
GATA
ガタ
...DANDY.
MROW...?

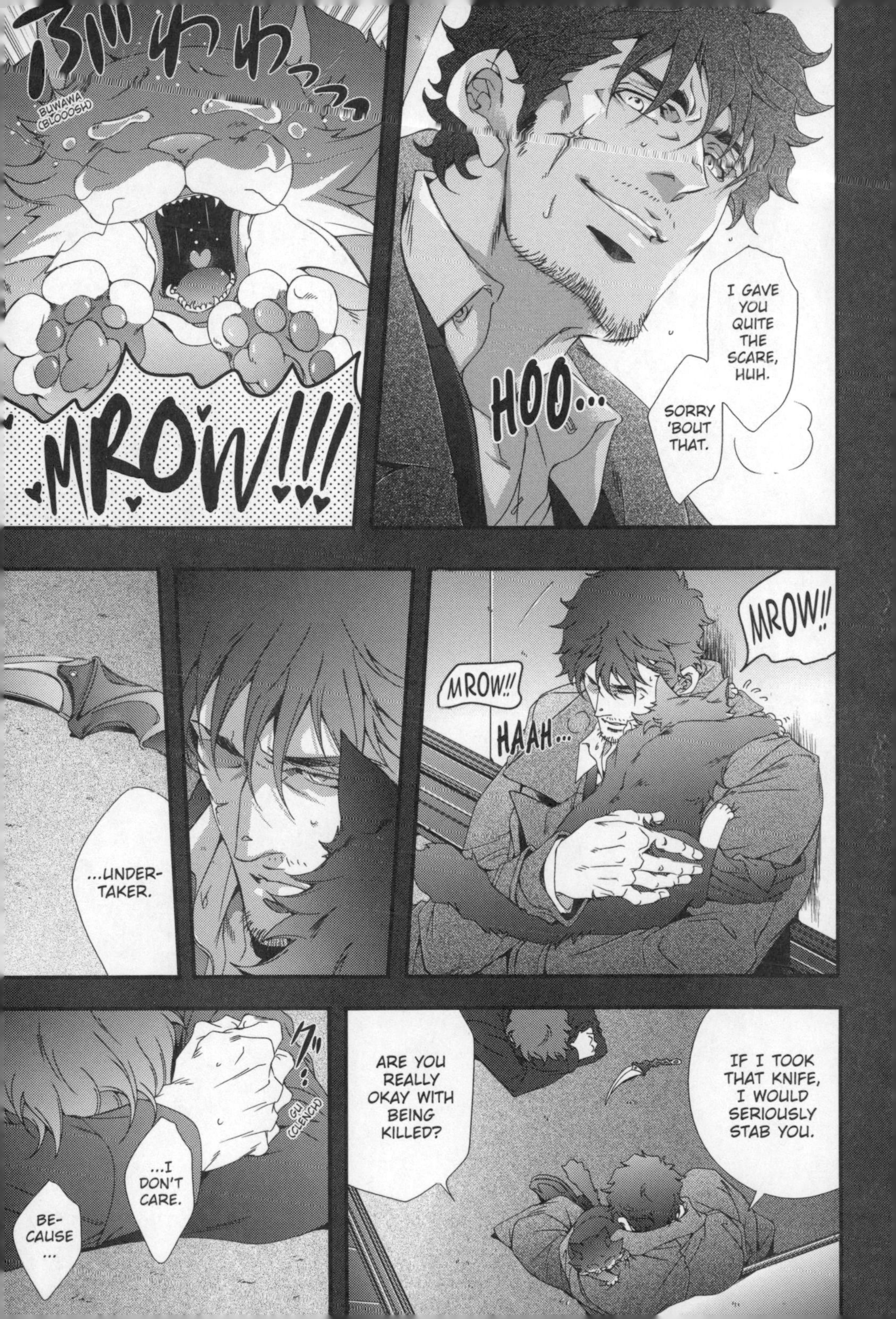
I GAVE YOU QUITE THE SCARE, HUH.
SORRY 'BOUT THAT.
HOO...
ぶわわっっっ
BUWAWA (BLOOOSH)
MROW!!!
MROW!!
MROW!!
HAAH...
...UNDER-TAKER.
IF I TOOK THAT KNIFE, I WOULD SERIOUSLY STAB YOU.
ARE YOU REALLY OKAY WITH BEING KILLED?
グ
GU (CLENCH)
...I DON'T CARE.
BE-CAUSE...

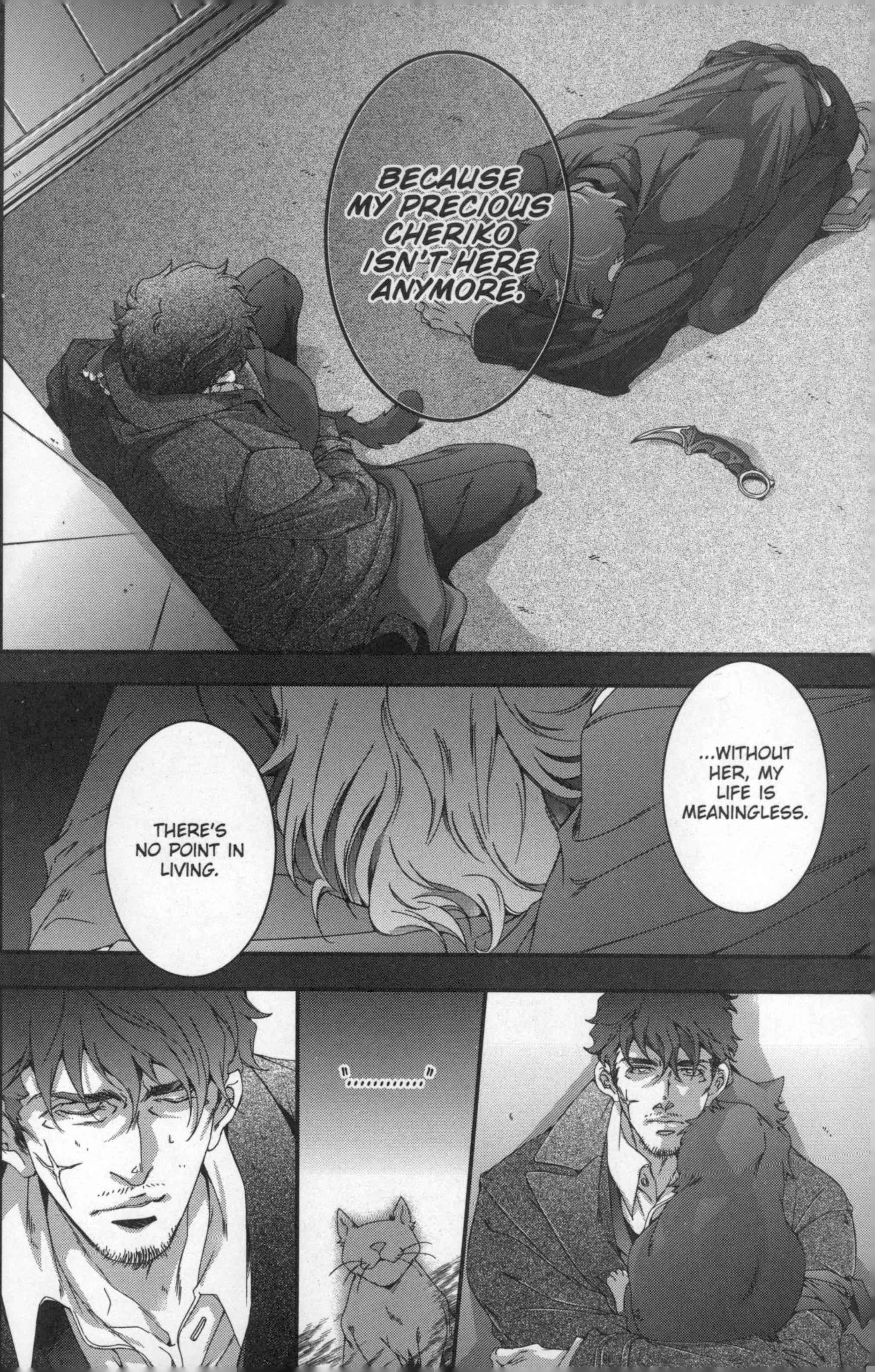
BECAUSE MY PRECIOUS CHERIKO ISN'T HERE ANYMORE.
...WITHOUT HER, MY LIFE IS MEANINGLESS.
THERE'S NO POINT IN LIVING.
"............"

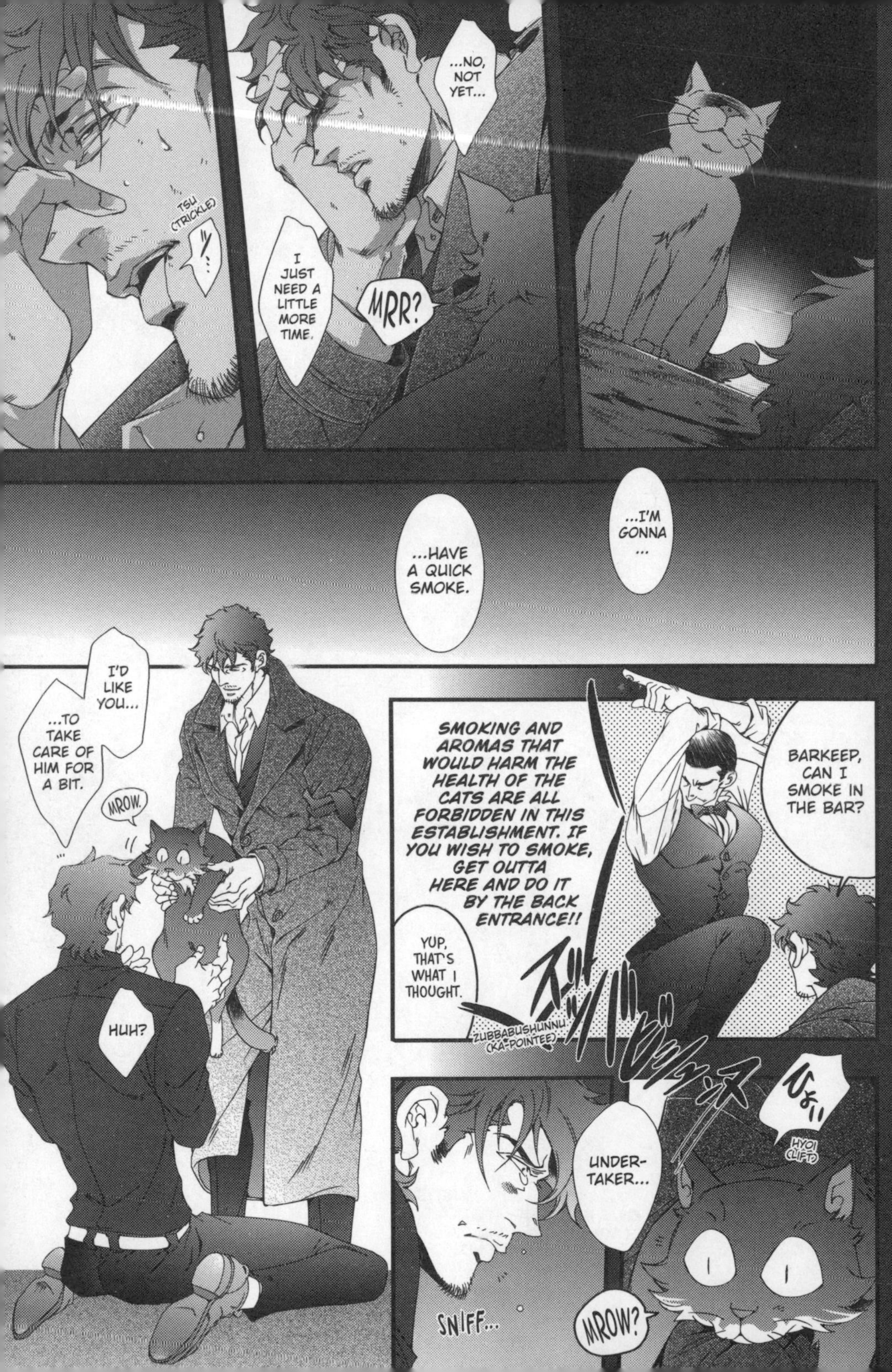
...NO, NOT YET...
I JUST NEED A LITTLE MORE TIME.
MRR?
TSU (TRICKLE)
...I'M GONNA ...
...HAVE A QUICK SMOKE.
BARKEEP, CAN I SMOKE IN THE BAR?
SMOKING AND AROMAS THAT WOULD HARM THE HEALTH OF THE CATS ARE ALL FORBIDDEN IN THIS ESTABLISHMENT. IF YOU WISH TO SMOKE, GET OUTTA HERE AND DO IT BY THE BACK ENTRANCE!!
YUP, THAT'S WHAT I THOUGHT.
ZUBBABUSHUNNU (KA-POINTEE)
HYOI (LIFT)
UNDER-TAKER...
MROW?
SNIFF...
I'D LIKE YOU...
...TO TAKE CARE OF HIM FOR A BIT.
MROW.
HUH?

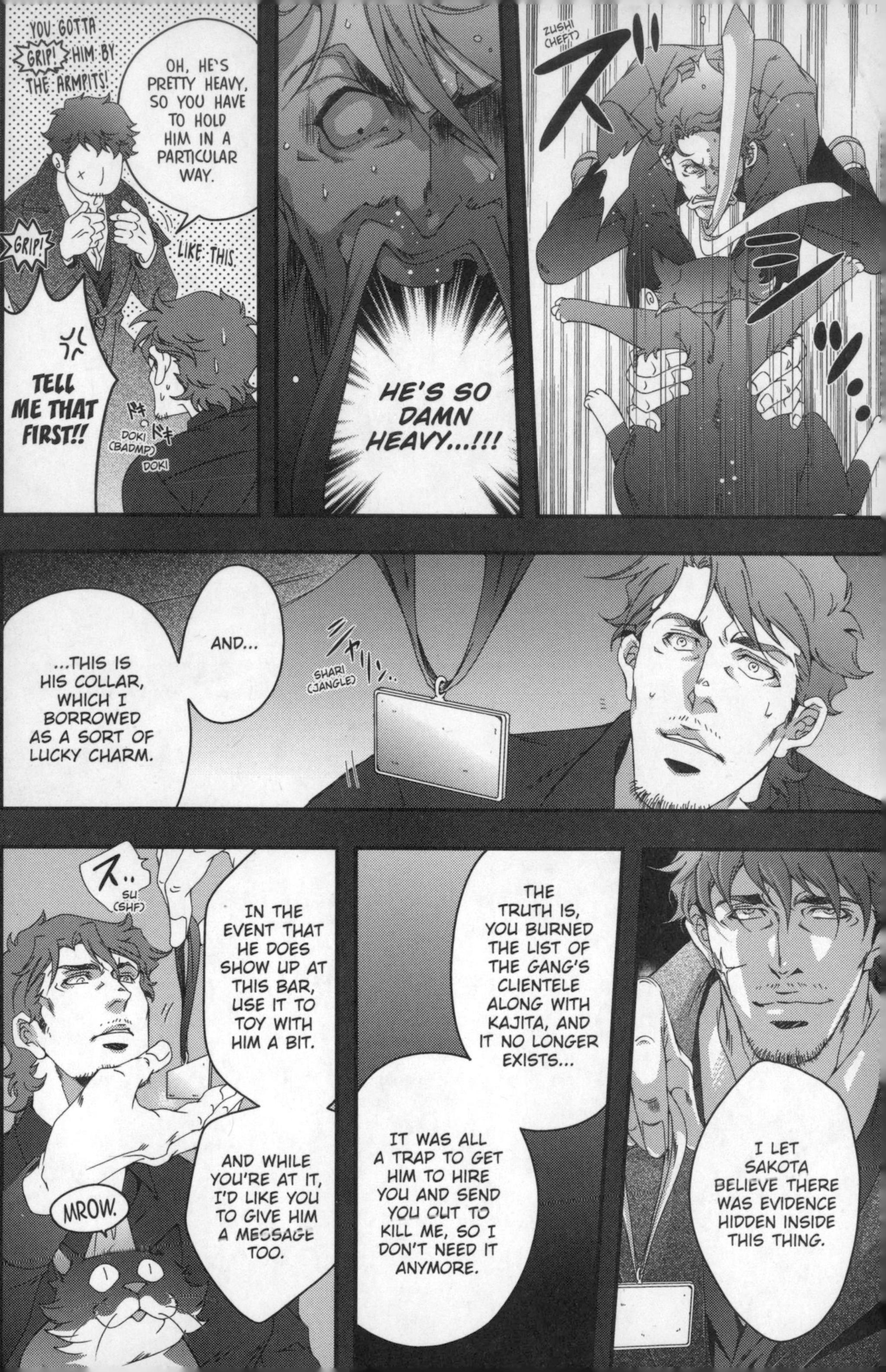
ズ
ZUSHI (HEFT)
HE'S SO DAMN HEAVY...!!!
OH, HE'S PRETTY HEAVY, SO YOU HAVE TO HOLD HIM IN A PARTICULAR WAY.
YOU GOTTA GRIP! HIM BY THE ARMPITS!
GRIP!
LIKE THIS.
TELL ME THAT FIRST!!
ドキ ドキ
DOKI (BADMP) DOKI
シャリン..
SHARI (JANGLE)
AND...
...THIS IS HIS COLLAR, WHICH I BORROWED AS A SORT OF LUCKY CHARM.
I LET SAKOTA BELIEVE THERE WAS EVIDENCE HIDDEN INSIDE THIS THING.
THE TRUTH IS, YOU BURNED THE LIST OF THE GANG'S CLIENTELE ALONG WITH KAJITA, AND IT NO LONGER EXISTS...
IT WAS ALL A TRAP TO GET HIM TO HIRE YOU AND SEND YOU OUT TO KILL ME, SO I DON'T NEED IT ANYMORE.
ス..
SU (SHF)
IN THE EVENT THAT HE DOES SHOW UP AT THIS BAR, USE IT TO TOY WITH HIM A BIT.
AND WHILE YOU'RE AT IT, I'D LIKE YOU TO GIVE HIM A MESSAGE TOO.
MROW.

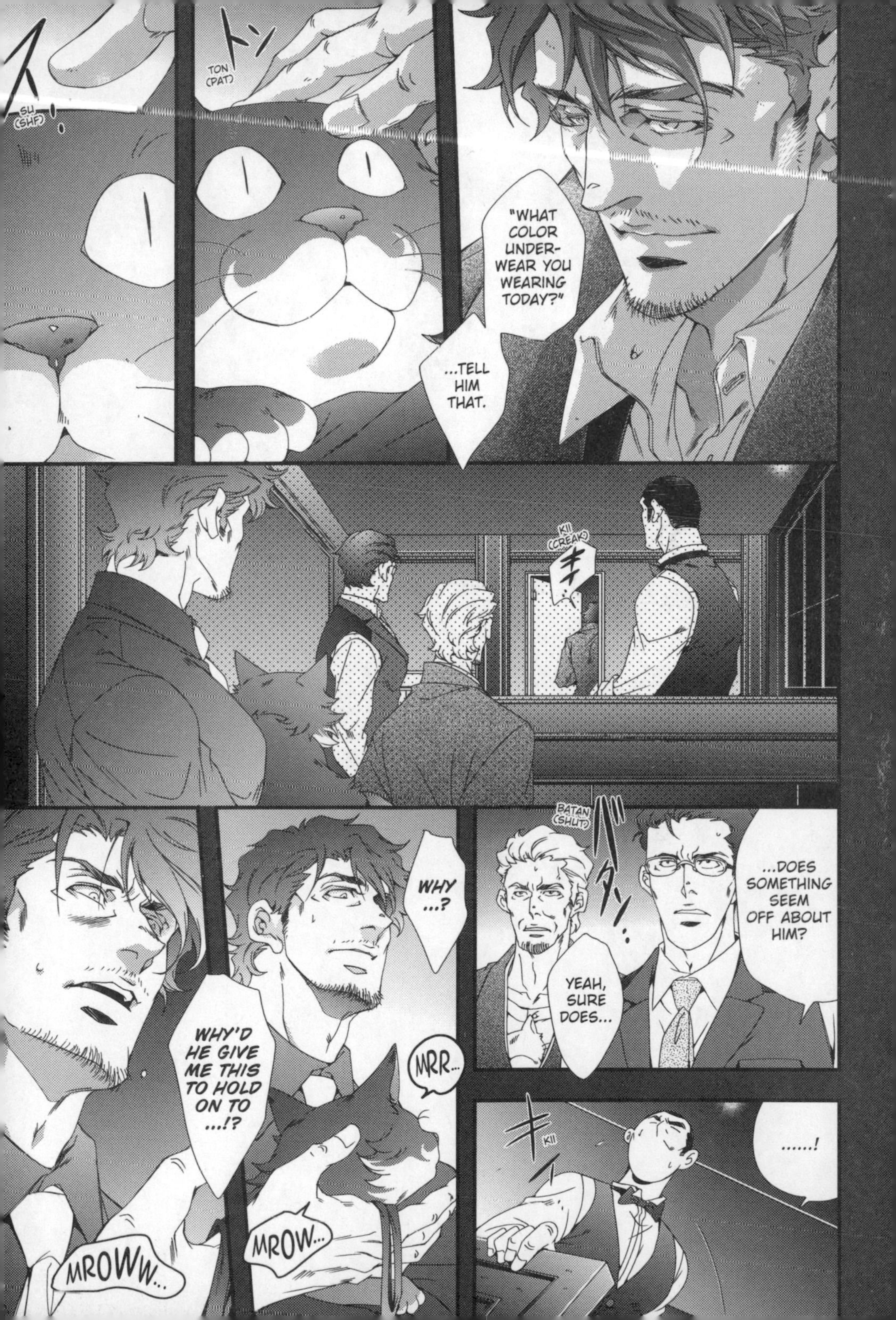
"WHAT COLOR UNDER-WEAR YOU WEARING TODAY?"
...TELL HIM THAT.
TON (PAT)
SU (SHF)
KII (CREAK)
...DOES SOMETHING SEEM OFF ABOUT HIM?
BATAN (SHUT)
YEAH, SURE DOES...
......!
KII
WHY ...?
WHY'D HE GIVE ME THIS TO HOLD ON TO ...!?
MRR...
MROW...
MROWW...

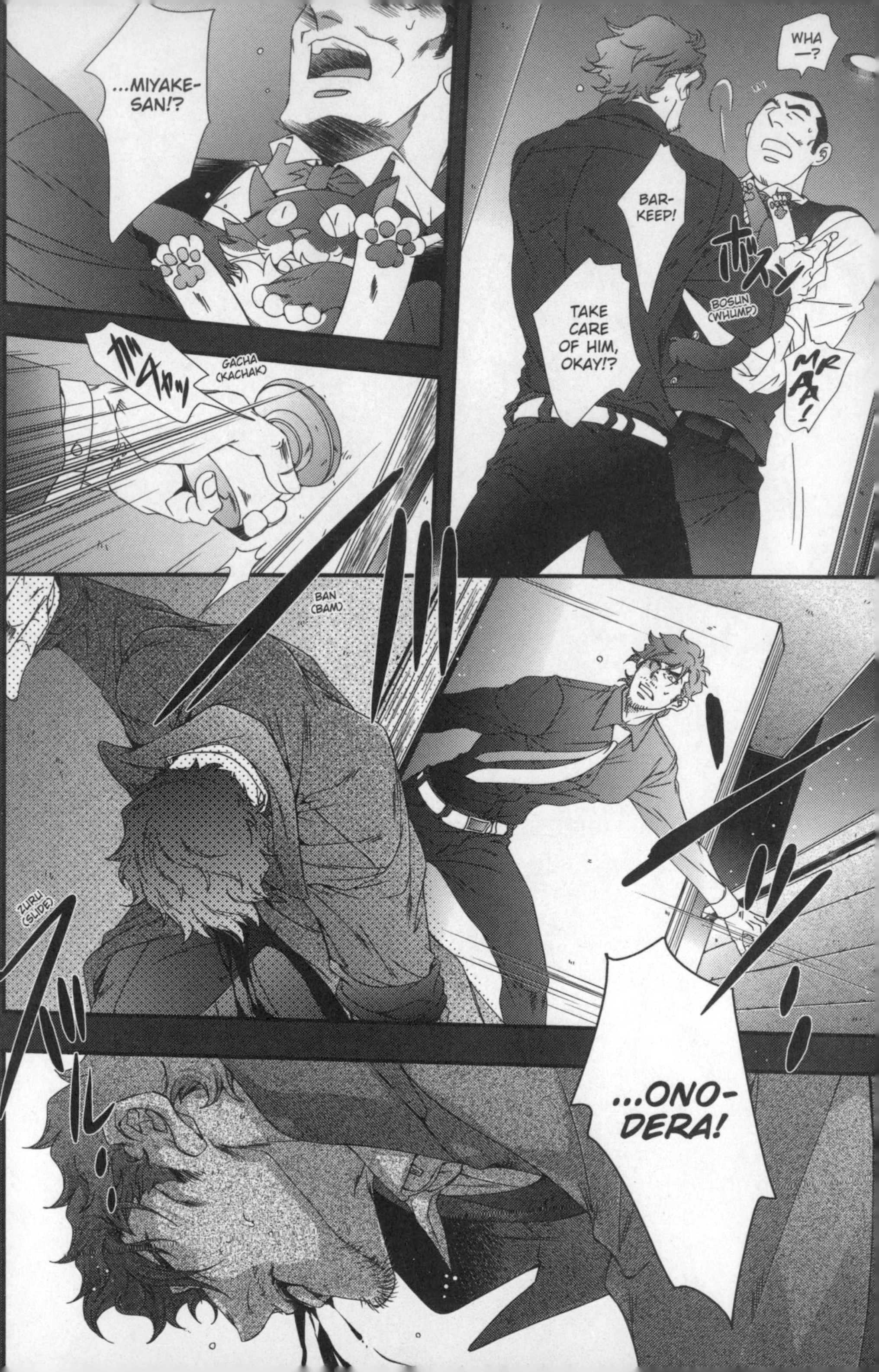
WHA—?
BAR-KEEP!
TAKE CARE OF HIM, OKAY!?
BOSUN (WHUMP)
MRAA!
...MIYAKE-SAN!?
GACHA (KACHAK)
BAN (BAM)
ZURU (SLIDE)
...ONO-DERA!

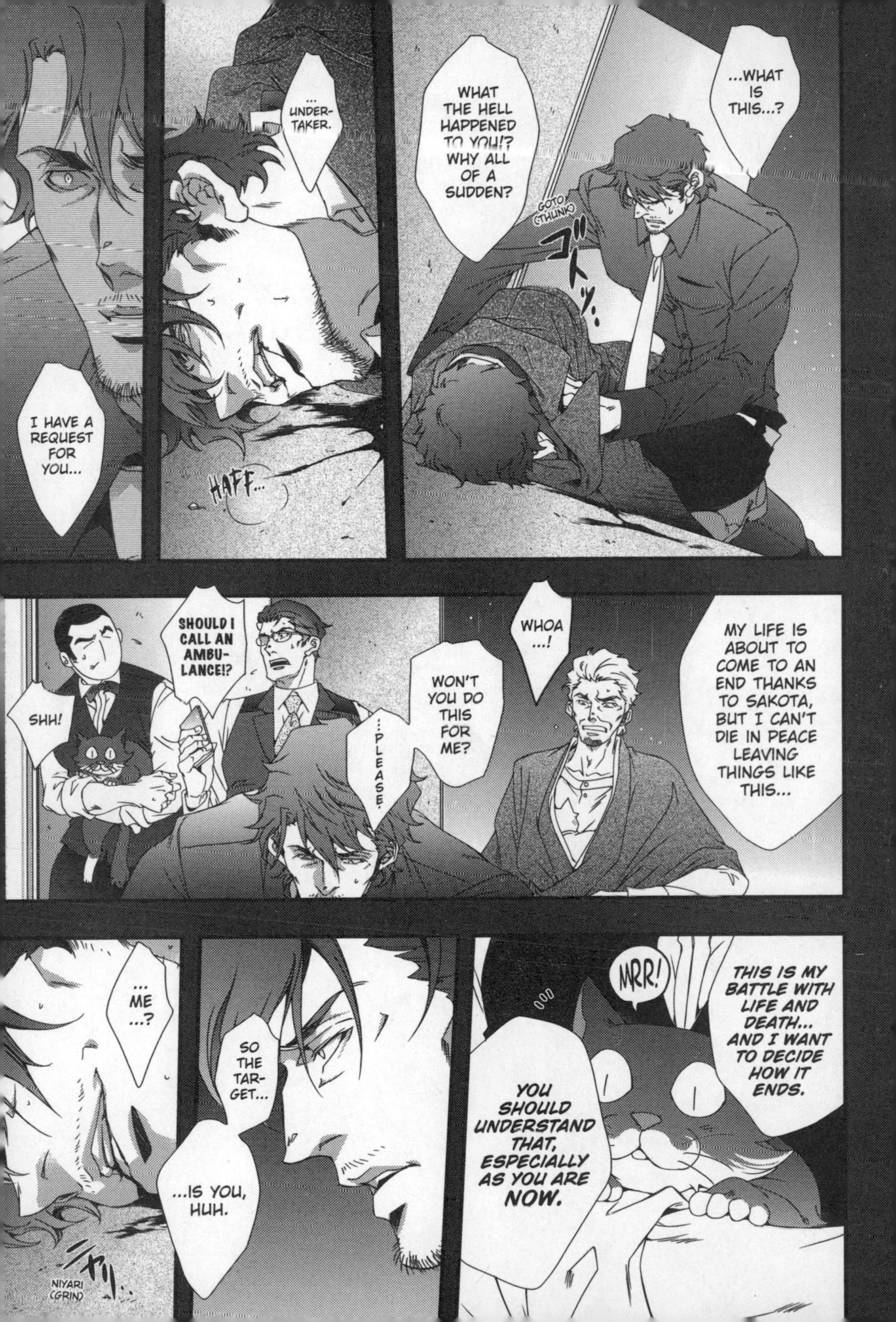

...WHAT IS THIS...?
WHAT THE HELL HAPPENED TO YOU!? WHY ALL OF A SUDDEN?
GOTO (THUNK)
... UNDER-TAKER.
HAFF...
I HAVE A REQUEST FOR YOU...
MY LIFE IS ABOUT TO COME TO AN END THANKS TO SAKOTA, BUT I CAN'T DIE IN PEACE LEAVING THINGS LIKE THIS...
WHOA ...!
WON'T YOU DO THIS FOR ME?
...PLEASE.
SHOULD I CALL AN AMBU-LANCE!?
SHH!
THIS IS MY BATTLE WITH LIFE AND DEATH... AND I WANT TO DECIDE HOW IT ENDS.
MRR!
YOU SHOULD UNDERSTAND THAT, ESPECIALLY AS YOU ARE NOW.
SO THE TAR-GET...
...IS YOU, HUH.
... ME ...?
NIYARI (GRIN)

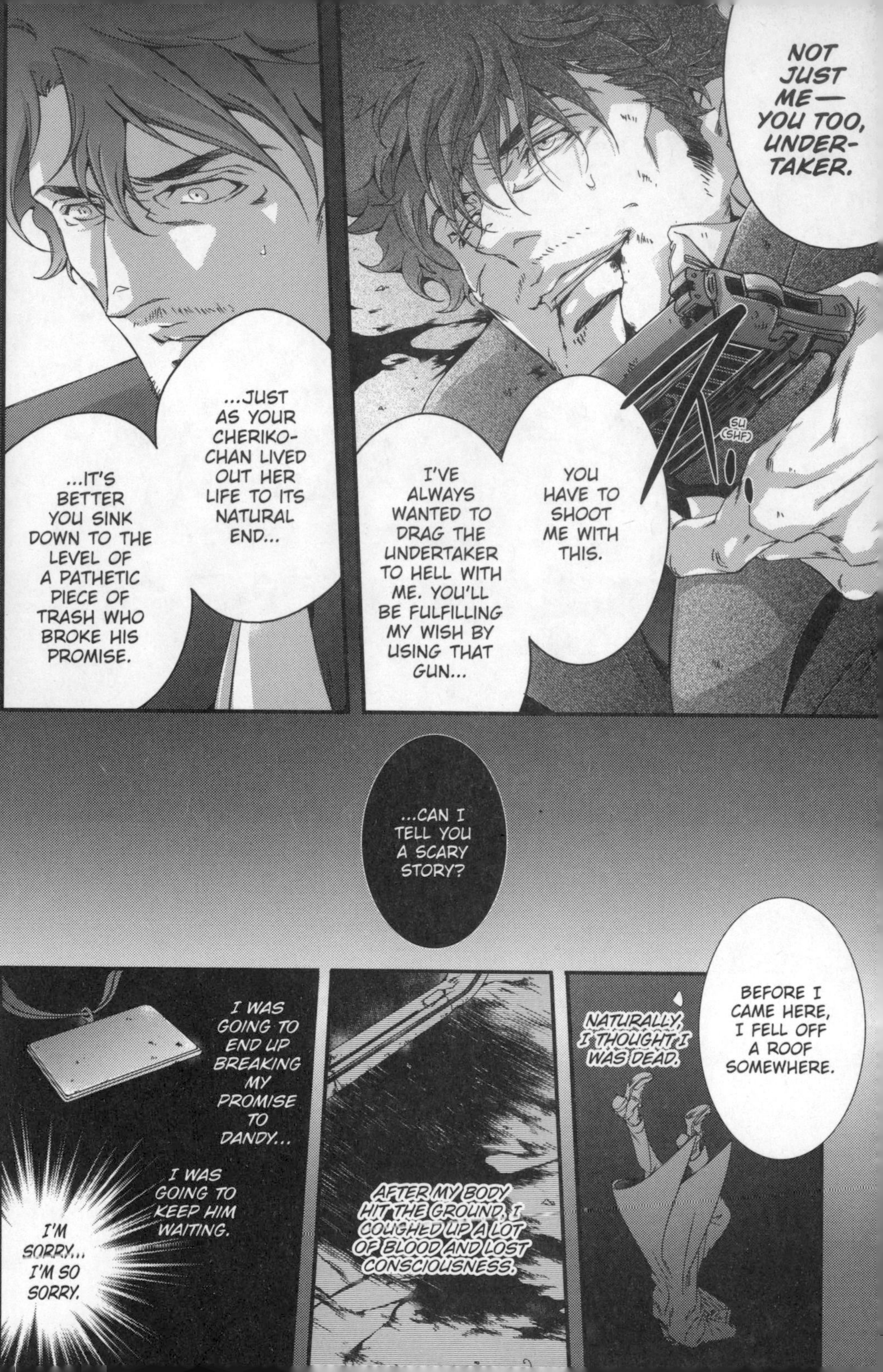
NOT JUST ME—YOU TOO, UNDER-TAKER.
YOU HAVE TO SHOOT ME WITH THIS.
SU (SHF)
I'VE ALWAYS WANTED TO DRAG THE UNDERTAKER TO HELL WITH ME. YOU'LL BE FULFILLING MY WISH BY USING THAT GUN...
...JUST AS YOUR CHERIKO-CHAN LIVED OUT HER LIFE TO ITS NATURAL END...
...IT'S BETTER YOU SINK DOWN TO THE LEVEL OF A PATHETIC PIECE OF TRASH WHO BROKE HIS PROMISE.
...CAN I TELL YOU A SCARY STORY?
BEFORE I CAME HERE, I FELL OFF A ROOF SOMEWHERE.
NATURALLY, I THOUGHT I WAS DEAD.
AFTER MY BODY HIT THE GROUND, I COUGHED UP A LOT OF BLOOD AND LOST CONSCIOUSNESS.
I WAS GOING TO END UP BREAKING MY PROMISE TO DANDY...
I WAS GOING TO KEEP HIM WAITING.
I'M SORRY... I'M SO SORRY.

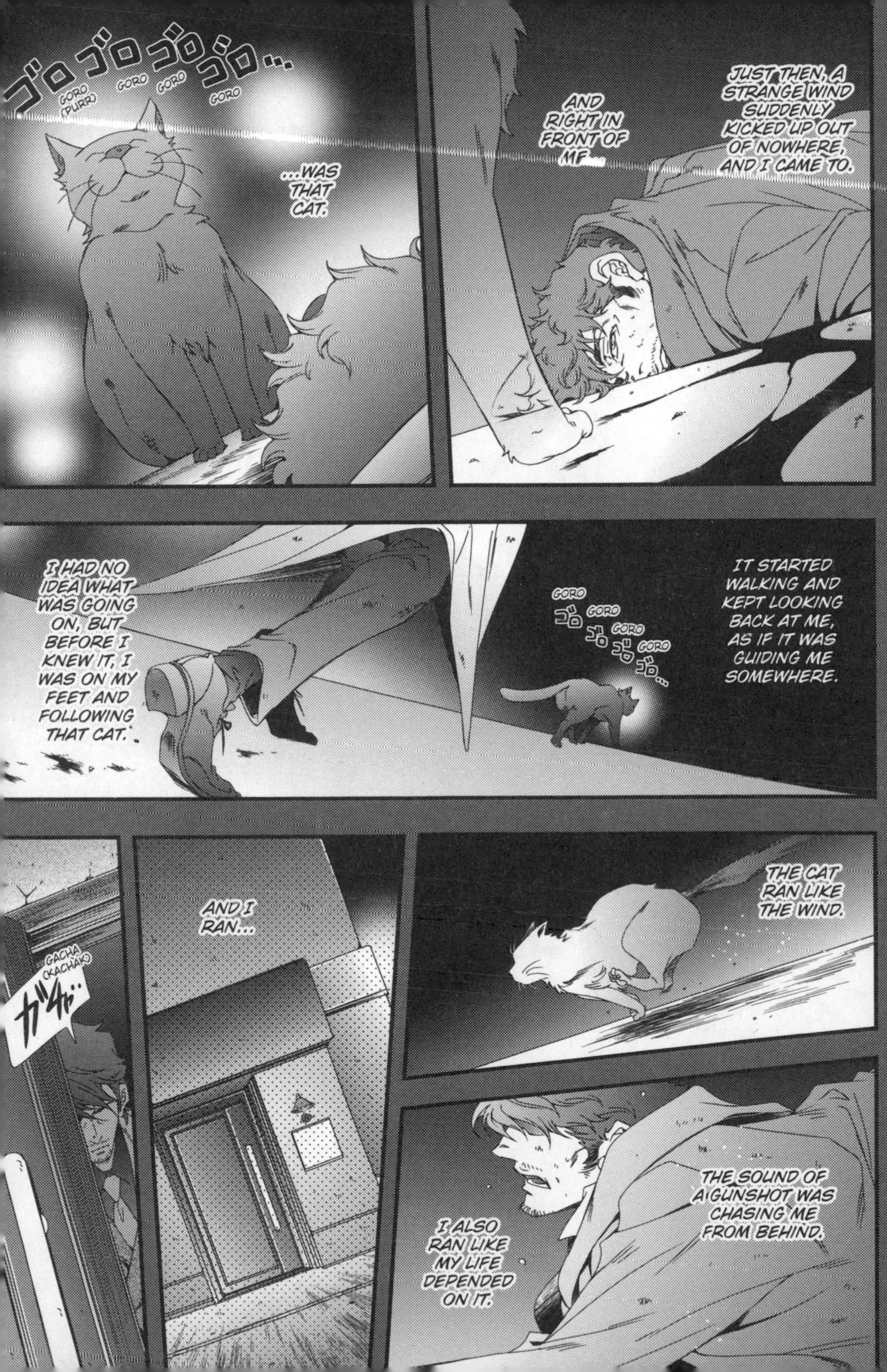
JUST THEN, A STRANGE WIND SUDDENLY KICKED UP OUT OF NOWHERE, AND I CAME TO.
AND RIGHT IN FRONT OF ME...
ゴロゴロゴロゴロ...
GORO (PURR) GORO GORO GORO
...WAS THAT CAT.
IT STARTED WALKING AND KEPT LOOKING BACK AT ME, AS IF IT WAS GUIDING ME SOMEWHERE.
ゴロゴロゴロゴロ...
GORO GORO GORO GORO
I HAD NO IDEA WHAT WAS GOING ON, BUT BEFORE I KNEW IT, I WAS ON MY FEET AND FOLLOWING THAT CAT.
THE CAT RAN LIKE THE WIND.
THE SOUND OF A GUNSHOT WAS CHASING ME FROM BEHIND.
I ALSO RAN LIKE MY LIFE DEPENDED ON IT.
AND I RAN...
ガチャ...
GACHA (KACHAK)

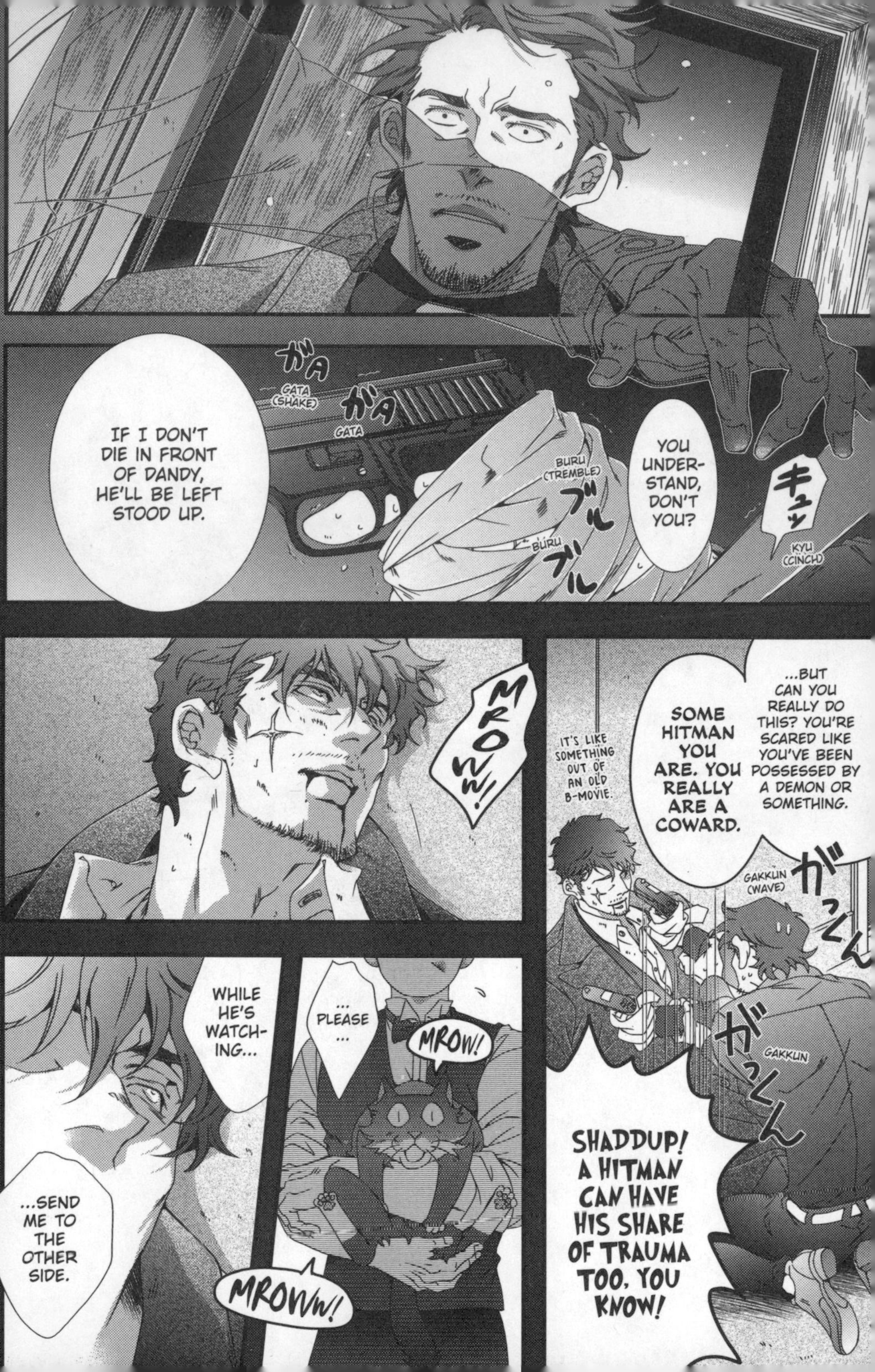

キュッ
KYU (CINCH)
YOU UNDER-STAND, DON'T YOU?
ブル BURU (TREMBLE)
ブル BURU
ガタ GATA (SHAKE)
ガタ GATA
IF I DON'T DIE IN FRONT OF DANDY, HE'LL BE LEFT STOOD UP.
...BUT CAN YOU REALLY DO THIS? YOU'RE SCARED LIKE YOU'VE BEEN POSSESSED BY A DEMON OR SOMETHING.
SOME HITMAN YOU ARE. YOU REALLY ARE A COWARD.
IT'S LIKE SOMETHING OUT OF AN OLD B-MOVIE.
がっくん GAKKUN (WAVE)
がっくん GAKKUN
SHADDUP! A HITMAN CAN HAVE HIS SHARE OF TRAUMA TOO, YOU KNOW!
MROWW!
... PLEASE ...
MROW!
MROWW!
WHILE HE'S WATCH-ING...
...SEND ME TO THE OTHER SIDE.

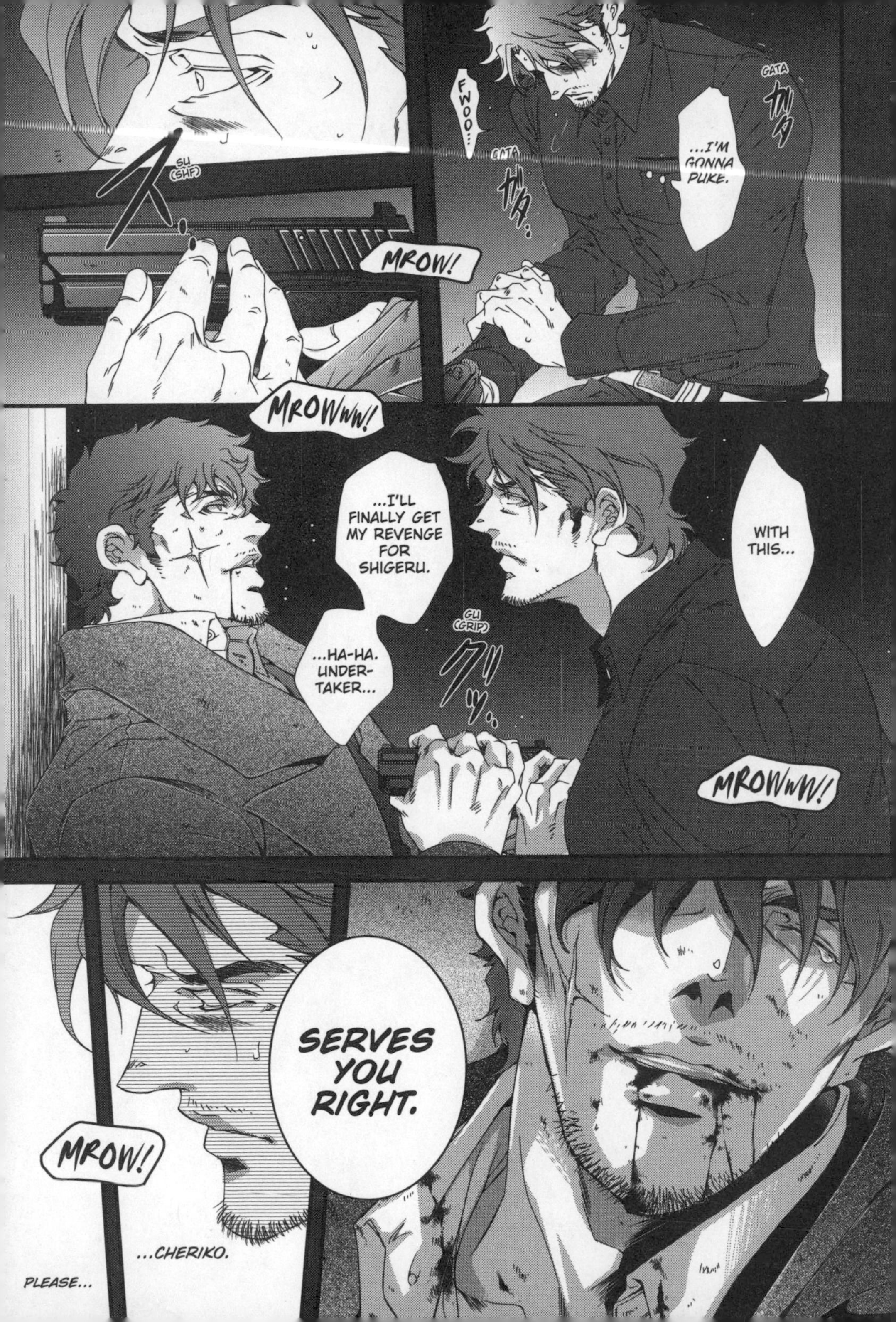
GATA
...I'M GONNA PUKE.
FWOO...
GATA
SU (SHF)
MROW!
MROWWW!
WITH THIS...
...I'LL FINALLY GET MY REVENGE FOR SHIGERU.
...HA-HA. UNDER-TAKER...
GU (GRIP)
MROWWW!
SERVES YOU RIGHT.
MROW!
...CHERIKO.
PLEASE...

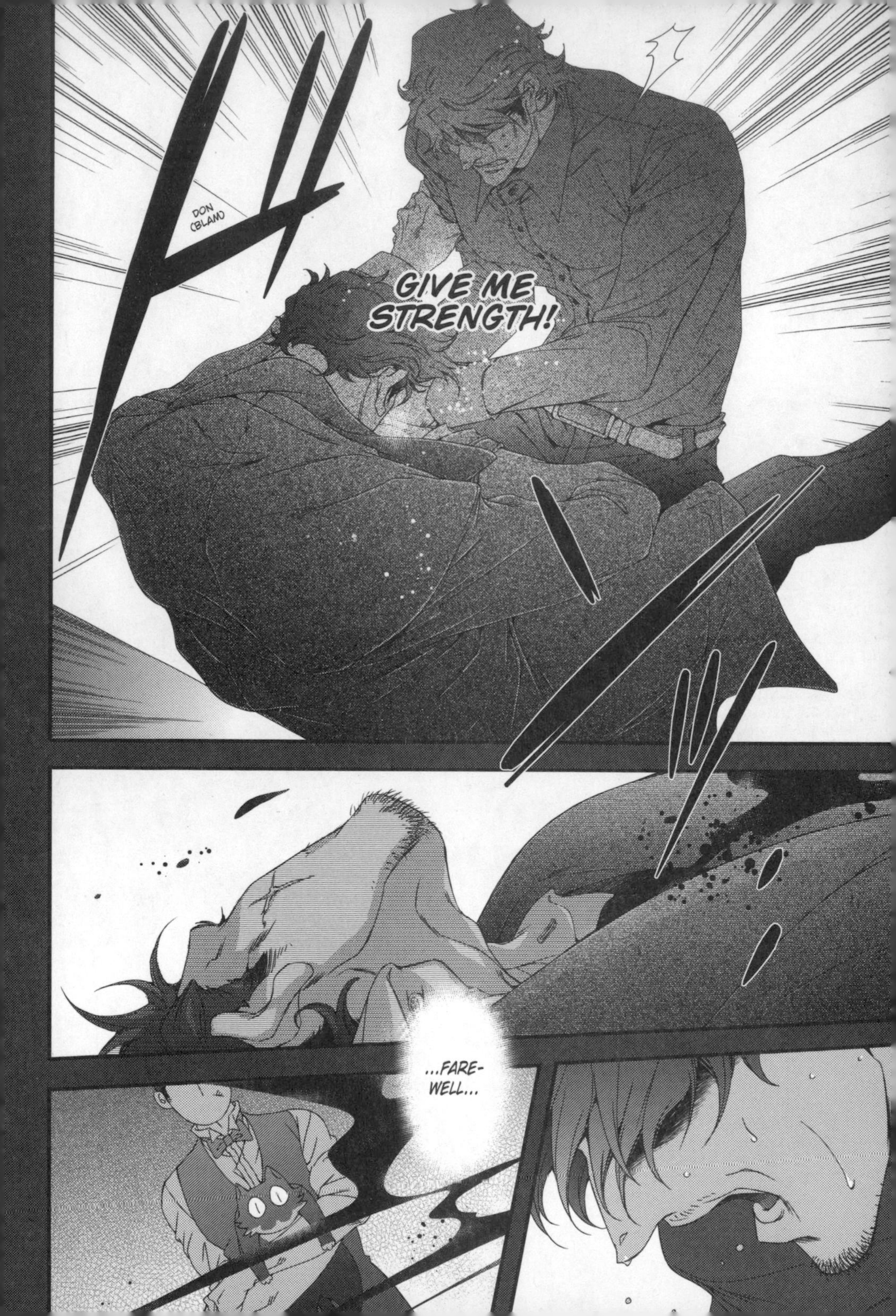
DON (BLAM)
GIVE ME STRENGTH!
...FARE-WELL...

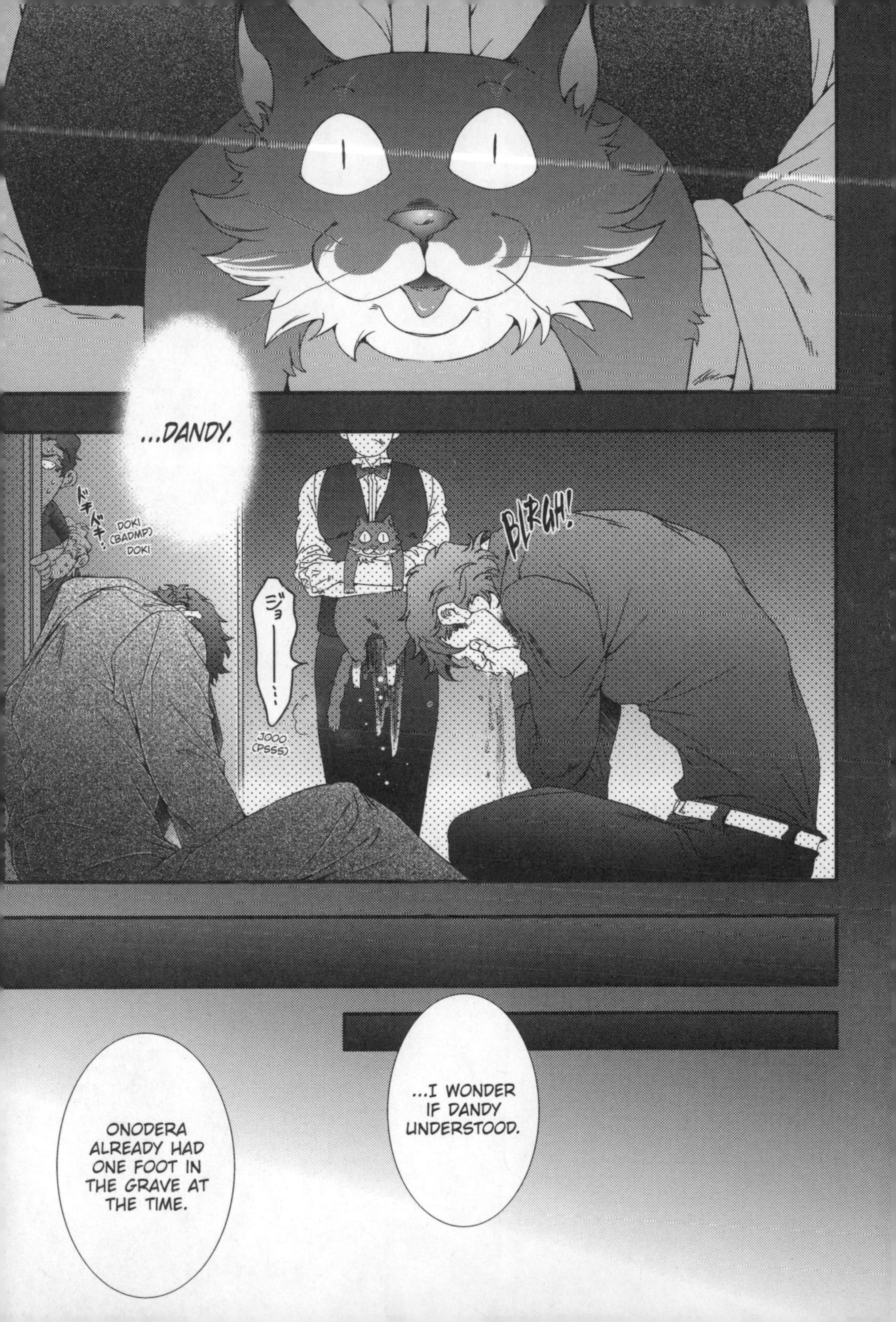
...DANDY.
BLRGH!
ジョーー…
JOOO (PSSS)
ドキドキ…
DOKI (BADMP) DOKI
...I WONDER IF DANDY UNDERSTOOD.
ONODERA ALREADY HAD ONE FOOT IN THE GRAVE AT THE TIME.

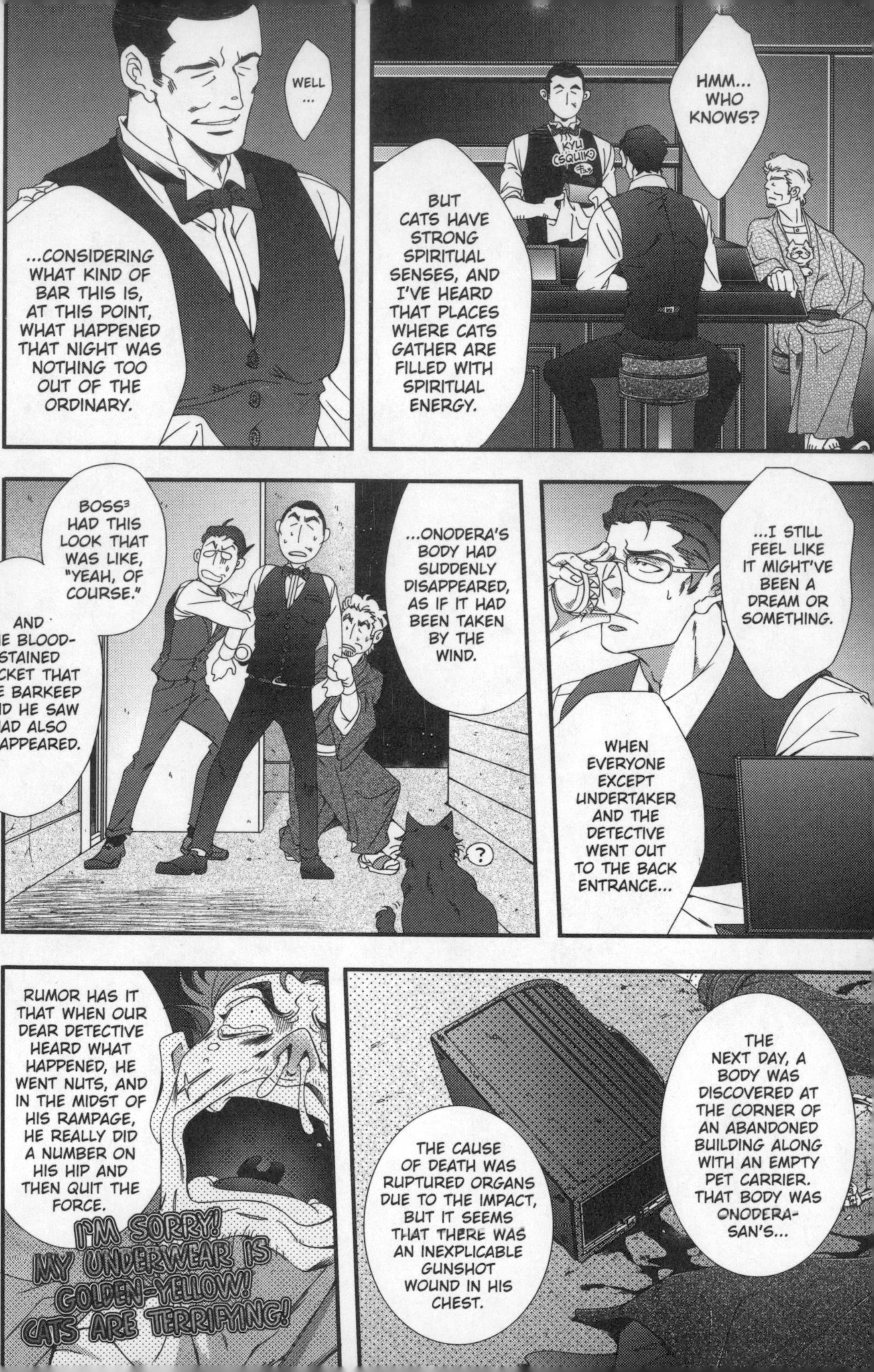

HMM... WHO KNOWS?
KYU (SQUIK)
BUT CATS HAVE STRONG SPIRITUAL SENSES, AND I'VE HEARD THAT PLACES WHERE CATS GATHER ARE FILLED WITH SPIRITUAL ENERGY.
WELL ...
...CONSIDERING WHAT KIND OF BAR THIS IS, AT THIS POINT, WHAT HAPPENED THAT NIGHT WAS NOTHING TOO OUT OF THE ORDINARY.
...I STILL FEEL LIKE IT MIGHT'VE BEEN A DREAM OR SOMETHING.
WHEN EVERYONE EXCEPT UNDERTAKER AND THE DETECTIVE WENT OUT TO THE BACK ENTRANCE...
...ONODERA'S BODY HAD SUDDENLY DISAPPEARED, AS IF IT HAD BEEN TAKEN BY THE WIND.
BOSS[3] HAD THIS LOOK THAT WAS LIKE, "YEAH, OF COURSE."
AND THE BLOOD-STAINED JACKET THAT THE BARKEEP SAID HE SAW HAD ALSO DISAPPEARED.
?
THE NEXT DAY, A BODY WAS DISCOVERED AT THE CORNER OF AN ABANDONED BUILDING ALONG WITH AN EMPTY PET CARRIER. THAT BODY WAS ONODERA-SAN'S...
THE CAUSE OF DEATH WAS RUPTURED ORGANS DUE TO THE IMPACT, BUT IT SEEMS THAT THERE WAS AN INEXPLICABLE GUNSHOT WOUND IN HIS CHEST.
RUMOR HAS IT THAT WHEN OUR DEAR DETECTIVE HEARD WHAT HAPPENED, HE WENT NUTS, AND IN THE MIDST OF HIS RAMPAGE, HE REALLY DID A NUMBER ON HIS HIP AND THEN QUIT THE FORCE.
I'M SORRY! MY UNDERWEAR IS GOLDEN-YELLOW! CATS ARE TERRIFYING!

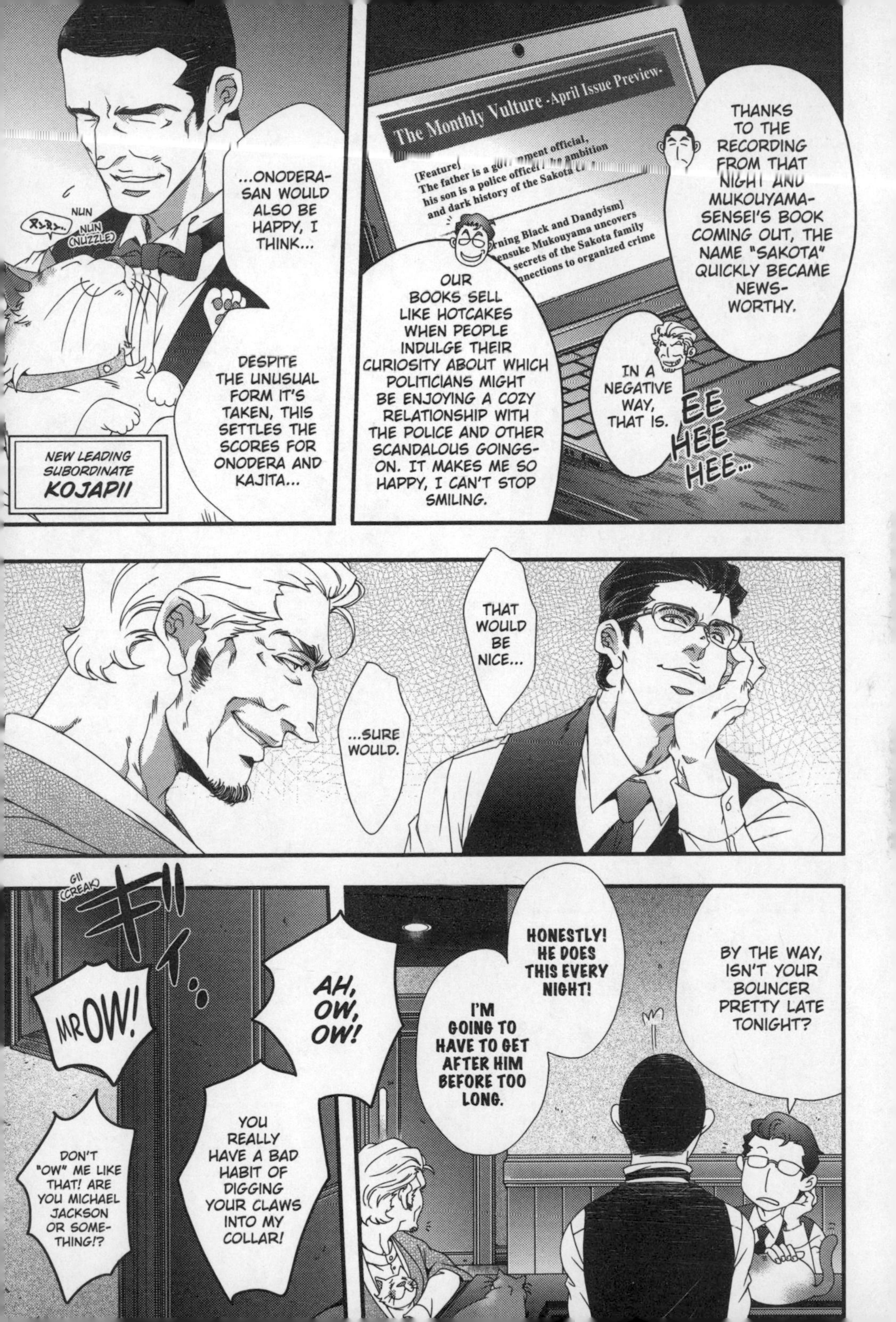
The Monthly Vulture -April Issue Preview-
[Feature]
his son is a police officer
and dark history of the Sakota
secrets of the Sakota family
THANKS TO THE RECORDING FROM THAT NIGHT AND MUKOUYAMA-SENSEI'S BOOK COMING OUT, THE NAME "SAKOTA" QUICKLY BECAME NEWS-WORTHY.
IN A NEGATIVE WAY, THAT IS.
EE HEE HEE...
OUR BOOKS SELL LIKE HOTCAKES WHEN PEOPLE INDULGE THEIR CURIOSITY ABOUT WHICH POLITICIANS MIGHT BE ENJOYING A COZY RELATIONSHIP WITH THE POLICE AND OTHER SCANDALOUS GOINGS-ON. IT MAKES ME SO HAPPY, I CAN'T STOP SMILING.
...ONODERA-SAN WOULD ALSO BE HAPPY, I THINK...
DESPITE THE UNUSUAL FORM IT'S TAKEN, THIS SETTLES THE SCORES FOR ONODERA AND KAJITA...
NUN NUN (NUZZLE)
NEW LEADING SUBORDINATE KOJAPII
THAT WOULD BE NICE...
...SURE WOULD.
BY THE WAY, ISN'T YOUR BOUNCER PRETTY LATE TONIGHT?
HONESTLY! HE DOES THIS EVERY NIGHT!
I'M GOING TO HAVE TO GET AFTER HIM BEFORE TOO LONG.
GII (CREAK)
MROW!
AH, OW, OW!
YOU REALLY HAVE A BAD HABIT OF DIGGING YOUR CLAWS INTO MY COLLAR!
DON'T "OW" ME LIKE THAT! ARE YOU MICHAEL JACKSON OR SOME-THING!?

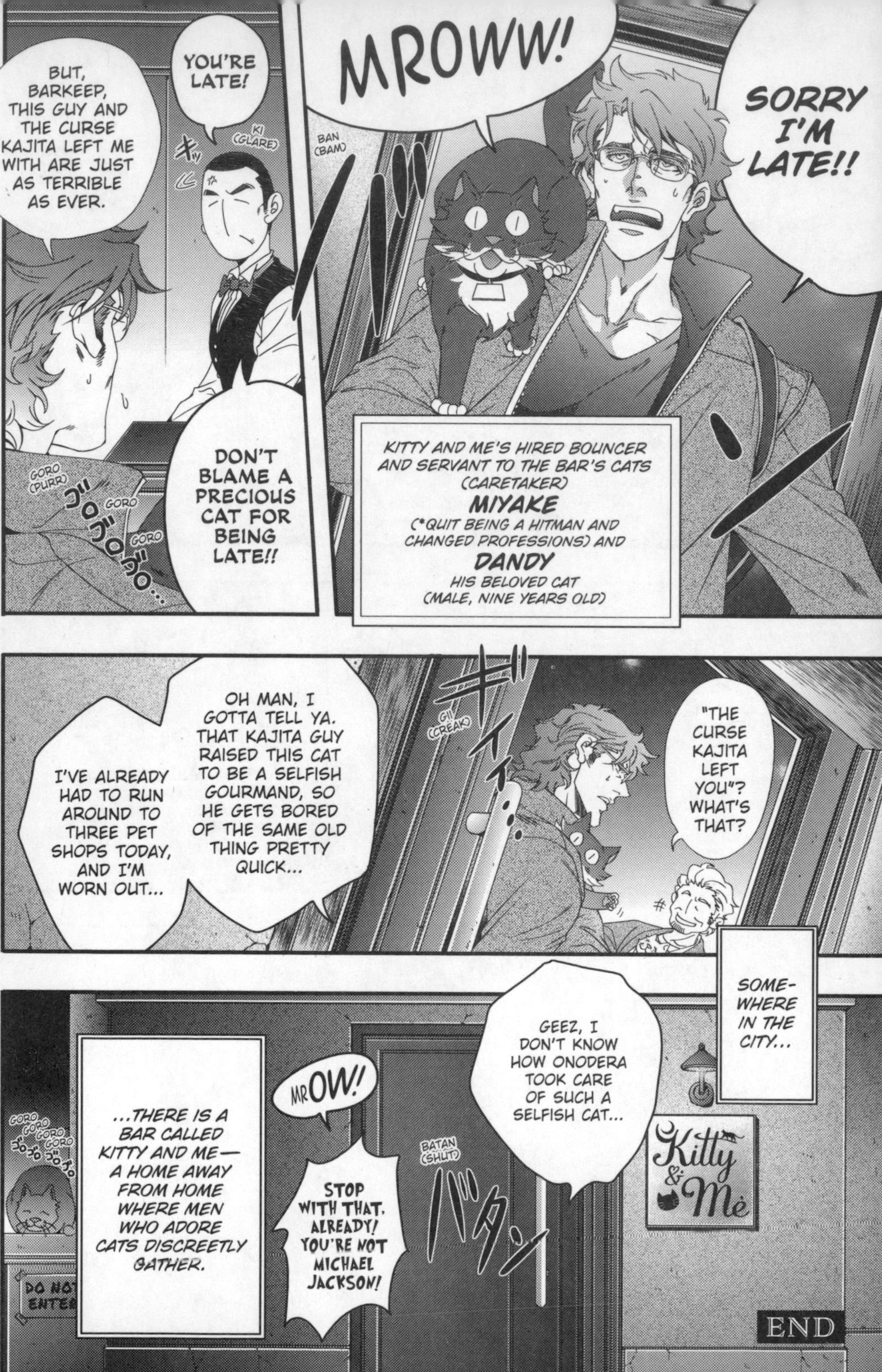
SORRY I'M LATE!!
MROWW!
BAN (BAM)
KITTY AND ME'S HIRED BOUNCER AND SERVANT TO THE BAR'S CATS (CARETAKER) MIYAKE (*QUIT BEING A HITMAN AND CHANGED PROFESSIONS) AND DANDY HIS BELOVED CAT (MALE, NINE YEARS OLD)
YOU'RE LATE!
KI (GLARE)
BUT, BARKEEP, THIS GUY AND THE CURSE KAJITA LEFT ME WITH ARE JUST AS TERRIBLE AS EVER.
DON'T BLAME A PRECIOUS CAT FOR BEING LATE!!
GORO (PURR) GORO GORO
"THE CURSE KAJITA LEFT YOU"? WHAT'S THAT?
GII (CREAK)
OH MAN, I GOTTA TELL YA. THAT KAJITA GUY RAISED THIS CAT TO BE A SELFISH GOURMAND, SO HE GETS BORED OF THE SAME OLD THING PRETTY QUICK...
I'VE ALREADY HAD TO RUN AROUND TO THREE PET SHOPS TODAY, AND I'M WORN OUT...
SOMEWHERE IN THE CITY...
GEEZ, I DON'T KNOW HOW ONODERA TOOK CARE OF SUCH A SELFISH CAT...
Kitty & Me
MROW!
BATAN (SHUT)
STOP WITH THAT. ALREADY! YOU'RE NOT MICHAEL JACKSON!
...THERE IS A BAR CALLED KITTY AND ME—A HOME AWAY FROM HOME WHERE MEN WHO ADORE CATS DISCREETLY GATHER.
GORO GORO GORO GORO
END

Onodera [43]

DANDY AND ONODERA AT THE VERY, VERY, VERY BEGINNING. A MISCHIEVOUS CAT THAT HAS A WEARY MIDDLE-AGED COP WRAPPED AROUND HIS LITTLE PAW...IS WHAT I HAD PLANNED FOR THIS STORY.

Dandy ♀ 5 y.o.

Nice to meet you! I'm Yourei Ono.

Thank you so very much for taking the time to read *Hard-Boiled Stories from the Cat Bar*.

This is my debut as a manga artist, but I've been overwhelmed with emotion over the fact that this story could be made into such a wonderful book...! When I first started drawing this manga, my beloved cat, who had been by my side for twenty years and five months, died of old age, and I was right in the middle of an intense period of grief that came from that loss. But by witnessing her death, I got to experience a cat's view of life and death and their earnest attitude toward life itself. This changed something inside me and probably gave birth to this manga. I hope that I've adequately conveyed my respect for cats and the pathos of older men who love cats way too much—to the point that cats run their lives. It would please me to know that I was somehow able to convey those sentiments to all you readers and that you were able to enjoy this manga. And finally, I want to give my heartfelt thanks to so many people. To Editor-in-Chief Kato of the *Young Age* editorial department, who picked me out of the vast sea that is the internet, gave me a chance to draw manga, and patiently guided me as my editor. To Akihara-san, who made cool designs for me. To all the production people involved in the work that got it to its current form. To my friends who cheered me on, my family who showed me their understanding, and the cats that watched over me... And to all the readers who pressed the support button and tweeted while I was being serialized, as well as those who cheered me on and gave me tons of support through letters, etc.!

I hope that all the cats in the world and everyone who loves cats can be happier.

Yourei Ono

Translation Notes

COMMON HONORIFICS

no honorific: Indicates familiarity or closeness; if used without permission or reason, addressing someone in this manner would constitute an insult.

-san: The Japanese equivalent of Mr./Mrs./Ms. This is the default honorific if politeness is required.

-kun: Used most often when referring to boys, this honorific indicates affection or familiarity. Occasionally used by older men among their peers, but it may also be used by anyone referring to a person of lower standing.

-chan: Affectionate honorific indicating familiarity used mostly in reference to girls; also used in reference to cute persons or animals of any gender.

-sensei: A respectful term for teachers, artists, or high-level professionals.

PAGE 2

The chapter titles are taken from popular film titles. The French drama *7 ans* (*7 Years* in the US) was released in Japan as *Waiting Girl*. *Retaliation* is the US title for the British drama *Romans*, which was later released in Japan as *Cross of Vengeance*. The Robin Williams documentary *Come Inside My Mind* was released in Japan as *Behind the Smile*. *Still, the Morning Comes* is the Japanese title for *12 Years a Slave*. *Say Hello for Me* is the film adaptation of the Takuji Ichikawa novel *Sono Toki wa Kare ni Yoroshiku*, which translates literally to "Say Hello to Him When the Time Comes."

PAGE 10

Hachiko was a dog who would wait every day at Shibuya Station for his master to commute home. After his owner died in 1925, Hachiko continued to wait at Shibuya for his master every day until his own death in 1935 and became known nationwide as a symbol of loyalty.

PAGE 168

A *hannya* mask depicts the face of a jealous female demon with a large snarling mouth.

Hard-Boiled Stories FROM THE CAT BAR

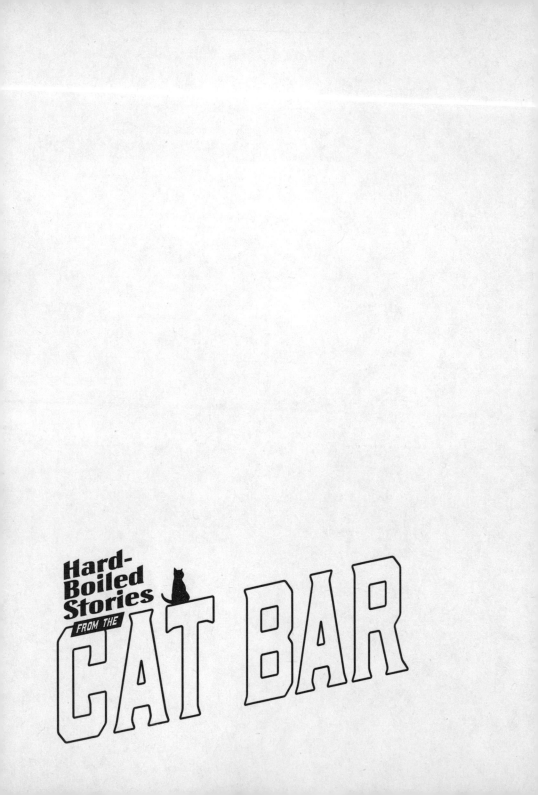

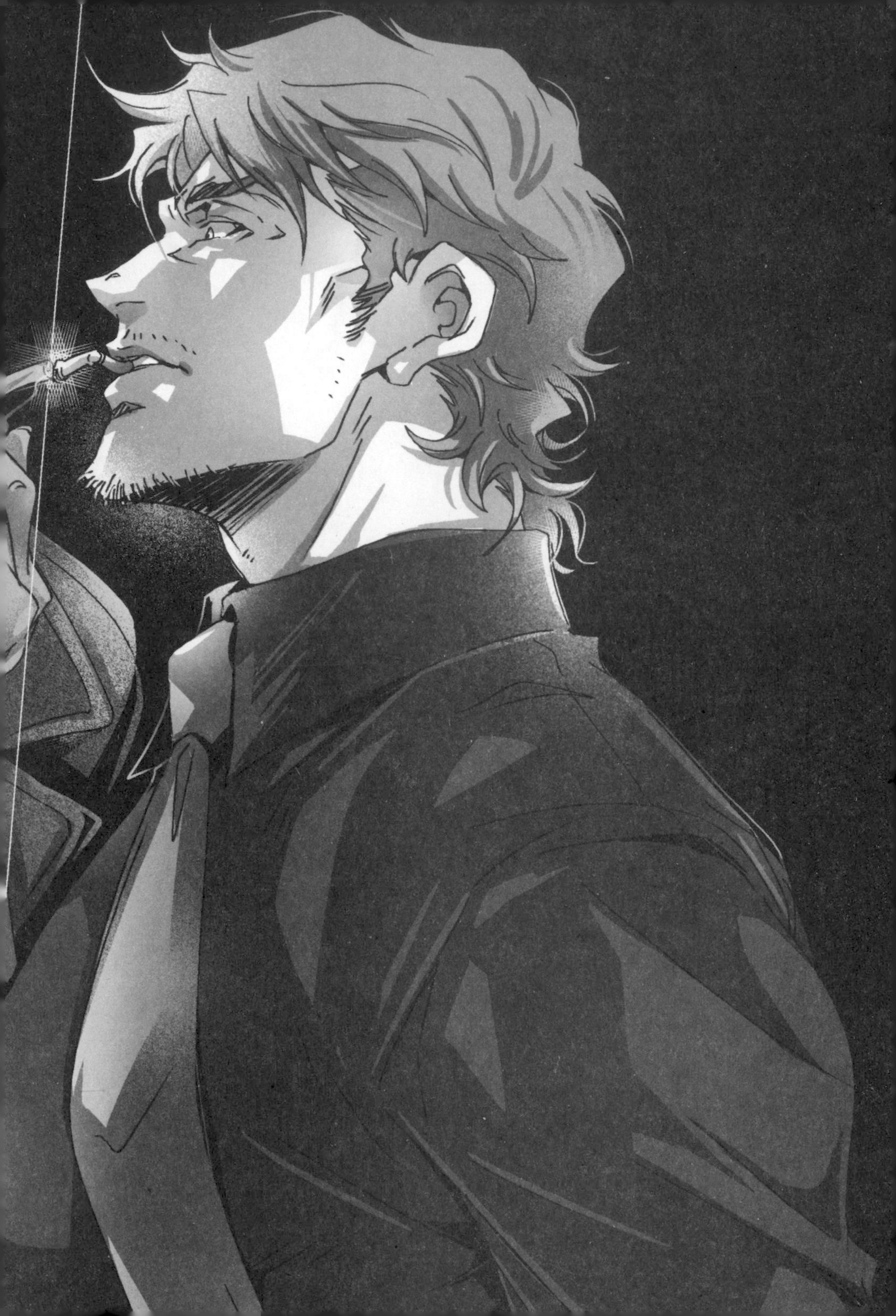

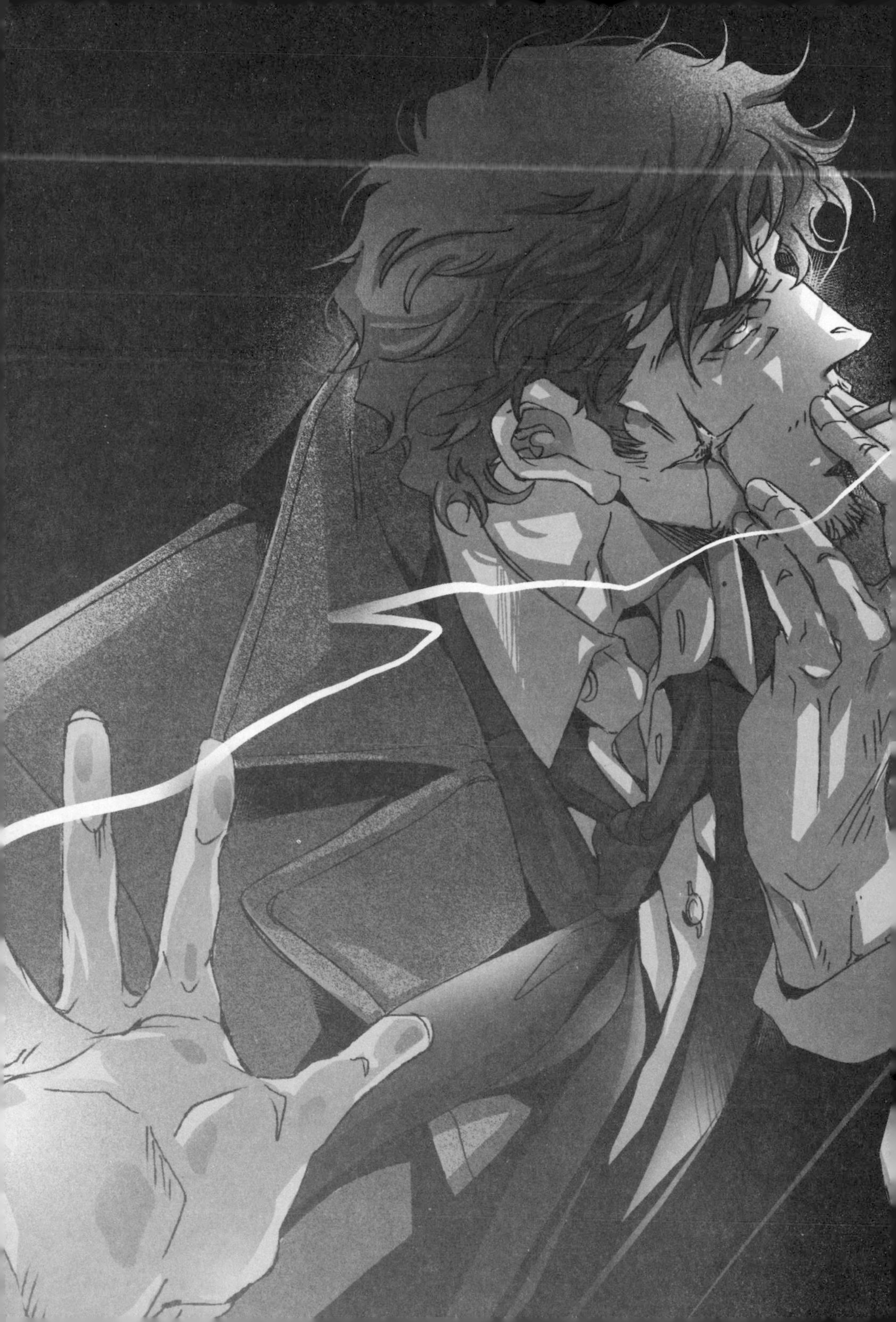

Hard-Boiled Stories FROM THE CAT BAR

Yourei Ono

Translation: **Ajani Oloye**   Lettering: **Abigail Blackman**

SAKE TO NAMIDA TO OTOKO TO NYANKO
©Yourei Ono 2020
First published in Japan in 2020 by KADOKAWA CORPORATION, Tokyo.
English translation rights arranged with KADOKAWA CORPORATION, Tokyo
through TUTTLE-MORI AGENCY, INC., Tokyo.

English translation © 2021 by Yen Press, LLC

Yen Press
150 West 30th Street, 19th Floor
New York, NY 10001

Visit us at yenpress.com
facebook.com/yenpress
twitter.com/yenpress
yenpress.tumblr.com
instagram.com/yenpress

First Yen Press Edition: May 2021

Yen Press is an imprint of Yen Press, LLC.
The Yen Press name and logo are trademarks of Yen Press, LLC.

The publisher is not responsible for websites (or their content) that are not owned by the publisher.

Library of Congress Control Number: 2021930395

ISBNs: 978-1-9753-2101-7 (paperback)
978-1-9753-2102-4 (ebook)

10 9 8 7 6 5 4 3 2 1

WOR

Printed in the United States of America